Convergences: Inventories of the Present

EDWARD W. SAID, *General Editor*

Secularism, Identity, and Enchantment

AKEEL BILGRAMI

Harvard University Press

Cambridge, Massachusetts

London, England

2014

Library of Congress Cataloging-in-Publication Data
Bilgrami, Akeel, 1950–
[Essays. Selections]
Secularism, identity, and enchantment / Akeel Bilgrami.
pages cm
Includes bibliographical references and index.
ISBN 978-0-674-05204-8
1. Secularism.   2. Identity (Philosophical concept)
3. Political science—Philosophy.   I. Title.
BL2747.8.B53 2014
211'.6—dc23
2013034472

To
Noam Chomsky
and
Prabhat Patnaik

Contents

REFLECTIONS ON EDWARD SAID

Preface

It is hard to give a descriptive label to the words on these pages. If asked to, I can't do better than to say that they are on "the moral psychology of politics" and hope that there is not much further scrutiny on the rhetoric I have ventured.

Though these essays are, to some measurable extent, various in topic and even in disciplinary perspective, there is also a quite readily apparent integrity discernible among them, enough at least not to require of me the heart-sinking form of bureaucratic harness of them for which "Introductions" to books sometimes reach. Instead, I have left to cross-referencing notes an extensive, frequent, and, I hope, conscientious stitching that threads the relations between the ideas that run through all the essays.

All but the last two essays have been substantially supplemented with additional writing since their initial appearance; and since each essay declares its own background of assumptions and motivations pretty much at the outset, I will eschew the redundancy of presenting them in forewords here as well, except to say this: The thematic trio of secularism, enchantment, and identity all speak to the issues of the relation between religion and politics. Though there is a concern as well as serious and detailed effort to place those issues in a framework that is attentive to both history and intellectual history, the approach of the

book is governed by a philosopher's interest in viewing them through
the lens of considerations of "reason," *practical* reason; and in particular to broaden that interest by studying the extent to which practical
reason is or is not efficacious in navigating the prima facie conflicts that
secularism is confronted with—conflicts that spring from the notion of
identity as it enters politics and the notion of enchantment as it has been
conceived in terms of the grip that religion and magic have over the lives
of ordinary people.

Salman Rushdie once said,[1] no doubt under duress, that secular
humanism was itself a religion, a judgment that sells short both religion
and secular humanism in one breath. I reckon (this is a conjecture) that
he made that equation so that he could repudiate the charge of apostasy.
One cannot, after all, be committing apostasy if one is only opposing one
religion with another. Under the threat of execution, one may be allowed
resort to an unconvincing equation, and my point in mentioning it now
is to say that, wrong though I believe that judgment to be , some of the
essays in the book pursue, with some variation, a theme it opens up: the
question whether there might not be in some conceptual and historical
continuities between religion and the secular a possibility of a distinctive
kind of radical politics, for instance, a politics whose origins go back to
the experiments in thought and action in that remarkable period of English history in the fourth and fifth decades of the seventeenth century.
Much of the potential for such radicalism feeds my mutually fortifying
interest in the otherwise conflicting relation between secularism and
enchantment.[2]

I hasten to add that what I mean (and elaborate in some essays here)
by "enchantment" as a *conceptual* resource within which to explore
the possibilities of a radical politics is thoroughly revisionary and the
recovery of intimations from the seventeenth century is not intended
as revivalist, but rather as an instructive bit of genealogy that may shed
light on urgent issues for our own time—such as for instance threats to
democratic attitudes in contemporary American political life, considered at length in the essay "Occidentalism, the Very Idea," which has
been vastly expanded since its initial publication to traverse this subject,
and the vexed contemporary issues of the environment, considered at
some length in the essay "Gandhi (and Marx)." There is, in general, a

dismaying complacence in much of our contemporary thinking about politics, which seems poised always to dismiss any appeal to figures such as Gandhi and Marx or to the very notion of enchantment, however secular, as an exercise in nostalgia. These qualms are squarely addressed in the last half of the essay "The Political Possibilities of the Long Romantic Period" (also very substantially expanded for this volume).

There is occasional overlap in some essays that I have not removed because, where it occurs, it comes to a common theme from *different* locations. Thus, enchantment is approached not just via the glance back to seventeenth-century dissent in England, but via the canon (and periphery) of the European Romanticist tradition, as well as from a detailed drawing into affinity—despite their vast differences—the ideas of Gandhi and Marx, who, as I say somewhere with only the merest exaggeration, are in fact philosophers in the Romantic tradition. So also, an argument central to Mill's liberalism is first presented by way of contrast with Gandhi's political philosophy and then later identified as generating much fallacious thinking in the academy's aspiration to latitude in speech. Or again, the argument in Gandhi for his initial opposition to secularism occurs first in presenting the merely *contextual* relevance that secularism has, but it also surfaces elsewhere in elaborating Gandhi's striking and unusual thought that there is an impertinence in modernity's efforts to transform the idea of "human beings" into the idea of "citizens." I give these examples not as an advance apology for the overlaps that will sometimes be encountered by the reader, but to explain how there may be consolidation of ideas to be had by the gaze upon them from different angles and in different philosophical and historical settings.

Some essays are longer than others, some more heavily freighted with analysis and argument than others. That is no doubt because they were initially called for on occasions and by editors with different audiences and goals in mind. I can only hope that this is not a source of irritation or distraction for the reader and that it provides instead for the sort of modulation that puts each essay in relief against the other and thereby eases some of the strain of reading the work of a (salaried) philosopher.

It gives me particular pleasure to have this book published in a series at Harvard University Press for which the late Edward Said had invited (actually, imperiously demanded) it some fifteen years ago. I am grateful

to the supportive forbearance of Lindsay Waters, whose patience I fear
I have much fretted with unconscionably long delays in gathering these
essays for publication. The reasons for the delay are entirely bad and,
looking back at them, even a little obscure to myself. For some years I
had simply not felt motivated even to snatch brief moments for the tasks
at hand because I think I was under an entirely false impression that
revisions to work already done would consist mostly of non-intellectual
labors. As I finally began reading the essays recently, I found that the
revisions needed would almost entirely be *additions* and, as it happens,
the additions came to be quite voluminous. So the labors have turned
out to be quite as absorbing and challenging as the pursuit of new ideas
and arguments can be. One perhaps good outcome of the delay has been
that because it is apparently the last book in a series that must now close
because of the death of its editor, Lindsay Waters has asked me to include
in the collection a closing section of "Reflections" geared to Said's work,
something I am very happy to do.

The book is divided into four parts, and although the division is mostly
a natural one, I should take just a few words to explain the presence and
placement of three essays that might, on the face of it, seem anomalous in
the parts in which they occur.

The part on secularism ends with an essay on liberty in the academy.
The issue of secularism, tied by the very meaning of the term to issues
of religion and politics, also has less analytical but nevertheless intimate
ties to liberal doctrine and basic liberal values. Though secularism, as I
argue in the first essay of the book, is certainly to be found in non-liberal
polities, much of our interest in secularism is proximate to our interest
in liberalism and the liberal value of freedom which surfaces in each of
the essays in that part. This proximity is visible not merely in countries
of Northern Europe and North America, but also in many others such
as, for instance, India and South Africa. And freedom, though vital to
the practice of religion in liberal societies is, obviously, vital more generally too in the matter of belief, and not just religious belief. The essay on
academic freedom considers a distinctive way in which there is a threat
to freedom of belief and inquiry in liberal societies, one which involves

no discernable forms of coercion or interference as is found in other less liberal societies.

The part on enchantment opens with an essay on Gandhi's moral thought, which bears on the subject of enchantment only indirectly, providing a distant but nevertheless useful and illuminating background for the two essays that follow in which enchantment is a central diagnostic concern. And then the essays that bear on the subject of enchantment spill over into the opening essay of the part entitled "Reflections on Edward Said." Said himself was not explicit about how that subject emerged from his critique of imperialism and his frustrations with orthodox forms of liberalism in the West which, as we know, in perpetrating imperial conquest found no conflict between its liberalism and the paternalism which pervaded its stated motivations for empire. The opening essay on "Occidentalism" in this part is a severely critical scrutiny of one work that makes an inverted appeal to Said's eponymous notion, aggressively asserting liberal values (which I myself cherish) in a manner that is complacent and self-congratulatory by visiting a shallow and uncomprehending disdain on notions of enchantment. The essay, thus, has a natural place in a cluster of reflections on Said's work.

I owe thanks to a mass of people, ranging from the anonymous in audiences in many parts of the world to more constant intellectual companions who have been generously gregarious in ongoing conversation (often electronic) over some years on the subjects of these essays. I have mentioned many of them specifically in the essays on which I have especially relied on them. But I could not introduce these essays as a collection without registering a more pervasive intellectual debt that I owe to exchanges with Carol Rovane, Steve White, Prabhat Patnaik, David Bromwich, Noam Chomsky, Isaac Levi, James Tully, and the late Adrienne Rich and Edward Said.

Secularism, Identity, and Enchantment

Secularism

ONE

Secularism

Its Content and Context

1.

I begin with three fundamental features of the idea of "secularism." I will want to make something of them at different stages of the passage of my argument in this essay for the conclusion—among others—that the relevance of secularism is contextual in very specific ways.

If secularism has its relevance only in context, then it is natural and right to think that it will appear in different forms and guises in different contexts. But I write down these opening features of secularism at the outset because they seem to me to be invariant among the contextually different forms that secularism may take. It is hard to imagine that one hasn't changed the subject from secularism to something else, something that deserves another name, if one finds oneself denying any of the features that I initially list below. Though I say this is "hard to imagine," I don't mean to deny that there is a strong element of stipulation in these initial assertions to come. I can't pretend that these are claims or theses about some independently identified subject matter—as if we all know perfectly well what we are talking about when we speak of secularism—and the question is only about what is true of that agreed upon concept or topic. The point is rather to *fix* the concept or topic. But, on the other hand, such talk of "fixing" should not give the impression that it is a matter of free choice, either. Once the initial terminological points about "secularism" are made, the goal of the rest of the essay will be to show why they are *not arbitrary* stipulations. So the reader is urged to be unreactive about these initial topic-setting assertions until the dialectic of the essay is played out.

First, secularism is *a stance to be taken about religion*. At the level of generality with which I have just described this, it does not say anything very specific or precise. The imprecision and generality have two sources. One obvious source is that religion, regarding which it is supposed to take a stance, is itself, notoriously, not a very precise or specifically understood phenomenon. But to the extent that we have a notion of religion in currency—however imprecisely elaborated—"secularism" will have a parasitic meaning partially elaborated as a stance regarding whatever that notion stands for. Should we decide that there is no viability in any notion of religion, and should the notion pass out of conceptual currency, secularism too would lapse as a notion with a point and rationale. The other source of imprecision is that I have said nothing specific or precise about *what sort* of stance secularism takes toward religion. One may think that it has to be in some sense an adversarial stance since surely secularism, in some sense, defines itself against religion. This is true enough, but still the very fact that I find the need to keep using the qualifier "in some sense" makes clear that nothing much has been said about the kind of opposing stance this amounts to. Part of the point of this essay is to add a little precision to just this question.

Second, for all this generality just noted, "secularism"—unlike "secular" and "secularization"—is quite specific in another regard. It is the name of a *political* doctrine. As a name, it may not always have had this restriction, but that seems to be its predominant current usage. So to the extent that it takes a stance vis-à-vis religion, it does so only in the realm of the *polity*. It is not meant—as the terms "secular" and "secularization" are—to mark highly general and dispersed social and intellectual and cultural phenomena and processes. Unlike the term "secularization," it is not so capacious as to include a stance against religion that requires redirection of either personal belief or, for that matter, any of a range of personal and cultural habits such as dress or diet. Thus it is not a stance against religion of the sort that atheists and agnostics might wish to take or a stance that strikes attitudes (to say nothing of policies) about the hijab. The increase in a society of loss of personal belief in God or the decrease in church- or synagogue- or mosque-going or the surrender of traditional religious habits of dress or prohibitions against pork may all be signs of increasing "secular*ization*" but they are irrelevant to the idea of secular*ism*. The reason for this is rather straightforward and obvious. It should be possible to think that a devout Muslim or Christian or Hindu can be committed to keeping some aspects of the reach of his religion out of the polity, without altogether giving up on being a Muslim, Christian, or Hindu. And it seems natural today to express that thought by saying that such a person, for all his devoutness, is committed to secularism. And one can say this while noticing and saying something that it is also natural to think and say: Such a devout person, in being devout, is holding out against the tendencies unleashed by the long social and ideational processes of secular*ization*. And we can appreciate the naturalness of this restriction of the term "secularism" to the polity when we observe that the slogan "separation of church and state" (which, whatever we think of it, is part of what is conveyed to many by the ordinary usage of the term "secularism") *allows* one the church, even as it separates it from the *state*, or, more generally, from the polity. If we did not believe that the term was to be restricted in this way, we would either have to collapse secularism with secularization or—if we insisted on some more subtle difference between those two terms—we would have to invent another term altogether (a term that has no cognate relation to this family of terms—secular, secularization, secularism) to capture the aspiration of a polity to seek relative independence from a society's religiosity. I believe that any such neologizing would be a stipulative act of far greater strain and artificiality than reserving one of these terms ("secularism") for this aspiration since, as I said, it is anyway implied by the slogans that accompany the term. What then of the contrast of "secularism" with "secular"? Unlike the latter term which is often said to refer innocuously and indiscriminately to all things that are "worldly" in the sense of being *outside* the reach of religious institutions and concerns (outside the cloister, in the mundiality of the world at large, as it were), "secular*ism*" aspires to be more concentrated in its concern— to not merely *refer* to anything that is outside of that reach, but to focus on something specific (the polity) and attempt to *keep* it or *steer* it outside of some specified aspects of that reach.

Third, secularism, as a stance regarding religion that is restricted to the polity, is not a good in itself. It seeks what is conceived, by those who favor it, to promote certain other moral and political goods, and these are goods that are intended to counter what are conceived as harms, actual or potential. This third feature may be considered too controversial to be regarded as a defining feature, but its point becomes more plausible when we contrast secularism with a more cognitive (rather than political) stance regarding religion, such as atheism. For atheists, the truth of atheism is sufficient to motivate one to adhere to it and the truth of atheism is not grounded in the claim that it promotes a moral or political good or the claim that it is supported by other moral or political values we have. By contrast, secularists, to the extent that they claim "truth" for secularism, claim it on grounds that appeal to other values that support the ideal of secularism or other goods that are promoted by it. Secularism as a political doctrine arose to repair what were perceived as damages that flowed from historical harms that were, in turn, perceived as owing, in some broad sense, to religion. Thus, for instance, when it is said that secularism had as its vast cradle the prolonged and internecine religious conflicts in Europe of some centuries ago, something like this normative force of serving goods and correcting harms is detectably implied. But if all this is right, then it follows that one would have to equally grant that, should there be contexts in which those goods were not seen necessarily to be goods, or to the extent that those goods were being well served by political arrangements that were not secularist, or to the extent that there were no existing harms, actual or potential, that secularism would be correcting, then one could take the opposing normative stance and fail to see the point and rationale for secularism.

2.

I want to now turn from features that *define* or characterize secularism to features of its *justification and basis of adoption.*

In a paper written in the days immediately following the fatwa pronounced against Salman Rushdie, called "What Is a Muslim?,"[1] I had argued that secularism had no justification that did not appeal to substantive values, that is to say, values that some may hold and others may not. It was not justifiable on purely rational grounds that anyone (capable of rationality) would find convincing, no matter what substantive values they held. I had invoked the notion, coined by Bernard Williams as "internal reasons," to describe these kinds of grounds on which its justification is given.[2] Internal reasons are reasons that rely on specific motives and values and commitments in the moral psychologies of individuals (or groups, if one takes the view that groups have moral-psychological economies). Internal reasons are contrasted with "external reasons," which are reasons that someone is supposed to have quite independent of his or her substantive values and commitments, that is, independent of elements in the psychologies that motivate people. Bernard Williams, recapitulating Humean arguments against Kantian forms of externalist rationality and the universalism that might be expected to emerge from them, had claimed that there are no such things as "external reasons." Whether that general claim is true or not, my more specific claim had been that there are no external reasons that would establish the truth of secularism. If secularism were to carry conviction, it would have to be on grounds that persuaded people by appealing to the specific and substantive values that figured in their specific moral-psychological economies.[3] Such a view might cause alarm in those who would wish for secularism a more universal basis. Internal reasons, by their nature, do not provide such a basis. As I said, internal reasons for some conclusion that will persuade some people may not persuade others of that conclusion, since those others may not hold the particular substantive values to which those reasons appeal and on which those reasons depend. Only external reasons could persuade everyone since all they require is a minimal rationality possessed by all (undamaged, adult) human minds and make no appeal to substantive values that may be variably held by human minds and psychologies. Alarming though it might seem to some, there is no help for this. There are no more secure universal grounds on which one can base one's argument for secularism.

Charles Taylor has convincingly argued that in a religiously plural society, secularism should be adopted on the basis of what Rawls called an "overlapping consensus."[4] An overlapping consensus, in Rawls's understanding of that term, is a consensus on some policy that is arrived at by people with very different moral and religious and political commitments, who sign on to the policy from within their differing points of view, and therefore on possibly very different grounds from each other. It contrasts with the idea that when one converges on a policy one must always do so for the *same* reason.

What is the relation between the idea that secularism should be adopted on the basis of an overlapping consensus and the idea presented in the earlier paragraph about internal reasons being the only reasons available in justifying secularism? A very close one. The latter idea yields (it lies behind) the former. The relation is this. Internal reasons, unlike external reasons, may vary from person to person, group to group. This may give the impression that there simply cannot be a consensus if we were restricted to the resources of internal reasons. But that does not follow. Or at any rate, it only follows if we assume that a consensus requires that all sign onto something (some policy or political position, such as secularism) on the same grounds or for the same reason. In other words, on the basis of an external reason or reasons. But such an assumption is a theoretical tyranny. Without that assumption, one could say this. *If* there is to be a consensus on some political outcome on the basis, not of external but of internal reasons, it will presumably *only* be because different persons or groups subscribe to the policy on their own, different grounds. This just is the idea of an *overlapping* consensus. If there were external reasons for a policy, one could get a consensus on it of a stronger kind and would not need to hold out hope for a *merely* "overlapping" consensus.

Perhaps all this is obvious. However, for reasons having to do with Rawls scholarship, I have been a little wary of this use of the notion of overlapping consensus since in Rawls it has always been a notion embedded in the framework of his celebrated idea of the "original position," i.e., the idea that one contracts into policies to live by without knowledge of one's substantive position in society. I find myself completely baffled by why the idea of the original position is not made entirely redundant by the notion of an overlapping consensus. If one did not know what one's substantive position in society is, one presumably does not know what one's substantive values are. If so, the very idea of internal reasons can have no play in the original position. It follows that if one were to adopt an overlapping consensus on the basis of divergent internal reasons that contractors may have for signing onto a policy, then the original position becomes altogether irrelevant to the contractual scenario. Of course, if one were to completely divorce the idea of an overlapping consensus from Rawls's conceptual apparatus within which it has always been formulated (even in his last published work, *The Law of Peoples*),[5] then it would be exactly right to say, as Taylor does, that secularism should be adopted in a pluralistic society on the basis of an overlapping consensus. But now, the only apparatus one has to burden the contractors with is the capacity for internal reasoning, that is, with psychological economies with substantive values that yield internal reasons. Rawls would not be recognizable in this form of contractualist doctrine. Indeed one would be hard pressed to say that one was any longer theorizing within the contractualist tradition at all, which is a tradition in which serious constraints of an "original position" or a "state of nature," etc., were always placed as methodological starting points in the making of a compact. Shorn of all this, one is left with something that is the merest common sense, which it would be bombastic to call "a social contract." We now need only say this: Assuming no more than our capacity for internal reasoning, i.e., our capacity to invoke some substantive values we hold (whatever they may differentially be in all the different individuals or groups in society), we can proceed to justify on its basis another substantive value or policy—for example, secularism—and so proceed to adopt it for the polity. If this path of adoption by consensus, invoking this internalist notion of justification, works in a religiously pluralist society, it will be just as Taylor presents it, an overlapping consensus, with none of Rawls's theoretical framework.

3.

The last two sections have respectively presented points of definition of secularism and points of its justification and basis of adoption. I think it is important to keep these two things separate on the general ground that one needs to have a more or less clear idea of what we are justifying and adopting before we justify and adopt it.

In a very interesting recent paper, Charles Taylor has argued that we need to *redefine* "secularism."[6] It is a complex paper with highly honorable political and moral motivations that underlie it. But, speaking more theoretically, I don't think it is quite as well motivated.

The paper begins by saying that there have been two aspects to secularism—one, the idea of the *separation of church and state,* and the other that the *state maintain a neutral equidistance from different religions within a plural society.* The paper wishes to correct an overemphasis on the first by stressing the importance of the second aspect and wishes to modify the second too along the following lines.

In modern societies, we seek various goods and the three in particular (echoing the trio of goods expressed in a familiar slogan) that remain relevant to secular aspirations are the *liberty* of worship, the *equality* of different faiths, and finally, more than just equality, the need to give each faith a voice in determining the shape of the society, so there must be *fraternal* relations within which negotiations, with each voice being equally heard, are crucial. What is more, because the first aspect's stress on separation of church and state is too focused on religion, the second aspect's stress on religious diversity should be modified and expanded to include the fact that in late modernity, the diversity of pluralist societies contains not just a variety of religious people, but non-religious people as well. Their point of view must also be included in the mix. *All* this is now included in the idea and ideal of a redefined secularism.

So to sum up his explicit motivations for seeking this more capacious definition of secularism: There is the importance of the state maintaining a neutrality and equal distance from each religion. There is the importance of a society allowing the democratic participation of all religious voices in shaping its polity's commitments. And there is the need to turn one's focus away from just religion to acknowledging and respecting wider forms of cultural diversity and a variety of intellectual positions, including non-religious ones. These are all worthy motivations and a society that pursues them would be measurably better than one that doesn't. The question is how does thinking so make a difference to how we theorize about the meaning or definition of secularism? There is no denying that it makes *a* difference to secularism, but it is not obvious to me that it is just as he presents it.

One of the things that he finds distorted about secularism while defined along the unrevised lines that he is inveighing against is that, so defined, it has been too focused on "institutional arrangements." Slogans such as "separation of church and state" become mantras and as they do, they suggest institutional arrangements that are fixed. Once done, it is hard not only to change the institutions, but also to reconceptualize secularism. What is better in order to maintain both theoretical and institutional flexibility is to allow the ideals in questions (the echoes of liberty, equality, and fraternity mentioned above) to determine what is needed rather than these slogans, which point to institutional arrangements and stop or preempt conversations about how to theorize secularism. In keeping with this point, he applauds Rawls for starting with certain ideals such as "human rights, equality, the rule of law, democracy" rather than anti-religious (or for that matter, religious principles) and then proceeding to consider the question of secularism to be in line with them (see Taylor, p. 37, note 6).

This is just right, I believe, as are the general moral and political instincts that prompt Taylor's appeal for a redefinition of "secularism": the desire for greater flexibility, the desire not to tie "secularism" to the polemical sense of "non-religious" or "anti-religious," the desire to establish secularism on the basis of an overlapping consensus of internal reasons. The question is, is it wise or necessary to redefine secularism to pursue these instincts and motivations?

4.

Let me, then, turn to a way of characterizing (I say characterizing because perhaps "defining" is too constricting a term for what both Taylor and I are interested in, but I will not always avoid talk of "definition" since it is the word Taylor himself uses) secularism that is, or to put it more cautiously, that may be at odds with Taylor's. (I add this caution because, despite what it seems to me at present, it may turn out that we are not much at odds and it is really a matter of emphasizing different things.)

I have said that it is a good idea, as Taylor suggests, to *start* with certain ideals that do not mention religion or opposition to religion, and *then* move on to talk of political and institutional arrangements involving the role of the state and its stances toward religion. So, just because it is what is most familiar to us in our tradition of political theory and philosophy, let us start within a liberal framework, let us start with some basic ideals and the fundamental rights and constitutional commitments that enshrine them, just as Rawls and Taylor propose. Starting with them as the basic, though tentative, givens, I suggest we embrace Taylor's account only up to a point and then add something that does not seem to be emphasized by him, indeed something that he may even wish to be de-emphasizing in his redefinition.

I propose, then, something like the following non-arbitrary stipulation as a characterization of secularism that contains all of the three features I had mentioned at the outset.

(S): Should we be living in a religiously plural society, secularism requires that all religions should have the privilege of free exercise and be evenhandedly treated *except when a religion's practices are inconsistent with the ideals that a polity seeks to achieve* (ideals, often, though not always, enshrined in stated fundamental rights and other constitutional commitments) *in which case there is a lexicographical ordering in which the political ideals are placed first.*

Much commentary is needed on this minimal and basic characterization.

Here are some miscellaneous points of commentary, in no particular order, that help to situate and motivate (S), thereby showing why, as a stipulation, it is non-arbitrary, and where it may seem to depart in emphasis and implication and significance from Taylor's redefinition.

(a)

One difference between (S) and the sort of redefinition Taylor is seeking is that when characterizing secularism, (S) squares with his urge to be non-phobic and accommodating toward religion as well as with his idea to have the state keep a neutral and equal distance between all religions—but then emphasizes something else as well: the lexicographical ordering. The point of this latter essential element of the characterization is that (S) is a stance that *can* be *adversarial* against religious practices and laws, but *only* when, from the point of view of the ideals one starts with, it needs to be that, i.e., when those practices and laws go against the very thing that Taylor himself thinks we should start with—the ideals and goals (formulated without reference to religious or anti-religious elements) that a society has adopted.

The fact that one's starting point lies in certain ideals helps (S) to avoid the charge that Taylor makes against some contemporary formulations of secularism, viz., that they start with an assertion of certain institutional arrangements with slogans or mantras such as "the separation of church and state." Rather, in the Rawlsian manner of which Taylor approves, (S) starts with certain ideals and goals that the society wishes to adopt, and the lexicographical ordering suggests that the institutions should be shaped and distributed in such a way that certain priorities articulated in the lexicographical ordering get implemented. There is certainly more of a stress than in Taylor on the priority over religion of certain goals and ideals formulated in terms independent of religion. Religion and its practices come second to these, if there is ever a clash between them. But, just as Taylor would have it, it is these goals rather than any institutional arrangements that form the starting point.

(b)

I had said that the first basic defining feature of secularism is that it is some sort of a stance regarding religion. What sort of stance is (S)? The point, which I have just made in (a) above, brings out how, as a stance, it is more adversarial than Taylor wishes secularism to be, but it is by no means obsessively seeking religion out as a target. It is certainly not trying to polemically remove it root and branch from public life, in all its social, cultural, and intellectual aspects, in a way often suggested in recent writings by today's doctrinaire atheists. This is because (S) keeps strict faith with the second elementary feature of secularism mentioned at the outset, viz., that it is only, and precisely, a political stance, a stance regarding religion only as it affects the polity. It is not dismayed by or concerned with the presence of religiosity in the society at large or in the personal beliefs of the individual citizens as so much of the ideological urge for secularity in the modern period is. The lexicographical ordering merely says that if and when there is an inconsistency that arises

between certain goals sought to be achieved in a polity that are formulated independently of religion and the practices of a religion, the former
must be placed first and the latter second.

Quite apart from the fact that it is restricted to political matters, the
antecedent in the conditional "if and when there is an inconsistency"
makes it clear that *even within this restricted domain,* there is no harm
to be found in the presence of religion, so long as it does not clash with
certain fundamental ideals and commitments of the polity.

What sorts of things are clear examples of the political domain and of
the priority being proposed within it by the lexicographical ordering?
The examples are hardly exotic.

Take a society in which the commitment to free speech is a fundamental ideal of its polity. Assume, then, that it is our starting point, in just
the way Taylor urges, whereby the formulation of the ideal is not from
within any religious doctrine nor indeed from within an opposition to
any religion. It is formulated without any mention of religion. Let's, then,
also assume that there are religions and religious practices in that society, those of Christianity and Islam, say, but not Buddhism, which, as it
happens, have commitments to censorship of blasphemy. (S) says that it
is important to see secularism as requiring the state to be evenhanded
toward religions in general, but not in any case when the lexicographical ordering comes to have application. And this is such a case. In this
case, the lexicographical ordering requires one to spoil the neutrality
by favoring Buddhism over Christianity and Islam since the state must
place the commitments to blasphemy in these religions second and the
commitment to free speech first, in the context, say, of the publication
of novels such as *The Last Temptation of Christ* or *The Satanic Verses* in
a society such as Britain's with a polity defined upon basic liberal commitments. (It is interesting to note that Britain took a non-neutral stance
in a quite different sense than the one I am recommending, weighing
down only on Islam but, as a result of Mary Whitehouse's campaigns,
not on Christianity. It is a question whether this points to an extent to
which established religion is more than merely nominal in Britain.) I will
discuss free speech and another example involving gender equality again
later, but for now, I offer this as a rather straightforward example of the
occasion on which (S) seems to depart from Taylor's understanding of

secularism, by emphasizing the "lexicographical ordering" ideal over the "neutral and equidistant" ideal of secularism that he favors.

I think in late modern societies committed to liberal ideals of this sort, it is a theoretical *loss* rather than gain to allow that a polity has been impeccably secular in *any* case in which it capitulates to the banning of a novel on the grounds that it is blasphemous by the lights of a religion's customs or laws. One may—even in late modern liberal societies—find good moral and political reasons to ban the novel. That is not the theoretical issue at stake. What is theoretically questionable is only that we should describe the ban as falling well within the secular ideal. It may well be that good politics or morals sometimes requires us to put the secularist policy aside. But it is *secularist* policy that we would be putting aside. If a redefinition of secularism were to deny this, that would be a questionable theoretical outcome of the redefinition. The stress on the neutral equidistance ideal over the lexicographical ordering ideal in a characterization of secularism may well lead to just such a questionable theoretical outcome in cases such as this. A society whose polity banned *both* the Kazantzakis *and* the Rushdie novel on grounds of their being blasphemous by the lights of two different religions that were being treated neutrally in this twin banning meets the neutral and equidistant state ideal of secularism, but fails to meet (S).

It cannot really be argued on Taylor's behalf that such a twin and symmetrical banning does *not* satisfy the state neutralist ideal of secularism, by pointing out that he has allowed into the groups that the state must be neutral toward non-religious people as well. What these religions find blasphemous is not just the expression of a point of view described innocuously as "non-religious," it is the expression of views that trash and cartoon and satirize their most cherished and deep commitments with contempt as Rushdie or Kazantzakis (or, to take other examples, Bunuel or Arrabal) did. So a state that decided to keep all these things (even-handedly for both—indeed all—offended religions) out of circulation in bookshops and cinemas would not be failing to be neutral and fair toward a group under the description "non-religious" people. It would be failing to be fair toward "blasphemers," not exactly a natural or routine category or grouping by any pluralist count of society. So, I assume, that the only protection that *blasphemers* can properly expect to get is from secularists who believe in (S), not secularists who wish to be neutral and equidistant between religious and "non-religious" people. Those last two or three words of the last sentence are too bland a description in the state neutral-ist ideal to warrant our saying that such an ideal has the very particular focus needed to count the censorship of something so specific as hurt-ful and contemptuous writing against a religion as anti-secular.[7] What is clearly moving Taylor is that a genuine pluralism in many *contemporary* societies has to acknowledge, as a natural grouping in the plural mix, not only Hindus, Muslims, Christians, but also non-religious people. Taylor is concerned to respect this development in the pluralism of our time. And what I am saying is that we should certainly grant him that that is a natural group to add as a modification of the "neutral and equidistant" ideal of secularism he favors, but then say, even so, that when we speak of pluralism and its groupings today, *"blasphemers"* is *not* a natural group-ing. As a result, his pluralist motivation here in adding to the mix of things toward which the state must be neutral is not sufficient (not sufficiently particular) to make the case that such censorship would be anti-secular by the lights of a state neutralist ideal of secularism.

If he were to go beyond what are broad and natural groupings to some-thing much more indefinitely detailed in its pluralist count in a society, counting as a group any group (however specifically described, blas-phemers being just one example) that could claim that there has been a lapse in neutrality by the state, after the fact of some state action, it is very doubtful that there can be anything at all that a neutralist state secular-ist ideal would yield by way of policy. That is to say, there would hardly be any policy that would be sanctioned as secular policy when there are an indefinite and limitless number of conflicting groups whose points of view have to be equally respected. Indeed unless there was some *ex ante* specification of the pluralist elements that a state was to be neutral between, the ideal amounts to nothing that can be interestingly speci-fied at all. What I think we must assume such an ideal envisages, if it is to envisage something plausible, is not that "blasphemers" are ex ante counted as a group who must be protected when devising state policies, but rather something like this: Muslims, Christians, Jews, Hindus, etc., as well as "non-religious" people (*a fragment among whom* will be novel-ists, filmmakers, etc., who satirize, vilify one or another religion) all must equally have a voice in the policies that a polity will adopt. Whatever policy is adopted once this fraternal deliberation takes place must count as the policies of a secular state according to this ideal. After all it is the outcome of a state allowing evenhanded voice to all groups. Now *it may turn out* that non-religious people will want protection for the fragment among them who have offended religions deeply in the novels they write or the films they make. And if they carry the day in the deliberation, then the outcome of this state neutralist ideal process of decision-making will *coincide* with the outcome of a lexicographical ordering imposed by (S), i.e., they will be co-*extensive*, (not co-intensive) outcomes. But *it may turn out instead* that the fraternal deliberation with all voices involved yields a policy that evenhandedly bans novels and films considered blasphemous by various religions, and if it does, the policy will *also* count as secular since Taylor's criterion of *fraternal* and *equal* participation of *freely* speaking voices will be satisfied. The point is that (S), however, will *never* count such an outcome as secular, so long as free speech is an ideal one begins with. The adoption of the policy will *always* fall afoul of the lexicographical ordering that is essential to (S)'s formulation of secularism. And just for that reason, I am saying, (S) has things more theoretically right about what secularism is.

(c)

In a clarifying response in personal correspondence to a draft of this essay, Charles Taylor makes a point of real importance and relevance for the present in explaining why he thinks a characterization of secularism should not incorporate the first feature of secularism that I had mentioned at the outset, viz., that it is a stance regarding religion. He expresses the anxiety that the sort of lexicographical ordering I propose which mentions explicitly the importance of placing one or other ideal or goal of a polity before some *religious* practice or custom or law might sometimes have the effect of having the secular polity equate some *unrepresentative* element of a religious population with "the religion" in question. The woeful effects of just this sort of thing are familiar from the present cold war being waged against "Islam" on the basis of a few acts of atrocity by a small fraction of Muslims. This is what Taylor says:

Here's where the hard-line secularist focus on religion alone leads to tragic and destructive moves. They attack "Islam" for instance for female genital mutilation, and for honor killings. And they seem to have a semblance of justification in that the communities who prac-tice these can see them as religiously sanctioned. They tar the whole community with this brush, and drive moderates into the arms of fundamentalists. Whereas, as Anthony Appiah has argued, the most effective way of ending these practices involves making allies with the more orthodox who can effectively convince Islamic societies that they are deviant to the message of the prophet.

As with everything else that prompts him on this matter, this is a humane and politically perceptive concern. But I don't find myself con-vinced that these considerations, despite their great importance today, are to be diagnosed as flowing from a characterization of secularism that incorporates the lexicographical ordering in the terms that I have pre-sented it. As I presented it, there is nothing in (S) that constitutes an "attack" on religion as a generality. In particular, when female genital mutilation or honor killings are identified as practices to be placed sec-ond in the lexicographical ordering, Islam, as a generality, is not "under attack." Rather, the claim is entirely conditional: *If* there be a claim by those who practice them that these practices owe to a religion and *if* that claim is correct, then the placing of the practice lower in the lexicograph-ical ordering than the moral and political ideals they run afoul of would be properly called a "secularist" policy on the part of the state. That is all that a characterization of secularism as (S) amounts to. I don't see that, so understood, secularism as a stance regarding religion has the effects that Taylor thinks it does. If it should turn out that nothing in the religion in question sanctions these practices, then the ideals and goals of the polity may supersede these practices in a lexicographical order-ing, but that lexicographical ordering would not be the lexicographical ordering characterized in (S) which specifically mentions religion. In that case, secularism, being a stance regarding religion, is not a notion that descriptively applies to such a case.

Moreover, though the anxiety that a whole community is being tarred by the brush of these practices of a fractional group in the community is a genuine and justified anxiety to have, it is not clear how (S) as a characterization of secularism is responsible for its happening. True, as a formulation of secularism, (S) mentions religious practices without distinguishing between the numbers that do and do not practice them. But it is not such a general understanding of secularism that gives rise to the public impression that the religion in question is itself to be identified with the practice. What is really responsible for it is an irresponsible media that doesn't care to distinguish finely enough between the practitioners and the rest of the community. And it is not as if states are completely innocent of responsibility since states, for familiar statist reasons, track whatever the media calls or fails to call attention to. But that a state should be implicated in that sort of thing is independent of whether the state has adopted secular policies as characterized by (S). One of the real sources of difficulty is that states, including liberal states, have no (and, by the nature of the case, cannot have any) political mechanisms by which to introduce *intra*-community democratization that would show the practitioners to be an *unrepresentative* minority within the community. Liberal politics has institutions which, via mechanisms like elections, calibrate representation with numbers of people. This happens, as we know, at the federal, state, regional, and even municipal level, but unlike these levels, religious communities are too dispersed and too imprecisely defined to have such mechanisms. Whether there can be intra-community democratization of a kind that does not depend on such representative institutions is a subject that needs much more study than it has had in political sociology. Until such democratization, a small fraction within a community which has the shrillest voice and the most activist presence may often get to be seen as more representative of the community than it deserves, by its numbers, to be, since the media will typically pay the most attention to the most audible voices, and the state, for typical reasons of state, will do so as well. This, not secularism as formulated in (S), should, at bottom, be the diagnosed source of Taylor's quite proper anxiety.

Taylor is rightly anxious too that when there is an equation of a religion with a small fragment of its members and its practices, it can sometimes have the effect of driving ordinary devout people, as he puts it, "into the arms of the fundamentalists." But again it is not clear why secularism as (S) elaborates it has any role to play in this. It is a complex question why non-practitioners of the practices in question do not always distinguish themselves vocally and explicitly from (the far smaller number of) the practitioners. Speaking more generally, it is a complex question why ordinary devout people remain a large but silent majority and don't speak out against the relatively small numbers of extremists and fundamentalists in their community, with whom they share so little by way of ideas and ideology. The answer to such questions would have to invoke a whole range of factors, all of which, I think, are at some distance from (S)—factors that make them feel as if they are letting the side down if they were to be openly critical of anyone in their community, even those whose views and practices they have no sympathy for. In the case of Islam, this defensively uncritical psychology has been bred by years of colonial subjugation, by continuing quasi-colonial economic arrangements with American and European corporate exploitation of energy resources of countries with large Muslim populations, by immoral embargos imposed on these countries that cause untold suffering to ordinary people, by recent invasions of some of these countries by Western powers, and finally by the racialist attitudes toward migrants from these countries in European nations. It is these factors that are responsible for ordinary Muslims, who might have otherwise been more willing to criticize fundamentalists in their community, focusing instead primarily on an enemy perceived to be external rather than internal.[8]

One might think that today the rhetoric of "secularism" (like the rhetoric of "democracy") plays a role in the anti-Islamist drumbeat of propaganda that accompanies these other factors and, therefore, it in turn plays a role in making the vast majority of ordinary Muslims unwilling to be critical of the offending practitioners in their midst. That might sometimes be so. But if and when it is so, the right thing to do is not to ask that secularism be redefined, but to demand that one should *drop* talk of secularism and focus instead on trying to improve matters on what is really at stake: the effects of a colonial past, a commercially exploitative present, unjust wars and embargos, racial discrimination against migrants in Europe, and so on. It is a change in these things, not a redefinition of secularism, that will draw ordinary Muslims out of "the arms of the fundamentalists," that will give the vast majority of non-practitioners the confidence to come out of their silence and their defensive psychologies to distinguish themselves from those whom they find to be a small but extreme and unrepresentative minority in their community's midst.

In the quoted passage, Taylor implies that secularism, as for instance defined by (S), would spoil the chances of making alliances with the orthodox in a community whose voices would have the most chance of bringing about an end of the offending practices. It is perfectly possible for a state to sometimes judge that it would be better for it to forge alliances with the orthodox element in a community to get it to speak up for an end to a certain offending practice rather than adopt a policy like (S) that opposes the practice that the orthodox element gives support to. That would be to surrender secularism for a more effective pragmatic strategy. It would not be to adopt a different ideal of secularism. I myself think that what is needed is for a secular state, as defined by (S), to help provide *internal* reasons to the community, including the orthodoxy that supports the practice, to persuade it to change some of its commitments. Such a strategy is perfectly compatible with a secularism defined in terms of (S) and I discuss how that is so at length in Sections 5 and 6 below (see particularly note 16 and the text in the main body of this essay to which it attaches). What is required in order to make this possible is for secularism not to give up on its lexicographical ordering as formulated in (S), but to seek a *conceptual vernacular* within which it can attempt to provide internal reasons that speak to even the orthodox element in a community. Too often secularism adopts the universalist rhetoric of rights in its efforts at persuasion rather than seeking *local* concepts and commitments within the community (including even among the orthodox in the community) that might put pressure on the community's own practices and thereby eventually provide the source of internal reasons for change. This is the entire theme of Sections 5 and 6 below.

(d)

Though (S) insists sturdily on the invariance of the lexicographical ordering in all contexts where there is secularism, it allows for much contextual differential in the form secularism may take because it allows for much variation in the ideals that are placed first in the lexicographical ordering.

Thus, for instance, the values and rights may vary from constitution to constitution, but one can assume that if it is liberal democracies in late modernity one is concerned with, then there will be substantial overlap of the basic and familiar values—freedom of speech, say, or racial and gender equality, and so on. In other sorts of societies, the ideals may be substantially different and there may be less stress on the basic freedoms and social forms of equality. Thus some socialist societies have stressed *economic* equality and the right to work more than they have stressed merely social equality and the basic freedoms. And there will no doubt be yet other forms of ideals and commitments in yet other societies that the lexicographical ordering mentioned in the stipulated characterization of secularism will place before the religious practices inconsistent with them. The point is not to lay down very specific ideals that form a definite list. The point rather is to stress the role of the priority over religious practices (whenever there is a clash with them) that such ideals (whatever they may be) will have in *the lexicographical ordering that forms the heart of the characterization of secularism.*

The last point has wider implications that distinguish between (S) and Taylor's redefinition in a rather sharp way. One should be able to characterize secularism independently of whether a polity is authoritarian or liberal in its fundamental orientation. Taylor, as I said, mentions with approval Rawls's starting point in certain rights and other liberal ideals. This is an approval one may share without actually insisting that there cannot be variation in the form that the ideals take or the ideals themselves. The theoretically important requirement is not that there be this or that ideal but that there be ideals that do not get articulated in terms that mention religion or the opposition to religion. All the opposition to religion that the characterization in (S) demands is in the notion of a lexicographical ordering that follows the initial starting point in these ideals. Thus, by these theoretical lights, so long as there were such ideals motivating a polity and they played such a role in the minimal demands of a lexicographical ordering, then (whatever other properties that polity possessed) it meets the necessary and sufficient condition of secularism. So, for instance, on the assumption that there were such ideals that were motivating the political regime that Ataturk imposed on Turkey, and on the assumption that religion and religious practices were always placed second in the lexicographical ordering as formulated in (S), the authoritarian properties of that regime do nothing to cancel the secularist nature of the regime, whatever else they cancel—for instance, the *liberal* nature of the regime. Not all secularism need be liberal secularism. So also, then, many communist regimes should get counted as secular by this criterion. Someone may find the authoritarian methods by which secularism was imposed in both Ataturk's Turkey and the Soviet Union to be wrong without denying they were committed to secularism. Taylor, who *explicitly* takes it to be an advantage of his redefinition that it rules out Ataturk's Turkey as secular (see note 6, Taylor, p. 37), is on this point at least, quite visibly at odds with (S) as a characterization of secularism. There is a further and symmetrically converse point to be made: Just as secularism may bypass liberalism, liberalism may outrun secularism when the liberal goals and ideals one might begin with, such as free speech, say, are concerned to protect those who offend *non*-religious sentiments and concerns, over and above protecting blasphemers. It can't be a reason to redefine secularism that the goals that it begins with (when they are liberal goals), which seek to protect one from the illiberality of some religious demands, would also protect one from illiberality coming from *other* sources than religious demands. Liberalism is a wider notion than secular liberalism, which qualifies liberalism to a restricted domain, just as liberal secularism qualifies secularism to a restricted set of cases of secularism.

It is also true that Turkey and some other nations did much else besides meet the minimal requirements of the lexicographical ordering as articulated in (S). They sought to rule out religion not just in the polity, but in a much more general way, intruding into the cultural life and the intellectual and artistic productions of their citizens. In doing so, they went far beyond the requirements of the lexicographical ordering. And in doing so they were not merely enforcing secularism in authoritarian fashion, they were enforcing secular*ization* as a broader social process. All this too may be acknowledged without it falsifying the observation of a more minimal property of these polities, which is that they were secular*ist*. As I said in (c) above, the characterization of secularism on offer in (S) is not by any means committed to rooting out religion in society. The lexicographical ordering that is the core of the

characterization is perfectly compatible with a society that has a great
deal of religiosity in its culture and practices. The ideals that are placed
first in the lexicographical ordering could be such as to find acceptable a
wide range of religious practices. But equally, on the other hand, it is not
a requirement of secularism, as defined by (S), that secularism should
be *in*compatible with determined and authoritarian efforts at imposing
secularization in addition to secularism. I had said earlier that because
secularism, restricted as it is to the polity, is a narrower notion than secularization, which extends as a process to society at large and its cultural
and intellectual life, polities may be secular*ist* with or without the society
at large being proportionately secular*ized*. The separateness of these two
notions would also have it, of course, that just because there is extreme
secularization enforced, as in Ataturk's Turkey, that is not necessarily a
sign that secularism must exist. In Turkey, as it happened, secularism
did exist, but there can be a society—Tel Aviv society, unlike Jerusalem,
I suspect, is one such—which is highly secularized but is embedded in
a national polity that is not secularist. Moreover, the separateness of the
two notions guarantees that the existence of secularization via authoritarian methods, as in Ataturk's Turkey, is not a sign that secularism does
not exist. Authoritarianism, whether it imposes secularism or secularization, is orthogonal to the criterion by which secularism is defined.

Quite apart from Ataturk, even Richard Dawkins and Christopher
Hitchens would not get counted as secularists but *anti*-secularists by
Taylor's redefinition since they repudiate neutrality between religions
and unbelief, the very thing that Taylor demands of secularism, when
he says: "Indeed, the point of state neutrality is precisely to avoid favoring or disfavoring not just religious positions but any basic position,
religious or nonreligious. We can't favor Christianity over Islam, but
also religion over against non-belief in religion *or vice versa*" (p. 37, my
italics). But I do think something simple yet deep is under theoretical
strain, if these are the implications of a semantic stipulation. I—despite
being an atheist—hold no brief for Dawkins and Hitchens, who, in my
view, represent one of the least appealing and most irrelevant intellectual
stances on religion today. Still, the idea that they and, also, the idea that
Ataturk should be counted as anti-secularists is too counterintuitive and
the redefinition seems to go against our most ordinary understanding

and instincts about secularism for reasons that have to do with values that have nothing much to do with secularism at all.

(e)

In the last comment, I urged that we allow that not all secularism is liberal secularism, implying more generally that secularism is only one value among many and, as a result, it may in some contexts be accompanied by properties that put aside many of the other values that we might cherish. But there is a more radical point to be made: We might, having begun with certain goals and ideals—which make no mention of religion or opposition to religion, just as Rawls, Taylor, and (S) require—find that *secularism is a quite unnecessary political doctrine or policy to adopt.* We might find that religious practices and customs promote those goals and ideals quite satisfactorily and that it would be a fetish of modernity to think that secularism nevertheless must be adopted by a polity. This is the scenario whose possibility I wanted to leave space for when I was outlining the third defining feature of secularism.

It is how Gandhi thought of the ideal of secularism for India in the early part of the twentieth century and there was wisdom in that view, then. India, because of its distance from Europe, not merely physical but cultural and political, was a good test case for contemplating both secularism's content and its relation to its own history.

If we step back and look at secularism's history from a distance in order to try to view its larger trajectories and patterns, we notice that much of the consolidations of secularism, that is, much of its coming to be viewed as a *necessity* in modern societies, occurred in the context of slowly and long-forming features of European societies. One particular trajectory was central.

In the post-Westphalian European context, there emerged a need for states to seek their legitimacy in ways that could no longer appeal to outdated ideas of the divine rights of states as personified in their monarchs. This new form of legitimacy began to be sought by the creation of a new form of political *psychology* in a new kind of subject, the "citizen," of a new kind of entity that had emerged, the "nation." It was to be done, that is, by creating in citizens a *feeling* for the nation, which generated a legitimacy for the state because the nation was defined in tandem, in hyphenated conjunction, with a certain kind of increasingly centralized state. This nation-state was to be legitimized by this feeling among its subjects, a political-psychological phenomenon that would somewhat later come to be called "national*ism*." In European nations, such a feeling was uniformly created in their citizens by a very standard ploy—by finding an *external* enemy *within,* the outsider in one's midst, "the other" (the Irish, the Jews, to name just two) to be despised and subjugated. In a later time, with the coming of a more numerical and statistical form of discourse, these would come to be called "minorities," and the ploy that I am outlining would be described as "majoritarian-ism." Often *religion* was either central to or was implicated in the way that minorities and majorities were defined, and it was to *repair* the deep and severe damages and scars caused by *this* process that secularism was consolidated as an indispensable necessity in the political life of nations. It came to be seen as a politically constructed guarantee of toleration in this context, that is to say, in a context of modernity in which a very spe-cific trajectory of nation-state formation was central. It is not that intoler-ance did not exist in prior times, but the structural necessities set up by new national boundaries and political institutions made the intolerance generated by the self-consciously adopted ploy I have sketched as some-thing seemingly quite impossible to alleviate in any other way but by the formulation of secularism and the devising of state policies in order to promote it.

Now it should be possible to say, as Gandhi did, that where such a trajectory had never occurred as it had in Europe, no such repair was needed. It was his view that religions had long pervaded the political life of India but it was within an ethos of quite un-self-conscious pluralism, a syncretic religious culture, within which politics was conducted in *scattered* loci of power, with no highly centralized state seeking to legiti-mate itself by creating the wrong basis for unity by a self-consciously constructed majoritarian feeling among its citizens. A unity which was instead an outgrowth of a rooted and syncretic culture within which diverse religions were, without too much strain, in any case relatively tolerant of each other, required no artificial measure and policies, no doctrinal formulations of modernity, under the name of "secularism."

Whatever the other shortcomings of such a culture (and there were no doubt many, as Gandhi himself often acknowledged), there was nothing measurably damaging of this specific sort to repair, and to impose secularism on one's people under these circumstances would be a mimicry of its colonial masters, a form of cognitive slavery. So it seemed to Gandhi. And, in fact, his greatest anxiety was that the eager modernizers around him in the Indian freedom movement which he led would fall into a form of thinking in which the post-Westphalian European path to modernity, conceived via this new form of state, was seen as compulsory for India as well. When he wrote first about it in the early part of the twentieth century, he declared explicitly that it was quite *un*compulsory.

Savarkar, who very deliberately and articulately formulated such a European path of politics for India, with majoritarian methods to achieve feelings of unity in his vision of a modern Indian nation of the future, was Gandhi's chief ideological opponent, and it is not surprising that it was one of his followers who would later assassinate him. Everything Gandhi stood for also stood in the way of such a conception of Indian modernity.[9] As it turned out, Savarkar's thinking had a great deal of influence in India, even some influence within the Congress Party that Gandhi led, and the openly vocal and activist form of majoritarian Hindu nationalism that has emerged in the country since the passing of Gandhi, Nehru, and some of the other leaders of the older generation, has made something like secularism seem much more obviously relevant for India than it seemed to Gandhi when he was writing about these matters during the very early period of the freedom movement. The point I am laboring in all this is that there may be many ideals—of pluralism, of toleration—that we start with, just as Taylor asks, but in many societies, there may be no work for the lexicographical ordering and for secularist doctrine, in general, to do in order to promote those ideals. Secularism is a normative position, which is shaped by these ideals in very specific contexts where the ideals and goals require it. It is not a goal in itself. Were the ideals present in other political forms and arrangements, the need for secularism would not so much as arise. In my view, it is theoretically sounder to say this than to redefine secularism so that it becomes the appropriate doctrine for all contexts and occasions and always serves the ideals we wish to pursue.

Still, I think one can explore these matters a little more by voicing a protest on behalf of Taylor's redefined ideal of secularism. One might do this by saying that what I am suggesting is the wrong lesson to learn from Gandhi's reaction to the situation in early twentieth century India. After all, what Gandhi was pointing out was that there was toleration by each religion of the other and there was equal and free participation of all religions in the syncretic religious culture of the time, and that just *is* secularism in the fraternal as well as the liberty and equality sense that Taylor has outlined. So if Taylor is right, Gandhi was in favor of, not against, secularism, and his view was that India was always secularist. It may be that once there is a more centralized state than existed in India in that earlier time, then this earlier secularism would have to be recast a bit to be seen as a centralized state being neutral and evenhanded among different religions, trying to steer modern society to replicate the syncretism of past times by encouraging all religions to be mutually respectful of each other's freely chosen religious practices. But it would essentially be a secularism that was continuous with the past.

A response on behalf of (S) to such a protest will help to bring out, in a little more depth, the history by which (S) has come to seem necessary.

The view voiced in the protest, I think, would be a quite mistaken reading of Gandhi, who was more clear-eyed about how secularism emerged from a certain history in the West and had certain distinct functions of meeting specific goals that needed to be met as a result of certain developments in Europe in the modern period.

The fact is that the goals and ideals that Gandhi articulated were merely those of toleration and pluralism. But toleration and pluralism, though they obviously have some relation with secularism (as they do with any number of other political notions and doctrines) are by no means identical with it. And secularism is not a guarantee for those ideals in all contexts. It is neither a necessary nor sufficient condition for toleration and pluralism. Secularism is a doctrine that is also introduced to further goals of a quite different sort that were not in the forefront of Gandhi's mind, and even when toleration and pluralism were at the core of what secularism sought to promote, it was within a context that I have just sketched above, in which this core came to be surrounded by other goals as well. Thus, for instance, it would never occur to Gandhi to be anxious to allow blasphemy to go uncensored. Nor did it particularly worry him that one or other religion, Hinduism or Islam, had personal laws that ran afoul of the ideals of gender equality in its family laws. These were not goals that were central to what he thought politics should be responding and pursuing in the context in which he lived and wrote.[10] On the matter of religion, his focus was instead on keeping India away from a politics in which Hindu majoritarianism entered as a way of creating nationalist feeling in India, thus giving rise to a trajectory in which secularism would be the natural outcome, introduced to repair the damage in this.

Now one might think that a state conceived as neutral among different religions, as Taylor envisages it, *is the best method by which to deal with the damage done by this trajectory.* So why am I resisting calling it "secularism"?

This is a good question and the answer is that once this trajectory takes its course, the damage is so deep and pervasive and so easily and constantly revived and revisited that minorities are simply not in a position to ensure that the state, even in a democracy (obviously even less so in more authoritarian regimes), will be able to be evenhanded. Political parties will constantly appeal, for electoral gain, to majoritarian tendencies and will not be able to eschew these tendencies after electoral success when they are tenants of the state. This, in turn, gives rise to a *reaction* among minorities to fall into identity politics as a defense since the state is often unable to withstand majoritarianism and remain neutral. When majorities and minorities are defined in terms of religion in this familiar scenario, there inevitably arises a sense that religion (in the political sphere) *itself* is the problem, even though the historical source of the problem lies in majoritarianism.

This point about religious majoritarianism and minority backlashes against it is a very crucial part of this essay's effort at elaborating the defining relevance of secularism. It stresses the historical context in which secularism emerged as *built into* how we understand its rationale. Any definition of a normative concept such as secularism must pay attention to *two things at once* that pull in different directions but must be kept in balance. One is to recognize that, being normative, the concept is after all an *ideal.* The other is the one that I have just stressed, viz., that the ideal itself has emerged in a historical context and our *conceptual* understanding of it must not lose sight of that history. Historical understanding and conceptual analysis are not to be seen as entirely separable cognitive enterprises. So when I say that secularism emerged to repair certain damages done by the rise of religious majoritarianism in European nation-building exercises (and minoritarian backlashes to it), I am not merely making an historical and genealogical point—I am building that genealogy *into the very content of secularism* because I am claiming that in that history the repair came to be viewed as impossible to carry out unless *religion itself* became the issue and that is why secularism was formulated as a stance to be taken (in some sense) in opposition to religion. To say that it is built into the very content of secularism is to say that it is not an aspect of its formulation that one can now simply refuse, as Taylor does, in his alternative formulation. So that is one rather deep methodological contrast between Taylor's position and (S). But this aspect of (S) as a definition comes with an important implication about its relevance and application. If it is the case that there are societies in which no such harms are present as emerged in the nation-building exercises of Europe and the (neutrally formulated) ideals we wish to pursue in a polity can, as it turns out, be found in religion itself, then there is no reason to adopt (S)—for, as I said, to do so would be to adopt an (historically understood) concept in a form of pointless mimicry when the historical circumstances are not present. That was Gandhi's claim about secularism in India and generally for many countries of the South.

Recent developments in India have increasingly shown that circumstances are now considerably different from when Gandhi first wrote about these issues, a victory, as I said, for the forces of Savarkar over Gandhi, even within the Congress Party, leave alone the Hindu nationalist party. For this general reason (and not merely in India), something more radical came to be seen as needed to keep under control this entire tendency toward domination by a religious majority and religious identitarian reactive responses by minorities. This radical policy keeps religion out of the polity, so that the temptation of the appeal to religious majoritarianism is preempted at the outset as a legal or constitutional transgression, something that the courts of an independently constituted judiciary are there to ensure (though as it turns out in some recent decisions in India, it is not obvious that the courts are willing always to do so). So it is these recent developments in India (present also in other countries of the South) which replicate in recognizable ways conditions in Europe that I've been describing at some length which give rise to an ethos in which something like a lexicographical ordering of the sort I have formulated tends to come to the forefront in how a modern polity is conceived. Once conceived this way, the term "secularism" is and has been the natural name for it. And once the conception comes into place, it begins to seem, in this increasingly and *very specifically* modern political ethos that had its origins in post-Westphalian Europe, that it is *not* sufficient to be neutral and evenhanded among religions.

Moreover, in such an ethos where religion itself comes to be seen as the source of the problem, whether in its majoritarian exploitation or in its minoritarian reaction to that, new goals (that is goals beyond merely toleration and pluralism) emerge; and these new goals, though they are defined independently of religion (goals such as free speech, say, and gender equality), turn their scrutiny on religion and focus on how religions *in particular* thwart the pursuit of the goals. Thus free speech is now seen not merely in its generality but more particularly free speech in the face of a religious requirement to suppress deliberate and brazen blasphemy; and gender equality too is steered, in particular, toward gender equality in the face of gender-unjust religious family laws; and so on. This specifically radical direction of thinking generated by this ethos can certainly lead up to an intemperate and unconstrained attack on religion in public life. My formulation of (S) is an effort to give a sober formulation of this radical step, respecting a range of Taylor's anxieties about such an attack on religion that leads him to redefine secularism, without actually embracing that redefinition. The point remains though that something like (S) alone comes to seem like the policy that could provide the repair of these historical damages and constraint on religion, because neutrality and evenhandedness among religions cannot possibly promote these new goals and ideals. It is not enough to neutrally and evenhandedly allow each religion in society its free speech–denying blasphemy laws or its gender-discriminating family laws. These laws are trumped only by the first-placed lexicographical ordering of free speech and gender equality. Of course, one can still insist that the state neutrally and evenhandedly apply the lexicographical ordering to each religion, but that still means that the ideal of neutrality and evenhandedness is embedded in (S); it does not constitute a secularism that is independent of (S).

Let me say again, however, that none of this was relevant in Indian politics when Gandhi wrote in the early part of the twentieth century. Neither issues of blasphemy laws nor of gender inequality were in the forefront of the public agenda surrounding the local, syncretist religious cultures and the politics that surfaced in them. (And this may well be the case in many parts of the world to this day—in many regions of Africa, say, even possibly in parts of the Middle East, though the intense material and therefore cultural gaze on—not to mention interventions in—the latter by Western interests may be comprehensively and decisively changing that.) But they are much more relevant now and, along with the need for the reversal of social and political damages of religious majoritarian sources for nationalism, they form part of a trajectory that emerged in India *since* the time Gandhi expressed his qualms against a very specific path in European modernity.[11] To describe Gandhi's position of an earlier time in India than the present as secularist, therefore, is to quite fail to see the relevance of a range of developments in India since the time in which he first wrote (the developments of what I had called a specific post-Westphalian trajectory) regarding which he had very prescient anxieties about what might be visited upon India, if the trajectory was adopted there. If we pay close attention to his anxieties in that period, we can recognize that he was not a proto-secularist but rather that he did not want the conditions to occur in India in which secularism would seem a necessity at all.

Before closing this section, let me qualify the general direction of these points that I have been making. It is important to do so, without actually reversing their direction. A little earlier I had said: "Any definition of a normative concept such as secularism must pay attention to *two things at once* that pull in different directions but must be kept in balance. One is to recognize that, being normative, the concept is after all an *ideal*. The other is the one that I have just stressed, viz., that the ideal itself has emerged in a historical context and our *conceptual* understanding of it must not lose sight of that history." In the foregoing remarks

I have focused on the important methodological difference between Taylor and (S) in that the latter resists the dispensability of the history to the conceptual understanding and, in resisting it, opposes Taylor's efforts at redefining secularism. But I want to close this exposition by saying just a bit about the first element (the element of an ideal) in the balance to be maintained because it points to another (less important) contrast that (S) offers as against Taylor. If I am right that addressing the damages of religious majoritarianism and minoritarian backlashes are central to the formulation of secularism, it strictly follows that secularism has particular relevance to societies in which there is more than one religion. Be that as it may, once erected as an *ideal*, the characterization of secularism must, at least as a limiting or degenerate case, allow it to have application in societies which are relatively homogenous in their commitment to religion. That is why I began my characterization of secularism in (S) with the words "Should we be living in a religiously plural society." Given the historical context in which secularism emerged and which I have outlined above, this conditional beginning of (S) lies idle. But qua ideal, (S) should—even if at most notionally—be formulated so as to have application to societies, should they exist, where where there is not much plurality of religion. The opening words of (S), as I have formulated it, ensures that it *does* have application to a society that is religiously homogeneous. If there are neutrally described ideals that the polity of such a religiously homogeneous society wishes to pursue and that require the lexicographical priority that (S) gives to them over a certain religious practice of such a society, then (S) has application to that society. And if it turns out there are *no* religiously homogeneous societies, the ideal does not lose its point because those opening words of (S) are merely in the form of a conditional. They don't assert that there are such societies; they only conditionally allow for the application of (S) to them, *should* there be any. One would not understand the nature of an ideal if one did not understand that ideals are to be formulated for conditions which may not hold in a particular time. Now Taylor's redefinition of secularism *cannot*, by its very conception, have any relevance or application to societies which may be relatively homogeneous in religious commitment because it is defined upon neutral equidistance between a plurality of religions. (S), by contrast, I am saying, *does* have such a relevance. Of course, I am not claiming that this is any great advantage of (S) over Taylor's redefinition because I am myself claiming that secularism cannot be understood except as having a certain genealogy in which more than one religion is present with a dominant majority religion and minoritarian defensive backlashes to it. But I am also saying that a definition or characterization must respect the fact that once it is understood in these historical terms, secularism does also take on the aspect of an ideal, and *qua ideal,* it can get a general formulation that at least in a limiting or degenerate sense has application to cases where the lexicographical priority it seeks may have relevance even though there is relative religious homogeneity. That is the minimal balance between contingency and history on the one hand and conceptual idealization on the other that any characterization of a normative concept such as secularism must try to achieve.

To sum up, then, it has, in general, been the burden of these several comments, (a) to (e), that I have been making on the nature of (S), to say that its stipulated form of secularism, in terms of a certain lexicographical ordering, gives a certain theoretical bite and specificity to secularism, such that it is not all goods in all contexts but only a good in some contexts, and therefore not always to be embraced even in our own time, if the conditions don't require it for the pursuit of other worthy goals. This specificity also allows one to say that secularism can often be accompanied by bad political and institutional arrangements such as in Ataturk's Turkey or in Baathist Iraq or in the aggressively authoritarian secularist policies of some communist regimes. It does not see those bad political arrangements and institutions as a reason and occasion to try to redefine secularism so that these don't count as secularist polities at all. Such redefinitions take the bite out of the concept, in much the same way that the redefinition attempted in the idea of "people's democracy" to counter "free democracy" took the bite out of the notion of "democracy."[12] The specific formulation of the lexicographical ordering, moreover, has the strict advantage over the "neutrality and equidistant state" ideal of secularism in disallowing things that would in our own time, if not earlier, intuitively count as anti-secular—for example, censorship of works of art and literature on grounds of "blasphemy" against a religion, something that the latter ideal would permit in a given case, on the grounds that it was ready and willing to neutrally permit it in all other cases of blasphemy against all other religions in the society.

I've spent a considerable time on these semantic matters with a view to bringing out the content of secularism, using Taylor's interesting and challenging ideas of a redefinition of secularism as a foil. I had said that though I think Taylor's redefinition has worthy moral and political motivations, it is not as well motivated, theoretically. (S), by contrast, does not make any attempt at redefinition; it merely tries to elaborate along modest, and minimalist lines, the rationale underlying the instincts behind dogmatic-sounding metaphors such as "the separation of church and state." As such, (S) seems to contain crucial elements that Taylor is trying to redefine secularism *away* from.

I want to turn now from semantic matters, from questions of what is the more plausible and non-arbitrary stipulation by which we define or characterize the content of secularism, to questions of how to implement (S), if and when its implementation is necessary.

5.

One way to bring out some essential points about the implementation of (S) would be to present some qualms I myself have about how (S) lends itself to coercive conceptions of its own implementation. And some of these qualms are best expounded if we first sympathetically present why it might theoretically and philosophically seem to many that Taylor's ideal of a state, neutral and equidistant between religious and non-religious points of view, is a better position to adopt than (S).

In Section 2, I took up the question of what *justified* secularism over and above what defined or characterized it, saying that it was important to distinguish between the two. And while discussing the justification of secularism, I had invoked Bernard Williams's distinction between two types of justification, one which appealed to internal reasons and the other to external reasons, and had claimed that there are only internal reasons for embracing secularism. I have not argued for nor will I argue for this claim in this essay, partly for reasons of space but partly also because I have done so extensively in previous papers.[13] The point of interest at present, as I say in Section 2, is that this view is entirely compatible with and indeed lies behind the claim that secularism should only be adopted on the basis of an overlapping consensus. On these issues of justification and adoption (rather than those of definition just discussed in Section 4), there is complete accord between Taylor's views and the ones expressed here.

To political philosophers and theorists, it might seem natural to conclude from these commitments on which there is complete accord between us that secularism is fated to be mired in a form of *relativism* regarding moral and political values, and such a relativism may well suggest, in turn, that something like a "neutral state" version of secularism is what we should retreat to, whereas any secularism such as (S) that seeks a somewhat more adversarial stance against religion, should be counted not as secularism but as one non-religious standpoint among other standpoints, including religious standpoints, between which the state is neutral.[14] This approximates Taylor's own favored understanding of secularism.

So we must ask, whichever we think is best to call "secularism," is the neutralist ideal shown to be better than (S), as a consequence of the relativist implications that seem to follow from the stress on internal reasons in the justification of secularism?

The idea is this. If there are no external reasons which support a moral or political standpoint or value (such as secularism, say, or to keep things even more specific and focused, secular liberalism), if internal reasons are the only reasons one can bring to bear when there is a deep disagreement over values (between, say, such a secular liberalism and one or other religious point of view), then it might seem that something like relativism about these values and points of view is necessarily in the offing. Recall that external reasons are reasons that all will agree on, no matter what their values and substantial commitments may be, and internal reasons appeal only to substantial moral and political commitments of individual citizens, which are likely to vary among the citizens. If internal reasons are the only reasons there are for justifications of such values as secularism, the thought that (S) in its secular liberal form will even have the resources to effectively offer such internal reasons to a strongly held religious standpoint (say, for example, a position with strong Muslim identitarian political values) to change its mind might seem too optimistic; and that, in turn, will make it seem as if some anti-secular Muslim commitments, such as to the value of censorship of blasphemy, may have their own sort of truth (*relativistically* characterized truth) on their side.[15] And if that is so, then it would seem only right that a state having to now navigate these different *true* standpoints—(S) in its secular liberal form as well as various religious standpoints such as Islamist and other strongly held religious views—should be neutral and evenhanded with each of them, since each has the prestige of *truth* on its side. This would reduce (S), even in the eyes of those who subscribe to it, to one among other true points of view, including religious ones. Thus the relativism that seems to emerge as a consequence from the points of philosophical *agreement* between Taylor and me on the primacy of internal reasons and the inefficacy of external reasons may seem to suggest that the state neutrality ideal is *theoretically* quite well motivated (by this relativism) and (S) less well so, despite all the theoretical points I made in the last section.

Can this be right? Does this specific argument, via a relativism that flows from the primacy of internal reasons, which I make on sympathetic behalf of Taylor's view, give us a reason to adopt the state neutralist ideal he favors over (S)? Or to put it differently, does this specific argument give a state committed to adopting (S) any reason to yield to a more state neutralist ideal?

I think it is arguable that it does not.

Notice, first, what exactly is meant by relativism, as it seems to follow from the denial of external reasons and the claim that only internal reasons will justify secular liberalism. It means something quite strong. What is meant is that when there are no external reasons and two parties are disagreed over some value commitment, *there may in principle be no scope for either party to give even internal reasons to one another.* Internal reasons are dependent on support coming from our substantive values, not something given to us by the very fact of our rationality. Therefore unlike external reasons, there is no guarantee that internal reasons to subscribe to (S) will be available since they are dependent on further values which may not be present—in the case under consideration, present in the values held by Islamists. And, in general, it is prima facie possible that in some sorts of value-disagreement, there will, *in principle,* be no such further values for the parties in the disagreement to appeal to. In that case we will have the kind of impasse mentioned in the formulation, just given, of relativism. The expression "in principle" is doing some serious work in this formulation of relativism. Relativism is a theoretical or philosophical position; it is not just a practical difficulty about how it is sometimes very hard to persuade someone you disagree with on some matters of value. The theoretical position is that each party in the dispute may be utterly unreach*able* by the other. This may indeed be cause for alarm to subscribers to (S), and, to the extent that we are alarmed, a concession and retreat to Taylor's redefinition of secularism shows the appropriate respect for each position that has truth on its side because (S) cannot claim greater truth on its side for the ideals it begins with and, therefore, must drop its claim to a lexicographical ordering that places those ideals first and religious laws and customs and practices second, when they clash. Thus relativism requires that not only are there no external reasons for justifying secular ideals, reasons that all can share and find to be reasons, but that there are *no* reasons (not internal ones either) that it can, in principle, find to justify secular ideals to other more religious points of view. Secular liberalism is one truth among many, and not merely one standpoint among many. The latter claim (one standpoint among many) is uncontroversial. But for a secular liberal to allow the former claim (that religious points of view that it often wants to place second in a lexicographical ordering have the *truth* on their side) would undermine the very priorities asserted in the lexicographical ordering. A relevantly neutral state of the kind that Taylor recommends is a better form of polity for such a scenario than (S), which has to concede that secular liberalism is just one truth among many. So these considerations of relativism might well motivate the adoption of Taylor's neutralist state rather than a state that adopts the lexicographical ordering ideal.

But before we concede that this relativism is the fate of (S), given the primacy of internal reasons, some more detailed understanding of what exactly internal reasons are is required.

What is it to find internal reasons to persuade another? Internal reasons are reasons we give to another that appeal to some of *his own values* in order to try to persuade him to change his mind on some given value, such as, say, a commitment to censorship of blasphemy. So if a Muslim does have such a commitment, a secular liberal subscribing to (S) can only appeal to some other value of *his* which is *in tension or in conflict* with his commitment to the censorship of blasphemy. To put it very explicitly, one will have to find that such Muslims are committed a) to censorship of blasphemy and yet that they are also committed b) to various other values which may lend support to the value of free speech. And for (S), to use internal reasons against such Muslims, is to stress b) to them in an effort to bring them around to discarding a). Of course if (S) was justifiable on grounds of external reasons, one couldn't appeal to considerations such as b), which is a substantive value. But, in that case, one would not *need* to appeal to such a consideration. It is only because one takes the view that both Taylor and I, following Williams, take, that there are no external reasons, that one is forced to appeal to considerations such as b).

In general, then, the strategy of internal reasons is a strategy that can only work when those against whom it is brought to work are *internally conflicted*. (It is important to add that conflicts within values need not always take the form of there being blatant inconsistencies among them. In fact it may seldom be that. Much more likely and much more pervasive are conflicts of a more subtle kind, tensions or dissonances between values.)

We can now pull the strands together. Relativism, as I've defined it for the purposes of this essay's concerns, is a doctrine that holds if there is a certain kind of impasse. It holds if there are, *in principle,* no internal reasons that two parties in a disagreement over values can give to one another. And if the prospect for giving internal reasons turns on the possibility of there being an internal conflict in at least one of the parties involved in a disagreement over values, then that implies that relativism would hold only if both parties in such a disagreement are *completely unconflicted,* that is, if they have perfectly and maximally coherent value-economies. In other words, in order for relativism, of the sort we are worrying about, to be true, it would have to be the case that someone with whom one disagrees over values is not merely never inconsistent (as I admitted blatant inconsistency might be hard to attribute to political and moral subjects), but they would also have to be *wholly* without any tension or dissonance in their values and desires. That alone makes for a *principled* impasse.

But it is hard to think that ordinary human subjects are so completely without internal conflict in this broad sense. The idea of such a total lack of inner conflict is an extraordinary condition to find in any value-economy. Relativism, conceived on this condition, would find instance, it seems, only when two parties in a dispute over a value were *monsters of coherence*. Perhaps some imagined rational automata are maximally coherent in their value commitments but the idea that ordinary human moral-psychological economies are so is barely conceivable. Thus, so long as Islamists with commitments to blasphemy laws are susceptible to conflicting relations among their commitments, so long as they are not possessed of maximally coherent value-economies, the scope of internal reasons to establish secular liberalism even in the face of identity politics is maintained. Maximal coherence being a barely conceivable condition, there is no need to despair about the scope for secular liberal politics to succeed without externalist reasons and arguments.

The point cannot be quite left where it is.

Let it even be conceivable that, at a given time, a particular illiberal moral-psychological economy is highly coherent and unconflicted—at any rate, let it be conceivable, as it surely is, that any conflict or tension that it *does* contain among its value commitments is not as a matter of fact helpful in bringing it around to shedding its anti-liberal commitments. It is perfectly possible that even if Islamists are internally conflicted on some matters, these may be matters which are not relevant to (S)'s efforts to give internal reasons to them to get them to change their minds on censorship of blasphemy. This *still* does not hobble the scope of secular liberalism. Why not? The answer to this question, I think, is central to the epistemology of political and moral values. The answer is: *because political philosophy cannot consider moral subjects and political citizens as standing outside of history, in some timeless, unconflicted psychological economy.*

Since citizens are historical subjects, history and the incoming states of information that it provides to these subjects, in its course, may well *introduce* conflict in them by introducing tensions and dissonance in the relations between their value commitments. Let me just give one example, at some distance from the dispute on issues of blasphemy, to illustrate what I have in mind. It is now fairly well documented that the large increase in pro-choice attitudes among hitherto even relatively conservative women in America in the third quarter of the last century was a result of their having deliberated their way out of a conflict in their own commitments, a conflict that *emerged* fully only in that period of history, when as a result of the rise of service industries and the relative decline of heavy manufacturing goods industries, the possibility of a more gender-distributed work force was created. An historical change, which provided for greater prospects for employment for women, introduced conflict into the values of even hitherto conservative women, and this in turn gave rise to internal deliberation on their part that resulted in many of them revising their views on the issue of abortion. The point, then, is that even if, at a given time, a value-economy seems relatively unreachable by internal reasons because it is relatively coherent and unconflicted, so long as we think of moral-psychological economies as necessarily being *in history*, internal conflicts may be injected by historical developments into moral-psychological economies.

The point is essentially Hegelian, though in Hegel himself (despite all the recent efforts by scholars to say that Hegel was relatively innocent of this) it is unfortunately marred because it is nested in terms that were more deterministic than is necessary. But it is a point of the utmost importance for those who think both that (S) can only be justified on the basis of internal reasons and that thinking so entails *no* relativism of the sort we are considering.

This Hegelian idea goes deeper than it might seem. It might seem that all the idea amounts to is that at some later time, we might be able to persuade someone with whom we are disagreed by giving him internal reasons, but *for now* at least, there is an impasse and so relativism about reasons is true. But this deflationary description misses the real theoretical status of the appeal to the subject-*in*-history. That appeal is precisely intended to repudiate the idea that we should think of subjects as being in slabs of time, with relativism about their values holding in one slab, and possibly passing away in the next. Despite the talk of different times, that would *still* be to conceive the subject essentially synchronically at each slab of time. A genuinely diachronically conceived subject (hardly ever the subject that is considered by analytical philosophers and political theorists writing about morals and politics, or anything else), a subject conceived neither synchronically nor in discretely periodized times, but rather a subject conceived of as essentially historically open-ended, is exactly intended to replace the subject relativized to a time, when his values may have a "relative" truth, or his reasons a relative closure. Hence the inclination to say, "Relativism *for now,* but not perhaps *later!*" is to not yet quite be on board with the depth of the point which Hegel's stress on the importance of history for our conception of human subjectivity is making. To be fully on board is to see that *no* sort of relativism is sanctioned for subjects conceived essentially diachronically and therefore open to the internal conflicts that history may provide.

I will admit again, however, that my appeal to Hegel here is highly selective since the fact that history should play this kind of role in our understanding of moral subjectivity—paradoxically—opens things up against the very sort of historical determinism that historicism has suggested to many (though, as I said earlier, not all) readers of Hegel. The select element in Hegel which I am applauding is the idea that Reason (what I, following, Williams call "internal" reason) does its work in a human subject by bringing about changes of value via deliberation on her part to overcome internal conflicts among values (something that popularizing Hegelians—never Hegel himself—describe overly schematically in dialectical terms of the trio of "thesis, antithesis, and synthesis"); and that one does so very often as a result of conflicts (what in the popular Hegelian representation is called "antitheses") that emerge because of incoming states of information provided by specifically historical encounters. Once viewed this way, there is no reason to think that relativism follows upon the loss of external reasons, and so no reason to be pessimistic about the scope of *internal* reasons to be a resource for secular liberal political outcomes. Within this selective Hegelian view of the importance of history and of diachronic subjectivity, the right way to describe what has wrongly been described as this "pessimism" is simply to say that there is no Whiggish *guarantee* of a consummation of the historical process in a secular liberal outcome. That is not pessimism; it is just a recoil from a *deterministic* historicism. One can be as optimistic as one wishes and hold out for history to introduce conflict in the points of view that one wishes to offer internal reasons to in order to change their commitments. Thus secular liberalism can remain committed to its ideals with confidence and a secular state need not retreat to neutrality between secularism and other religious points of view, even in the face of the most vexed disagreement with these other points of view.

That we should see the significance of history for subjectivity along these lines is, however, not a merely metaphysical position; it is in a rarefied sense itself an *evaluative* position. This point is crucial. After all someone else may see history as having a rather depressing record in resolving conflict between groups and resist my repudiation of relativism, a repudiation which has *the default* lie in the view that it is always at least possible that new conflicts *internal* to an individual or group will—via internal reasoning—help resolve conflicts *between* individuals or groups. Such a person will simply not find the record in history sanctioning this default position. The default says that when there is an intractable value-disagreement between two parties, history may always inject, in one of the parties, the sort of internal conflict necessary for the other to provide internal reasons to it. The interlocutor here will deny this, saying that the record of history does not justify this to be the default position. I have no purely philosophical or metaphysical argument against such an interlocutor who does not agree with me about how to view the significance of history for moral subjects in conflict with one another. To find this interlocutor wrong is, in the end, to assert a value. In fact we cannot find him wrong without asserting a value; we cannot find him wrong by a non-evaluative argument. And to say that is to assert the priority of the evaluative over the metaphysical.

This needs more patient exposition.

The default position says we must see the significance of history for subjectivity to be as follows: that one always see it as at least *possible* that a dispute in values may be resolved by internal reasoning as a result of the requisite *internal* conflict being introduced into one or other of the disputing parties by the incoming states of information that historical changes provide to their psychological and value-economies. It is when the significance of history is viewed along these lines (as allowing such a default position) that we are in turn allowed to turn our back on the claim of relativism that the deepest disputes in value might constitute an impasse. That is to say, such a default allows one to make *no* concession to a possible right or truth or correctness on the side of one's opponent, in cases of interesting and deep moral and political dispute. So the hard question, which I raised above, remains: *What gives us the right to view the significance of history for moral subjectivity along these lines?* Why may we not see its significance along quite different lines, see history as providing too much evidence for *disallowing* what I just claim as at least a necessary and permanent *possibility?* The nested modalities are complicated here, but my interlocutor's idea will be that what I am insisting is a possibility might only be contingently so, and there may be no necessity that such a possibility always exists. History is simply not to be viewed in the optimistic way I am viewing it. It is possible that such dispute-resolving internal conflicts are introduced into moral subjects by history but it is possible also that they are not. Why, then, am I insisting that history must be viewed in a way that it *necessarily* leaves it as an open possibility that such a conflict is introduced?

As I admitted, there is no answer to this question (and so there is no justification for taking the default position I do on the significance of history) along lines that are *non*-normative or purely metaphysical. There is nothing in history, nothing in the concept of history and our place in it, when that is conceived in purely descriptive and non-normative terms, which could instruct us to view history as offering us the default position I insist on. To take the default position I do, therefore, is *itself* to take a higher-order *evaluative* stance. And it is only by taking such an evaluative stance that a secular liberal can express the confidence that disputes in identitarian contexts with illiberal tendencies need not ever produce the despondency of saying that perhaps both sets of principles (liberal and illiberal) may have their own sort of right on their side.

What do I mean by saying that it is in the end an *evaluative* stance which gives a secular liberal the confidence to insist on the exclusive rightness of secular liberalism against illiberal opponents, *despite* the loss of externalist reasons and the loss of externalist justifications of liberalism? I mean simply that it reflects a value, a value central to what I think is best conceived as a special and unusual version of *humanism*.

Here is how I have allowed myself to think of it.

When one is in a moral dispute with another, even if it is a bitter and vexed dispute, it is far better to be have an attitude of *inclusiveness* toward one's foe that makes one strive to share the truth as one sees it with him, rather than to adopt an *excluding* attitude and say that he may have his own sort of truth or right on his side. The latter is what the relativist pluralist says, and it will be said by anyone who does not see the philosophical and methodological force and insight of the Hegelian notion of a subject and its significance for morals and politics, as I am seeing it. For someone who does see that force and that significance, the attitude will be quite the opposite, the value of inclusiveness. This is the value which claims that it is far more attractive to say to even one's bitterest foe in a moral or political conflict, "You must be my brother," than it is to say, "You can never be my brother." To insist that he must be your brother, to refuse to allow him his own truth and to strive to convince him of the truth as you see it and judge it, is to show the requisite attitude of inclusiveness toward him. This may seem paradoxical since one is *refusing* him his own sort of truth for his views in the name of seeing him as *one's brother*. But that is just how it is. Perhaps only a subject as perverse and abstract as philosophy can see in this no paradox at all.

I will admit that the rhetoric of "must" versus "never" in my last paragraph to express the contrasting values does not present the best options. I did use the flamboyant rhetoric even so and presented the options in their most extreme form, in order to bring out the contrast vividly. To care about the truth, as one sees it and judges it, and to care enough for others who do not see it to strive to share it with them, need not take on the vocabulary which has it that one thinks that they "must" be one's brother and embrace the truth we see. But that vocabulary captures something of the caring that I want to stress here against the relativist form of pluralism, which precisely does not care in this way. Opposing such a relativistic form of pluralism, I am saying, involves not merely appealing to the Hegelian notion of subjectivity in the way I do, but also seeing that appeal as an assertion of a value of caring about the truth (as one sees it and judges it), rather than showing an indifference to others who disagree with one, as the relativistic pluralist does when he says that they may have their own sort of moral truth on their side. Such a way of caring for truth therefore itself reflects a caring for *others*, caring enough to want to convince them of the truth. That is the point of the talk of "brotherhood" as a value, a humanist value, which, in this specific sense, is missing in the relativist cast of pluralism.

To many humanists, such talk of brotherhood—flowing as it does from an ideal of caring for something so *abstract* as truth, and wanting to share that abstract thing with others—will seem too intellectualized a way of talking compared either to the down-to-earth ways in which we talk of the humanist values of brotherhood or to the sentimental, literary cast it had taken on ever since the rhetoric of "sweetness and light." It is brotherhood based on an epistemological value rather than on the usual sorts of moral values of solidarity and support that are articulated in standard versions of humanism. To such traditional humanists, the paradox of denying one's moral foe his own sort of rightful moral view, in the name of brotherhood, will seem to undermine the doctrine from within. But, as I said, there is no paradox here. It is a sign of greatly respecting someone, of including him in humanity, that you deeply want him to believe what you believe to be the truth rather than grant him as a truth (*his* truth) what you take to be deeply false. I admit that this is a very abstract way of configuring the ideal of human inclusiveness. But why should humanism not have highly abstract sources? These sources are precisely what might give the doctrine some further muscle and rigor, and therefore make it less dismissible as a musty and pious doctrine.

If I am right, it is, in the end, this abstractly humanistic and evaluative interpretation of the role of history in the constitution of human subjectivity in morals and politics that underlies the repudiation of relativism in the realm of moral and political values.[16] (In the realm of science, the situation is somewhat different. Even if one took a cognitivist conception of moral values, as I happen to do, issues regarding relativism in the *more purely* cognitive realm of science are distinct, and responses to relativism there would need to be constructed along different lines, a complicated form of difference that I cannot possibly take up here.)

What are the implications of this understanding of the Hegelian argument, for our specific subject of secularism in this essay?

6.

The goal has been to show that this repudiation of relativism allows a state that has adopted (S) to remain committed to its idea of a lexicographical ordering. It was intended to preempt the need for a state to abandon (S) and retreat to a neutrality between non-religious and religious points of view.

If the argument of the last section is convincing, the idea of an overlapping consensus on some policy such as (S) need only commit one to a pluralism about *reasons* for subscribing to (S), it does *not* commit one to a pluralism about the conclusions and outcomes based on those reasons. Thus even if (S) is the outcome of an overlapping consensus, with individuals signing onto (S) for a plurality of quite different reasons, the argument of the last section establishes that this does not require any one of them to say that their commitment to (S) is merely to a relativistic truth. Each can be committed to its truth simpliciter. With right (a right given by the entire Hegelian dialectic I am presenting), (S) is a secularism that takes its own commitments to be true and holds out for them against opponents, given the possibility that history will inject conflicts in their opponents' thinking so as to make them come around to (S)'s commitments by the internal reasons that those conflicts might introduce into their opponents' moral-psychological economies. It holds out for fully secular outcomes, and in no way wavers in confidence about the truth of (S), even if it grants that (S) might not be implementable until internal reasons, as a result of historical developments, are available to religious points of view that, in the present, contain illiberal commitments. So in the examples we considered earlier, it would insist that something like religious laws requiring censorship of blasphemy or gender-unjust family laws of a religion must be placed lower in the lexicographical ordering than free speech and gender equality. It would not grant that these laws possess truth, relativistic truth, from within their own larger religious points of view. The whole point of the stress on a Hegelian framework for understanding the role of internal reasons is to ensure that (S) need not make any such concession or compromise on the *exclusive* truth or rightness of its commitments to free speech and gender equality, giving it the right to assert the lexicographical ordering it favors. Thus (S) will not allow secular liberalism to be demoted to just one truthful standpoint amongst others, as was suggested would happen if relativism were true. This makes all the difference to the question whether we should hold fast to (S) or concede the superiority of an ideal of state neutralism toward different religions that Taylor has proposed as being better.

The issue can be usefully explored by looking at a very well-known and much-discussed example from India as a test case. In the aftermath of Indian independence, Muslims in India, after much fascinating discussion during the constituent assembly debates, were allowed by constitutional provision to live by their own personal and family laws. (I am going to consider this case, ignoring the fact that there *has* been a reform of the Hindu code as it applies to family laws. What this asymmetry between Muslims and Hindus shows is that granting Muslims their own personal laws runs afoul of *both* (S) *and* the state neutrality ideal that Taylor has advocated. But I am concerned for now only with the fact that Muslims were granted their own personal laws and how that falls short of (S).)

How exactly that awarded outcome of an exception to Muslims in India is to be interpreted is actually a rather delicate matter, and one may see in it two possible ways of conceiving of what the state intended and therefore two possible ways in which the state conceived of itself.

One way to look at this case is to see it as a triumph of the kind of pluralism that is suggested by the relativist position. What pluralism, in the relativist form, allows for is the idea that a liberal democratic state, will, in the name of minority cultural rights, grant to minorities (in the Indian case, to Muslims) their own special personal laws on divorce, marriage, alimony, etc., even if some of these laws are illiberal in various respects. On this reading, the state may grant to a minority Muslim community their own *alternative nomic or customary system,* which is a rival system to liberal law, with its own sort of right or truth on its side, and the pluralism that the constitution was committed to must acknowledge this fact.[17] So interpreted, the state can be viewed as approximating a neutralist position, not favoring secular ideals over Muslim personal laws as a lexicographical ordering would, but instead granting the Muslim demand in the constituent assembly debates that they be allowed to live by their own personal laws. *Some* of the *Muslim* voices in the debates over the constitution took this view of how to conceive of this exception to be granted to Muslims to live by their own personal laws, arguing that the very idea of minority rights was to be interpreted as allowing, along these lines, for a minority to be awarded such an exception.

But the Hegelian considerations I have presented allow another possible reading of the concession to Muslims, which I also think is the more historically accurate one, the one that the *preponderance* among the framers of the constitution actually had in mind. On this reading, it is not that the Muslim community is being granted its demand for living by its own personal and family laws on the grounds that their standpoint, as a minority with rights, like the secular standpoint, has truth on its side, which must be acknowledged by a state conceived of as neutral between these two standpoints. Rather the thinking was this. In the aftermath of independence the Muslims who remained in India and did not migrate to Pakistan lost a great deal—they lost their count in numbers not only due to migration to Pakistan, but due to the killing of Muslims in the pogroms on the Indian side of the newly partitioned borders, they lost jobs, they lost land, and, in the vital sense of its wide availability in instruction in schools and colleges, they even lost their language, Urdu. In the face of these losses and the demoralization it generated, depriving them of the cultural aspects of their lives that are centered in their family and personal laws would be an inhumane blow for a state to deliver to a minority community. What a secular state, subscribing to something like (S), must, therefore, do is to wait for history to bring into Muslim thinking the sorts of internal conflict that might give them internal reasons to come around to secular ideals of gender equality and put aside their family and personal laws. But until then, the lexicographical ordering that places those laws second to gender equality may be put in *abeyance*—which is not at all the same as putting the lexicographical ordering *aside*. One would put it aside only if one thought that the state thinks that there is *truth* on the side of those laws, equal to the truth of ideals of gender equality. But one would put it merely in abeyance on quite different grounds—because it would be *coercive* to implement (S) until the necessary internal reasoning takes place among Muslims. Without being too misleading, this could be thought of as a kind of affirmative action policy rather than a minority right granted to Indian Muslims, a policy of bias in favor of them in the cultural sphere—personal law, in particular—given the deprivations they suffered in other spheres of their lives as a result of partition. And like many affirmative action efforts, it was conceived as a temporary measure with the explicit goal of eventually giving them the confidence to stand as equals and, via their own internal reasoning, embrace the commitments of the rest of the polity in the matter of law and, therefore in turn, in the matter of secularism in the lexicographically prior sense that this essay is presenting as the right understanding of secularism. On this reading, Indian secularism is a very clear example of (S) as it sits within the Hegelian framework which I have constructed for its application.

(I should add as an aside that this issue has been excruciatingly complicated at present by the fact that the demand for reform of Muslim personal law usually comes these days—and for some years now—not from anything recognizable as allowing Muslims to reform them as a result of their own internal reasoning, but rather from a kind of harassment of a minority by the Hindu right-wing in the country. That Muslims could be reasonably expected to deliberate their way to allowing a reform of their personal laws in the face of such harassment would be to utterly fail to understand the psychological preconditions for how internal reasons usually work in a historical context. A group's capacity to change via internal reasoning requires a great deal of psychological security and self-confidence, precisely what is undermined by the demoralization and defensiveness caused by such harassment.)

Returning from the details of this example to the general point: This second reading reveals that a Hegelian framework for thinking of justification by internal reasoning and the adoption of political outcomes by an overlapping consensus preempts any need to think that a state *must* be neutral between secular ideals and religious standpoints. It allows for a full and confident adherence to (S), confident not only about it having the exclusive right on its side on the liberal outcomes at stake, but in the hope that it will provide internal reasons eventually to other opposing illiberal points of view to embrace those outcomes.

How does this point nest with my applause for Taylor's motives for redefining secularism, while resisting the redefinition itself? It does so by echoing the distinction between matters of definition and matters of justification made at the outset, in another closely related distinction: between what is the right *outcome* for a secularist to seek, on the one hand, and, on the other, what is the right way of *implementing* this outcome.

One half of the idea, here, is that certain forms of justification suggest the relevance of certain forms of implementation. If secularism had an externalist justification, i.e., if secularism could assume that those who oppose it are not merely possessed of different substantive values but are failing by the light of a more general and universal rationality, then a secular state could perhaps regard itself as having more right to proceed in the implementation of secularism, without awaiting the consent of those who oppose it. But if secularism is stuck with only the resources of internal reasons for its justification, i.e., if secularism must acknowledge that those who oppose it may be fully rational from within their own substantive value commitments, then a secular state has greater obligation to exercise more carefully the scruple of seeking first to persuade them with internal reasons before proceeding with its adoption and implementation.

But the other half of the idea is that just as questions of the justification of an ideal are distinct from what the ideal is (from definitions of the ideal), questions of how best to implement an ideal are also distinct from what the ideal is and need not alter our understanding of which is the better or best ideal to adopt. It has been the argument of the first four sections of this essay that questions of justification of the ideal of secularism need not set us on the path of redefining the ideal, and it has been the burden of Sections 5 and 6 that the scruple of awaiting the implementation of secularism till internal reasons are provided to those who oppose it need not make a difference to what we think is the best ideal of secularism that needs to be implemented. Or to put it the other way round, if (S) is, in the appropriate context, the right ideal for a secularist polity to adopt, that may still leave open the possibility for us to say that in *implementing* (S), we should do exactly as Taylor suggests. We should involve, in the fraternalist manner he rightly proposes, all the voices in the polity, including the anti-secularist religious voices, just as happened in the constituent assembly debates in India where the Muslims were able to make their demands and argue for them. It may turn out that, in its wisdom, the fraternal collective of those voices concludes that— on the matter of some particular set of religious laws or practices—until some group finds the *internal* reasons to accept the state's implementation of (S), the implementation must be held in abeyance. If so, it should be quite possible to allow—without conceding anything theoretically or defintionally amiss with (S)—that (S) remain temporarily unimplemented, just as happened with Muslim family laws in post-independence India, on the *second* reading I gave.[18]

Why exactly should it be possible to allow this? Because the deepest concern behind Taylor's demand of fraternal involvement of all groups, I believe, is that a state must, as far as it is possible, be *non-coercive* in the adoption and implementation of the policies it views as justifiable. (Jeffrey Stout wisely advises me that since states have sanctions backing the laws they make and implement, they are, by their very nature, going to be coercive no matter what, and so a better term to use to describe Taylor's motivation is that he would like the state to be, as far as is possible, *non-dominating.* I am happy to follow his advice.) Taylor's concern here is a moral one and it speaks for a certain conception of politics. What it properly motivates, indeed what it forces us to do, is to look for the right forms of adoption and implementation of (S). It would be wrong to think that, in doing so, what it motivates and forces are merely things in the practical rather than in the theoretical domain. The entire construction of the role and relevance of the Hegelian notion of subjectivity in the dialectic of this essay was intended to provide a *theoretical* solution to the problem posed by Taylor's search for a non-coercive and overlapping consensus for the secular outcome or, to put it in my own favored terms, to the problem of implementing a secularism whose justification is based only on internal rather than external reasons. But what the essay has nevertheless insisted on is that this theoretical solution requires neither a theoretical redefinition of secularism nor any concession to the superiority of state neutrality ideals over (S). It is an avoidable inference that the non-domination in the adoption of secularism that motivates Taylor's arguments makes a difference to what it is we are adopting or should adopt. It does not lead to another *conception* of secularism.[19] Such secularism as is worth believing in is well characterized by (S).

Yet I have also said that it is not required to believe (S) in all contexts. The relevance of a doctrine of the sort that (S) exemplifies emerged in certain historical contexts when certain political goals could not be pursued without something like the lexicographical ordering (S) formulates. (S), therefore, is a valuable doctrine to embrace and implement in contexts which approximate those historical conditions and which contain those political goals. It is not a doctrine that holds without regard to context, purely on the basis of abstract philosophical arguments or on the basis of glib assertions of the universal reach of a certain familiar form of modernity.

Taylor's own desire to redefine secularism is based—as we saw in Section 3—on the argument that a context of modernity has now emerged in which his redefinition is needed. This, as he sometimes puts it, is the context of multiculturalism, in which talk of *"toleration"* is no longer appropriate. A state neutral between different religious cultures and also non-religious cultures should constitute the new meaning of secularism in such a multicultural context. I will end with some closing remarks on the relation between (S) and the idiom of "toleration."

What is it about the idiom that seems inappropriate in the present multicultural West? The answer is obvious. It is a familiar and repeatedly made observation that the very idea of toleration presupposes *disapproval* of what is tolerated, and a condescending acceptance of what one disapproves. If, in the context of an aspiring multiculturalism, one wants to improve on or replace the attitude of disapproval with some other moral psychological attitude that cultures (including secular cultures) must exhibit toward one another, it might seem that we have two choices. One is to emphasize a different, less hostile, kind of negative attitude: *indifference* rather than disapproval. And his redefined secular ideal of state neutrality toward different religions might be seen as precisely maintaining such an indifference toward them, neither favoring nor disfavoring any of them, allowing each culture, in turn, to thrive in relative autonomy and with indifference rather than hostility toward one another. The other is to stress a more positive attitude: *respect* rather than disapproval.

Now it must be admitted that it is exactly indifference that is opposed by the humanism underlying the Hegelian ideal of historical subjectivity in the understanding of secularism as defined by (S). When one finds something appealing in the attitude expressed by "You must be my brother" toward someone with whom one is in moral conflict, it is the appeal of *not* being indifferent to his views. Respect is another matter. As I said earlier, it *is* showing (a rarefied form of) respect of this abstract humanist kind to someone with whom one is morally disagreed, when one seeks to change his mind and make him one's brother. But *for just that reason* one is not showing indifference toward him and his views. So if indifference is a crucial ingredient in the way in which one must (in multicultural societies) supersede the disapproval implicit in "toleration," does this repudiation of indifference by (S) mean that (S) is retaining the element of disapproval that is presupposed by the idiom of "toleration"? And if so, should we conclude that the state neutralist secularist ideal is more apt than (S) for a context in which multiculturalism has taken us beyond the ideal of toleration? I think it would be a mistake to infer that. The moral psychology involved in (S) is more subtle than that conclusion suggests.

First of all, because (S) replaces indifference with a concern to register disagreements and attempt to change the minds holding those points of view with which one is in moral and political disagreement, its assumption of disapproval of one point of view for another is never accompanied by any condescension whatever. Even if disapproval of another point of view is present, (S) demands the sort of positive engagement between points of view that leaves no place for condescension. But for the same reason, it is not at all obvious that there really is even an assumption of disapproval that it really makes, and here is why not. The sorts of efforts that are needed to reach others (with whom one is deeply conflicted) by providing them with *internal* reasons and arguments requires one not merely to get past indifference toward their views, but also, in a sense, to get past the disapproval of their views. Now this idea of "getting past" disapproval could, of course, still be interpreted as meaning that the disapproval of others is a necessary condition, even if not a sufficient condition, when one seeks to change their minds in situations of moral and political conflict with them. That is, it could be interpreted as saying that the disapproval must throughout be in place, but it must be *supplemented* by some rational engagement with (rather than merely toleration of) those whom one disapproves of. However, such an interpretation of "getting past" disapproval would not be up to the tasks at hand as I have sketched them in the last many pages. "Getting past" the disapproval would have to really amount to *overcoming* the disapproval and *replacing* it (rather than merely supplementing it) not just with respect but with further more detailed attitudes toward the other, if one is to engage the other with something as *empathy*-demanding as the search for *internal* arguments, arguments in *their conceptual vernacular,* in order to change their minds—since as these last two sections of the essay make clear, nothing less than that are the tasks at hand.

What these further attitudes that are needed exactly are is a searching question in the moral psychology of politics and part of the exercise in these last two sections has been to bring us to the point of raising it. There is not enough space to explore this question in any detail in an essay that is already far too long. But one can convey in a general way the sorts of considerations that will matter in any answer we might give.

Take one sort of example, particularly relevant to one of the points that Taylor raised in his response to me that I cited earlier. To tap the conceptual vernacular of those one opposes in providing them with internal reasons to change their minds on some particular matter (censorship of blasphemy, say) may often (though not necessarily always) involve tapping elements in their tradition that are themselves religious, even sometimes elements in the orthodox aspects of their religion. There is no reason to think that a secularism such as (S), even though it does in some sense take a stance *against "religion,"* cannot display its own wisdom and appeal by showing how the ideals it seeks have their echoes (or presentiments) in *religious traditions.* The (occasionally Habermasian) demand that in the public sphere one should always be able to translate away any thick religious elements that may exist in the conceptual vocabulary and argumentative dialectic of such internal reasoning by which one works up to secularist policy is, therefore, quite uncompulsory. As I have said, (S) tends to be most pressingly required when religion emerges in the political arena in a specific way—in the context of majoritarianisms that are peculiarly the product of modern nationalism (to take a contemporary example, Hindu nationalism—and the Muslim identitarian backlash against it—in India of the last twenty years or more). And so, in particular, there is no reason to think that various ideals that (S) seeks to promote in the face of such religious majoritarianism cannot sometimes be argued for by appealing to the commitments of ordinary people that flow from some of the remnants of their *older* religious traditions that are still relatively uncontaminated by the modern contexts that have been marked by majoritarianism. It is not as if these traditions are totally erased in the lives and mentalities of people in modern society. However ruthless modernity's trajectory might be in some parts of the world, so long as it is human mentality and culture that it acts upon, its surface will be more like a palimpsest than some sort of brand new and blank slate. If that were not so, we would have no use or application for the concept of "tradition." And so, the thought is that it is quite possible that sometimes religious *tradition* may provide someone the grounds for internal reasons to change his mind away from the *new* and majoritarian forms that religion takes in its appearance in political modernity. Secularists have sometimes been almost neurotically anxious about mobilizations that appeal to the religious elements in a society, even if it is for goals that might be impeccably secular or for ideals indifferent to the entire debate between the secular and religious. The Indian independence movement offers examples of such mobilization, such as for instance Gandhi's inspired Khilafat movement and then later the Congress Party's "Muslim Mass Contact Programme," which were both highly dynamic and generative of entirely secular, anti-imperialist effects in Indian society, but which made various segments of the political leadership nervous, even so. Nothing in (S), despite the lexicographical priority it gives to certain ideals over religious practices and commitments, reflects this anxiety.

I particularly want to stress this for two reasons. First, and less important, because it may seem that just because the entire Hegelian argument of these last two sections is based on a subject's capacity to be redirected in his or her values by incoming considerations in one's historical future, those considerations can't turn on elements of one's past thinking and traditions. But that would be an elementary fallacy. It is a childish non sequitur to think that considerations that cause one to change one's mind in the *future* cannot contain elements of one's *past* traditions. But the more important reason to stress it is that such a reliance (as I have been stressing in the last page or two) on the conceptual vernacular in the

providing of internal reasons necessarily generates elaborately empa-
thetic attitudes of engagement with the traditions and mentalities of
those one opposes. If the implementation of a doctrine such as (S) is
theoretically elaborated along these lines, it cannot possibly be faulted
for failing to have relevance in a context in which we have gone "beyond
toleration" to multiculturalism. Being based on a very specific form of
humanism, (S) admittedly does eschew indifference toward those it
opposes, but what it replaces it with—in the sort of detailed engagement
that I have been trying to convey—equally takes it decisively beyond the
chronic assumption of disapproval that has made the idiom of "toleration" come to seem so off-beam in the pluralist contexts of multiculturalist modernity.

Secularism, Multiculturalism, and the Very Concept of Law

Unlike secularization, which is a large and general cultural and intellectual process of the declining hold of religious belief and practice, secularism, as I have expounded it in the previous essay, is a very specific doctrine about the polity that gained its particular point and purpose in the aftermath of European nation-building after the Westphalian peace. As such, it is intricately caught up with a nation's laws. But given the uneven development of secularization and an abiding religiosity in many parts of the world even where secular*ism* as a political doctrine has been embraced, a question that has vexed liberal polities in recent years is: Can culture and religion, in particular, provide grounds for *exemptions* from a secular liberal nation's laws?

This familiar question arises just as much for European nations with large immigrant populations as it does for liberal democracies outside of Europe with substantial religious and cultural minorities such as, for instance, India and Canada. And the question itself is situated in a somewhat gnarled set of historical as well as terminological developments that need to be briefly presented first, before one can address it.

One theoretical motivation (amongst others) for introducing the term "multiculturalism" in the discussions of recent decades is to describe issues that arose as a result of the special attentiveness that *immigrant* minority cultures call for in demanding some of these exceptions to the law within a secular polity. And it is no small irony that multiculturalism as a special form of attentiveness to the needs and demands of minority cultures came to be seen as a necessity because *secularism* was insensitive to those needs—for it was secularism that was initially intended to repair the damage of majoritarianism in Europe's nation-building exercises, as I tried to show in my last essay. What explains this irony? As a repair for the ravages of majoritarian tendency, secularism has come to be seen as too blunt since it was not merely taking a stand against religious majoritarian domination but equally against religious minoritarian backlashes opposing that domination. It was a stand, therefore, against *all* religious practices—whether that of a minority or that of a majority—placing those practices second whenever they clashed with the nation's laws. In other words, because secularism addressed religious practice only as a generality, without differentiating between majority and minority religions, it did something to protect the minorities from previous forms of domination by a religious majority, but it did so at a level of abstraction from the detail of a minority's felt need to preserve its own religious sentiments. This problem was then later exacerbated in European nations by their deliberate policy of admitting large immigrant populations, often with religious commitments, from erstwhile colonies to meet their labor shortages in reconstructing their economies after the loss of potential manpower in the Second World War. For these immigrant communities, who found themselves in a new setting, frequently facing racial hostility, their religion often became a collective zone of comfort and so the demand for preserving their religion as their only source for cultural dignity and solace in an alien and seemingly hostile secularist polity began to be acutely articulated. "Multiculturalism" became the term to describe the form of diversified cultural autonomy that underlies such a demand, a doctrine intended to supplement secularism, i.e., to pick up the slack created by secularism's insensitivities to specifically minoritarian culture. However, in the last decade or more, there has been a serious backlash against multiculturalism and in a new and curious development, the terms "multiculturalism" and "secularism" are increasingly viewed as being in tension rather than supplements or complements to one another. Especially since the hostilities generated by a trigger-happy "war on terror," all over Europe and indeed more widely in the West (in countries such as Canada, for instance) it is *majoritarian* sentiment that has increasingly appealed to secularism as a stick with which to beat the very ideal of multiculturalism, an ideal that they view as being soft on minority religious cultures, and under such an assault, multiculturalism has been put on the defensive for it has become something of a term of abuse and scorn not only among brazenly right-wing nationalists of an older and familiar European sort but among the secular liberal intelligentsia. It is this development, I believe, that underlies Charles Taylor's recent efforts to redefine secularism as a kind of religious multiculturalism (a neutral stance toward all religions allowing them to live and practice freely side by side in equality and fraternity), a terminological move made with a view to grab this stick away from these majoritarian forces. If secularism is redefined so as to be just another name for religious multiculturalism, it cannot possibly be invoked against multiculturalism. As I tried to convey in my last essay, such a redefinition of secularism may be very well motivated in such ethical and political terms, but it makes for little clarity and sense in substantial theoretical or indeed historical terms.

All this makes it all the more urgent to get some clarity as to what is at stake in these intellectual and political developments. The subject has many sides and angles. some of which I tried to present in my previous essay. In this essay, I will keep my focus on questions of the law, and particularly on the question I began with, the question of secularist polities accommodating a religious minority's demands for exceptions to some laws. But despite the narrow focus, I want to work up to how the larger *conceptual and philosophical* issues that underlie the debate between secularists and multiculturalists reveal something interesting and fresh: nothing less than two ways to understand the law and legislation.[1]

Before embarking on this, it will be good to get a preliminary and elementary point of clarification out of the way. The general debate I will focus on is about *secularism* in the face of multiculturalism, and "culture" in "multicultural," as I use that term, will be restricted to religious cultures and communities. But many (though perhaps not all) of the points made here will be applicable without strain to other sources of culture, having to do with nationality, ethnicity, indigenous native populations, and so on. That is all to the good, since in explanation more generality is to be preferred to less, where it is plausible, that is, where it does not trample over good distinctions.

To repeat, our question, at its highest level of generality, is about whether religion gives ground for exemption from liberal laws. Sometimes the laws in question can be about relatively marginal issues such as how to dress, as in the demands of Sikhs in Britain that they be allowed to wear their turbans while riding their motorcycles—despite safety laws requiring helmets—because their religion requires it. Or it can be about somewhat more important matters such as with the Sikh demand that they be exempt from laws about carrying dangerous weapons in public, so as to allow them to wear their kirpans in public religious ceremonies. Or it can be about even larger issues having to do with laws of divorce and alimony, as in the (successful) Muslim demand during the -Constituent Assembly debates in India that Muslims be allowed to live by the personal laws prescribed in the sharia. Finally, they can also be about the most fundamental of issues in liberal doctrine, such as the Muslim demand both in Britain and in India that constitutional rights to free speech be put aside when it comes to blasphemy,[2] as for instance in the case of Salman Rushdie's book *The Satanic Verses*. Though the law in each of these may differ in weight and importance, the basic structure of the arguments and issues is the same in all the cases.

What I want to look hard at is the extent to which the issues at stake in this debate between the secularist and the multiculturalist might be over something as deep and philosophical as how to understand the nature of law itself.

The traditional and classical secular position has tended to be that the very notion of law, law by its very nature, seems to be the sort of thing that demands equality in its application. A law is not a law unless it holds for everyone. Yet the multiculturalists, with their sympathy for the religious demands for exemptions, seem to be questioning precisely this claim. Do they, then, understand the nature of the law differently? If so, because it seems so natural to think that the law should apply to everyone equally, the multiculturalist is, at least prima facie, stuck with the task of showing that what seems so natural here might not in the end be justified.

Why, then, *does* it seem so natural that a law, by the very kind of thing it is, applies equally to everyone? It is shallow to simply say in a very general and unilluminating way that equality is a fundamental value and it applies to the law as to other things. What is natural about the claim we are considering has to do much more specifically with how we think legislation proceeds or should proceed.

Let's look at a prominent recent secularist position on the law. Brian Barry, in his book *Culture and Equality,*[3] takes an unambiguous position on the matter and since Barry writes with great clarity and force and with detailed arguments for conclusions that echo what is only instinctively and inarticulately held by a very wide swath of secularists, I will allow his particular dialectic to stand in for the secularist stance on this question. Here is what he says: "If there are good reasons to formulate the law, then those very reasons repudiate the demand for exemptions. And if, on the other hand, there are good reasons to grant exemptions to the law, that puts into doubt that there should be such a law in the first place."

This is a very tidy view, a view, as I said, shared by a lot of secular liberals. By "good reasons," it is presumably meant "reasons which, upon reflection, are decisive." Why is Barry and why are secularists, generally, so convinced that if there are decisive reasons to support a law, then it should not allow for exemptions? The answer is clear—because if there was something decisive to be said on the part of granting the exemptions, then there are no decisive reasons in favor of the law.

What seems too tidy is just this assumption that if there is something to be said in favor of the exemptions, then that puts into doubt that there are decisive reasons for favoring the law. But one should be careful that in calling this too tidy, one is not misunderstanding the secularist position. The secularist does allow that one could go on to grant exemptions if one wishes, but when one does so, it is on purely *"pragmatic"* grounds, grounds which have nothing to do with the law except insofar as how people will respond to it. So, for instance, a state might grant exemptions to a law in order to keep the peace, knowing that there will be great dissatisfaction, even perhaps violence, if one insisted on applying it across the board. But these are all pragmatic considerations that the state might invoke—for statist reasons, like keeping the peace. But in these cases the exemptions are not *principled* exceptions; they are merely a bit of special pleading on grounds quite irrelevant to whether the law—*qua law*—is a just and good law. (A case of a principled exception would presumably be something like the escape clause for self-defense in a homicide law. There is nothing pragmatic about having this exception; it is not a result of taking into account, once the law is exceptionlessly formulated and already in place, how people are responding to it. It has nothing at all to do with people's feelings and responses, religious or otherwise. It is dictated entirely by considerations internal to the law. It is therefore an exception *built into* the law, and not a pragmatic afterthought.)

What the secularist rightly and shrewdly sees here is that the multi-culturalist is not going to grant that only and purely pragmatic reasons justify exceptions to a law about traffic safety, public order, etc. He (or she) is going to insist that there are principled reasons that religious considerations might provide for having the exceptions. And secularists are anxious that this insistence really questions something rather basic about the nature of law itself. So they have nothing per se against grant-ing exceptions to the law. So long as the exceptions are always seen as being granted on pragmatic grounds *after* the event of legislation, the secularist is prepared to tolerate exceptions. What she will not tolerate philosophically is the multiculturalist way of claiming the exceptions. And, if I am right in the way I have set things up, the reason for this seems to be that that way of claiming the exception threatens the very conception of law which the secularist assumes.

So one must ask: What is this conception of law that the secularist assumes? What is philosophically and jurisprudentially at stake in say-ing that there are no principled but merely pragmatic reasons underlying the granting of exceptions on religious grounds?

This is what seems to be at stake. According to the secular liberal, when making a law, legislators look *only to the subject matter of what the law is about*—safety on the road, as it might be, or the threat to public order which carrying dangerous weapons bring to it. If they find, when considering that subject matter, that there are good reasons to formu-late a law regarding helmets or the ban on carrying dangerous weapons in public, then those reasons rule out any principled exceptions based on people's religious feelings and sentiments. So the answer to the question—why is it so natural to think that the law applies equally to all citizens?—is that laws are formulated with a view to addressing issues (subject matters), consideration of which dictate what is just and right, quite independently of what this or that group of citizens' response to the law will be. Quite possibly people will hate wearing helmets, paying taxes, etc., but if considerations of safety and political economy, the subject matters addressed by those laws, dictate that it is right that people should wear helmets and pay taxes, then that is that.

To multiculturalists, that is precisely the underlying view of law, the underlying view of the task of legislation, that is bound to appear too tidy. It leaves out of legislation and the considerations that go into it any sensitivity to the deepest human commitments and sentiments of people. It may be, they will grant, that when thinking only of safety (the subject—or one subject—of traffic laws), one should not be bothered by religious considerations of the male Sikh's religious obligation to wear a turban instead. But the context of legislation is always part of a much larger human and social context. Laws are *for* people, even if they are *about* subject matters, and when the commitments and sentiments of people go as deep as they sometimes do over questions of religion, one cannot restrict one's gaze to just the subject matter of the law in question and what is right for that subject matter. One has to think of how the law will affect the people who live under it in ways that may have nothing to do with safety in traffic.

Here, then, is one way I would propose of formulating the alternative picture of legislation that the multiculturalist is assuming. (There could be other models proposed to capture the multiculturalist assumptions about legislation, but this seems to me the one that is clearest and least conceptually cluttered.) When legislators devise laws they confront a vast *decision problem*. As with any decision problem, we must proceed via a governing constraint, which is often called "the total evidence requirement." And if legislators look at the *total* evidence, when considering a law on motorcyclists' safety, whether in Bombay or Bradford, they would inevitably have to ask themselves, among other things, how to weigh the gain in safety against the loss in offense caused to a sizable minority of citizens. Now it is possible that here, as with any decision procedure, the weights we attach in these considerations lead us to quite *uncertain* deliberative outcomes; and when that happens we may well think that the best solution is to have *both* the law of safety *with* the exemptions for the relevant religious community. The uncertainty dictates this ecumenical decision, the very ecumenism which Barry repudiates when he says disjunctively *either* the law had good reasons for it *or* it is a bad law because there are good reasons for the exceptions. It's only if the deliberative procedure weighing the total evidence yielded a more *certain* outcome one way or another that we would disallow exceptions and have the law, or see the point of the exceptions and conclude that there was no need for the law. But in the deliberative weighing of *total* evidence on matters in which considerations of safety are vital *and* religious sentiments run strong, it is quite likely that the deliberation will often *not* produce outcomes with any certainty. If so, the ecumenical or conjunctive legislation of law *and* exception will prevail over Barry's disjunctive view.

This conception of legislation is alternative to the one that the secularist is presupposing because it is no longer possible to dismiss the granting of exceptions as merely "pragmatic" afterthoughts. It is true that we did not want to offend the relevant minority of citizens' feelings, but that consideration was *at the outset* one of the things to be weighed in solving the decision problem about what sort of law to adopt under the total evidence requirement. It was not as if we first arrived at the law, on some independent and more principled grounds, and then on subsequent more pragmatic considerations of not offending the minority, granted the exceptions. Not offending minorities was, as I said, weighing in right at the outset of deliberation.

It won't do to object on behalf of the secularist by saying that this way of thinking about legislation as a vast decision problem taking in the total evidence in deliberating toward a decision does not allow for the fact that some people might find it *unfair* that the sentiments of a religious minority are being seen as *relevant* evidence in the decision. Thus, for instance, this objection might invoke the fact that teenagers also want exemption from wearing helmets because it is uncool to do so, and they might say, "We too have strong sentiments about this, why are you paying more attention to the Sikhs?" There is a simple failure on the part of this objection to see that the whole point of taking the view of legislation as a vast decision problem is that the protest made by the teenagers *can also be thrown in as one more consideration into the pot of the total evidence,* and weighed in the deliberation toward the decision. And it may turn out that *even after* throwing that in as a bit of evidence, our deliberation tells us that the Sikh case is more urgent than the teenagers' and therefore the same uncertain outcome which dictated both the law *and* the exemption granted to the Sikhs from the law is the best decision. So protests about what is and is not fair, and therefore what is and is not the relevant evidence in the total evidence, are just *more* evidence in the *total* evidence on which the decision is made by legislators.

Exactly the same thing can be said in response to other sorts of objections to this decision-problem format for thinking about legislation. So, for instance, secularists might object that there will be something too *unstable* about laws if they are arrived at on the basis of taking into account what people's sentiments are regarding the law. Well, here too, let the threat of this instability *also* be thrown into the pot of total evidence, for the legislators to weigh. They may still come to the conclusion, after weighing it along with everything else, that we should after all have both the law with the exception rather than Barry's tidier disjunctive view of the matter.

It simply misses the point to say that once we throw the point about unfairness to other groups who want exemptions and the point about instability of laws into the total evidence, legislators are very *unlikely* to find themselves adopting the ecumenical law-plus-exemption outcome. Even if that is in fact so, the point is it need not be so. Let us even grant that because of throwing in the considerations of unfairness and instability into the total evidence, legislators—proceeding as if they were undertaking a decision problem of the kind I outlined—came up with laws which were exemptionless, i.e., with laws which were *co-extensive* with the laws that legislators working with the model underlying the secularist's view—who consider only the subject matter of the law and what it dictates—came up with. That does nothing really to show that the models are not radically different. For it is quite *possible* that even if you allow considerations of unfairness and instability to be weighed along with considerations of the strong sentiments of minorities and how they will respond to the laws, the latter might trump the former in our deliberations, and in that case we will adopt the law-cum-exemption outcome.

This demonstrates that even if in fact the two models come up with the same laws, they are only co-extensive; they are not co-intensive.

The point is that those wedded to the legislative model assumed by the secularist are going to cry foul at the very idea that considerations of religious sentiments at the outset of legislative deliberation are being allowed. No amount of co-extensiveness of this with their own model will soothe them. That is to say, no amount of reassurance that the same laws are likely to be devised by the decision-problem model will soothe them. And that is only right. Given their view of legislation, this *should* seem to them to constitute a wholly different and unacceptable legislative model. Even if it *happens to* yield the same laws, it might not do so if decision-making deliberative outcomes turned out to be different.

I have been trying to contrast two different models of legislation as underlying the debate between the secularist and the multiculturalist. Whichever one we prefer in the end, there is nothing *obviously* wrong or incoherent with either model. But we must ask a deeper question at this point. So far we have only asked what conception of legislation underlies the secularist finding it so natural to think that the law applies equally and without exception to everyone and what conception of legislation underlies the multiculturalist way of questioning what seems so natural to the secularist. We must now ask whether something deeper underlies these different models of legislation themselves. Whichever side we take on the dispute between the two underlying models of legislation, it would be premature to take it without noticing a deeper layer of what is at stake.

There is something rather more abstract and methodologically significant that lies behind what the secularist is aspiring to, and it is worth a brief exploration. Barry himself does not explore it and at this point one must leave Barry behind and dig somewhat deeper into the foundations of the secularist position he propagates.

A good place to try to unearth it is by diagnosing why his position seems to him so obviously to have the moral and philosophical high ground. And I do not doubt that Barry (whose book—thick though it is, thick with rigorous arguments—is filled with a pervasive indignation against any sympathy shown toward multiculturalism) will be raised to new heights of denunciation by the very idea of the notion of legislation

I am presenting on behalf of the multiculturalist. One can hear it: "This is no way to go about devising laws! It is not a decision problem taking in as considerations all those messy details of people's feelings toward prospective laws *right at the outset!* It is to misunderstand the very nature of laws to conceive of their devising in these terms! It may be that some subject matter regarding which a law is sought will be a difficult one on which to decide what will be a just law. But if that is so that is because of the intrinsic difficulty of resolving the legal aspects of the subject matter; it should not be because we have an eye out for how this or that group will respond to it. We would never get any laws without exceptions if we proceeded along the lines of the proposed method!"

While reading and thinking about his position, I tried hard to diagnose this impatience he is bound to show toward the multiculturalist assumptions about the law. What deeper methodological assumption is he implicitly adopting which makes it seem so obvious to him that his way of thinking of law is the only right one? At first I thought it was simply this: Barry, in his own mind, has started with a paradigm of what a law is by looking to cases in which we are not prepared to countenance any accommodations and exceptions (at any rate not because of considerations coming from the sentiments of groups affected by prospective laws),[4] laws of homicide for example. And then he extrapolates and elevates this into the very *concept* of law. That is to say, he extrapolates it to cover *all* laws. But I then abandoned this diagnosis because it was too uncharitable to him. It is uncharitable because the extrapolation from the one sort of law to all others is too obviously illicit. Multiculturalists and every other sensible person would be happy to concede that homicide laws and a few other such laws are very different in that one should not countenance the sort of exemptions on religious grounds which are being claimed for other laws. But they will certainly find it an extraordinary and unacceptable inference to go from this concession to saying that all laws are like homicide laws in this respect.

But what other diagnosis is there, if this one is uncharitable? What other deeper underlying methodological assumption motivates the secularist notion of law and legislation?

Let me start trying to say something on the secularist's behalf now. Someone who finds the decision-problem approach to devising a law (as

I have spelt it out briefly) to be missing the very point of law, may be thinking something like this.

I will begin with a crude, very abstract, and almost sentimentally philosophical statement of the idea. The idea of a law derives from something more basic than law itself, something like the idea of a principle, something of greater generality, greater abstraction, something which is more transparent to us, whose point and rationale shines forth from the very kind of thing it is. There is a greater self-evidence about it. That notion of principle underlies our most basic understanding of laws. So understood, laws do not try to cope right at the outset with the messy details that may lead to accommodations and exceptions. They stand above those messy details and in fact it is the point of laws to bring clarity to the messy details and put them in their place.

The point becomes less crude if we point to an analogy that might exist with the basic laws, say of Newtonian science, and their relations to particular engineering applications, or (a better analogy) their relations to the details and *highly* qualified (by ceteris paribus clauses) generalizations of some of the special sciences such as psychology or meteorology or even biology where much messier details have to be dealt with. We do not spoil or give up on the idea of the most general explanatory laws of fundamental physics just because of the messy details of the engineering applications or because the special sciences throw up recalcitrant details for them. On the contrary. It is part of the prestige of the fundamental sciences that we try to constantly *subsume* the particulars at the lower levels of the special sciences under their higher-level laws. We may not always succeed, but that is the aspiration, and the prestige of the laws is reflected in the aspiration and is unaffected by the occasional failure to fulfill the aspiration.

Why should morals and the law be any different from science? Here too we might seek an analogy with the distinction between basic physical laws versus engineering detail or the laws of the basic sciences and the messy phenomena and highly hedged generalizations of the special sciences. I believe that secularists presuppose something like the analogy in the background when they relegate the messy details of people's sentiments to pragmatic afterthoughts following upon what is decided at a higher plane of the law itself.

Someone might protest: Practical life is too messy to hold this stratified view of higher laws under which lower-level messy details are always
sought to be *subsumed,* and that is why the decision-procedure approach
suits better the situation of the devising of laws.

But I think we can try to do better, on the secularists' behalf, to
explain why things might not be that dissimilar in morals and the law,
and this finally is the crucial point which should remove some of the initial impression of crudeness and of an overly remote and abstract philosophical diagnosis.

In law and morals too we often find that some of our lower-level, much
more contested and controversial and messier questions can be decided
or come closer to being decided if we can find similar *subsumptions* under
higher-order principles. This happens often. Thus for instance, we may
often find ourselves uncertain about how to think of pornography, say.
We may worry about the effect of shops in our neighborhood selling por-
nographic materials, we may think of our children having easy access to
them, and so on. These messy and controversial points about the matter
are given a clarification and put in their place as soon as we notice, however, that questions regarding pornography are to be *subsumed under
the much more general principle of free speech.* Similar messy questions
may be raised about the health and safety issues surrounding abortion,
which may leave legislators uncertain about its legality, and again the
same clarity and decisiveness is brought to the matter if we see that it
can perhaps be *subsumed under a higher-level principle of privacy.* Both
these subsumptions have indeed occurred as any basic survey of the history and sociology of these legal issues will tell us. Someone who was
undecided while looking at the controversial details about abortion or
pornography might find that the subsumption to these more general and
basic principles adds just the clarity that will help him or her decide.
*The process is quite parallel to that I was describing as a certain sort of
aspiration in science.*

In fact there occurred recently a somewhat farcical episode in my
university, which provides a gorgeous illustration of the point I am
making. A couple of years ago it was reported in the newspapers that
my colleague Edward Said threw a stone on a recently liberated site
in Lebanon in the direction of a building housing some Israeli guards.

He was with his son, and he did so in order to let off steam and express some satisfaction at the liberation of an area, which the occupying Israeli forces had evacuated. Some professors and students at Columbia University demanded that action be taken against Said for a violent act, suggesting that he even be asked to leave the university. There was a lot of discussion and much controversy was exchanged in the student newspaper. Now even if one thinks as I do that the demand was preposterous and farcical (though I am sure it did not seem particularly farcical to poor Edward Said who was harassed—as he so often was— by the most disagreeably malicious and false propaganda about it), it was interesting to see what a lot of calm and clarity was brought, even among those making the preposterous demand, when the provost wrote in the newspaper to say that Said's throwing the stone is to be subsumed under the principle of free speech and expression.

On this diagnosis then the secularist is impatient with other models of law and legislation than his own because those models cannot keep faith with this essential underlying feature of the law, a feature which sees their point and rationale to be one of clarifying (or being capable of clarifying) what before the subsumption under them seem like messy and controversial details.

Now of course, we may not always succeed in these subsumptions, and when we do not, though we will not give up on the aspiration to subsume them eventually, we will still in the meanwhile have to acknowledge the messier details as having to be dealt with in some way. But *now,* with *this* understanding of the underlying point and rationale of law in place, there will be a perfectly good justification for dealing with them pragmatically, just as the pure sciences deal with the details of engineering or the basic sciences deal with the seemingly recalcitrant phenomena of some of the special sciences. It is clear on this view that in neither the legal nor the scientific case does acknowledging the messy details cancel the fact that we do still *aspire* to the subsumption of the low level to the high, and it is the presuppositions of this *aspiration* (of the clarity and transparency imparted by the more abstract notion of principle) which I think underlies the secularist refusal to countenance the decision-problem approach to legislation, as I presented it. That approach falls afoul of precisely these stratified presuppositions about subsumption of the lower level to the higher and tries to deal with the mess right from the start without this stratified picture.

It may seem that in my effort to unearth what underlies the secularist conception of the law, what I am proposing is a mere analogy between subsumption in the one case (the law) and the other (science), and analogies, it might be thought, only get us so far.[5] It is true that I had used the word "analogy" to make the comparison above. But in fact it is much more than an analogy. I am actually claiming that there is a genus—the aspiration to illuminate via a subsumption of detail under a general principle. And I am claiming that it contains two different species: 1) illumination gained by the subsumptions of the messier details studied by the special sciences to the general laws and principles of the more basic sciences and 2) illumination and clarification gained about what is at stake in particular moral, religious, legal issues and their attendant controversial details, when they are, once again, seen as instances of more general laws and fundamental constitutional principles. It would be quite uncomprehending, then, to think that I am trading on the superficial similarity of the use of the word "law" or "general laws" in the two cases to say that what legislators and scientists are concerned with must be thought of as analogous when they are not. That is not the point at all. Of course, the "laws" of science and the laws adopted by a society's legal system are very different animals. One's point is to explain, the other's to provide normative constraints backed by sanctions. Nobody sensible would fail to see that distinction. The claim I am making despite these differences is that inquiry in general is often governed by a theoretical urge, which is gratified when we find something to be a special instance of something more general. This happens in both science and the law in ways that I was specifying. That in the one case the laws are explanatory and in the other the laws are rules to live by does nothing to spoil the point since the point is not to say that the laws are the same at all. It is rather to say that in both forms of inquiry, scientific and moral, the theoretical gratification which comes from subsumption is pervasive and motivating. It may turn out on reflection that we ought to discard this theoretical urge (see next note) and cease to find it gratifying if it suppresses the acknowledgement of other forms of illumination than this one. I take no stand on that issue here, though I have views about it. But whatever we say about that issue, it would be wrong to claim on its basis that the tendency to find subsumption illuminating is not in fact a very strong and pervasive tendency among inquirers, whether in scientific or practical inquiry. It is this tendency, I am saying, which helps to explain why the decision-problem approach to legislation underlying the multiculturalist view seems so unappealing to many secularists. One does not even have to be convinced by the particular examples of subsumption I cited (of pornography and abortion being assimilated respectively to more general laws and principles about free speech and privacy) in order to grasp that this tendency to find subsumption illuminating goes very deep in inquiry in the moral and legal sphere just as it does in the scientific sphere.

Having said that on behalf of the secularist, we must also be clear that it is this very underlying stratified picture of laws which is much disputed[6] not only by multiculturalists who might adopt the decision-problem approach as I presented it, but by those who might adopt instead (to take just one example) the "virtue-theoretic" stance that such a higher notion or level of principles do not underlie the moral life in this way, that the entire aspiration to subsume is misguided, that the notion of moral *perception* and moral judgment in the sense of *phronesis* should be brought to center stage instead, and talk of principles and subsuming the particular judgment under more general principles is the wrong underlying paradigm in the practical domain of morals and the law. This virtue-theoretic view, going back to Aristotle, and flourishing under a recent philosophical revival, is of course very different from the decision-problem approach as I am presenting it. Decision-theoretic reasoning is after all also anathema to virtue-theorists who stress a sort of moral perception instead of the codifications and constraints of decision theory. For them codification of reasoning in the realm of value is just as bad as the idea of moral principles. In fact these two approaches have little in common other than opposing the subsumptionist picture, which I am claiming underlies the secularist conception of law.

Though I have strong views on the subject, I am not interested here in taking a stand on which of these conceptions of the law is the right one. As I said, in this essay I am only raising what some of the deeper issues at stake are in the general debate between the secularists and the multiculturalists. What I am sure of is that at some point these broad underlying methodological issues about the nature of law itself will have to be eventually addressed before we can conclusively decide on which side to take in the debate. Until we address them, the multiculturalist will always seem to the secularist to be conflating and confusing questions of justice and the law with cultural politics, and the secularist will always seem to the multiculturalist to be tendentiously and coercively ushering out people's religious sentiments from center stage and presenting them as afterthoughts, considerations relevant only pragmatically, and relevant only to *governments'* having to face the problem of keeping the peace, once the *lawmakers'* more pristine job is essentially done.

THREE

Liberalism and the Academy

1.

Though there is much radical—and often unpleasant—disagreement on
the fundamental questions around academic freedom, these disagreements tend to be between people who seldom find themselves speaking
to each other on topics such as this or even, in general, speaking to the
same audience. On this subject, as in so much else in the political arena
these days, one finds oneself speaking only to those with whom one is
measurably agreed, at least on the *fundamental* issues. As proponents of
academic freedom, we all recognize who the opponents of academic freedom are but we seldom find ourselves conversing with them in academic
conferences. We only tend to speak to them or *at* them in heated political
debates when a controversy arises, as for instance at Columbia University over the promotion of faculty in Middle Eastern studies, or in those
states where the very idea of a curricular commitment to modern evolu-
tionary biology is viewed with hostility. I will not be considering such
controversial cases of overt political influence on the academy. This is
not because they are not important. The threats they pose are very real,
when they occur, and the need for resistance to these threats is as urgent
as anything in the academy. But they raise no interesting intellectual

75

issues at a fundamental level. If there is disagreement, it is likely to be on relatively *marginal* questions, such as, for instance, whether academic freedom is a special case of the more basic constitutional right to free speech or whether instead it is a distinct form of freedom tied to the specific mission of universities.

What might philosophy contribute to these more marginal questions? In this brief essay, I would like to make a fuss about a standard argument for a conception of academic freedom to which there is widespread subscription when it is coarsely described but which, when we describe it more finely and look at the arguments more closely, is quite implausible and leads indirectly to thoroughly confused ideas about displaying "balance" in our classrooms and our pedagogy quite generally. I will then use some of the points and distinctions I make in this critique to explore the exact nature of more subtle and interesting (and actually more pervasive) kinds of threat to academic freedom than the obviously controversial ones that I mentioned above, which many academics, I assume, find an abomination, and which, as I said, raise no interesting issues, even if they ring urgent alarms. At the very end, I will venture to advocate imbalance of a very specific kind in the "extra-mural" domain, when it is neither inquiry nor classroom curriculum that is at stake but the effort to engage the intellectual and political culture at large.

2.

No matter which stand is taken on the marginal question as to whether academic freedom is a special case of the constitutional right to free speech or something special and apart, there is a great and recurring tendency in the literature on the subject to appeal to the *same* broad arguments and metaphors and intuitions to present the justifications for academic freedom as is done for the justification for freedom of speech in general. And it takes roughly the following lines. First, there is a statement of purpose or *goal:* Academic institutions are sites for intellectual inquiry and research and therefore one of their chief goals is the pursuit of truth and the pedagogical project of conveying the truth, as one discovers it and conceives it in one's research, to students, and to set students on the path of discovering further truths in the future on their own.

And then second, there is a statement of the *conditions for the pursuit of that goal:* This pursuit of truth is best carried out, it is said, under conditions where a variety of opinions are allowed to be expressed on any subject, even if one finds some of them quite false, since it is possible that they might be true and one's own view might turn out to be false. Often, the metaphor used to capture this ethos and it's efficacies in the matter of truth is that truth surfaces in a *"marketplace of ideas."*

When Justice Holmes first put that phrase into the air, he was not particularly thinking about the academy, but quite generally about the shape of a free society.[1] In fact, as two Columbia historians (Richard Hofstadter and Walter Metzger)[2] pointed out, Holmes was really expressing in more intuitive and metaphorical terms the justification for tolerance in speech quite generally, for which John Stuart Mill had earlier in *On Liberty* given a more structured argument with premises and a conclusion.[3] So even if one thought that academic freedom was set apart from the articulations of the First Amendment, the structure of the *underlying* philosophical argument is the same as to be found in Mill's more general argument for liberty of speech as a fundamental principle of the polity at large. I want to spend some time on this underlying argument but before I do, it is worth emphasizing that it is not just given by professional and lay philosophers; it is found in the case law of this country in which universities have figured, repeatedly. Thus for instance in *Keyishan vs. Board of Regents of the State University of New York* (1967), the language of the Supreme Court of this country explicitly cites the phrase "marketplace of ideas" and talks of the "robust exchange of ideas which discovers truth out of a multitude of tongues." That is just one example. There are literally scores of cases in the lower courts as well that appeal to Millian considerations, and they too begin by defining the goal of universities as being one of seeking the truth in intellectual inquiry.

What is Mill's argument and why does it have such a strong appeal for law, philosophy, and even our everyday understanding of the justifications for academic freedom? Its appeal is the appeal of a certain fallibilist epistemology that widely underlies the classical and orthodox liberal mentality. Curiously, this form of fallibilism clashed starkly with the pragmatist epistemology of American thinkers like Peirce and also with the heterodox form of liberalism that one finds in American thinkers like

Dewey. Yet the American courts and American quotidian opinion cite Holmes and Mill like a mantra.

Mill's argument has two premises and a conclusion. The premises are:

> *Premise 1:* Many of our past opinions, which we had held with great conviction, have turned out to be false.

> *Premise 2:* So some of our current opinions that we hold with great conviction may also turn out to be false.

From these premises, he drew a conclusion about tolerance and free speech:

> *Conclusion:* Therefore, let us tolerate dissenting opinions just in case our current opinions are wrong and these dissenting opinions are right.

The idea is that the "marketplace of ideas" keeps us honest. Since we can never be sure that we are right, a marketplace of opinions, many of which may oppose our own opinions, may well throw up the truth, displacing our own convictions about it. Metzger and Hofstadter make this connection between Holmes and Mill explicit and there is no doubt that something like this justification, if true, would hold for free speech in the academy with particular force, even if we saw the academy as standing apart from constitutional contexts for free speech, because the academy is specially geared to pursue the truth in its various disciplinary pursuits.

Let's, then, stare at the argument for a while.

Mill's argument is based on an induction. It is often called Mill's "meta-inductive argument." The induction is found in the transition from the first premise to the second. It is called a *meta*-induction presumably because whereas most inductions go from observations about the *world* in the past to conclusions about the future, his induction goes from an observation about our past *beliefs* about the world to a conclusion about our present and future *beliefs* (viz., that they may be false).

There is an extraordinary ambition in this argument. It hopes to persuade us of a value, the value of free speech, as something for a polity or a university to embrace, on the basis of something that is pure rational argument. By this I mean that it does not aim to convince us to adopt a political value (the value of free speech) *on the basis of any other moral or political values.* It hopes to convince us on grounds that are, in that sense, value-free. It does not matter what moral or political values we have, so long as we are capable of induction, we are supposed to see the force of the argument. And since inductive capacities, like deductive capacities, are part of general rational capacities, possessed by all (adult, undamaged) human minds, if the argument is right, everyone should see the value in free speech, just in virtue of their rationality. To fail to do so, therefore, is nothing less than irrational. Mill gives quite other arguments for free speech in that careless masterpiece—such as for instance that free speech is a value to live by because it encourages diversity as well as creativity in society, and that a willingness to submit to the clash of ideas is essential to the moral courage of human beings and prevents their mental pacification. But such arguments are inherently less ambitious. Their appeal is confined to those who value individual creativity, or variety, or what Blake called "mental fight." There is a risk in any argument that comes to an evaluative conclusion by appealing to another value. Values are things that tend to have variable appeal. And so those who do not subscribe to the other value will not be convinced by it. The meta-inductive argument, by contrast, if successful, is supposed to knock us down with a much more general logical force: induction, a capacity possessed by all, so the argument is intended, thereby, to fetch universal conviction.[4]

But is it successful? The incessant sloganeering about the "marketplace of ideas" depends centrally on its success. Deep though it goes in liberal culture and sensibility, I think Mill's argument is a numbing fallacy.

To begin with, even at a cursory glance, you will notice that the judgment in the first premise is made from the point of view of one's current opinions and convictions. It is from our present point of view, from what we *currently take to be true,* that we are able to say that our past opinions are false. But the judgment in the second premise is telling us that our current point of view may contain false views and therefore to be unsure and diffident about them. Now if we are unsure about our current beliefs and our judgment in the first premise is made on the basis of our current beliefs, then to that extent we must be unsure of our first and basic premise. Any conclusion based on it therefore is bound to be, to that extent, itself shaky and uncertain.

Am I being too quick or unfair with Mill's argument?

Someone may seek to defend it by saying that Mill does not think that *any and all* of our current beliefs might be wrong. In particular, he does not require that we have any lack of confidence in our current judgments about our past beliefs being false. So the first premise is not shaky. According to this defense of Mill, we make epistemological *progress,* and cumulatively build up a fund of truths via rejecting past convictions in the course of the history of inquiry. It is just that there are still a vast number of present beliefs of which we are convinced, but which may well be false, given the meta-induction. So just to give an example, it might be said that there is no need to lack confidence in our judgment that our past belief that the earth is flat is false. As was claimed by Karl Popper (another philosopher, who—like Mill—tried to display the virtues of a free and open society on the basis of abstract arguments that all rational subjects would accept) we make epistemological progress by confidently rejecting certain convictions (such as the one about the earth being flat) as false. So, in general, this line of defense of Mill says that adopting freedom and tolerance opens up our convictions to falsification via the allowing of dissenting views and once we do so, we can then make progress in knowledge by this process of falsification, which tolerance enables, and come to hold with confidence at least some beliefs, such as, in our example, the belief that the earth is *not* flat.

But this way of defending Mill's epistemological assumptions in his argument for freedom is of no real help to him. It should follow, from this defense, that Mill would now allow that at least as far as the belief that the earth is *not* flat (i.e., the belief that we confidently hold, the belief that our epistemic progress has established conviction in via the falsification process made possible by tolerance) is concerned, we should not tolerate dissent toward it. This is because we do not have any diffidence in this belief—and it was diffidence in our convictions that was the basis on which he argued for free speech. It is only because beliefs are not something we are confident in having established as true that the argument for free speech is supposed to go through. So if there *are* beliefs about whose truth epistemic progress via falsification allows confidence, then to that extent, free speech (as argued for by Mill) need not be necessary, regarding at least them. But, of course, Mill will *not* allow that there be *exceptions* made to freedom of speech for some beliefs. He is not going to say, "Go ahead and tyrannize and censor the speech of flat-earthers since the belief that the earth is not flat is something we have no diffidence about." That is to say, he is not going to allow that our convictions (now held with *confidence*) that certain beliefs are false are immune from his conclusion about tolerance and free speech. That is simply not a ground in Mill for putting tolerance aside. So the defense may be right in trying to free Mill of a non-credible epistemology, but even if it is right in doing so, it has not done so in a way that strengthens a weak argument.

There is another even more fundamental internal problem with the argument.

In characterizing it, I have said that it comes to a value conclusion on the basis of premises that appeal merely to an induction, and not on the basis of any other political or moral value. But the fact is that though it appeals to no moral and political values, it does appeal to a cognitive value, the value of truth. Since it says that one should adopt free speech because it creates a marketplace of ideas from which the truth, even if it goes against one's convictions, will emerge, one is assuming at least that there *is value* in pursuing the truth. So it *does* appeal to another value (the cognitive value of truth) to justify the value of free speech.[5] It is only because we value truth and have it as a goal that we will be moved by the idea that a marketplace of ideas engendered by freedom of speech is something that we should adopt.

But now, if that is so, there is something internally peculiar about an argument that appeals to the value of truth and the goal of pursuing the truth, as it does, while also implying, as the second premise does, that we can never know that we have achieved the truth. How can we claim to have a goal that we can never know we have achieved, when we have achieved it? What sort of goal is that? It is not perhaps as peculiar as having a goal that we know that we can never achieve. That is outright incoherent. You cannot coherently strive to achieve what you know to be impossible. But to allow that we can achieve a goal and yet insist that we can never *know* we have achieved it when we have, though not perhaps outright incoherent, is a very peculiar understanding of what goals are.

To put it explicitly, the internal tension is this: The argument's second premise says that beliefs whose truth we are utterly convinced about may turn out to be false. This strictly implies that we can never be sure that we have achieved the goal of truth, not even when we are quite convinced we have. And yet the argument presupposes that the pursuit of truth is a value and that we have it as a goal to pursue. If the goal of inquiry into the truth that all academic institutions embrace is really to pursue in this way something that we never can be sure we have achieved, then we must be assuming that what we do, in pursuing it, is a bit like sending a message in a bottle out to sea. We never know what comes of it, we never know that it has arrived. What sort of epistemological project is that? It is a conception of inquiry in which we have no control over its success. If inquiry is successful, that success is, from our hapless point of view as inquirers, necessarily some sort of bonus or fluke.

The argument demands that our point of view of inquiry have a built-in diffidence: We are supposed to be diffident even about our most well-established claims. But such diffidence yields no instruction. The doubt expressed by the thought "for all one knows even our strongest convictions as to what is true might be false" is an idle form of doubt. Consider the paradox of the preface, in which the author says coyly, "Something or other that I say in the next four hundred pages is bound to be erroneous or false" (and then typically adds, and "for those errors I alone am to blame and not all those nice people I have just acknowl-edged as having aided my thought and argument"). The author's decla-ration of impending falsity in the pages to come is idle because it gives him or her no instruction about what to do to remedy things. It is not as if she knows what it is that is bound to be false, and why. Like Mill and Holmes she just thinks that that is the tentativeness and diffidence with which she must hold the views she has written down. But a doubt that gives no instruction in her practice of writing is a doubt that does not make any epistemic difference. And as pragmatists say, something that makes no difference to practice (not even to cognitive practice, as in this case) makes no difference to inquiry and epistemology at all. Any argument which arrives at a commitment to free speech on the basis of a conception of inquiry that has such precarious coherence hardly deserves the centrality that it has been given in the liberal tradition of political thought.

It will not do, in the face of all these difficulties being presented against Mill's argument, for liberalism to say, "You are right. There is no need to think that inquiry will have truth as a goal, if we can never know when we have attained any particular truth. But perhaps then we should cease to think that truth *is* a goal of inquiry. We simply try to achieve something less than truth." This view (taken by Richard Rorty though not at all in the context of these questions I am raising about Mill's argument) does not help Mill at all because now the question will arise: What then is Mill's argument for tolerance targeting in the meta-induction? Is it not essential to the argument that it find one, or place one, in a position of never being confident that we have what we epistemologically seek? If truth, the property of beliefs we never are confident we have achieved, is no longer a goal of inquiry, if it is replaced by something weaker which we *can* be confident of having achieved when we have achieved it, then Mill loses his premises in the argument altogether and so he cannot come to his conclusion for free speech—at least not on the basis of *that* argument or anything resembling that argument. In general, Mill seems to presuppose as a value that it is good to seek the truth and that it is a goal of ours that we seek it, and the argument for tolerance turns on our never being sure that we have achieved it. And in my criticisms, I have been saying that the idea that we are never sure that we have achieved it is in deep tension with the presupposition of the argument that truth *is* a value and that we have it as a goal of inquiry that we seek the truth. To respond to the critique by saying that we do not have truth as a goal of inquiry is to give up on Mill's premises and argument altogether. Even if that is the right way to go in epistemology (which I don't believe it is, i.e., I don't believe we should give up truth as a goal of inquiry, but rather we should not conceive of truth in these ulterior ways that Mill does and that Rorty acquiesces in, in taking his view of the goal of inquiry), it does no favors to Mill on the question of liberty.

I am afraid there is no rescuing Mill's meta-inductive argument. As an attempt to lay a superlatively rational foundation for a liberal commitment to freedom of inquiry, it is a dud—even if a noble dud.

I have been resisting Mil's argument for the political and academic value of free speech by finding fault with its underlying epistemological assumptions, but I cannot rest with these purely negative points about the mistaken epistemology within which Mill's political argument is made without saying something, at least very briefly, in more positive terms about what the contours of an *alternative* epistemology look like. The alternative epistemological assumptions that my criticisms are making derive from a combination of philosophical views that go back to the American pragmatists, to philosophers such as Wittgenstein and Austin, and eventually to Kant's doctrine of "transcendental idealism." The general tendency of the epistemological position which surfaces in these philosophers is often described by contemporary philosophers as a denial of a view called "realism," a view that is committed to an objectivity in how truth must be conceived, an objectivity that the pragmatists and Kant cannot accommodate in their epistemology. But that, I think, is a mistake. The alternative epistemology found in pragmatism and indeed in Kant's transcendental idealism can perfectly well and quite innocuously be understood as a form of realism. In fact it is, in my view, the only sane form of realism worth our subscription. Please don't be put off by these grand-sounding "isms" (pragmatism, transcendental idealism, realism) that I have just pronounced. They all amount to a quite commonsensical philosophical outlook and that is how I will present it here in a summary encapsulation though, of course, they must in the end be elaborated and defended (and have been elaborated and defended by the pragmatists and Kant himself) in large doctrinal philosophical structures.

Against Mill, I have insisted that when we achieve the truth in inquiry we must not be blinded to the fact that we have achieved it. We can know when we have achieved the truth. Now to say we achieve the truth and know that we have done so does not mean that we cannot revise our beliefs which we think amount to the truth. We can certainly revise beliefs, even beliefs that we currently hold with conviction and take to be true. But the idea that we can revise a given belief we hold with conviction is not properly expressed (indeed it is incoherently expressed) by saying, as Mill would have us say, "My belief that p is true, but for all I know it might be false," or "I know that p, but for all I know, p is false." This is a point and distinction that was much stressed by the greatest of

all pragmatists, Charles Sanders Peirce, and also by philosophers such
as Wittgenstein and Austin. And such a pragmatist point is very closely
linked with Kant's epistemology.[6] If pragmatism is right, the word
"belief" means two different things in inquiry. First there are beliefs held
with conviction and certainty. Second there are beliefs held as hypotheses. In inquiry, the former form a background and the latter are in the
foreground of inquiry. And when we test and assess beliefs qua hypotheses in the foreground of inquiry, we do so taking for granted without
any doubt the truths of the beliefs in the background because it is these
background beliefs that provide *the lights by which we assess* the foreground beliefs or hypotheses.[7] They are simply not, therefore, subject to
Mill's philosophical and fallibilist forms of doubt. Now Kant had made
a similar point when he said that reality is in some sense not entirely
independent of our own world-view, our own concepts and categories of
understanding. That is the rudimentary expression of his "transcendental idealism." This means that when we state the conditions in the world
which make any particular proposition true or false, the conditions are
always something that are specified by the lights of our own background
beliefs. What I have outlined above is the pragmatist development of that
claim in Kant. In the pragmatist (and Wittgenstein's and Austin's) idea
of inquiry, our beliefs, held with certainty and conviction, provide the
background lights of assessment, i.e., *the world-view from within which*
we, as inquirers, can assess foreground hypotheses or specify the reality (the conditions in the world) which makes any specific proposition
true. That is the marriage of pragmatism and transcendental idealism
that makes for a sane realism.

But someone in the name of "realism" and the objectivity of truth
might protest: Your position does not allow truth to be sufficiently
independent of belief and without that truth loses its objectivity. I think
the only sense in which independence of this kind is required by realism is the independence which says truth is independent of belief in the
sense that a belief is true *whether we believe it or not*. And the pragmatism of Peirce, as Isaac Levi has pointed out to me, *does* allow this. Suppose we believe that p is true. This means that it meets the standards of
correctness provided by our background beliefs. But now the standard
of correctness provided by our background beliefs in inquiry is such

that we also know that, were we to suppose that we judge something to be true which is not dictated by those standards, we would be wrong to do so. Thus were we to suppose that we judge that not-p is true, we would conclude that that judgment was wrong. In other words p is true whether we believe it or we don't believe it and believe its negation. And that, as I said, is all that is needed to establish the requisite independence that makes truth objective. No greater independence of truth from belief is required to make truth objective. And no other realism is needed than one based on this ideal of truth's objectivity.

So much for the epistemology that confronts Mill's argument for liberty. What alternative politics of inquiry does it allow within the academy? In the immediate context of the political controversies we find ourselves in, in university life, the conception of academic freedom based on Mill's classical liberal form of argument leads *directly* to the advice we often get, sometimes even from university presidents, about how we should be *balanced* in what we say in our classrooms, showing consideration to all points of view, even those which from our point of view we confidently know to be wrong. This directive wholly fails to understand what sort of role the ideal of "balance" ought to play in the academy. It is a worthy ideal but we have to understand the right place and context for it in the academy.

Let's go along, as we have been doing, with the assumption that a primary aim of universities is to pursue the truth in our various disciplinary inquiries and that the point of pedagogy is to try to present the truth we have found by presenting evidence and argument for it. Now if "balance" has any role to play in all this, its role is entirely *nested within* this primary goal, *not* something *independent* of this goal. And within this primary goal, the only thing that "balance" *could* mean is that one must look at *all* the evidence that is available to one in our inquiries. (This is the cognitive counterpart to what decision theorists call "the total evidence requirement.") What "balance" cannot possibly mean is the nonsensical thing that the directive we are considering tells us, viz., the equal presentation in the classroom of two contradictory views. No educator with any minimal rationality would do that on the elementary grounds that if there are two contradictory views, only one can be right. Of course if she cannot make up her mind on the evidence as to which one is right, she might present the case for both views evenhandedly. But presumably such undecidedness is an *occasional* phenomenon. If so, balance cannot be put down as a *requirement* for pedagogy in the classroom. Hence, the constant demand that we always present both sides of a disagreement presupposes a conception of education as a sort of chronic dithering. It is far more sensible to say that "balance" allows that an educator presents her judgment with complete conviction because "balance" in the academy is nothing other than a synonym for the idea that we must look at *all* the evidence before coming to our convictions. It has no other role or meaning. Attempts to give it another meaning (as in the directive with which I am finding fault) are drawn from a fault-line that has its beginnings in the canonical Millian form of liberal argument for free speech.

It might be thought that there is no very direct link between the broad liberal mentality toward freedom of speech and academic freedom that I am situating in Mill's argument and this talk of "balance" in the university's classrooms. So take, for instance, the demand that we show balance when discussing Middle Eastern politics, presenting the Israeli viewpoint as much as the Palestinian, in classrooms. About this demand, it might be said that there are *much more straightforward political motives* underlying the demand such as protecting Israel from the harsh criticisms that it deserves for its brutalization of Palestinians. If both sides are constantly being presented equally, as is demanded by "balance," then the force of such decisive criticism can be softened. I don't deny that there are these political motives for demanding balance in cases of this kind as well as other cases. But we can't forget that many political motives of this kind are cloaked in high-sounding intellectual arguments so that their nakedness, qua political motives, is hidden. Just think of the way slaves were said to be not quite "persons" by ideologues rationalizing slave ownership or the way natives were said to be lacking "rationality" by colonists. These philosophical arguments are a constant factor in rationalizing the pursuit of political motives and goals. Mill's argument for liberalism with its underlying assumptions that I have tried to expose is similarly often invoked and underlies (as a *rationalization*) these other political motives for demands for balance in pedagogy. It is partly at least for this reason—and not merely as a philosophical exercise—that I have subjected Mill's argument to this critical scrutiny.

3.

I have been inveighing against a very standard liberal argument and a
metaphor that it yields about truth emerging from a marketplace of ideas,
which goes deep in the sensibility of our self-understanding in the academy and in the courts that have pronounced judgment in controversial
cases that the academy has thrown up. This may have given the impression that I am recommending more dogmatism regarding our own
convictions than a commitment to academic freedom can allow. That
impression would be wrong.

The criticisms I have just made of Mill's argument are quite compatible with the view (which is my own view) that there is far too much
dogmatism in the academy, especially in the social sciences and even in
the humanities. (And if it is less so in the natural sciences, still, as Kuhn
pointed out almost five decades ago, there is some there too.) As a matter
of fact, my view is that if we could characterize more or less exactly what
this dogmatism is, we would have identified the most pervasive as well
as the most insidious and interesting form of threat to academic freedom.

As I said at the outset, this essay was going to raise a typical philosopher's fuss about how to rigorously characterize the arguments by which
we justify academic freedom and I have said that I find Holmes's metaphor and Mill's argument less than exact and plausible and this implies
that theirs is not the way to understand the dogmatism that thwarts academic freedom. To be fussy is to demand that one gets certain distinctions carefully right. And I am claiming that to diagnose and combat
the far too high levels of dogmatism in the academy, we do not have to
assume a fallibilist notion of diffidence and doubt. It is one thing to be
undogmatic in the way that academic freedom demands, quite another
to have the sort of notion of inquiry suggested by Millian and classical
liberal arguments for academic freedom.

Let me convey what I have in mind by the dogmatism that constitutes
a threat to academic freedom by returning to the paradox of the preface.
The paradox offers us a site for locating a useful taxonomy via which we
can identify what sort of dogmatism amounts to such a threat.

I had said about the paradox that the *generalized,* that is to say, the
unspecific form of doubt that is stated in the preface ("Something or

other that I say in the next four hundred pages is bound to be erroneous or false," echoing Mill's argument that our strongest convictions may turn out to be false) gives the author no instruction as to what to do about it. He cannot possibly be moved to do anything about his text by a doubt such as this. What the author will be moved and instructed by is not this sort of doubt but rather—if he or she is not dishonest and not obtuse—by some *specific* evidence or argument that is provided against one or other of his *specific* conclusions or claims. Now both these qualifications—"if he or she is not dishonest and not obtuse"—are revealing.

They show that there is no direct relevance of this issue I have just raised (about ignoring *specific* counter-evidence and counter-argument presented to one) to the question of academic freedom. Suppose someone failed to recognize counter-evidence that was presented to him. That would be a sign of his obtuseness. Suppose again that someone did recognize that counter-evidence had been presented to him by some colleague and he simply ignored it. That would be a sign of his intellectual dishonesty. But both these things are quite *separate* kinds of wrong from thwarting academic freedom. Now it is true that sometimes those who are dishonest in this way are caused by this dishonesty to suppress or hound out someone who presented that evidence and that would, of course, be threatening to academic freedom; but suppressing or hounding someone out is a matter quite separable from what we are concerned with, the ignoring of evidence that is provided against what one takes to be the truth.

If this is right, we have identified so far three different phenomena. *First,* there is academic *dishonesty*—to recognize evidence or argument that goes against one's conclusions but ignore it. This in itself is *not* academic unfreedom. *Second,* there is the inability to even recognize the force of counter-evidence and counter-argument. Let's call this academic or intellectual *obtuseness*. And even more obviously, that is not a case of academic unfreedom either. *Third,* there is the suppression of those who present counter-evidence and counter-argument that one has recognized to be so and one has dishonestly evaded. This, I have said, *is* a case of academic unfreedom. But as I said at the beginning of the essay, it is a very obvious case and not a very interesting one, so I will simply put such cases aside since they raise no difficult questions. It is not even clearly characterizable as a case of dogmatism though it bears some relations to dogmatism.

We, then, still do not have the kind of academic unfreedom that is genuinely and clearly also a case of dogmatism. So now, finally *fourth* in our taxonomy, I want to present that kind of dogmatism and show why it is a far more interesting and unobvious and also a more pervasive threat to academic freedom than is identified in the third; and in presenting it, it will become clear what its relation is to the first and second phenomena in the taxonomy, from which it is also important to distinguish it, especially the first phenomenon with which it is too often conflated.

The dogmatism that interests me is found in submerged forms of academic *exclusion* when we circle the wagons around our own frameworks for discussion so that *alternative frameworks* for pursuing the truth simply will not even become visible on the horizon of our research agenda. This form of dogmatism is distinguishable from the first of our four phenomena, academic dishonesty of the kind that refuses to accept counter-evidence and counter-argument presented in refutation of some specific conclusion of our inquiry. Why? Because alternative frameworks *do not refute our conclusions directly* with counter-evidence or counter-arguments, so much as point to other, possibly deeper and more interesting ways of looking at what we are studying. And here is the absolutely crucial point. *If* they *do* contain counter-arguments and counter-evidence to our own claims and convictions, those will only surface *further downstream,* well *after* the frameworks are recognized by us upstream as possibly fruitful forms of investigation. But it is this recognition *upstream* that the dogmatist in us finds so hard to confer and it is in this failure that academic unfreedom (rather than intellectual dishonesty) is located.

These are cases in which a discipline discourages the development of frameworks outside of a set of assumptions on which there is mainstream consensus—and the political influence on the formation and maintenance of these exclusive assumptions, where it exists, is very indirect indeed, so indirect that it would need a fair amount of diagnostic work to reveal it since the *practitioners themselves are often quite innocent of the influence.* On the other hand it is not as if this is a rare or unusual phenomenon. It is widespread and is quite well known and many know it closely. That is why an academic institution like The New School in New York is one of the more valuable institutions of higher learning in this country, having valiantly housed—indeed it has been something of a hospice for—those suffering from an exclusion of unorthodox frameworks for thinking about a range of themes in a range of different disciplines.

Dogmatism of this kind is also distinguishable from the third sort of flaw, obtuseness. To be dogmatic in this way is not at all to be lacking in the acuity that would recognize the force of counter-evidence and counter-argument. If one has failed to recognize any counter-evidence (downstream, in my metaphor), that is because one has (further upstream) not even so much as recognized the possibility of the framework from which it flows. It is not as if the counter-evidence is there for us to see downstream and we are not perceptive enough to see it. Rather it is *not there for us to see* downstream because we have not recognized the *framework* upstream, from *within which it is visible*. And this last failure is a kind of dogmatism, not stupidity.

Among disciplines, economics provides the most gorgeous examples of this. It is perhaps the worst offender in inuring itself against alternative frameworks of thought and analysis. In fact, I will frankly say that I have never come across a discipline that combines as much extraordinary sophistication and high-powered intellect and intelligence with as much demonstrable falsehood. So, for instance (there are more sophisticated instances, I am mentioning only the most tiresomely familiar one), some of the most brilliant intellectuals I have known to this day make claims about the trickle down of wealth in capitalist economies and present them with the most sophisticated formal and quantitative methods, despite the plain fact that wealth has not trickled down (at least not to the places where it needs to trickle down), *anywhere in the world* in the *entire history of capitalist political economy.* If a physicist were to make some of the claims that economists have made which have been falsified as repeatedly as they have, they would not only have their careers terminated, they would properly be the laughing stock of the profession. In Economics, they often win Nobel prizes. Now there is no direct political influence that forces this sort of refusal to question, leave alone give up, one's assumptions in a discipline such as economics. The regulation is wholly *within* the discipline's profession and even there, there may be very little browbeating or intellectual bullying, that is to say, very little *explicit* regulation. It is largely unconscious self-censorship—often done with career advancement in mind—that threatens academic freedom in such disciplines.

On the very evening after I wrote these words in a draft of this essay, I was over at dinner at my economist colleague Joe Stiglitz's apartment and I impertinently told him that I was going to raise this point in a lecture I was to give at a conference on academic freedom the next day. His response was memorable. "Akeel, I agree with you about economists but I don't understand why you are so puzzled. One would only be puzzled if one were making the wrong assumption about economics. What you should be assuming is that—as it is done by most economists—economics is really a religion. And so why should you be puzzled by the fact that they cling to and never give up their views despite their frequent falsification." So I will rephrase my point: One apparently makes one's way up in a church hierarchy by clinging fast to the orthodox faith.

But there is the following difference. The church has had a history of explicit and rigid regulation of what may or may not be said and pursued in its fold. But, as I said, if there is political (or corporate) influence in play in the sort of dogmatism I have described in economics, it is not obviously visible and direct, and the protagonists in economic inquiry in universities would be quite genuinely clueless about it and, with no dishonesty, deny its influence. Sometimes, as in my own subject of analytic philosophy, where there is a great deal of exclusion of alternative frameworks for discussion, there is no political influence, *however indirect,* in play. If there is a question of power and politics involved it is entirely internal to the discipline, the power that is felt and enjoyed simply in keeping certain ways of thinking out of the orbit of discussion, forming small coteries of people referring to each other's work with no concern that the issues they discuss are issues that have no bearing on anything of fundamental concern to any of a number of disciplines with which philosophy had always been concerned before, say, even fifty years ago, and from which it has now managed to isolate itself for the most part. Richard

Rorty had tried to raise Kuhnian questions for the discipline of analytic philosophy[8] and spoken with eloquence about its insularity and he was certainly right to notice just how exclusionary the subject had become, the more it had become a *profession in universities*.

Moving away from specific disciplinary examples, the general point that emerges from these examples can be made if one recalls that De Tocqueville famously said, "I know of no country where there is so little independence of mind and real freedom of discussion as in America." And here is a wildly curious thing. At the same time, it is America that has more free institutions (including academic institutions) than anywhere else in the world. How can this extraordinarily paradoxical duality co-exist? What explains this paradox? I can't possibly try to provide an explanation here,[9] but whatever it is that explains it will provide a very good sense of the deep, that is to say, submerged forms of academic unfreedom that exist in this country. When the freest academic institutions co-exist with some of the highest levels of academic unfreedom in the democratic world, the sources of unfreedom are bound to be far subtler than is captured by the standard vocabulary of "suppression," "brainwashing," "political pressure," "manipulation," and so on. That is why this fourth phenomenon, this pervasive sort of dogmatism, is a far more interesting case of academic unfreedom than the third phenomenon in our taxonomy. When a person working with unorthodox frameworks of research is looked upon, with *perfect sincerity* by professionals, as someone unfortunate and alienated and to be pitied as irrelevant or outdated rather than bullied and hounded, we know, not only that the political influences on these professionals are not even easily identified, leave alone easily confronted, we also know that this kind of thwarting of academic freedom needs a quite different descriptive vocabulary than I used in describing the third phenomenon.

Equally, I would insist that it is different from the first phenomenon of academic dishonesty as well because to accuse these professionals of *dishonesty* (rather than in their dogmatism unconsciously perpetrating academic *unfreedom*) would be to be glibly moralistic since (if I am right in making the upstream/downstream metaphor) it is not *honesty* that requires that people should be willing to allow frameworks of investigations other than their own. At any rate it is not honesty in the sense that is required to admit that one's views have been refuted, when one has been shown evidence against them and one is not too obtuse to recognize the evidence. To insist that they are both a case of dishonesty would be to perpetrate a (not very good) pun.

The interest and subtlety of this exclusionary phenomenon, then, lies in its distinguishabilty from all of the other three in our quartet: academic dishonesty, academic stupidity, and straightforward and obvious forms of academic suppression. Despite its subtlety, it *is* a recognizable assault on academic freedom, and it is the more important to analyze in detail precisely because there is nothing as obvious (or infrequent) about it as there is about the efforts at external influence of Christian groups on science curricula or of Zionist groups on Middle East studies departments, in some universities. Being much more subtle it is also much more pervasive than these more obvious phenomena—and much harder to resist. Different people feel it differently at different times. Frameworks for serious research in race and gender felt it constantly for decades till as late as the 70s of the last century. Quite possibly more old-fashioned forms of humanistic scholarship in a range of literary disciplines began to feel it since the late 80s and 90s of that century. And I daresay, research programs which pursue seriously socialist forms of analysis feel it more than ever today in economics departments.

I have tried in this essay to shift attention away from the fallibilist epistemological presuppositions of metaphors such as "the marketplace of ideas" and its classical Millian arguments for academic freedom, and I have tried to focus it instead on the need to diagnose the sorts of unconscious attitudes that make for unwitting disciplinary mandarins and gatekeepers, "normal scientists" as Kuhn called them. One doesn't need to be diffident in the conviction with which one holds one's views in order to resist such attitudes. We should allow alternative frameworks not because we have some generalized doubt that we ourselves might be holding false views. We should allow alternative frameworks for quite different kind of reasons, also found in Mill's writing on liberty, as I said, having to do with the fact that if we allow for frameworks of investigation other than our own, we make for an attractively diverse intellectual ethos and in doing so allow the creativity of different sorts of people and minds to flower. These sorts of consideration in favor of academic freedom, unlike Mill's argument considered in Section 2 which appeals to all those capable of inductive reasoning and in pursuit of the truth, gives rise to a picture of academic freedom that appeals *only* to those who think that there is value in creativity and diversity in the academy. The appeal therefore is frankly disadvantaged by its less than universal reach. But, on the other hand, the picture can claim the advantage of not being landed with a bizarre conception of inquiry presupposed by Mill's more ambitious argument and the metaphorical cliché that it has yielded about the "marketplace of ideas."

The vital point I want to repeat in marking this difference from Holmes's metaphor and from Mill's meta-inductive argument on which that metaphor is based, is that if considerations about truth and falsity enter this picture, it is only, as I said, *further downstream* when something that other frameworks deliver might claim to be a truth that clashes with ours and provides some evidence or argument for us to give up some of our own convictions. But since those considerations do not surface upstream where we are pursuing the goal of inquiring into the truth in our investigations, that goal of pursuing the truth need never be conceived of as a goal whose success is necessarily opaque to its seekers, as in Mill's argument for freedom. In our own pursuits toward the truth, we may be as confident in the truth of the deliverances of our investigations as is merited by the evidence in our possession, and we need feel no unnecessary urge to display balance in the classroom, if we have shown balance and scruple in our survey of the evidence on which our convictions are based, the only place where balance is relevant in the first place.

4.

Having said that, I should like to conclude with a point that rotates the angle a bit on the question of balance.

One of the questions that has most exercised scholars of academic freedom is the extent to which the concept and the policy applies to the utterances of a scholar not within the university but in what is called the *"extra-mural"* context. Is a professor free to say things outside the university in public forums that would be unsuitable for one reason or another in the classroom or at official university events? There is a lot of interesting writing on this subject, some of the most interesting by scholars of the law. But I want to say something here that is a bit off that beaten track.

When it is not classroom curriculum and intellectual inquiry in the university but political debate in general outside the study and the classroom that is in question, there are good reasons why the views one expresses can and often should be substantially *im*balanced. And by imbalance here, I don't just mean that they should speak with conviction for one side of a disagreement, if that side has the preponderance of evidence on its side. That form of imbalance is what my critique of Mill and Holmes has tried to establish as perfectly appropriate in the classroom. But for extra-curricular and extra-mural public speech by academics, I have in mind the moral appropriateness of a *further* and more *willful* kind of imbalance. To conclude in one's thought what the evidence in one's investigations dictates is not really a matter of choice or will.[10] The evidence *compels* us, as it were. But to be imbalanced in the *further* way I am about to mention *is* a matter of will and moral decision. Let me explain.

I find it not only understandable but honorable, if someone speaking and writing in America finds it important to *stress much more* the wrongs of the American government and its allies and clients, like Israel, Saudi Arabia, Egypt, Pakistan (now even India), Indonesia under Suharto, Chile under Pinochet, and so on, rather than speak obsessively, as is so often done, about the wrongs done by Muslim terrorists or Islamic theocratic regimes or, for that matter, Cuba and North Korea. But if the same person was speaking or writing, say, in the Palestinian territories or in Arab or Middle Eastern newspapers, it would be far more admirable if he were to criticize Hamas or Islamic regimes like Iran's. So also, unlike the many who were abusive toward him for not doing so, I find it entirely honorable that Sartre, living in Paris in the Cold War ethos, refused to spend his time criticizing the Soviet Union and instead criticized Western governments for the most part.

It is said that whenever Sakharov criticized the Soviet Union's treatment of dissidents in the 50s, he was chastised by his government for showing an imbalance and not speaking out against the treatment of blacks in the American South. That is precisely the kind of imbalance that courageous academics are going to be accused of by the enemies of intellectual freedom in this country, and I hope that all of us will have the courage to continue being imbalanced in just this way.

Secular Enchantment

FOUR

Gandhi, the Philosopher

1.

I was once asked by a literary magazine to write a review essay on Nehru. Some weeks later, the editor asked me if I would throw in Gandhi as well. As it happened I never wrote the piece, but I remember thinking that it was like being asked while climbing the Western Ghats whether I would take a detour and climb Mount Everest as well. I am not now trying to scale any great peak or to give a defining interpretation to Gandhi. It's generally foolhardy to write about Gandhi, not only because you are never certain you've got him right, but because you are almost sure to have him wrong. There is a lack of plain argument in his writing and there is an insouciance about fundamental objections, which he himself raises, to his own intuitive ideas. The truth of his claims seems to him so instinctive and certain that mere arguments seem frivolous even to readers who disagree with them. Being trained in a discipline of philosophy of a quite different temperament, I will try to not get distracted by the irritation I sometimes feel about this.

In reading Gandhi recently I have been struck by the integrity of his ideas. I don't mean simply that he was a man of integrity in the sense that he tried to make his actions live up to his ideals, though perhaps in fact he tried more than most to do so. I mean something more abstract: that his thought itself was highly integrated, his ideas about very specific political strategies in specific contexts flowed (and in his mind necessarily flowed) from ideas that were very remote from politics. They flowed from the most abstract epistemological and methodological commitments. This quality of his thought sometimes gets lost because, on the one hand, the popular interest in him has been keen to find a man of great spirituality and uniqueness and, on the other, the social scientist's and historian's interest in him has sought out a nationalist leader with a strikingly effective method of non-violent political action. It has been common for some decades now to swing from a sentimental perception of him as a "Mahatma" to a cooler assessment of Gandhi as "the shrewd politician." I will steer past this oscillation because it hides the very qualities of his thought I want to uncover. The essay is not so much (in fact hardly at all) inspired by the plausibility of the philosophy that emerges as by the stunning intellectual ambition and originality that this "integrity" displays.

2.

Non-violence is a good place to get a *first* glimpse of what I have in mind.

Violence has many sides. It can be spontaneous or planned, it can be individual or institutional, it can be physical or psychological, it can be delinquent or adult, it can be revolutionary or authoritarian. A great deal has been written on violence: on its psychology, on its possible philosophical justifications under certain circumstances, and of course on its long career in military history. *Non*-violence has no sides at all. Being negatively defined, it is indivisible. It began to be a subject of study much more recently and there is much less written on it, not merely because it is defined in negative terms but because until it became a self-conscious instrument in politics in this century, it was really constituted *as* or *in* something else. It was studied under different names, first usually as part of religious or contemplative ways of life remote from the public affairs of men and state, and later with the coming of Romantic thought in Europe, under the rubric of critiques of industrial civilization.

For Gandhi, both these contexts were absolutely essential to his conception of non-violence. Non-violence was central in his nationalist mobilization against British rule in India. But the concept is also situated in an essentially religious temperament as well as in a thoroughgoing critique of ideas and ideologies of the Enlightenment and of an intellectual paradigm of perhaps a century earlier than the Enlightenment. This is a paradigm in which science became set on a path which seemed destined to lead to *cumulative* results, building to a *progressively* complete understanding of the world in which we lived, a world which we could as a result control. It is a familiar point that there is no understanding Gandhi, the anti-colonial nationalist, without situating him in these larger trajectories of his thought.

The strategy of non-violent resistance was first introduced by him so as to bring into the nationalist efforts against the British an element beyond making only constitutional demands. On the face of it, for those reared on Western political ideas, this seems very odd. Constitutional demands, as they are understood in liberal political theory, are the essence of non-violent politics; as is well known the great early propounders of liberal democratic thought conceived and still conceive of constitutions and their constraints on human public action as a constraint against tendencies toward violence in the form of coercion of individuals by states and other collectivities, not to mention by other individuals. So why did Gandhi, the prophet of non-violence, think that the Indian people, in their demands for greater self-determination, needed more than constitutional demands? And why did he think that this is best called "non-violent" action? The obvious answer is the instrumental and strategic one: He knew that making demands for constitutional change had not been particularly effective or swift in the first two decades of this century and that since the conventionally conceived alternative was violent revolutionary action—which found advocates on the fringes of nationalist sentiment in India—he instead introduced his own strategy of civil disobedience, at once a non-violent and yet a non- or extra-constitutional strategy. But, of course, he had more in mind than this obvious motive.

First, Gandhi wanted all of India to be involved in the movement, in particular the vast mass of its peasant population. He did not want the nationalist achievement to be the effort of a group of elite, legally and constitutionally trained, upper-middle-class Indian men ("Macaulay's bastards"), who argued in assemblies and round-table conferences. He almost single-handedly transformed a movement conceived and promoted along those lines by the Congress Party into a mass movement of enormous scale, and he did so within a few years of arriving from South Africa on Indian soil. Non-violent action was the central idea of this vast mobilization. Second, he knew that violent revolutionary action could not possibly carry the mass of people with it. Revolutionary action was mostly conceived hugger-mugger in underground cells and took the form of isolated subversive terrorist action against key focal points of government power and interest; it was not conceived as a mass movement. He was not unaware that there existed in the West ideologies of revolutionary violence which were geared to mass movements, but he was not unaware, either, that these were conceived in terms of middle-class leadership *vanguards* that were the fonts of authority. Peasant consciousness mattered very little to them. In Gandhi there was not a trace of this vanguard mentality of a Lenin. He did indeed think that his "satyagrahis"—the non-violent activists whom he described, with that term, as "seekers of truth"—would provide leadership which the masses would follow, but it was absolutely crucial to him that these were not to be the vanguard of a revolutionary party along Leninist lines. They were to be thought of along entirely different lines; they were to be *moral exemplars,* not ideologues who claimed to know history and its forward movement better than the peasants to whom they were giving the lead. Third, Gandhi chose his version of non-violent civil disobedience instead of the constitutional demands of the Congress leadership because he thought that the Indian people should not merely ask the British to leave their soil. It was important that they should do so by means that were not dependent and derivative of ideas and institutions that the British had imposed on them. Otherwise, even if the British left, the Indian populations would remain a subject people. This went very deep in Gandhi and his book *Hind Swaraj* is full of a detailed anxiety about the *cognitive* enslavement even of the nationalist and anti-colonial Indian mind, which might, even after independence, never recover from that enslavement.

These points are well known, and they raise the roughly political considerations which underlie his commitment to non-violence. As I said, they give only a *first* glimpse of the integrity of his ideas. There are deeper and more ambitious underlying grounds than these in his writing.

3.

The idea that non-violence was of a piece with the search for truth was central to what I have called his "integrity" and to these more ambitious and abstract considerations than the ones I have just discussed. Gandhi was explicit about this, even in the terminology he adopted, linking *ahimsa* (non-violence) with *satyagraha* (literally, "truth-force," or more liberally, a tenacity in the pursuit of truth). There is a standard and entrenched reading of Gandhi which understands the link as follows (and I am quoting from what is perhaps the most widely read textbook of modern Indian history, Sumit Sarkar's *Modern India*): "Non-violence or ahimsa and satyagraha to Gandhi personally constituted a deeply-felt and worked-out philosophy owing something to Emerson, Thoreau and Tolstoy but also revealing considerable originality. *The search for truth was the goal of human life, and as no one could ever be sure of having attained the truth, use of violence to enforce one's own view of it was sinful.*"[1]

I have no doubt that Gandhi says things that could lead to such a reading, and for years, I assumed that it was, more or less uncontroversially, what he had in mind. After scrutiny of his writings however, especially his many dispatches to *Young India*, it seems to me now a spectacular misreading. It fails to cohere with his most fundamental thinking.

Notice that according to this reading, or misreading, his view is no different from one of the most celebrated liberal arguments for tolerance—the meta-inductive argument of Mill's *On Liberty*.[2] Mill contends that since much that we have thought to be true in the past has turned out to be wrong, this in itself suggests that what we presently think true might also be wrong. We should therefore tolerate, not repress dissent from our present convictions just in case they are not true. According to Mill, and according to Gandhi on this widespread misreading of him, truth is never something we are sure we have attained. We must therefore be *made modest* in the way we hold our present opinions, and we must not impose our own conceptions of the truth on others. To do so would be a form of violence, especially if it was enforced by the apparatus of the state.

The modesty would appeal to Gandhi, but he would find something very alien in Mill's argument for it. There is no echo in Gandhi of the idea that the source of this modesty is that however much we seek truth, we *cannot attain* it, which is what Sarkar contends is the ground of his non-violence. In fact, it makes little sense to say that truth (or anything else) is something we should *seek,* even if we can never attain it. How can we intend to attain what we know we cannot attain? It would be bootless to protest that Gandhi and Mill are not saying that we can never attain the truth, only that we cannot know if we have attained it—so there is still point in the search for truth. That does little to improve matters. What sort of a goal or search is that? On this epistemological view, our inquiry and search for truth would be analogous to sending a message in a bottle out to sea, a search that is blinded about its own possible success, making all success a sort of bonus or fluke.

In any case, there is something rather odd in Mill's argument for tolerance. There is an unsettling tension between the argument's first two premises. The first premise is that our past beliefs have often turned out to be wrong. The second is that this is ground for thinking that our present opinions might be wrong. And the conclusion is that we should therefore be tolerant of dissent from current opinion. But the fact is that when past opinions are said to be wrong, that is a judgment made from the *present* point of view, and we cannot make that judgment unless we have the conviction in the present opinions which Mill is asking us not to have. It is all right to be asked to be diffident about our present opinions, but then we should, at least to that extent, be diffident about our judgment made on their basis, viz., that our past opinions are wrong. And if so, the first premise is shakier than he presents it as being.

The pervasive diffidence and lack of conviction in our opinions, which is the character of the epistemology that Mill's argument presupposes, is entirely alien to Gandhi; and though he is all in favor of the modesty with which we should be holding our opinions, that modesty does not have its source in such an epistemology and such a conception of unattainable truth.[3] What, then, is its source?

It is quite elsewhere than where Sarkar and everybody else who has written on Gandhi has located it; its source is to be found in his conception of the very nature of moral response and moral judgment. The "satyagrahi" or non-violent activist has to show a certain kind of self-restraint, in which it was not enough simply not to commit violence. It is equally important not to bear hostility to others or even to criticize them; it is only required that one not follow these others, if conscience doesn't permit it. To show hostility and contempt, to speak or even to think negatively and critically, would be to give in to the spiritual flaws that underlie violence, to have the wrong conception of moral judgment. For it is not the point of moral judgment to criticize. (In the section called "Ashram Vows" of his book *Hindu Dharma,*[4] he says, "Ahimsa is not the crude thing it has been made to appear. Not to hurt any living thing is no doubt part of ahimsa. But it is its least expression. It is hurt by hatred of any kind, by wishing ill of anybody, by making negative criticisms of others.") This entails the modesty with which one must hold one's moral opinions and which Mill sought in a quite different source: in a notion of truth which we are never sure we have attained and therefore (from Gandhi's point of view) in a quite untenable epistemology. The alternative source of the modesty in Gandhi has less to do with issues about truth and more to do with the way we must hold our moral values.

Despite the modesty, one could, of course, *resist* those with whom one disagrees, and Gandhi made an art out of refusal and resistance and disobedience. But resistance is not the same as criticism. It can be done with a "pure heart." Criticism reflects an impurity of heart and is easily corrupted to breed hostility and, eventually, violence. With an impure heart you could still indulge in non-violent political activism, but that activism would be strategic, merely a means to a political end. In the long run it would, just as surely as violence, land you in a midden. Even the following sensible-sounding argument for his own conclusion, often given by many of his political colleagues who found his moral attitudes obscure, did not satisfy Gandhi: "Let us adopt non-violent and passive resistance instead of criticizing the British colonial government because to assert a criticism of one's oppressor would usually have the effect of getting his back up, or of making him defensive, and so it might end up making things harder for oneself." Gandhi himself did occasionally say things of that sort, but he thought that colleagues who wanted to *rest* with such arguments as the foundation of non-violence were viewing it too much as an instrument and they were not going deep enough into the spiritual nature of the moral sense required of the satyagrahi. One did not go deep enough until one severed the *assumed theoretical connection* between moral judgment and moral criticism, the connection which, in our analytical terms, we would describe by saying that if one judges that "x is good," then we are obliged to find morally wrong those who, in relevant circumstances, judge otherwise or fail to act on x. For Gandhi this does not follow. The right moral sense, the morally pure-hearted satyagrahi, sees no such connection between moral judgment and moral criticism. Of course, we cannot and must not cease to be moral subjects; we cannot stop judging morally about what is and is not worthy, cannot fail to have moral values. But none of that requires us to be critical of others who disagree with our values or who fail to act in accord with them. *That* is the relevant modesty which Mill sought to justify by a different argument.

This view of the moral sense might well seem frustratingly namby-pamby now as it certainly did to those around him at the time. Can't it be argued, then, that Gandhi is shrewdly placing a screen of piety around the highly creative political instrument he is creating, both to confuse his colonial masters and to tap the religious emotions of the Indian masses? This is the oscillating interpretation I have been inveighing against, which, finding his religiosity too remote from politics, then fails to take his philosophical ideas as being intended seriously and views him only as a crafty and effective nationalist politician. It sells short both his moral philosophy and his politics. The fact is that his view of moral sense is of considerable philosophical interest, and is intended entirely earnestly by its author. It is given a fascinating theoretical consolidation in his writing which may be lost on his readers because it is buried in a porridge of saintly rhetoric, of "purity of heart."

4.

What is the assumed theoretical connection between moral judgment and moral criticism, which Gandhi seems to be denying? It has a long history in the Western tradition of moral philosophy. Our moral judgments or

values are the basis of our moral choices and actions. Unlike trivial judgments of taste which are the basis, say, for choosing a flavor of ice cream,
moral judgments have a certain feature which is often called "universalizability." To choose an action on moral grounds under certain circumstances is to generate a principle which we think applies as an "ought" or
an imperative to *all* others faced with relevantly similar circumstances.

Strictly speaking, though the two are closely related, universalizability is not to be confused with universality. Universality is the idea that a
moral value, whether or not someone in particular holds it, applies to all
persons. Universalizability suggests merely that if someone in particular
holds a moral value, then *he* must think that it applies to all others (in
relevantly similar situations). Yet despite the fact that it is weaker than
universality in this sense, it still generates the *critical* power which Gandhi finds disquieting. If moral judgments are universalizable, one cannot
make a judgment that something is morally worthy and then shrug off the
fact that others similarly situated might not think so. They (unlike those
who might differ with one on the flavor of ice cream) must be deemed
wrong not to think so.

Gandhi repudiates this entire tradition. His integrating thought is that
violence owes to something as seemingly remote from it as this assumed
theoretical connection between values and criticism. Take the wrong
view of moral value and judgment, and you will inevitably encourage
violence in society. There is no other way to understand his insistence
that the satyagrahi has not eschewed violence until he has removed criticism from his lips and heart and mind.

But there is an interpretative challenge hidden here. If the idea of a
moral value or judgment has no implication that one find those who disagree with one's moral judgments to be wrong, then that suggests that
one's moral choices and moral values are indeed rather like one's choice
of a flavor of ice cream, rather like one's more trivial judgments of taste.
In other words, the worry is that these Gandhian ideas suggest that one
need not find one's moral choices and the values they reflect relevant
to others at all, that one's moral thinking is closed off from others. But
Gandhi was avowedly a humanist, and repeatedly said things reminiscent of humanist slogans along the order of "Nothing human is alien to
me." Far from encouraging self-enclosed moral subjects, he thought it

the essence of a moral attitude that it take in all within its concern and its relevance. Thus despite the emphasis on individual conscience over universalized principle, the last thing Gandhi wanted to do was to sequester the relevance of one's religious and moral convictions to oneself. In a most interesting, if sometimes harsh, profile of Thoreau, Robert Louis Stevenson says of him, after describing the great virtue of the man, that "Thoreau was a skulker. He did not wish virtue to go out of him among his fellow men, but slunk into a corner to hoard it for himself. He left all for the sake of certain virtuous self-indulgences."[5] Well, for Gandhi, in spite of his admiration for Thoreau, virtue should be the exact opposite of a *self*-indulgence. The virtuous person should be the exact opposite of a "hoarder" of virtue, a "skulker." How, then, to reconcile the rejection of universalizability and of a value's potential for being wielded in criticism of others with this yearning on Gandhi's part for the significance of one's choices to others? That is among the hardest questions in understanding the philosophy behind his politics, and there are some very original and striking remarks in his writing which hint at a reconciliation.

So far, I have presented the challenge of providing such a reconciliation as a philosophically motivated task. But it is more than that. It is part of the "integrity" that I am pursuing in my interpretation of Gandhi that it also had a practical urgency in the political and cultural circumstances in which he found himself. We know very well that it was close to this man's heart to improve India in two ways which, on the face of it, were pointing in somewhat opposite directions. On the one hand there was the violence of religious intolerance, found most vividly in the relations between Hindus and Muslims. This especially wounded him. Religious intolerance is the attitude that the other must not remain other; he must become like one in belief and in way of life. It is an *inclusionary*, homogenizing attitude, usually pursued with physical and psychological violence toward the other. On the other hand, for all his traditionalism about caste, there was something offensive to Gandhi within Hinduism itself. The social psychology of the Hindu caste system consists of an *exclusionary* attitude. For each caste, there was a lower caste which constituted the other and which was to be *excluded* from one's way of life, again by the most brutal physical and psychological violence. When I think sometimes about caste in India—without a doubt the most resilient form of exclusionary social inegalitarianism in the history of the world—it's hard to avoid the conclusion that even the most alarming aspects of religious intolerance are preferable to it. To say "You *must* be my brother," however wrong, is better than saying "You will *never* be my brother." In religious intolerance there is at least a small core which is highly attractive. The intolerant person cares enough about the truth, as he sees it, to want to share it with others. Of course, that he should want to use force and violence in order to make the other share in it spoils what is attractive about this core. It was Gandhi's humanistic mission to retain the core for it showed that one's conception of the truth was not self-enclosed, that it spoke with a relevance to all others, even others who differed from one.[6] How to prevent this relevance to others from degenerating into criticism of others who differed from one and eventually violence toward them is just the reconciliation we are seeking.

In the philosophical tradition Gandhi is opposing, others are potential objects of criticism in the sense that one's particular choices, one's acts of moral conscience, generate moral principles or imperatives which others can potentially disobey. For him, conscience and its deliverances, though relevant to others, are not the wellspring of principles. Morals is only about conscience, not at all about principles.

There is an amusing story about two Oxford philosophers which makes this distinction vivid. In a seminar, the formidable J. L Austin, having become exasperated with Richard Hare's huffing on about how moral choices reveal principles, decided to set him up with a question. "Hare," he asked, "if a student came to you after an examination and offered you five pounds in return for the mark alpha, what would you say?" Predictably, Hare replied, "I would tell him that I do not take bribes, on principle!" Austin's acid response was "Really? I think I would myself say, 'No thanks.'" Austin was being merely deflationary in denying that an act of conscience had to have a principle underlying it. Gandhi erects the denial into a radical alternative to a (Western) tradition of moral thinking. An honored slogan of that tradition says, "When one chooses for oneself, one chooses for everyone." The first half of the slogan describes a particular person's act of conscience. The second half of the slogan transforms the act of conscience to a universalized principle, an imperative which others must follow or be criticized. Gandhi

embraces the slogan too, but he understands the second half of it differently. He too wants one's acts of conscience to have a universal relevance,
so he too thinks one chooses for everyone, but he does not see that as
meaning that one generates a principle or imperative for everyone. What
other interpretation can be given to the words "One chooses for everyone" in the slogan, except the principled one?

In Gandhi's writing there is an implicit but bold proposal: "When one
chooses for oneself, *one sets an example to everyone.*" That is the role of
the satyagrahi. To lead exemplary lives, to set examples to everyone by
their actions. As he once wrote: "Faith does not admit of telling. It has
to be lived and then it becomes self-propagating."[7] Even more explicitly,
in a letter to Ramachandra Kahre, he says that "the correct reasoning,
however, is this. If we do our duty, others also will do theirs some day.
We have a saying to the effect: If we ourselves are good, the *whole world*
will be good."[8] This is not just a casual remark in a letter. It is an idea
that surfaces in many places in his thought and is the basis of an entirely
different way of thinking about religion and the moral life. The good,
conceived in this way as exemplarity, breaks out of the subjectivity of
one's own conscience. Goodness begins in that subjective experience of
conscience, but by exemplary action it asserts its humanistic relevance of
what begins there, no longer now something subjectively limited (as matters of trivial taste are), but reaching out to "the whole world," making
possible a humanistic universalism—the very opposite of what Stevenson describes as "hoarding" ones virtues, "skulking" in one's own moral
"self-indulgence."

And the concept of the exemplar is intended to provide a wholesale
alternative to the concept of principle in moral philosophy. It retains
what is right in Mill (the importance of being modest in one's moral
opinions) while rejecting what is unsatisfactory (any compromise in our
conviction in them). There is no Millian diffidence in one's beliefs conveyed by the idea that one is only setting an example by one's choices, as
opposed to laying down principles. One is fully confident in the choices
one wants to set up as exemplars, and in the moral values they exemplify.
On the other hand, because no principle is generated, the conviction and
confidence in one's opinions does not arrogate; it puts us in no position
to be critical of others because there is no *generality* in their truth, of

which others may fall *afoul*. Others may not follow. Our example may not set. But that is not the same as disobeying an imperative, violating a principle. As a result, the entire moral psychology of our response to others who depart from us is necessarily much weaker. At most we may be disappointed in others that they will not follow our example, and at least part of the disappointment is in ourselves that our example has not taken hold. And the crucial point is that disappointment is measurably weaker than criticism, it is not the paler shade of contempt, hostility, and eventual violence.

This is a subtle distinction, perhaps too subtle to do all the work we want from morals. But that there is a real distinction here is undeniable as is its theoretical power to claim an alternative way of thinking about morals. It is a commonplace in our understanding of the Western moral tradition to think of Kant's moral philosophy as the full and *philosophical* flowering of a core of Christian thought. But Gandhi fractures that historical understanding. By stressing the deep incompatibility between categorical imperatives and universalizable maxims, on the one hand, and Christian humility on the other, he makes two moral doctrines and methods out of what the tradition represents as a single historically consolidated one. And discarding one of them as lending itself ultimately to violence, he fashions a remarkable political philosophy and national movement out of the other.

I want to stress how original Gandhi is here as a philosopher and theoretician. The point is not that the idea of the "exemplary" is missing in the intellectual history of morals before Gandhi. What is missing, and what he first brings to our attention, is how much theoretical possibility there is in that idea. It can be wielded to make the *psychology* surrounding our morals a more tolerant one. If exemplars replace principles, then it cannot any longer be the business of morals to put us in the position of moral*izing* against others in forms of behavior (criticism) that have in them the potential to generate other psychological attitudes (resentment, hostility) which underlie interpersonal violence. Opposition to moralizing is not what is original in Gandhi either. There are many in the tradition Gandhi is opposing who recoiled from it; but if my interpretation is right, his distinction between principle and exemplar, and the use he puts it to, provides a theoretical basis for that recoil, which otherwise would simply be the expression of a distaste. That distaste is a distaste for something that is itself entailed by a moral theory deeply entrenched in a tradition, and Gandhi is confronting that *theory* with a wholesale alternative.

This conception of moral judgment puzzles me, even while I find it of great interest. It has puzzled me for a long time. Before I became a teen-ager (when I began to find it insufferably uncool) I would sometimes go on long walks with my father in the early mornings. One day, walking on a path alongside a beach we came across a wallet with some rupees sticking visibly out of it. With a certain amount of drama, my father stopped and said, "Akeel, why should we not take that?" Flustered at first, I then said something like "Gee" (actually I am sure I didn't say "gee"), "I think we should take it." My father looked most irritated and asked, "Why?" And I am pretty sure I remember saying words more or less amounting to the classic response: "Because if we don't take it then I suppose someone else will." My father, looking as if he were going to mount to great heights of denunciation, suddenly changed his expression, and he said magnificently, but without logic (or so it seemed to me then), "If *we* don't take it, *nobody* else will." As a boy of twelve, I thought this was a non sequitur designed to end the conversation. In fact I had no idea what he meant and was too nervous to ask him to explain himself. Only much later, in fact only while thinking about how to fit together the various elements in Gandhi's thought, did I see in his remark the claims for a moral ideal of exemplary action. But notice how puzzling the idea is. Here is a wallet, abandoned, and we should not take it. This would set an example to others, though no one is around to witness it. The romance in this morality is radiant. Somehow goodness, good acts, enter the world and affect everyone else. To ask how exactly they do that is to be vulgar, to spoil the romance. Goodness is a sort of mysterious contagion.

The idea is as attractive as it is romantic. The question is, how attractive? I will leave the question hanging since all I want to do in this short essay is to present Gandhi's highly "integrating" suggestion that there is no true non-violence until criticism is removed from the scope of morals. This is to see the ideal of non-violence as being part of a moral position in which moral principles, by the lights of which we criticize, are eschewed. Exemplary action takes the place of principles. If someone fails to follow your example, you may be disappointed but you would no longer have the conceptual basis to see them as transgressive and wrong and subject to criticism. So the integration Gandhi wishes to achieve (the integration of non-violence with total non-criticism) is as plausible as is the moral position stressing exemplars. The plausibility of the moral position depends a great deal on the degree to which the moral action and judgment is made visible. How else would an example be set except through public visibility? Gandhi was of course fully aware of this as a political thinker and leader, which is why it is even possible to integrate the detail of his political ideas with the moral philosophy I have been sketching. He was fully aware that the smaller the community of individuals, the more likelihood there is of setting examples. In the context of family life, for example, one might see how parents by their actions may think or hope that they are setting examples to their children, rather than bearing down on them with articulated moral principles. Gandhi's ideal of peasant communities organized in small *panchayat* or village units could perhaps at least approximate the family, where examples could be visibly set. That is, in part, why Gandhi strenuously argued that flows of populations to metropoles where there was far less scope for public perception of individual action was destructive of the moral life. Indeed, once such metropolitan tendencies had been unleashed, it is easy to understand his habit of going on publicized fasts. It was a way of making visible some moral stance that could reach a larger public in the form of example rather than principles.

5.

I have been arguing that the standard view, which presents Gandhi as essentially applying Mill's argument for tolerance to an argument for non-violence, is very wide of the mark. They exhibit diverging attitudes toward the concept of truth and the epistemology it entails. Gandhi, like Mill, wants our own opinions to be held with modesty, but, unlike him, with an accompanying epistemology that does not discourage conviction or confidence. To that end, Gandhi rejects the notion of truth that Mill seems to presuppose in his argument for tolerance. He replaces the entire argument, as I have been indicating, with another that seems to

have less to do with the notion of truth per se than with the nature of
moral judgment.

But now a question arises. How can this argument have less to do with
truth and one's search for it, when the term "satyagraha" with which
"ahimsa" is constantly linked in his thinking, has truth as its target?

It is in answer to this question that his final and most audacious step of
theoretical integration takes place. For him, truth is a moral notion, and it
is *exclusively* a moral notion. So there is no possibility of having misrep-
resented his argument in the way that I am worrying. The worry I have
just expressed is that once Gandhi repudiates Mill's basis for tolerance
and non-violence (that we may never be confident that we have arrived at
the truth in our search for it) and once he replaces it with his own basis
(the separability of moral value and judgment from moral principle and
moral criticism), truth then drops out of the Gandhian picture in a way
that seems un-Gandhian. It in fact does not drop out since truth in the
first place is not, for Gandhi, a notion independent of what his argument
rests on, the nature of our own experience of moral value.

What this means is that truth for Gandhi is not a *cognitive* notion at all.
It is an experiential notion. It is not propositions purporting to describe
the world of which truth is predicated; it is only our own moral experience which is capable of being true. This was of the utmost importance
for him. It is what in the end underlies his opposition to the Enlightenment, despite the undeniably Enlightenment elements in his thought,
including his humanism and the concern that our moral judgments be
relevant to *all* people. Those who have seen him as an anti-Enlightenment thinker usually point to the fact that he was opposed to the political
and technological developments which, he insists, issue inevitably from
the very conception of Reason as it is understood in scientific terms. So
understood, sometime in the seventeenth century, with the rise of the scientific method in Europe, all the *pre*dispositions to modern government
and technology came into place. All that was needed for those predis-
positions to be triggered in our sustained efforts to organize and control our physical and social environment was for the Enlightenment to
articulate the idea of Reason as it affects social life and the polity. But this
familiar understanding of his view of the Enlightenment does not take in
what I have called his "final and audacious integrating" philosophical

move. This conception which set in sometime in the seventeenth century *itself* owes much to a more abstract element in our thinking, which is that truth is a cognitive notion, not a moral one. Only if truth is so conceived can science become the paradigmatic pursuit of our culture; without it the scientific outlook lacks its deepest theoretical source. And it is a mark of his intellectual ambition that by making it an exclusively and exhaustively moral and experiential notion instead, Gandhi was attempting to repudiate the paradigm at the deepest possible conceptual level.

What I mean by truth as a cognitive notion is that it is a property of sentences or propositions that describe the world. Thus when we have reason to think that the sentences to which we give assent exhibit this property, then we have knowledge of the world, a knowledge that can then be progressively accumulated and put to use through continuing inquiry building on past knowledge. His recoil from such a notion of truth, which intellectualizes our relations to the world, is that it views the world as the object of study, study that makes it alien to our moral experience of it, to our most everyday practical relations to it. He symbolically conveyed this by his own daily act of spinning cotton. This idea of truth, unlike our quotidian practical relations to nature, makes nature out to be the sort of distant thing to be studied by scientific methods. Reality will then not be the reality of moral experience. It will become something alien to that experience, wholly external and objectified. It is no surprise then that we will look upon reality as something to be mastered and conquered, an attitude that leads directly to the technological frame of mind that governs modern societies, and which in turn takes us *away* from our communal localities where moral experience and our practical relations to the world flourish. It takes us *toward* increasingly abstract places and structures such as nations and eventually global economies. In such places and such forms of life, there is no scope for exemplary action to take hold and no basis possible for a moral vision in which value is not linked to "imperative" and "principle," and then, inevitably, to the attitudes of criticism and the entire moral psychology which ultimately underlies violence in our social relations. To find a basis for tolerance and non-violence under circumstances such as these, we are compelled to turn to arguments of the sort Mill tried to provide in which modesty and tolerance are supposed to derive from a notion of truth (cognitively understood) which is always elusive, never something which we can be confident of having achieved because it is not given in our moral experience, but is predicated of propositions that purport to describe a reality which is distant from our own practical and moral experience of it.

All these various elements of his opposition to Mill and his own alternative conception of tolerance and non-violence were laid open by Gandhi and systematically integrated by these arguments implicit in his many scattered writings. The only other philosopher who came close to such a sustained integration of political, moral, and epistemological themes was Heidegger, whatever the fundamental differences between them, not least of which is that Gandhi presents his ideas in clear, civil, and bracing prose.

There remains the question whether such an integrated position is at all plausible. It should be a matter of some intellectual urgency to ask whether our interests in politics, moral philosophy, and notions of truth and epistemology are not more fragmented or more miscellaneous than his integrations propose. Is it not a wiser and more illuminating methodological stance sometimes to recognize that there is often a *lack* of connection in our ideas and our interests and that to register that lack is sometimes more important and revealing than to seek a strained connection?

I will resist answering these questions, except to say that Gandhi's idea—the idea that it is a matter of great moment, both for epistemology and for society and politics and morals, that truth is not a cognitive notion—is impeached by the worst aspects of our intellectual culture.

If Gandhi is right and if truth is an exclusively moral notion, then when we *seek* truth, we are pursuing *only a moral value*. This leaves a great deal out of our normative interest in truth, which, as we have seen, Gandhi is perfectly willing to do. He is quite happy to discard as illusory our tendency to think that apart from the moral virtues involving truth (such as that of *telling* the truth, and living by and exemplifying our moral values) there is also in some sense *a value or virtue* in getting things right about the world and discovering the general principles that explain its varied phenomena. This latter is not a moral virtue; it is a cognitive virtue, and for Gandhi, cognitive virtues are a chimera. For him truth's relationship to virtue cannot consist at all in the supposed virtue of acquiring truths of this kind; it is instead entirely to be understood in how truth surfaces in our practical and moral relations. That is why truth itself will have no value for us *other* than the value of such things as truth-*telling*, which *does* involve our practical and moral relations. To tell the truth is among other things (such as, say, generosity or kindness or considerateness) a way of being moral, and it was an aspect of morals that Gandhi himself was keen to stress. But the point is that truth being *only* a moral notion, there is no *other* value to truth than the value of such things as *telling* the truth, no more *abstract* value that it has.

There is a palpable mistake in collapsing the cognitive value of truth into the moral value of truth-telling, a mistake evident in the fact that somebody who *fails* to *tell* the truth can, in doing so, still value *truth*. That is to say, the liar often values truth and often values it greatly, and precisely because he does so, he wants to conceal it or invent it. The liar indeed has a *moral* failing in that he disvalues truth-telling, but he still values truth, and what he values in doing so therefore cannot be a moral value. It cannot be what Gandhi (and more recently Richard Rorty)[9] insists is the only value that attaches to truth. To put it very schematically and crudely, truth has to be a more abstract value than a moral value because both the (moral) truth-teller *and* the (immoral) liar share it.

So what is this more abstract value of truth, which even the liar shares? If there is this abstract value to truth, and if *even* the liar values it, someone must surely in principle be able to *fail* to value it, else how can it be a value? How can there be a value if no one can fail to value it?

This is indeed a good question and only by answering it can we come close to grasping the value of truth that is not a moral value. The answer is: Yes, someone does indeed fail to value truth in this more abstract sense. But it is not the liar. It is the equally common sort of person in our midst, one whom Harry Frankfurt has called "the bullshitter."[10] This is the person who merely sounds off on public occasions or who gets published in some academic journals simply because he is prepared to speak or write in the requisite jargon, *without any goal of getting things right* nor even (like the liar) concealing the right things which he thinks he knows.

The so-called Sokal hoax,[11] on which so much has been written, allows this lesson to be sharply drawn. I don't want to get into a long discussion about this incident both because it is remote from Gandhi's interests but also because I think that it has become a mildly distasteful site for people making careers out of its propagandist and polemical potential. Everything that I have read on the subject of this hoax, including Sokal's own contribution, takes up the issue of how Sokal exposed the rampant and uncritical relativism of post-modern literary disciplines. I don't doubt that literary people in the academy have recently shown a relativist tendency, and yet I wonder if that is really what is at stake. The point is analogous to the one I just made about the liar. The relativist also does value truth in the abstract sense I have in mind, even if he has a somewhat different gloss on it from his opponents. In fact it is because he does value truth in this sense that he wishes to urgently put this different gloss on it. I believe it quite likely that the journal in which Sokal propagated his hoax would have been happy (at least before the controversy began) to publish a similarly dissimulating hoax reply to his paper in which all kinds of utterly ridiculous arguments were given, this time for an anti-relativist and objective notion of truth, so long as these arguments were presented in the glamorous jargon and with the familiar dialectical moves that command currency in the discipline. If so, the lesson to be learned from the hoax is not that relativism is rampant in those disciplines but that very often bullshit is quite acceptable, if presented in the requisite way. To set oneself against that is to endorse the value of truth in our culture, truth *over and above* truth-telling, for a bullshitter is not a liar.

Living and working in the context in which I do—contemporary American academic culture—I feel almost as strongly about the value of truth in this sense as I do about moral values surrounding truth, such as telling the truth or indeed many of the other moral values one can think of. That it might have mattered less to Gandhi is of course a matter of context, a matter of the quite different and much more impressive political concerns and interests of the Indian nationalist movement. But the philosophical lesson is a perfectly general one, and the very fact that he himself had gathered the strands of his political concerns and interests and tied them into "integral" relations with these more abstract issues about truth and epistemology make it impossible for us to dismiss the lesson as being irrelevant to him. So I must conclude by saying that I don't think that Gandhi should have denied this cognitive value of truth. He should in fact have allowed that it defines the very possibility of his own philosophical undertakings and that it underlies his own yearning to find for his philosophical ideas the highest levels of what I have called "integrity." These undertakings and yearnings are all signs of a commitment to the very notion of truth which he wishes to repudiate. Whether allowing it will in the end have unraveled that integrity must remain a question for another occasion.

But I will end by saying that what that question will turn on is really the underlying question of this essay: How much integrity can these themes tolerate? It is Gandhi's essentially religious temperament that motivates the extraordinary ambitions of his integrations of these themes. What I mean here is that for all his romanticism about the power of exemplary actions to generate a moral community, Gandhi like many religious people is deeply pessimistic in one sense. He is convinced of the inherent corruptibility of our moral psyches. That is what lies behind his fear that criticism will descend inevitably into violence, and it is also what underlies his fear that the intellectualization of the notion of truth to include a cognitive value will descend inevitably into an elevation of science into the paradigmatic intellectual pursuit of our culture, and thus our alienation from nature with the wish to conquer and control it without forgiveness with the most destructive forms of technologies. The modern secular habits of thinking on these themes simply do not share this pessimism. Neither descent is inevitable, we will say. We can block the rise of bad technologies by good politics. There is no reason to see it as inevitable once we think of truth in cognitive terms, not even inevitable if we value scientific inquiry. So also we can block violence with good, constitutional politics and the rule of law, and there is no reason to think it inevitable just because we think of values as entailing the exercise of our critical capacities toward one another. The modernist faith in *politics* to control or at least to distract us from what might otherwise be seen as our corruptible nature is the real achievement, if that is what it is, of the Enlightenment. It is only this faith that can convince us that the integrations which Gandhi's pessimism force on him are not compulsory.[12]

I have raised the issue at stake at the highest level of generality. It is in the details, however, that it will be decided, and those really must await another occasion.

FIVE

Gandhi (and Marx)

There are many reasons to write on Gandhi and on Marx, not least because they are both being aggressively—and with the most brazenly ideological motives—discarded as irrelevant to our time.[1] But why write about them together, as a conjunction?

One reason to thematically conjoin the philosophies of two thinkers is to seek a synthesis of their ideas. I think it would be foolhardy of me to try to present such a synthesis of Gandhi and Marx. It is not that I doubt that it is a worthy ambition. But I do doubt that I have, indeed I am certain that I don't have, the intellectual abilities to attain it. A more tractable goal is to begin to provide a framework in which one could see some genuine and deep affinities between Gandhi and Marx. That is what I will try to do, speaking for the most part on Gandhi, but with an eye, in the frameworking remarks with which I shall begin and end, to seek overlaps of approach and substance in their thought.

It would be perverse not to admit, at the very outset, that the affinities between them are much the more interesting and worth pursuing only because there is so much substantial divergence in their thought. But that divergence is not only far more obvious than the affinities, it has also been very well mined over many decades, pretty much ever since Gandhi became prominent in Indian public life. Perry Anderson's recent invective against Gandhi merely (and rather misleadingly) recapitulates what had been said for a long time by Indian communists and, unlike the latter, is massively simplistic because it shows little understanding of the conditions of a predominantly peasant society in which and about which Gandhi wrote and thought. So it is largely the convergences with which I will be concerned, taking for granted a background of entirely familiar divergences that bring into relief their great interest.[2]

We are all aware that Gandhi was a great campaigner against imperialism, perhaps the greatest ever. It is perhaps less taken for granted that he was a great anti-imperialist *thinker*. And, as such, anyone who has read his remarks on the Lancashire cotton industry's effects on India cannot fail to notice how critical he was of the central element of capitalism in the imperialism that India suffered under British rule. One can speculate, then, about the failure of nerve, more likely of temperament, that prevented Gandhi from developing these shrewd and insightful remarks into a more elaborate analysis and appreciation of the notion of class and class struggle as is found in Marx. But I will not do so and merely rest with the thought that these and other remarks in his writings about imperialism carry with them an incipient form of such an analysis that never flowered into anything systematic in his thought.

Where else might we turn, then, to seek interesting affinities? I don't think that this can be done by just staring at their writings with a view to seeking common elements. Affinities that go deep are not worn on the sleeves of texts. There is intellectual spadework to be done before they become so much as visible. That is to say, one has to *construct a framework* within which some central elements in their writing can come into view as having a common significance. I will begin and end the argument of this essay by trying to do that, while in the body of the essay I will focus on Gandhi, developing some of the details of his thought within such a common framework.

1.

To begin with, two preliminary interpretative points, one each about Marx and Gandhi.

The writings of Marx that are most obviously relevant to such a construction as I am undertaking are those of the so-called "early" Marx,

in particular *The Economic and Philosophical Manuscripts of 1844.* I say
"so-called" deliberately. There is plenty of evidence that the ideas in this
early work were not restricted to that work or to his early writings; but for
reasons having to do with a compulsion on the part of some influential
interpreters to distinguish between the scientific Marx and the soft or
sentimental or (worst of all) "philosophical" Marx, there was a corresponding effort to have this echoed in a distinction between the early and
the more considered writings of the mature Marx with the clear intention
of presenting the former as disowned and irrelevant to his remarkable
and monumental analysis of capital. Proof (at any rate, as close to something like a proof as is possible in intellectual history) that there was no
real distinction between the early and the late Marx is found first of all
in the well-known fact that Lukacs in *History and Class Consciousness*
came to the ideas of the allegedly early Marx by reading only the allegedly late Marx since the early writings were not available to him; and
second in the now equally well-known fact that the *very* late Marx of the
last decade of his life wrote with an interest and sympathetic gaze on the
Russian peasant communes in a way that measurably qualifies the very
elements of the analysis in *Capital* which, in the first place, were said by
this offending interpretation to be the sign that the 'late' Marx had repudiated the allegedly 'early' Marx. These points of interpretation deserve
further elaboration that I will not try and pursue here and instead simply
register that this periodizing distinction has done an abiding disservice
to Marx's intellectual legacy and when I stress that early work, I do so not
with the intention of feeding any such distinction, but only because it is
where Marx most elaborately and explicitly says what I want to exploit
in the framework I am initially constructing. In fact, let me declare with
only the mildest exaggeration that I take Marx to be primarily a philosopher in the Romantic tradition, an understanding of Marx that should be
entirely compatible and comfortable with the rigors of the analytic and
systematic (misleadingly called "scientific") nature of his thought.

Gandhi's most important writings (*Hind Swaraj,* primarily) must be
seen in the very specific historical and political context in which they
were written. We know that *Hind Swaraj* was written in 1909 and we
know that it expressed urgent anxieties about the harms to be found
in modern Western civilization. These anxieties need to be properly

contextualized before they are understood. My own contextualization of them is roughly this. Gandhi was convinced that India in 1909 stood at the crossroads that Europe found itself in the early modern period. The harsh words that Gandhi reserves for Western modernity were expressive of the fear that India would go down the lamentable path of some of the worst aspects of *politics and political economy* that have characterized the passage in Europe from early to late modernity. And the entire book tries to provide a genealogical and diagnostic account of the *cognitive and cultural sources and effects* of those aspects of politics and political economy of Europe's past and present that have never had any place in Indian society, however defective Indian society may otherwise be,[3] and which would do no favors to India were India to embrace them, an embrace that seemed to him very much in the offing, given the fact that India was not merely being subjected to imperial subjugation but to a determined effort to enslave it in cognitive and cultural terms. To preempt such an embrace was thus a matter of desperate urgency for him, especially since he feared that the Indian elites were beginning to exhibit a thralldom to European, particularly British, ways of projecting India's political and economic and cultural future. The insistently strident critical tone throughout the work is a reflection of this desperation. I will return a little later to tie a little more closely these two initial and seemingly separate set of interpretative remarks about Marx and Gandhi.

With these two preliminary points in place, let me step back a bit to present a rudimentary puzzle. Here is a remarkable, on the face of it almost bizarre, fact about the intellectual history of the European Enlightenment. It is familiar to every schoolchild that the great revolutionary political events in that period of the history of Europe, particularly in France, were mobilized side by side with the intellectual articulation of some sloganized ideals, the most prominent of which were—and continue to be—"liberty" and "equality." But—and this is the bizarre turn—just as soon as these two ideals were articulated, they were elaborated in theoretical and methodological developments that put them in a seemingly irresoluble tension with one another. This peculiar outcome is evident everywhere in the philosophical and political arguments and rhetoric ever since the Enlightenment. The rhetoric (if not the actual politics) of Cold War disputation was only a very late and very crude manifestation of the tension that has existed between these two ideals for well over two and half centuries of theorizing in the Western tradition of thought.

As a result, it is quite impossible to understand these two notions of liberty and equality any more without thinking of them in a zero-sum relation with one another, the very idea of an increase in the one being seen as only possible if one were to admit a proportionate decrease in the other.

Why should a tradition of political thought theoretically frame its two chief ideals in such a way that they are chronically (and acutely) pitted against each other? That is a question which cannot possibly get an answer that leaves out the much larger context of the sort of political economy that had developed in Europe and the effect it had on political theorizing in and since the Enlightenment. I cannot pursue that context and its effect in a brief essay, whose main theme lies elsewhere. I cannot, in fact, do much more than mention one or two features of the political theorizing that produce this tension between its two ideals and convey how—given the deep roots that these features have taken in our sensibility and our practice—we have come to see it as virtually impossible to question these features without seeming to be pursuing quite unintuitive or outdated lines of thought.

One feature is too well known and well mined to bear much more than the most minimal mention, and that is the linking of the notion of *property* to a notion of the personal liberty which its ownership bestows on one, a liberty that is carried in a "right" and therefore enshrined in the law of the land. How the possession of private property, when seen in these terms, undermines equality in the economic sphere (and therefore in other spheres) has been the subject of extensive commentary, and Marx was, of course, only its most famous and most powerful critic.

Less explicitly theorized is another feature, which I will call the *"incentivization of talent."* It is the most natural thing in the world to think that someone's talent should be acknowledged as *hers* and that it is *she* who should be praised and rewarded for it. We think it a failure to respect someone's individuality to fail to do so. Take any example of a poem or a scientific discovery or a fine test century. We praise individuals for such things and other such products of individual talent and expect them to be rewarded, whether it is a poet or a scientist or a batsman. We don't simply praise the *zeitgeist* for such productions; we praise the particular individuals and we think the rewards they get for it are deserved. Notions such as "dessert" thus also get linked to one, among other, rights possessed by individuals. This goes so deep in our thinking that it is likely to be considered an hysterical egalitarian ideologue's artifice to deny it. Denying it seems to fly in the face of our intuitive understanding of what it is to be an *individual* (rather than just a symptom of the zeitgeist in embodied human form), it violates what we conceive to be the *liberty* of an individual to reap the praise and rewards of the exercise and efforts of his talents, not to mention the liberty of *others to enjoy* the productions of these efforts at their most excellent because they are *incentivized* to be as excellent as they can be. But, like the liberty attaching to possession of property, this way of thinking of liberty as attaching to talent also promotes social and economic inequality. Just think of the entire range of practices from commercial endorsements associated with talented sportsmen to so-called "merit" raises in various professions, monetary prizes for every form of production including intellectual and literary production, to say nothing of bonuses to bankers and investors—you will, in particular, recall that after the financial crisis there was an outcry against the limits suggested on bonuses of investment bankers on the grounds that this would cause all the *talent* to leave the financial industry (fetching the obvious response that if it was the talent that got us into this mess, then let's have some mediocrity).

Historically this second feature was a later development than the liberty that attaches to property. It grew out of a commitment to a liberty to reap the fruits of something that was not quite property—one's labor (though there have been theoretical attempts to equate labor with property by viewing it as something we *own*). Initially talent was considered distinct from labor because a commitment to *natural* equality distinguished between labor (the capacity for which all human beings equally possess) and talent (which is unequally distributed in human beings). But with the entrenchment of a conception of liberty as a form of *individual* self-governance, one's liberty to reap the fruits of one's talent became quite as prominent and taken for granted as the other liberties. This second feature of liberty attaching to the idea of talent is less structurally central to our culture than the liberty that is tied to property, but

it perhaps goes even deeper psychologically and the dichotomy it generates with equality is, therefore, more subtly troubling; and it seems just
as impossible to overcome.[4]

There are several other features of the political philosophy we have
inherited that one could summon to present the tension between liberty
and equality, and I have mentioned only these two just to give a completely familiar sense of how far such thinking has gone into our sensibility, how entrenched it is in the very way we deploy these terms, and how,
therefore, it would seem almost to change the semantics of the terms if
we were to think that the tension could be removed or resolved. That
is to say, if we managed to see them as not being in tension, it would
only be because, as Thomas Kuhn might have put it, we have changed
the *meanings* of the terms "liberty" and "equality," not because we have
produced an improved theory or politics *within* the framework of the
Enlightenment. Within that framework things are, on this score, unim-
provable. In other words, what I mean by framework here is perhaps one
of the (diverse) things that Kuhn meant by his term "paradigm" and, if
so, clearly we need to shift to another framework if we are ever going to
remove the tension between these two notions. In such a new framework,
neither "liberty" nor "equality" would *mean* what they mean in the
framework of Enlightenment thought, no more than "mass" in Einstein's
physics meant what it meant in Newtonian mechanics, if Kuhn is right.

How might such a shift in framework be sought? To do so directly,
by brutely redefining the terms or announcing a new term (Balibar's
neologism "equaliberty," for instance) would be an act of sheer semantic
stipulation. And it would be an act in vain. This sort of willful dictation
of nomenclature seldom works, except perhaps in purely classificatory
exercises, which don't pretend to theory. To say: "From now on, I will
use the word" . . ."as follows" with a view to presenting an alternative
theory is to place the cart ahead of the horse. *Discourse* about human
concerns should be posterior to, a natural outgrowth of, a prior *conceptual* understanding; it can't by itself declare new forms of understanding
into existence. What makes language so central to our human concerns
is not that it can in itself dictate how we think but that it is the repository of how we think and how we have thought. So new frameworks for
thought built on existing concepts must be constructed first and this may

then have the effect of revising the meanings of terms by situating them in a new conceptual framework.

In keeping with this obvious suggestion, here is what I propose.

There is no improving our understanding of these notions of liberty and equality—as they stand—so as to resolve the tension between them. So let's, as a start, usher them off center stage entirely. If this is to disinherit the entire tradition of liberal thought of the Enlightenment, so be it. Once these are exeunt, we need to replace them on center stage with a third, more primitive, concept—that is to say, a concept more fundamental to our social and political life than even liberty and equality. And this is to be done with the idea that "liberty" and "equality" may *subsequently* be introduced once again—by the back door, as it were—but now merely as necessary conditions for the achievement of this more basic ideal that occupies the central position. So reintroduced, there is reason to think that these terms may have undergone substantial revision in their meanings, and thus may not any longer express concepts that are at odds with one another.

We need, then, to fasten on an appropriately more fundamental concept. To be more fundamental than concepts such as liberty and equality which have been so central to our theoretical understanding of politics, it would have to track something not necessarily older and more traditional in our political understanding so much as something that speaks more immediately to our experience and our ordinary lives. And it is here, I believe, that we can find—if we keep firmly in mind the two preliminary interpretative points I began with—that Gandhi and Marx both instinctively appealed to the same idea in their critical thought: the concept of an "*unalienated* life." Of course, by this I don't mean that they explicitly set up my dialectic of first noticing a tension in two existing ideals and then adopting the methodological strategy of addressing this tension by removing them from centrality and replacing them with the ideal of an unalienated life, which they can then be seen as necessary conditions for. I readily admit that this dialectic is my own constructed framework and not found in these terms in their writings. But my thought is that once it is constructed, we are given a way to interpret as essentially linked two, on the face of it, quite different things of which *both* thinkers were famously critical: Enlightenment liberalism and mass society of the modern period. To repeat, the link is that the former critique displays a tension within the two chief ideals of the liberal Enlightenment, which the latter critique helps to resolve by presenting the overcoming of alienation in the mass societies of modernity as the fundamental goal of politics, the achievement of which is only possible if the two ideals are also jointly attained; and since the two ideals are now merely necessary conditions for achieving an even more fundamental goal, they will be conceptually reconfigured without the crippling tension that afflicted them in the initial framework of the political philosophy of the Enlightenment. The so-called early Marx who lamented the alienation that afflicted modern capitalist civilization and the Gandhi who thought that India should not embrace the alienated culture of the modern West were thus intellectual partners in a common theoretical cause.

It is true that they had very different analyses of the sources of alienation, but the difference was really only over the level of specificity at which they analyzed its sources. Gandhi looked for very much more general—the largest visible—sources of alienation. Marx, by contrast, bearing down in particular on capitalism as an economic formation, located far more specific sources. That is to be expected, given the fact that Gandhi, unlike Marx, did not have a very detailed acquaintance with the structures and mechanisms of a relatively advanced capitalist society and the conditions of labor in it. Even so, there is a level of description one could give of the sources of alienation that they each respectively identified that would present them as diagnosing the same thing: the transformation of the human subject to an object or, to put it more elaborately, an increasing *detachment* of the wrong kind in one's relation to the world, including one's relations to others and, therefore, an increasing loss of genuine subjectivity and subjective engagement with the world and with others. To resist capitalism (in the case of Marx), to avoid for India the path of European modernity's civilizational tendencies in which capitalism was an acknowledged central element (in the case of Gandhi) were each essential to restoring us as subjects from the atomized anonymity we had come to feel in the form of modern mass society that must be overcome (in the case of Marx) or avoided (in the case of Gandhi's India standing at the crossroads that Europe had stood some centuries earlier).

2.

With these very large and basic affinities registered, I want now to focus on Gandhi in particular and briefly present his account of the sources of alienation, as it surfaces in *Hind Swaraj* and a scatter of other writings dispersed through many genres (letters, speeches, dispatches to *Young India* and other magazines, etc.).

Science, in particular modern science, is the target of much criticism in Gandhi's writings, beginning with *Hind Swaraj*. But to say that is to say something highly misleading, and what is misleading is often the result of some of Gandhi's own rhetoric which is often simplistically formulated and fails to capture his own much more intricate and fascinating critical stances. What Gandhi opposes is not science itself. There is no indication that he thought that the laws of modern science were false or that its methods, in the domain of study and explanation in which they are aptly exercised, are faulty. Rather his opposition is to a certain *dominant status* that modern science has tended to acquire in the cultures in which it flourishes under the watch of power- and profit-oriented wealth, and the *outlook* that this generates in those cultures. It is this outlook that gives rise to the forms of detachment mentioned earlier that are the sources of the alienation that comes from undermining our subjectivity and moral engagement with which we would otherwise inhabit the world.[5] When it begins to dominate a culture, science's methods are applied in domains where they are inappropriate and this is the basis for the creation of a mentality and eventually institutions that, in turn, generate the forms of detachment that threaten the subject-bearing and agentive elements of human life that are the basis for an unalienated life.

A conspicuous aspect of Gandhi so often placing the fault-line of Western civilization at the doorstep of *modern* science—he would have had no objection to Aristotelian science, for instance—is that he was basically giving or implying a *genealogical* account of the conceptual and material changes due to which the West has landed where it has and where he feels, with desperate urgency, as I said, India should not be headed. (By his genealogical method I mean two things at once: One, it is history mixed with conceptual history or the role of concepts in history;

and then, it is also openly practicing in this conceptual history, a herme-
neutics of suspicion, trying to reveal how the *standard* story, the self-
presentation of that history, is not innocent.)

It was in the *early modern* period in Europe that science began to
acquire its kind of dominant status in society—and India, which stood at
that very same juncture a few hundred years later when Gandhi was writing, had to make the choice as to whether or not to allow this to happen
in its own midst. And my own way of making sense of Gandhi's varied
writings on the subject has been to formulate his account by posing the
following genealogical question on his behalf, a question initially at a
very high level of generality: *How and when did we begin to think of the
world as not merely a place to live in but a place to master and control?*
The purpose behind posing such a question should be evident. It gives
a very omnibus and premonitional sense of the passage from engagement and subjective agency ("live in") to detachment and objectification
(something to "master and control") in our relations with the world, and
asks genealogically how and when it first occurred. But it is so general in
its formulation that it is hard to know how one may even begin to address
it, leave alone answer it.

At this level of generality, perhaps all one can do is to see a little better
what sort of issue is being raised in raising the question.

Thus consider a development in high philosophy from within which
the genealogical dimension of the question's point comes more into focus.
For some twenty hundred years, philosophers in the Western tradition of
philosophy have recurringly raised in epistemology skeptical questions
about our knowledge of the external world. But as historians of philosophy have often noted, sometime in the seventeenth century, primarily in
the hands of Descartes, a new conclusion was drawn: If one can doubt
our knowledge of the external world, quite possibly the external world
does not exist. No skeptic in the tradition ever drew this conclusion before
Descartes. The Ancients who formulated skeptical doctrines never concluded that the world may not exist from their assertion that there was
no knowledge of it. Why not? Because they did not assume that the only
way to relate to the world was via knowledge. They took it for granted
that if one were to doubt the possibilities of knowledge that would do
nothing wholesale to undermine the more ordinary relation we bear to

it, of merely *living in it.* It was Descartes' innovation, one that expressed a transformation in his time whose legacy is that of an increasing detachment of outlook toward the world we live in, elevating the idea of living in it *itself* into some highly cognitively mediated relation that *underlies* the mastery and control we are trying to genealogically diagnose.[6] As I said, this gives only a preliminary sense of what is being genealogically diagnosed but much more breakdown of the question is needed if we are to go beyond this generality to some more detailed answers and analysis.

It needs breakdown into more specific questions, and much of my writing on Gandhi has taken the form of formulating these more specific questions and answering them, with the intention of bringing together different aspects of his critique of the modern sources of alienation. Four questions in particular echo at a more specific level the purpose with which the initial question has been posed. 1) How and when did we transform the concept of *nature* into the concept of *natural resources?* 2) How and when did we transform the concept of *human beings* into the concept of *citizens?* 3) How and when did we transform the concept of *people* into the concept of *populations?* and 4) How and when did we transform the concept of *knowledges to live by* into the concept of *expertise to rule by?*

And the reason why each of these questions—echoing at a more specific and tractable register the highly general and omnibus question—hints at an underlying source of alienation is that each of them tries to genealogically uncover an increasing detachment or disengagement in the way one approaches its chief subject, whether it be nature or humanity or knowledge. In this respect, Gandhi's understanding of politics and its relations to metaphysics ideas was close to Heidegger's—and presented in far livelier and more appealing prose.

Let me say a little bit about each of these questions, though not in any linear presentation since they are deeply integrated with one another in Gandhi's thought.

The pervasive Bhakti influences on Gandhi made him think of nature in essentially sacralized and spiritual terms. To think of nature as shot through with divinity was an intrinsic obstacle to transforming it conceptually to the idea of natural resources. And—to make the historical and genealogical connection—this sacralized understanding was precisely how much of *popular* Christianity (sometimes this strand was described as a modified element of neo-Platonism in popular Christianity by intellectual historians) conceived of nature in the early modern period in Europe.[7] Thus, for instance, the radical Puritan sect the Diggers, among others in England, resisted the system of enclosures because it was transforming something sacred, something to live in, to make a life in and to respect, into a resource and a site for an early form of agri-*business*. The outlook that the new science of that period was shaping was precisely keen to undermine these sacralized conceptions so as to remove all conceptual obstacles to predatory commercial extraction from nature, and scientists were aligning themselves with commercial interests and with *High* Christianity (in England this was the established Protestant orthodoxy which opposed the "neo-Platonism" of the popular Christianity of the radical sects as dangerous "enthusiasm") to make this possible. These are the developments that Gandhi thought the outlooks around modern science was bound to bring to India and much of his writing is reminiscent of the *scientific dissenters* of the *late* seventeenth century and early eighteenth century in Europe who fought against such a desacralization of nature. These dissenters appealed to the neo-Platonism of the earlier radical sects as a form of resistance to the emerging outlook wrought by the new science that was (with the alliances it had formed with commercial interests) transforming the local, egalitarian, collective agrarian life—the transformation of merely *living* in nature to its mastery and control for large-scale profit and gain, whose agricultural surpluses would, as we know, feed into the creation of large metropoles, further destroying the life of agrarian communities.

Much of this was consolidated in political thought by familiar and celebrated ideas of a posited conjectural past in which social contracts were said to have been generators of norms and principles to live by. Thus, for instance, in one familiar strand of this tradition of thought (going from John Locke—there are other strands that are not relevant to what I am presenting), we are told: Suppose that we start in the state of nature. And suppose that there are as yet no policies or laws to live by. Nor is there any sort of institution of property. Then suppose that some of us join and come up with an agreement with which we resolve to keep faith, an agreement about rules for the private appropriation of property out of the common. We agree that if someone comes upon a stretch of ground, fences it, and enters it into a register in an elementary form of office that we set up, then it becomes his or hers. And (this is the punch line) we, then, say to ourselves that this may be *only done if, by doing so, no other is made worse off than they hitherto were—and we elaborate this crucial proviso by saying, in particular, that if one were to hire others at wages which enable them to live better, they would in fact be better off than they were in the state of nature.* The underlying claim of these theoretical posits of a contract (in all versions and strands of it) is to show one thing: how come we are, as a result of the contract, better off than we were in a state of nature. In the strand that I am focusing on in particular, the assessment of political principles by such a conjunction of mutual advantage (a pareto-improvement) both for possessors of land and those who work on it becomes the cornerstone of the economic outlook of liberalism even through a later period of industrialization when industrial capital rather than land was at stake. In its historical context, what the Lockean ideal consolidates and justifies is the system of enclosures, which, though it had begun fitfully a century earlier, had set in deeply and systematically in society only in Locke's time and led to the thoroughly predatory commercial attitudes toward nature and its bounty as well as to a very specific conception of governance and law to support them. Indeed my point in raising this is not merely to stress the 'possessive individualism' that has surfaced in commentary on Locke, but also crucially the accompanying attitudes toward nature that surfaced in tandem with it. The Lockean social contract, as a bit of political theory-construction, both *explains* these developments, while, in a carefully constructed *normative* façade, presents them as moral and political *achievements,* often even described as a form of social "scientific rationality" in what I have elsewhere (see the essay "Occidentalism, the Very Idea" in this volume) called a "thick" sense of that term. The entire doctrinal outcome of such a theorization appealing to a conjectural past is thus presented as having *both* an historical inevitability *and* a rational justification—with an appeal, therefore, on two quite different registers, the descriptive and the normative.

The historical embedding of social contract theory is more fully revealed if we take a look at some of its arguments and assumptions via criticisms implicitly found in the range of dissenters and "enthusiasts" I have mentioned above.

The radical critique of this hypothesised scenario would then go something like this. Such a contractual outcome as is expounded here has what might be called, what economists call, an *"opportunity cost."* What is that? An *avoided* benefit when you make a choice is counted as the opportunity *cost* of your having made that choice. This idea applies straightforwardly to our case. What the radical critique says is: Because the land is thus privatized we cannot set up a system for working the land in common and as a commons. *Thus, even though we agree that we are all better off than we* were **in the state of nature,** *it is still perfectly possible for us to say that we are worse off than we* **would have been** *had the private economy not been established.*

This is a simple and obvious enough counterfactual claim but it has a very significant and less than obvious theoretical result—it philosophically transforms the very notion of consent to something that is not even so much as recognizable from within the contractualist tradition. Consent, once this counterfactual is in place, should be viewed instead as a more complicated act than it might otherwise seem in that tradition. It should be viewed as follows: Whether someone can be said to have consented is not necessarily to be viewed as this contractualist tradition proposes but rather it may be a matter of what he or she **would** *choose in antecedently specified sorts of conditions that do not obtain*—in which case the entire Locke-to-Nozick tradition of thought may be assuming that we have implicitly rationally consented to something which we in fact have not. To put it differently, if there was an implicit consent by those who are hired to work for wages, it was coerced by a condition that they could not avoid, their non-possession of the land. Possession of the land by some and not others is thus a coercive condition and the contractualist tradition presents a *coerced* implicit consent falsely as a *freely chosen* implicit consent.

Such a revisionary understanding of the notion of consent can be understood as offering a counterfactual maneuver in order to *improve* upon the normative ideal that this tradition of contractualism offers, or if you find that a tendentious way of putting things, then, at the very least, to offer an *alternative* normative ideal. But really the point I am insisting on is that this entire line of criticism is, in any case, not just an idle theoretical counterfactual exercise at improving the normative ideal, because *history* gives considerable support to the counterfactual by recording a tremendously active and vocal dissenting tradition in the early modern period against these incipient liberal ideas about the economy and polity. Some of these dissenters—the early ones—were not targeting Locke, since they in fact predated Locke. I include them even so because the counterfactual I have presented should not be thought of as an argument from anachronism. It is counter to fact (as counterfactuals are), but the point is that it is not counter to all facts; it is counter only to facts which came to be because *others very much in the air* did not survive for reasons that need not by any means be described as having the force of rational necessity about them. Their failure to survive, far from being determined by rational force, was a matter of the success of particular worldly alliances that I mentioned which were formed, consciously and unconsciously, at a particular period of time which managed to silence a lively and systematic resistance to them by quite different dissenting ideas, a silencing that owed nothing to rational superiority but rather to the greater force of worldly organization of elite interests on the victorious side. And as a result of these alliances, a certain orthodoxy won out in this conflict and flowered eventually in the standard Enlightenment ideas that we have come to think of as "liberal" doctrine.

The dissenters—such as Winstanley and Walwyn, for instance, to name just two—gave serious elaboration of the ideas contained in the counterfactual I have proposed, ideas about precisely what might be possible for the economy and polity if one did work the land in common, and indeed not just theoretical elaboration but in the case of the sect known as the Diggers, even implementation, in local experiments, thereby raising, at least briefly for a period of a dozen years in mid-seventeenth century England, the possibility of preempting the entire trajectory of orthodox liberal doctrines that Locke's theoretical construct of the social contract was intended to generate.

If I am right, then this counterfactual with its own historical instances found in the dissenting traditions of the time shows that the normative ideal found in the very idea of a "social contract" is not only merely consolidating of the orthodox liberal doctrines that eventually won out, but it shows also first that the doctrines are presented, via the social contract, as having *a historical necessity and inevitability,* which, if the dissenting critique was right, they do not possess, and second, presented via the social contract's aspiration to a normative ideal as possessing the right of a *rational* force and conviction, that they need never be granted as possessing.

I am keen to put on record an entire historical dissenting tradition that goes from the mid-seventeenth century radical sectaries to the late seventeenth century and early eighteenth century *scientific* dissenters, whom I have written of elsewhere (again see "Occidentalism, the Very Idea" in this volume) and who invoked the neo-Platonist and Hermeticist ideas of the radicals of a half a century earlier; and I am keen to do so because they anticipated in uncanny detail all the instincts and anxieties that Gandhi expressed about India going down the European path of political economy and governance. He was only a latecomer in a long tradition of "freethinking" which pulled together a range of themes *not just* about political economy, but about governance, science, metaphysics, religion, and alternative notions of rationality, thereby making it a dissent from much more than the "possessive individualism" stressed by other critics of Locke. In other words, the ideas of this long dissenting tradition emerge not merely as an early version of what we in our time have come to describe as a critique of market society, but rather as a wholesale *ethical* alternative to the liberalism of the orthodox Enlightenment, forming a recognizable genealogical antecedent to what might rightly be called an alternative and "radical" Enlightenment unfolding eventually in some of the ideas to be found in Gandhi's critique of the Enlightenment, through a tradition of radical thought that included not only Gandhi's avowed influences, Tolstoy, Ruskin, and Thoreau, but also a literary and philosophical Romantic tradition in England and Germany that took seriously ideas of disenchantment and alienation and found, of course, in a powerful and recurring and familiar thread in Marx's thought.

It may seem that, though I am perfectly right to notice this affinity between Gandhi and early modern dissent (each in their different settings expressing anxiety and wishing to preempt the onset of a capitalist economic formation and a centralized form of government to facilitate it), I can't be right in assimilating *Marx* into this affinity, given that Marx seemed to think such an economic formation as *determined* by a historical pattern in the narrative of materialism he is so well known for. Though there *may* be a serious divergence between Marx and Gandhi here, I doubt very much that it is as obvious as it has come to seem. Marx only really spoke in fully deterministic terms about the tendencies of *capital*, its immanent "logic." The term "logic" in "the logic of capital" can't be projected into the past to talk of earlier logics that led up to capital. Prior to the onset of capitalism, the elements in the narrative of "historical materialism" were not the outcome of anything as strong as something that Marx would wish to describe as a "logic," even if there was a pattern in the development of various economic formations which "historical materialism" outlined. The Marxist economist Prabhat Patnaik, following Oskar Lange, speaks of the "spontaneous tendencies"[8] that are immanent in capital, deterministic tendencies on which no *humanly planned* constraint could be put on any permanent basis (say, for instance, the sort of constraints formulated in Keynes). The "logic" of capital would brook no constraint of this kind in anything but a temporary form. As Patnaik puts it, the logic is such that either capitalism will overcome these constraints or capitalism itself would have to be transcended by another economic formation. Those are the only two options. Such is the logic of capital. But neither he, nor Lange so far as I know, attribute any deterministic tendencies of this strict sort to any prior period or economic formation. These tendencies are described by Patnaik and Lange as "immanent to capital" precisely because they are specific to capital alone. They cannot glibly be generalized and projected back into all of economic history. It is precisely because they are specific, immanent only to capital, that talk of these deterministic tendencies has the explanatory bite it does. It powerfully explains and reveals something in a *particular* kind of economy. It would lose its explanatory illumination if it was dispersed as a general phenomenon present in all of history. Determinism of this strict kind is a feature only of modernity and the economic formation unique to it. If this is right, it is not so obvious that Marx would dismiss the idea that Gandhi expressed in the first years of the twentieth century (or the early modern dissenters in Europe expressed in the seventeenth century) that there is nothing preordained and compulsory about the adoption of capitalism in India (or in Europe). Of course, it is well known that Marx did occasionally express the thought that colonialism may have brought advantages to India and there is no doubt that he thought capitalism was an advance on previous economic formations. But, first of all, those are normative claims, not descriptive deterministic claims. And second, it is also well-known by now (though scandalously under-studied) that Marx did much to overturn those thoughts in his last decade of writing on the Russian peasant commune, arguing after a close scrutiny of the ethnological notes he had gathered on them, that countries like Russia and India may have within them the resources to proceed more directly to socialist ideals and avoid the oppressive 'developmental' aspects of capitalist (and large-scale industrialist) economic formations. Thus on the matter of determinism, regarding the inevitability of India's capitalist future, it is not at all clear, I am claiming, that Marx would have found Gandhi's resistance to such a future to be flying in the face of any logic that he detected in history. If this is right, it offers a reading of Gandhi that is worth making explicit and clear and I'd like to exploit some of the analysis I've just presented to do so, thereby linking my two interpretative points about Gandhi and Marx that I began with. It has been widely noted that Gandhi's *Hind Swaraj* is a rather shrill work of criticism of Western modernity. What explains this in someone who was not given to such harshness of tone in his writing or speech? I had earlier said that it was explained by the fact that he thought India was at the cusp that Europe had been in the Early Modern period and he was anxious that India not go down the path of Europe in its passage from Early to Late Modernity. There is no doubt that the onset of capitalism in this passage was one among other sources of that anxiety for him. And some of the harshness of his words gets a very specific justification once we understand the analysis that I have just presented. In the analysis I had said that prior to modernity, prior to the period of capitalism, there was no conceptual or empirical compulsion to attribute a *deterministic* historical tendency in the various

passages of economic formation. But equally, on this analysis, the determinism that is attributable to the period of modernity alone is marked by
so ruthless a 'logic' of capital (undermining, as Patnaik points out, any
constraints that might be put on its 'spontaneous' tendencies) that there
is *not that much comfort* to be gained by the idea that determinism is
not a mark of previous periods and that therefore capitalism is not itself
an inevitability for countries like India. The ruthlessness of the logic
ensures that *if capital so much as gets a toe-hold* in the political economies of any region, it has a force and forward movement that cannot be
constrained. Gandhi, I believe, understood this with great clarity and it
is *this* understanding that explains the desperation with which he wished
to avoid it and the consequences of its modernity for India, and therefore
the particularly strident tone of his criticisms. Thus the analysis owing
to Marx (including the last decade of Marx's work) brings out *both* that
capitalism is not inevitable and can be avoided but also that once it is so
much as an incipient presence, its tendencies have so forceful a logic that
they are simply not containable from within the economic and political
framework it allows. It is this very specific and local historicism of the
modern period to be found in Marx that is quite of a piece with Gandhi's
most famous text on the subject of modernity, which *both* envisioned for
India a life that by-passed European modernity, a possibility which as I
said Marx's analysis allows for, while noting with a detailed and desperate anxiety how if it got any sort of foothold, it would be entrenched, as
Marx's analysis equally insists on, with a logic that can only be described
in deterministic terms.

So far, in charting early sources of alienation, I have stressed the transformation of the concept of nature and its effects on generating a wholesale form of extractive *political economy,* with a dissenting tradition in
the same period that stressed a quite different conception of nature with
hopes of local forms of egalitarianism based on a collective ideal of the
cultivation of the commons. But, as I had said earlier, these issues of
nature and political economy were, for Gandhi and his dissenting antecedents in the West, closely integrated with questions of knowledge and
of political governance.

It was, once again, Gandhi's religion (based on a maverick mix of
Bhakti, Jain, Buddhist, New Testament passages on the trust we should

place in the judgment of the most humble, ordinary people, and Gujarati Vaishnavite influences, including the sant poets of Gujarat, such as Narsin Mehta) that also made him resist the idea that knowledge was something other than what we live by. It was not something that was meant for elite control, a form of expertise by which a privileged priesthood exercised its dominance. But there again—to make the genealogical connection—the very desacralization of nature by the outlooks shaped by modern science of that period in Europe also ensured that such an elite conception of knowledge as expertise would emerge there. To desacralize nature and matter was to exile God from the world, something essential to the official Newtonianism of the Royal Society in England, where God was responsible for motion, not by being present *in* nature and thereby providing an inner source of dynamism that made for the motion of the universe, but as a clockwinder, an *external* source of motion of an otherwise intrinsically brute and inertial universe. And this, in turn, had the consequence that now God, no longer present in matter and nature, was not available to all who inhabit His world. He was a distant, providential figure and access to Him was the exclusive prerogative of the scripturally learned in universities.[9] This complaint of the radical Puritan dissenters should not be confused with the orthodox cliché about Protestant ideals of an individual's relation to God bypassing the Catholic Church's mediation of those relations. In fact, it is that very Protestant orthodoxy which had converted this individualism to its "possessive" variety, with essential links to property and extraction from property for profit by way of a right, and it was the same Protestant establishment that had deemed "enthusiasm" to be dangerous and argued instead for the exile of God to an inaccessible place, available only to those trained in the formal learning of specialized scriptural knowledges. By contrast, it is the *democratization* of the sacred rather than possessive individualism which these Puritan dissenters were demanding. Their complaint, thus, was that the exile of God and these ideas of the *expertise* of a priesthood that it made possible reached out to the priesthood's secular counterparts (through the very same alliances between established religion, science, and commerce) giving rise to elite conceptions of medicine, the law, and political governance by the monarchs and their courts who were now said to stand in the same relation to the brute populace as God did to a brute and purely material and desacralized universe. The dissenters in England and parts of Europe vociferously objected to these developments, anticipating in detail Gandhi's objections in *Hind Swaraj* and other writings to elite medicine, to the expertise of lawyers, and to centralized forms of governance that would inevitably be based on expertise rather than the norms and needs of localities.

Expertise ceases to respond to people as people, converts them into populations, something to be studied in a detached way rather than to be engaged with for the needs they have. When aggregated in this way, Gandhi feared that their needs would not be perceived as palpable, but merely as statistics. Responses to them would be not immediate but conceived in abstract terms that would never come to fruition in actually fulfilling their needs. So to take just one obvious and simple and utterly familiar example,[10] wealth is supposed to "trickle down" to poor sections of the *population*, a typically abstracted and detached "expert" modern response to *people's* needs, an outcome which has never actually occurred in the history of capitalist political economy, but which, from this detached perspective of expertise, is supposed to occur according to the models and theories that it constructs. The reification of people into populations, thus, abstracts attention from particular effects and numbs the sensibility to the connection between theory and practice.

Examples of the effects of such detachment can be proliferated in every domain, even in the domain of violence that Gandhi abhorred. In an earlier time, prior to modern science, if one had to kill someone in battle one would have to face them and pierce them with a spear. The detachment of outlook and practice that modern science made possible allows one instead to go miles up in the air and bomb much of a city in minutes and there is nothing that remains on record but a statistic in the next morning's newspapers and the historical record of the destruction of a certain *number* or *percentage* of a *"population."* Drones are only the latest and most grotesque development in this trajectory of detachment. In fact, if I can stretch the point as far as I think it goes with only a little strain, things get much more detached than that—to a point that should be seen as *ad absurdum*, were it not for how seriously it is intended. One does not even have to bomb a population. Should sections of a population, invoking Gandhi, raise objections to these alienating forms of detachment in our attitude toward nature and people, one is simply told that we are not part of the modern world, nostalgic for another time, and so irrelevant to our time. Thus, consider the following report from the *Telegraph* (January 7, 2012) of what Chidambaram from his perch in the Indian cabinet had declared: "Union home minister P. Chidambaram today called for a rejection of the *counterculture* against the use of natural wealth, pitching the development debate as a choice between museums and modern societies at a time several mining and power projects are held up because of protests. 'I don't think we should allow the counterculture to grow, a counterculture which says that people in these areas should live as they lived 300 or 400 years ago. We are not building museums here, we are building a modern society, a modern state,' Chidambaram told the inaugural session of the Northeast Business Summit here." The purpose is clear. Those people who protest that the natural environment (and the people who "live in" it and are sustained by it in the modest ways that allow it too to be sustained) was not a mere resource for development had no future in what India is to become. An entire point of view and the people who propagate it are thus made inconsequential, a people without any place in a blueprint of the future as drawn up by "experts" at a "Business Summit," a people reduced to not mattering for what the world has become and where it will go. This is the ultimate form of detachment in violence, to remove a people by the stroke of an ideological declaration from a position of corporate and governmental power, a form of rarefied, cognitive (rather than bodily) genocide in the name of the forward march—or perhaps "the end"—of history.

I cite this not merely to give a rough picture of the *abstract and detached* ways in which people and points of view are eliminated, but also to convey how closely the dissenting voices of the early modern period that I sketched earlier are echoed in contemporary struggles in countries such as India (and in the countries of the South generally) in a way that Gandhi with his prescience had warned a century ago.

One might think: This is just to cite a minister with a mission of "development," but why attribute this outlook to an accumulating wider elite sensibility as I have been doing rather than merely to the state that promotes such "development" on the part of the largest corporations it serves. But there is plenty of evidence of the outlook's widespread elite subscription. Even one of the most humane of contemporary economists, Amartya Sen, has written against those who protested the dispossession of agricultural land (for corporate "development" projects) from those who worked on it, that England went through its pain to create its Manchesters and Londons, and India will have to do so as well. Such a claim, which appeals to an historical analogy, does not present the entire historical context, one which would show the analogy to be imperfect.[11] Those who were dispossessed from their land and way of life by the "primitive accumulation" of an earlier period in England moved in great numbers across the Atlantic to America. There is no place for the dispossessed of, say, rural Bengal to go, except to the already glutted cities and their slums, creating heightened forms of urban immiseration. When the mobility of labor had some sort of parity with the mobility of capital, remarks such as Sen's may have had a point. When there is complete disparity between them, with immigration laws on the one side constraining labor's mobility and the dismantling or re-mantling of the Bretton Woods institutions on the other side, releasing capital for far greater mobility than it ever had, Sen's remark comes off as being of a piece with Chidambaram's remarks and shows how entrenched the attitude is among the intellectual class and the intelligentsia.

On the question of the transformation of human beings into citizens, the issues are ripe for misunderstanding, given what are, in many aspects, by and large honorable commitments to Enlightenment ideals; but let me present them, as they seem to me to have motivated Gandhi— also, as I hope will come through in the presentation, in an entirely honorable way.

Given his instinctive religious understanding of human life on earth, Gandhi had little faith in the capacity for the politics of the modern period to address the deeper among human concerns. The assumption that lies behind the detailed codes and constitutions of the forms of polity in the West with which we are familiar is perhaps the Enlightenment's most fundamental assumption—that what is bad in us can be constrained and overcome by good politics. Gandhi, perhaps out of the pessimism of an essentially religious man, simply did not believe this. He found it at once a shallowness and an insolence to think that human beings can be made better by being made over into some abstract new form of being called "citizens."[12]

This skepticism was based on a shrewd genealogical understanding of the emergence of modern European polities which, perhaps more than anything else in that part of the world, he did not want India to mimic. As he saw it, Europe, in the late seventeenth century, as a result of some of the changes already mentioned above, had come to find outdated its earlier forms of legitimation of the state which had appealed to the divine rights of the monarch who occupied it. It, therefore, had to seek new forms of justification for the state and the power it exercises. And (since the Westphalian peace) it sought this justification by a quite different strategy, by looking to modern social psychology rather than a God-given right of the tenant of an exalted office. The strategy was complex. The state was now to be seen as one half of an undecouplable conjunction with a new form of entity. This entity that came to be called the "nation" could not sufficiently be defined in purely territorial terms and borders. If it was conceived merely territorially, it could only justify the state in terms of the power needed to protect it from other such entities, but that would not justify the state's power and authority over its own "population." A further element was needed, then, a commitment drawn from the populace. Contractualist accounts were presumably relevant to this commitment too, basing themselves on a conjectural fiction about an originary past of a willed, conventional compact among human beings, an act by which they were transformed into citizens. But this was high theory. A yet further and far more crucial element would have to be less fictional and less hypothetical, more grounded in an actual political psychology that had to be generated in this citizenry. The populace had to be made to develop a *feeling* for this new kind of entity, the nation; and because the latter was understood as being inseparable from the state (a "nation-state"), the feeling for the first half of this hyphenated conjunction would confer a justification upon the second half, which had no longer any independent significance except as part of this conjunction with the first, and which *because* of its conjunction with this abstracted ("imagined") entity took an increasingly *centralized* form unlike earlier forms of power which were relatively scattered. In due course, this feeling would come to be called "national*ism*," a phenomenon Gandhi detested and he willfully strived in the Indian context to make that term mean something *entirely* different, wholly synonymous with "anti-imperialism" and emptied of these historical European connotations.

What in the European idea of nationalism did he find repugnant and dangerous? To answer this question, we have to ask: How did post-Westphalian Europe go about generating this feeling to be instilled? All over that continent, it was done by a method whose notoriety only came to be fully understood by Europeans in the middle of the last century as a result of developments in Germany in the 1930s and 40s, but Gandhi, who wrote before that period, saw it as having much earlier roots. This was the method of finding an external enemy within the territory and the "population" and despising them as the "other" and subjugating "them" (the Jews, the Irish, Protestants in predominantly Catholic countries, Catholics in predominantly Protestant countries) and thereby instigating a feeling among the rest of the population of a sense of privileged possession of this new entity, the nation, as "ours." Later, when numerical forms of discourse emerged and statistical methods in the social sciences were applied, categories such as "majority" and "minority" would be deployed to describe this, and such a method of generating a feeling for the nation and thereby legitimating state power would come to be called "majoritarianism." Gandhi wanted this entire trajectory by which Europe came to be what it is, an assembly of modern "nation-states," to find no root in India. It is for this reason that he opposed Savarkar more than he opposed any other figure of modern India,[13] for it is "Hindutva" that stood for the European method of modern politics, invoking a religious majoritarianism to build a nation and to legitimize a centralized state.

This was how "citizenship" began in the modern West and it is to *repair* the ravages wrought by this method that the West had to adopt various civic measures and ideologies such as "secular*ism*" (a political doctrine, something distinct from the larger social, cultural process of "secularization"), and later "multiculturalism." Gandhi, I suspect, thought the ravages went too far and too deep to be repaired by such a shallow politics. However *necessary* secularist citizenship may be to repair it, it would not, he felt, be *sufficient*. When Gandhi expressed a disdain for the idea that human beings must be made over into citizens, it is this entire history of the emergent idea of the nation that he was rejecting, and when it was claimed that one could avoid that European path of the construction of a nation in India by adopting at the outset of Indian independence the ideal of a *secular citizenship*, his response was to say that secularism was an ideal meant and adopted to repair a form of damage that had occurred in Europe, and there was no reason for India to allow that damage to occur among its own people in the first place.[14]

Gandhi furthermore shrewdly integrated some of these criticisms of the aspiration to improvement via notions of citizenship and rights with his entire skepticism about the role of the effect of privileged and expert knowledges. As I have read him, his criticism of the rise of a certain outlook in which privileged status is given to specialized knowledges is of a piece with the privileged status given to *certain lifestyles and behaviors* around rule itself. This integration goes back to notions of civility that emerged in the same period and the same set of ideas and outlooks of the seventeenth century where Gandhi located the fault-line. There has been fine and detailed study of the rise of notions of civility in the work of such intellectual historians as Norbert Elias and, more recently, Keith Thomas and Peter Burke. In some of their descriptions one can gather a certain *semantics* that was essential to how the notion was characterized. Civility, which consisted in a range of things from comportment to dress and speech, was said to be a feature of the lifestyles of the monarch and his courts, and the propertied elites, who, as I've pointed out, were often said to rule over a brute populace by analogy with (indeed as a mundane version of) an exiled and distant God ruling over a brute and material and inert (Newton, in his *Opticks* had called nature and matter "stupid") universe.[15] And so, correspondingly, in this semantic stipulation, civility was contrasted with "cruelty" which was a feature particularly of the lifestyles and behaviors of the rude populace. (At times a sentimental Left radicalism buys into this semantic contrast when it almost wistfully attributes a sort of "jouissance" to the lifestyles and behaviors of the working class precisely because of its "incivility.") As Clarendon had said: "Nothing but joy in propriety reduc'd us from this barbarity, and nothing but security in the same can preserve us from returning into it again."[16] When I call this a semantics, I mean to suggest that these had nothing to do with empirical concerns of evidence and observation.

These were *stipulations* of how these words "civility" and "cruelty" were to be used and internalized.

The effect this usage had was remarkable, one of a deeply imbibed self-deception, a fact that the intellectual historians I mentioned do not register, though they are central to how Gandhi understood the culture of liberal democracy, which he dismissed and which he contrasted with his own notions of a democratized mentality that he claimed to have learned from the New Testament's deep commitments to the wisdom of judgment to be found in the most ordinary and humble of people. The self-deceptive effect of the semantics was to create a screen that hid from the European monarchs and their courts the cruelty of their *own* perpetration on the brute populace, who alone were counted, by the semantics, as capable of cruelty. And in Gandhi's understanding, in the modern West this screen of self-deception morphed over from the notion of civility into the more abstract domain of rights and constitutions and codes, whereby cruelty came to be understood by nations who possessed such rights and constitutions as only occurring in nations that do not possess them. Thus the cruelty perpetrated by the former on the distant lands of the latter were hid from the perpetrators because cruelty can only really happen in lands without rights and constitutions—an attitude quite prevalent to this day, when it is still pervasively assumed that cruelty can only really happen, say, in Mugabe's Zimbabwe or Saddam's Iraq but not in the metropolitan West. There is, I believe, no understanding the phenomenon of Guantanamo without this self-deceptive function that rights have come to have, no matter how rightly celebrated rights are for the great good that they have done where they have been adopted. Torture of that sort cannot be located on American soil because "we don't do torture" since cruelty only happens in other sorts of places. If Gandhi showed a studied indifference to rights and constitutions and the very idea of citizenship, it was partly at least because he saw it as emerging from these links with expert knowledges of codified rule whose self-deceptions had a genealogy in an earlier period of elite lifestyles and aspirations to civility.

In case I am misunderstood, I should add that for one to appreciate today all of these points I am attributing to Gandhi, one does not have to find either secularism or the commitment to rights and constitutions to be misguided. One can cherish these as much as one likes—and I do cherish them—and yet see the merit in Gandhi's view. All one has to appreciate is the second of the preliminary interpretative points with which I began this essay.[17]

I have briefly—really much too briefly—tried to give sketches of answers to each of the four questions I had posed and to convey through a genealogical story how *integrated* they are. There ought to be a book-length's elaboration of these very superficially sketched points. Let me just conclude this discussion of these four questions by saying that it is a measure of Gandhi's profundity that he saw these four transformations as being, at bottom, *the same* transformation. That is why the four questions to which these are answers are merely a breakdown of the single genealogical question of an intractably omnibus generality with which I began. For Gandhi, they were all manifestations of a single alienating process that began with a desacralization and the consequent adoption of an objectifying attitude of detachment toward *both* nature *and* its inhabitants that owed to outlooks developing around the rise of modern science and which—through worldly alliances formed between scientific ideologues, commercial interests, and established or "high" (rather than popular) religious institutions—gave rise to a form of political economy and of political governance that, for all the liberal pieties and high-sounding ideals that accompanied them, were destructively exploitative of nature and of its inhabitants, and were elitist and undemocratic in the apparatus of rule that they set up.

3.

I return now to the theme of the affinities between Gandhi and Marx and their fundamental emphasis on the ideal of an unalienated life that was defined against such forms of detachment.

Marx, of course, did not view *desacralization* to be the ultimate source of the detachment with which nature and human life and labor came to be reduced and objectified. He located the source quite elsewhere. But though the diagnostic fault-*line* was different, there was a common conception in both Marx and Gandhi of the *fault:* alienation engendered via the objectification of human subjectivity and of the world which it inhabited. Marx's analysis was just as elaborate as the four-fold integrating analysis in Gandhi that I have been trying to convey through my genealogical account, but it was not at such a high level of generality; it was more specifically focused on labor. Even so, the overlapping elements are salient. Like Gandhi, Marx stressed both 1) the objectification of the relations between nature and human beings such that nature was not seen any longer as prompting their practical and moral engagement ("living in"), but rather seen as the object of their detached and extractive gaze ("mastery and control"), and he also stressed 2) the objectification of the relations between human beings themselves whereby they are not mutually seen as *subjects* to be *engaged* with but rather—with detachment—as a source of production of a form of value that was at once abstract and material. Marx's rhetoric in speaking of these alienating relations ("commodification," "fetishism") was also substantially different from Gandhi's ("desacralization," "the making of ends into means"), but that difference is superficial. They both shared a vision in which each of these sources of alienation was overcome, whereby, regarding (1), "the naturalism of man and the humanism of nature are both brought to fulfillment," to use Marx's words, and where regarding (2) no subject is seen in a *detached* way as a means or an object but rather is viewed as a subject, as an end in himself, someone to be *engaged* with by one's own agentive subjectivity.

What alternative vision does it take to confront these two most fundamental forms of alienation –from nature, and from each other? I want to close this essay with some very compressed remarks about what I take to be the most *general and the most underlying* philosophical considerations by which we can at least begin to specify the alternative vision it would take. What I have to say will, because it is so general and underlying, not speak directly to the details of how Marx thought these sources of alienation should be confronted. But those details, I believe, are in the service of these more general and fundamental ways of conceiving the shape of an unalienated life. And vis-à-vis Gandhi too, what I have to say will try to reach past the specifically religious basis of his sacralized understanding of an unalienated life to the more general conception that underlies it.

Let me speak to each form of alienation in turn.

(1), as I said, has to do with the relations between human beings and nature, and (2) has to do with the relations among human beings.

What the desacralization of nature did as a result of the processes I briefly described above was—to use Weber's phrase—"disenchant the world." And, following Gandhi, I have described this as a transformation of the very idea of nature into the idea of "natural resources." But to describe it as resources is to describe a material consequence of the transformation, its availability for systematically extractive purposes. And so a prior question must be: What did desacralization achieve that released these possibilities for viewing it as a (re)source for systematic extraction. That is, we need an intermediate level of description of what nature became as a result of desacralization such that, given what it became, it could now be viewed with impunity as a resource.[18] A few additional steps of reasoning have, thus, to be added.

To see something as a mere resource and not as sacralized, we first need to see it as brute, as something that makes no normative demands of practical and moral engagement with us; we need to deny "the humanism of nature," to use Marx's expression, and instead see it as something we relate to only in completely detached terms. The paradigmatic way of viewing nature in a purely detached way ever since the mid-seventeenth century is to view it as natural science views it, as an object of study and explanation rather than as something to be engaged with in practical and moral terms, to see it primarily as following strict laws of its own ("laws of nature") that govern its events. So I would think that the first step toward the right intermediate description of what nature was transformed into by its desacralization, before it could be described as a "resource," is that nature is to be *exhaustively* characterized as *"that which the natural sciences study."* To describe it as a resource for material exploitation follows upon *first* transforming it into something that is viewed as *merely* requiring our detached gaze for this kind of objective study. There is real significance in this priority and sequence. In the last half century or more there has been much, as it is called, "critique" of "instrumental" reason and though that critique is surely correct and worthily motivated, it is not the primary purpose of this essay to simply rehearse it here. What is less obvious and less emphasized, and what I see myself as partly attempting to contribute to in my writings on Gandhi, is that the deeper and prior source of critique should be about the very understanding of nature itself along these detached lines—and, moreover, it is important to understand in detail *how* quite generally and how more or less exactly the notion of resources (whether natural or even human) and the instrumentalities they generate *emerge* from such an understanding of nature.

So, first, what is this understanding?

The answer I think has to be that if you see nature as exhaustively characterized as that which the natural sciences study, then it cannot contain any value properties. So, the Malabar Forest or the Narmada River contain chlorophyll and H_2O but contain no value properties. What, then, is the source of values, if they are not present in the world around us? The outlook of science that Gandhi decried has an answer, which philosophers such as Hume gave very explicitly: *values come entirely from our states of mind*, i.e., our desires, preferences, and subjective utilities, which when they are geared to, or reared in social relations, become somewhat loftier states of mind such as sympathy and the 'moral sentiments'. There is no basis for values but our states of mind. Nothing in the world, including nature, can contain value properties. By Gandhi's and Marx's lights, this would already amount to being alienated from nature. Marx, fully anticipating Gandhi's point about the transformation of nature into natural resources via the detachment issuing from the outlook around modern science, says, "For the first time, nature becomes purely an object for humankind, purely a matter of utility; ceases to be recognized as a power for itself; and the theoretical discovery of its autonomous laws appears merely as a ruse so as to subjugate it under human needs . . ."[19] Marx, unlike Gandhi, did not see the source of value in nature as coming from its being sacralized. But the remarks on nature's humanism and the idea of nature as 'a power for itself' rather than 'purely an object for humankind' exactly intended to repudiate this evacuation of value properties from nature since nature, for him, was something that man was responding to in terms that were normatively prompted by it, a view that John McDowell[20] has also attributed to Aristotle. It was nature 'for man' as Marx puts it. That is what he means by 'nature's humanism'. Nature is intrinsically something that our human capacities uniquely (and none other than *our species'* capacities for it is part of what he called our 'species being') were moved by in *normative* terms and it is this which triggered our unique kind of subjectivity to a praxis or practical agency vis-a-vis nature. (See the crucial note 22 for how this idea of nature's 'humanism' or nature being 'for human beings'—something captured in contemporary philosophical terms by analogies made with what Locke and Boyle called 'secondary qualities'—can be completely misunderstood and fallaciously interpreted as *denying* that nature contains value properties.)

However, one more step has to be filled in at this intermediate level, because a question arises: What is it about something which can only be the object of detached natural scientific study (rather than something containing values that prompts our practical and moral agency) that lends itself to then being viewed as a resource to be exploited?

If it is something only to be studied in a detached way, how do we then make the transition of going about the practical task of exploiting it? To exploit a resource is to go beyond merely studying its natural properties as the natural sciences do. It is a *practical* engagement with nature. So nature must contain something that *prompts* this *practical* agency. If we relate to nature merely as the natural sciences do, we can see the gold underground as merely Au, assigned the number 79, a chemical property; but when we see it in that detached way we do not yet see it as something that could be a resource to be mined. We also need to see nature containing such things as *opportunities* which are the sorts of thing that might prompt us to such extractive practical engagement. Thus the very same thing that is Au (that which natural science studies) is also something that the *natural* sciences do *not* study, an *opportunity*. So we have, on this picture, an interesting mix of conceptual ingredients. On the one hand, the world, including nature, contains the properties that natural science studies in a detached way. On the other hand it contains *no* value properties. (Values are entirely derived from our internal mental states; they have no existence outside our mentality.) But if nature only contains the former kind of properties, then we cannot explain how we can view nature as a resource and *act* upon it in practical terms to exploit the resource, over and above merely studying it in a detached way. So a third, intermediate kind of phenomena between "natural" properties and "value" properties is needed and it needs to be *in nature,* if the idea of nature is to be transformed into the idea of natural resources. These phenomena can be described as "opportunities." On the one hand they are *not values* because values are strictly to be found only as emerging from our states of mind and are not contained in the natural world external to us. On the other hand, though they are properties in the natural world external to us, they are *beyond* the province of the natural sciences to study.

It is exactly here I think that we find a role for the social sciences as they have come to be understood in the modern Western paradigm, a cognitive enterprise which navigates resources that the world offers ("opportunities"), for the satisfaction of our states of mind (values as they are conceived in terms of desires and utilities, constrained, when we are lucky, by socially sensitive moral sentiments). Hence this last step, at this intermediate level of description, reveals how the social sciences, quite apart from the details of their intellectual pursuits, came to have a broad underlying mission: to study how *our* desires and utilities (the basis of all values) combined with our probabilistic apprehension and calculation of the desire- (and utility-) satisfying properties *in the world* (opportunities) explain all human individual and collective behavior. And it is the same steps of reasoning that complete the transformation of nature to natural resources, which latter just *are* the opportunities or desire- and utility-satisfying properties in the world. To sum up and repeat: On this picture, nature contains nothing that itself is intrinsically valuable. It contains opportunities but no values. Values emanate wholly from our states of mind, and nature, apart from containing the natural properties that natural science studies, also contains the opportunities (resources) for us to satisfy those states of mind. If we speak of nature with the vocabulary of value, that is entirely a projection of our desires and utilities onto nature. Such a vocabulary describes no intrinsic properties of nature. And since nothing intrinsic in nature is valuable, nothing in nature can constrain our desires, utilities, and moral sentiments. Nature is conceived only as providing opportunities to fulfill, not as constraining our desires. Desires and moral sentiments can only be constrained by other desires and moral sentiments.

All these steps and levels of description go into how we understand the sources of alienation in our relations with nature. Gandhi, as I said, believed that the fault-line which set us on this path is the desacralization ("disenchantment" in Weber's term) of nature that came from the out-look of modern science. This might seem to imply that nothing short of *re*sacralization of our conception of nature would overcome the alienation he found endemic in modern European civilization. But my point in presenting these various steps and levels of description has been to suggest that even if in the historical past desacralization of our conception of nature was the fault-line, and even if we cannot in our historical present easily conceive of a return to sacralized nature to overcome this source of alienation, we nevertheless have a more *secular* conceptual repertoire by which to think of what it might even be conceived to re-enchant the world. The more general and underlying fault-line is not desacralization but the evacuation of *value* properties from the world and the reduction of the world only to a) properties that the natural sciences study and b) to opportunities, whose status as potential satisfiers of our desires and utilities (the bases of our values) it became the business of the *social* sciences to study—where the term *science* in "social science" is supposed to indicate a sphere of "expertise" to be contrasted with the *mere study* of society.

This entire picture, despite its pervasiveness and the sense of confident inevitability with which it is widely propagated, is quite uncompulsory. It is the cognitive universe of Western modernity that Gandhi presciently saw through and he saw it as encroaching on Indian ways of relating to the world, not just by material exploitation but by enslaving the Indian mind. He rightly saw it as a dogma; indeed, I would put it more strongly, he rightly saw it as a *superstition of modernity* that nature must be conceived only as that which these sciences study. (By superstition, I just mean a belief so accepted in the wider belief community that we take it on trust and forget when or how it was proved and why and in what ways it helps us to live.) However, in this case, among the intellectual classes, it is a dogma that has been maintained by sheer intellectual browbeating, dismissing all denials of it as an expression of an unscientific mentality. But there is nothing unscientific whatever about denying it. One can only be unscientific if one denies or contradicts some proposition in some science. But no science contains the proposition that nature is exclusively and exhaustively what falls within the purview of these sciences. That is a proposition asserted by *philosophers* and, if and when scientists assert it, they are doing so not qua scientists but on their own time, as philosophers. These are the ideologues who have wholly embraced the *outlook* that emerged around the new science in the late seventeenth century. When they express such a view of nature they are not uttering a scien*tific* proposition but expressing a scien*tistic* outlook, the preposterous elevation of science by claiming that all questions about nature are scientific questions and implying, therefore, that there exists nothing in nature that falls outside the business of science and its laws.

To deny this dogma is neither to express a phobia against science itself[21] (as opposed to the increasing effects of the outlook of scientistic detachment I have been elaborating in the various different manifestations of it, which Gandhi conflatingly blamed modern science for generating) *nor* an urge for resacralization. An atheist, which I confess to being, can deny the dogma. To say merely that values (not God) suffuse the world and nature may not constitute a form of enchantment or re-enchantment that Gandhi would have wished to countenance, but I believe it is what *underlies* his understanding of our relations with nature. The idea of a sacralized nature is a specifically religious manifestation of this more underlying ideal. The sacred was once thought by many to be a source of value in nature, but value in nature can be without a source; it can be *sui generis.* There is no reason to think that if we cannot any longer embrace the sacral in nature then we cannot embrace the idea that nature contains values that prompt our practical *moral* engagement with it over and above our detached scientific study of it and our practical opportunistic predatory exploitation of it.[22]

I have tried here to sympathetically glean from Gandhi's ideas possible sources of an unalienated relation to nature, allowing nature to contain properties of value and meaning, without necessarily identifying those sources in anything sacral. This would, of course, be entirely congenial to Marx, but there is a great deal to sort out, which I can't do at any length here, about how it relates to some basic ideas in Marx, particularly the early work of Marx that I have invoked in which there is much discussion of nature and species-being and labor as well as a frequent rhetoric of "fetishism" and "commodification" in the elaboration of issues of alienation. How does this discussion of nature square with the issues raised by the rhetoric? I think the right reading of Marx which shows how it squares with it requires us to see nature as containing value properties which we in our unique species-being, that is, which we alone as a species, are able to respond to. This is what makes for the idea of the "humanism of nature" and the "naturalness of man" in the words I have cited. We, as a species, alone are attuned by our sensibility to perceive the normative demands that the world, including nature, makes on us, and are triggered by these perceptions to respond to it with our engagement, that is, with our subjectivity and agency and, eventually, in the fully socialized version of these responses, with our labor. To see nature in this way is commended by Marx in the passages on our relations with nature, and it is *not to be confused* with something he criticizes rather than commends, his idea that we often bestow things with qualities they don't possess, fetishizing them as possessing occult qualities that, as mere things, they do not.[23] It is a grossly fallacious extrapolation of this *very specific* application of the idea of a fetish in Marx (say, to something like money) to see it as having a more general reach, as is done in the outlook that is generated by modern science to claim that we have falsely projected value properties onto nature, and in doing so bestowed it with occult properties that it does not possess. No such scientism can be attributed to Marx. It is fallacious because in the passages on the humanism of nature, Marx himself views nature as containing value properties which prompt the engagement of human subjectivity and agency, and would be astonished by the idea that this is to conjure something occult. It is this extrapolation that I was inveighing against above when I objected to our tendency in this context to throw away the baby (value properties in nature) with the bath-water (sacralized conceptions of nature). Marx, unlike Gandhi, would certainly count the latter as a generalization of his notion of a fetish, but he and Gandhi are one in embracing the former. And that is why I have described the deeper point that underlies both Gandhi's and Marx's notion of an unalienated relation in terms of considerations having to do with value rather than sacralization.

The master thought here, then, is the presence of value properties in the world (including nature) that we inhabit. I call it the master thought because I would myself go so far as to say that we cannot even make sense of the idea that we are *capable of practical agency*, unless we see practical agency as something responsive to value properties in the world. The idea that our practical agency is merely a matter of satisfying our desires and moral sentiments without seeing our desires and moral sentiments as themselves prompted by such responsiveness to value properties in the world, including nature, is a shallow conception of agency, one which cannot survive a deeper philosophical scrutiny. For consider the following simple point (well, "simple" is a bit of ostentatious rhetoric, so let me say instead, crucial point). If our desiring something (or valuing something) was always given to us or experienced by us *not indirectly via* our perception and experience of the desir*able* (or value) properties of the thing that was desired (and valued), but rather given to us and experienced by us *directly* in our observation of our own minds that contain those desires (and valuings), then they would always be given to us in the *third* person perspective on ourselves. They would always be given to us when we step back and look at ourselves from the outside as detached observers of ourselves and our desires. But when we have such a third person perspective on ourselves, we are precisely not being agents. To put it in other words, consider the difference between two things said by someone: 1) "X is desirable/X is valuable" and 2) "X is desired by me/X is valued by me." If every time I desired or valued something, it was given to me in the sense of (2), I would have no practical agency because my desires, so given to me, would not motivate me to act at all. They would lie in my experience as lead, inert, unable to prompt me to act, since they are viewed by me only when I think of myself and observe my mind in a detached way from the outside—where my mind is, as a result, an object rather than a subject. But that is exactly what is not so if my desiring something is given to me *indirectly* via my experience of the desirability (the value properties) of something in my perceptual ambient surroundings. I would then be in the *first* person mode, taking in the world around me and by the perception of its desirabilities and value properties, which make normative demands on me, prompted to act on the world, and in all this I would be experiencing my desires indirectly but in the first person mode. There is a deep and reciprocal relation to be remarked here. Desirabilities or values in the world prompt our desires, but our desires are our conduits, our paths to the desirabilities and values in the world. It is this mutual relation that constitutes—at the highest level of generality—our being *at home in the world* and it is what—of course, again, at this very high level of abstraction and general-ity—makes for an unalienated life. My first person mode of *agency* rather than a *detached* observation of myself is *only* triggered if my desires take desirabilities or values in the world as their objects. That first person mode of agency is exactly what is *de*activated if the objects of my desires are given to me as desir*ed* rather than desir*able*. If given only as desired, they are given to me in a mode or perspective of detachment that I have on my self and my mind.[24]

It is not surprising then that the enchantment of the world with value properties is what is set up to be opposed by the increasing detachment that Gandhi found in the four questions that I presented in my read-ing of him. That he should have himself found the enchantment of the world by values to have a sacralized source need not be what we see as essential any more. But that does not cancel the depth of his jitters about the detachment wrought by descralization, which these four questions signaled.

So the most *general and underlying source* of the unalienated life (one that stands behind the profound details of Marx's and Gandhi's analyses of alienation in modern society) lies in the idea that nature contains the sorts of things (values) that make normative demands on us, and when we exercise our subjectivity and our agency to be in tune with these demands, we are in an unalienated relation with nature.[25] If one wanted an encapsulated form of the ideal, here is a slogan: To be unalienated from nature is *for our subjectivity to be in sync with the normative demands upon it coming from the value properties of nature*. To try to achieve such a relation with nature would be to begin to confront some of the effects of the set of transformations that I have tried to present genealogically through an exposition of some of Gandhi's ideas. The thought encapsu-lated in the slogan needs much further elaboration than I can give here, but it is the most fundamental thought that can make for a sane relation to the environment and the world we inhabit. The idea that we can come to a satisfactory relation simply by invoking elements entirely from within our own interests and utilities and moral sentiments, independent of normative constraints from the world itself, is not merely shallow. It is a false optimism that makes no dent in the framework that has landed us (via the genealogy I tried to trace) with the alienation in which the urge for "mastery and control" has undermined the ideal of merely "living in" and morally engaging with the world. Wittgenstein once used the phrase "leaving the world alone" to propose a non-revisionary metaphysical attitude we might adopt toward the world. It is an essential aspect of such non-revision that we refuse a very specific revision, refuse to evacuate the world of its value properties in the name of science's comprehensive coverage of it, and with this refusal, allow it to make normative demands on our engagement; and, if I am right, it is also an essential outcome of such non-revision that it may eventually allow us to leave the world alone in a much more expanded sense than Wittgenstein had intended.

The idea that nature *makes demands* on us is, strictly speaking, a metaphor. Nature may contain values but those values don't get voice in the intentional sense. Quite obviously, their demands are not literally spoken or intentionally formulated, unless we redefine our ideas of speech and thought. Things in nature have meaning, but it is not linguistic meaning expressing intentionality. The reason for this is perfectly simple. It is a mark or an implication of what we mean by intentionality that subjects who possess intentionality are the sorts of subjects that are potentially appropriate targets of a certain form of criticism. I can criticize you for doing something wrong, making unreasonable normative demands, having destructive thoughts, as you can me. But it makes no sense to criticize elements in nature in the same sense. We can say of a hurricane that it is destructive but that is a "criticism" only by courtesy, not the sort of criticism that you and I make of each other's doings and demands and thoughts. Bruno Latour, Jane Bennett, and others have proposed that there is no reason to restrict intentionality to human intentionality, claiming that there are actants over and above actors and intentionality is a property that has wider application than I am suggesting. But it is one thing to suggest that a group or collectivity, something which does not coincide with an individual human animal, has intentionality, quite another to say that elements in nature, "things," have intentionality. A group or collectivity of individuals might be said, *qua group,* to have intentionality, precisely because it can engage in the deliberative structure of thought and decision that individuals do. (This happens when individuals in the group put aside their individual desires and beliefs and think *from the point of view of the group.*) That is precisely why we can criticize the group (a corporation, say) over and above criticizing individuals (its CEO, say). But elements in nature and things do not possess or carry out any such deliberative structure or process and so there is no similar ground for attributing intentionality to them. That is why talk of nature making normative demands on us is metaphorical in a way that it need not be in the case of a group of individual persons.

Unlike Latour and Bennett and others, I don't think there is any theoretical advantage in multiplying notions of intentionality, one that human individuals (and perhaps groups of human individuals) literally possess as well as *another* that "things" in the world (including nature) *also literally* possess, thereby making them "actants." There might have been an advantage in saying this if there was a *dis*advantage, something we lose, in conceding that the idea that nature makes normative demands on us is a metaphor. But nothing is lost in conceding something like that. Why not? Because it is not a metaphor that can be paraphrased away. It is *not* a *dispensable* metaphor. And the crucial point is that when we point out that a metaphor can't be paraphrased away, we are not *merely* putting forward a linguistic thesis about a certain figure of speech. The *linguistic* thesis that a metaphor is not paraphrasable away has a *metaphysical* counterpart. To make the linguistic claim is at the same time to make the following metaphysical claim: There is an aspect or a fragment of *reality* which can only be captured by *that metaphor.* And the reality that is captured by the *metaphorical* attribution of intentionality and voice, etc., to things, to elements in nature, is as authentic as any reality that literal attributions of intentionality describe. It is just not the same reality. It is not intentionality.

Thus, without compromising at all the significance of the fact that value properties are in nature, I can still disavow intentional vitalism just as I do the necessity of resacralization. Not all enchantments need to be seen as vitalist or sacral.

The idea that we should not take seriously the normative demands that value properties in nature make upon us, simply because they are not literally spoken or intentionally formulated in the ways that *our* normative demands on each other are, would be to take a quite narrowing *parochial* stance on the ethical and political possibilities that our relations with nature present, quite as narrow as white men of property saying no one but white men of property may have representative voice in the polity. These are ethical demands that we ought to be able to begin to conceive in terms that have *political* significance and it is a matter of the utmost urgency that we begin to do so. Clearly, we don't as yet have a conceptual (not to mention institutional) framework in which we can find a way to directly hear the normative demands coming from nature on institutions of political representation. Our frameworks hitherto have articulated our concerns about nature and the environment in terms having to do with the demands that *we* make for *our* well-being or protection whether it is for future generations or those most vulnerable in the present to the devastating effects of changes in climate. But that is what I was earlier describing as shallow and as not making a dent in the frameworks that are the source of the alienation we have identified. What is needed—if we are to get beyond the prejudice that all value comes from us alone and cannot be found as properties in nature—is to give *political voice to the demands coming from nature itself.* This is what we lack an articulated framework for. But that is not a reason to put into doubt that these genuinely are demands. We mustn't forget that it took centuries for us to articulate a framework within which we gave *representative* voice to *our own demands* when we painfully and with much blundering and much resistance constructed democratic institutions. It is, therefore, bound to take much careful and painstaking (and painful) effort to think toward what an intellectual and institutional framework would look like for giving actual representative voice also to something like the demands coming from value properties in nature. The mind may even boggle—in our current state of philosophical and institutional development—as to what such a framework of ideas and institutions would look like. But it would be to be faint of heart and mind (in the way that parochialism always has been) to conclude from our impoverished thinking on this subject so far that there must be something wrong or fantastical in the very idea of such a broadening of the ideas and institutions of representation. That would be to willfully ignore and perpetuate all the sources of alienation that I have been trying to present via my reading of Gandhi's philosophy, refusing to construct the possibilities for an unalienated life as inhabitants of nature. Gandhi apart, many will no doubt express skepticism as to whether Marx can be co-opted at all in these Gandhian reflections on nature and our unalienated possibilities of life in it since many have been highly and quite rightly critical of the fact that countries influenced by Marxist doctrine in the past—communist and socialist countries—have been just as guilty of the transformation of nature into natural resources as any. Still, Marxism, if one stresses the themes in Marx that I have in drawing the affinities with Gandhi, *has* the resources to say that social- ism possesses the *capacity,* even if it has not had the will, to constrain and even reverse some of the effects of this transformation, resources simply not available while capitalism has not been transcended.

So far I've discussed only an ideal of an unalienated life in our rela- tions with nature. What then of (2), the more *social* forms of alienation, alienation as Marx puts it, of "man from man" rather than man from nature? That must really be the topic of a whole and separate essay, but since it is what is most relevant to the issues of liberty and equality I began with, let me end by making the briefest and the most elementary of gestures toward what is involved.

Here again what I have to say will focus more on Gandhi than on Marx and it will be at a level of generality that is only found implicitly in Marx and not in the specific details of his penetrating discussion of how the conditions of labor in a capitalist society deracinate human beings from each other and from their "species-being," their identity as *human.*[26] But it is no bad thing for philosophy to step back and register things at a more general level so as to underscore what the scrutiny of specific structures elaborate and exemplify.

Alienation of the sort that Gandhi and Marx were concerned with has, as a central strain, the idea that when human beings are made anony- mous in a mass society within a capitalist economic formation that is typical of the modern West, we become individuals in a sense that is so atomistically realized and reified that the very idea of the social or of the collective becomes a mere abstraction. It has no palpable or phenomeno- logical place in the lives of individuals nor any reality which could be the basis of genuine unalienated relations between them. But we must ask: What is the idea or ideal of the social collective that makes for an unalien- ated life and which has been so undermined by these developments in the West that Gandhi and Marx have analyzed in such abundant detail?

In other words, those details apart, what is the most general thing we can say about it?—as a corresponding counterpart to the general thing we said when addressing (1) or man's alienation from nature, viz., that the unalienated life consists in one's agency being in sync with the normative demands that are made by the value properties in nature.

Here, then, is a capsule, a corresponding sloganized answer for (2), i.e., man's alienation from man, on which I will briefly elaborate before closing. The ideal is simply this, and it is something that Gandhi came close to formulating. What we aspire to, when we seek a socially unalienated life with one another, is the realization of the ideal that *nobody in society is well off if someone is badly off.*

Someone might think that this just *is* the idea of equality, so why was I so keen on saying at the outset that I would construct a framework in which equality would not be on center stage but a necessary condition for some other ideal that was on center stage such as the ideal of the unalienated life. All I have done, it might be said, is simply *equated* the social aspects of being unalienated with the idea of equality. I have not done the more complex thing that I had set out to do.

This response misses what the slogan is seeking to convey. What it misses is that the entire point of the slogan was to assert the importance of equality only at *second remove.* In a situation where some are well off and others are not, the idea of the slogan is not merely to say that this is a bad thing (as an assertion of the importance of equality that is *not* once removed would), but rather to say that even those who in a situation of inequality are *well* off are *in fact not so.* Subtle though the distinction is, it makes all the difference; it establishes the deep contrast between the idea of equality and the idea of a socially unalienated life, with the former now merely a condition for the latter (even if an indispensable condition).

There is a further analytical clarification to be made. It might seem that what this ideal of being socially unalienated articulates is that those who are well off should not be unconcerned about those who are not well off. So being unalienated from one another in this social sense is to be infused with a sense of social concern about others who are not well off. It is a *mentality,* a cast of mind in which concern for others less well off is central and the ideal of the collective is dependent on the existence of this mentality in individuals. Much of the eighteenth and nineteenth century stress on "sympathy" was about this form of mentality. It is also the sort of thing that Rousseau stressed when he said that "pity" (less condescendingly termed, "compassion," I think) was basic to human mentality until it was undermined in the trajectory he traced by which inequality was created in society through the emergence of self-love or amour-propre.

But this too is a mistaken reading of what the slogan is reaching for. If it were merely reaching for this, I would have begun this essay by saying that the more fundamental ideal that should replace liberty and equality on center stage should be the third ideal in that celebrated trio—fraternity. This kind of concern for others is merely the subjective basis of fraternal relations, as the Enlightenment understood it. And though fraternity is much to be desired, it does not dig as deep as the ideal of an unalienated life is meant to, in Marx and Gandhi.[27]

My slogan was reaching for a much more ambitious ideal. It is not merely claiming that we should feel this form of concern for others though, as I said, it would certainly not deny that it is a good thing to do so. Now this is not to say that mentality or subjectivity is *not* involved in this ideal as the slogan presents it. It is indeed involved and is central to the slogan's meaning. What, then, is this mentality?

One can identify it by first identifying the offending experience or mentality that it is *defined against* such that one is unalienated only when that offending experience or state of mind is *absent*.

I have said the important thing to emphasize when discussing this ideal is not the feeling of *concern* that the well-off person might feel for those not well off. Rather what one should be initially emphasizing is the fact that the person who is well off in fact also suffers or experientially partakes of a kind of *malaise,* when others are not well off. It is *that* malaise which is alienation. It is a generalized unease of the mind or, as metaphysicians like to say, of *being,* which affects all social relations. In a society where some are not well off, all feel and partake of this alienation, even those who are well off. Often people don't know the cause or the grounds of the malaise as having its roots in a society characterized by discrepancies in well-offness. Yet the malaise is manifest in a variety of different behaviors of theirs. Thus it is a subjective state of felt experience that can be said to have an objective presence in the minds of people whenever they live in societies with such discrepancies. Though I won't try to present it here, the empirical correlation between such discrepancies and the behavior that reflects this malaise is extremely well established.

Of course, the behavior which reflects the malaise is bound to be very different in those who are well off than it is in those who are not, and it takes some careful psychological integration of theory and evidence to show how these are both symptoms of the same malaise; but that ought not to be an insuperable difficulty. Just to take the most obvious examples: On the side of the badly off, the familiar sentiments of resentment and envy, as well as the attitudes of resignation and pacification are all symptom of the malaise. On the side of the well off, the tendency to cut themselves off from the worse off (consider the appeal that "gated communities" have), though very different from the alienated pathologies of the badly off, is an example of a recognizable symptom of the same malaise.

Katherine Boo in her *Behind the Beautiful Forevers* tries to capture some of these divergent symptoms in different groups (so called "well off" and "badly off") of the same pervasive malaise in contemporary Mumbai:

> She [Asha] had by now seen past the obvious truth—that Mumbai was a hive of hope and ambition—to a profitable corollary. Mumbai was a place of festering grievance and ambient envy. Was there a soul in this enriching, unequal city who didn't blame his dissatisfaction on someone else? Wealthy citizens accused the slum-dwellers of making the city filthy and unliveable, even as an oversupply of human capital kept the wages of their maids and chauffeurs low. Slum-dwellers complained about the obstacles the powerful erected to prevent them from sharing in new profit. Everyone, everywhere, complained about their neighbours. But in the twenty-first-century city, fewer people joined up to take their disputes to the streets. As group identities based on caste, ethnicity and religion gradually attenuated, anger and hope were being privatized, like so much else in Mumbai. This development increased the demand for canny mediators—human shock absorbers for the colliding, narrowly construed interests of one of the world's largest cities.[28]

But eloquent and gripping though her book is, even these, like the ones I myself mentioned earlier, are the most obvious and hackneyed symptoms. This is a subject on which social and moral psychology needs to keep a constantly alert eye for the changing (and more diverse and subtle) forms in which alienation surfaces in the behavior of groups and individuals in contemporary forms of unequal societies where, as Boo says above, traditional "group identities" that might have once provided a given framework of life for avoiding the malaise, have become "attenuated" and "privatized." A fascinating recent work by Macalaster Bell, for instance, argues that *contempt* can be a valuable and efficacious counter-emotion to adopt by those who have been made worse off by corrosive forms of disrespect shown to them in conditions of inequality.[29] The case she makes for contempt along these lines is, for the most part, powerful and unusual, despite how deeply it goes against both Kantian moral and liberal political ideas and attitudes. If it fails as an argument, it is only because the fact of having to adopt something like contempt as a form of moral defense and moral counter to inequalities of this kind *is itself a symptom of the malaise of alienation* that pervades the society where such inequalities exist. I say her argument "fails" with deliberate hesitation. Perhaps Bell would and could adhere to her views and claim to do so with justification, even as she concedes that the necessity of these counter-emotions that she has justified are symptoms of the pervasive malaise of alienation in such a society. If that is so, it would be just the sort of interesting moral-psychological phenomenology that I think the subject of social forms of alienation need to be descriptively embedded in.

Where does all this leave us with how to think of the slogan's ideal of an unalienated life? The answer is by now obvious. That is to say it turns, obviously, on negating what we have identified. To put it in a word, what the ideal expresses is precisely the kind or form of mentality in which this kind or form of malaise that afflicts both the well off (giving the lie to their being in fact well off in any but the most shallow sense) and the worse off is *absent*. Here too there is much more to be said by way of elaboration of this aspect of the unalienated life that I cannot do in an essay that is already too long and which I must bring to a close.

What Gandhi and Marx shared was a concern with alienation in the two basic forms described by (1) and (2) and I have tried to convey at a more general and underlying philosophical level than theirs what must lie behind their visions of a life without these two forms of alienation. An achievement of these visions—of our subjectivity being in responsive sync with the normative demands of nature's value properties and of a society that lives with the understanding that all fail to be well off if anyone is not well off—would, I believe, be quite impossible to conceive without also conceiving as achieved some of the basic liberties and forms of equality that we have come to regard as essential. But it would do so without generating any internal tension between them. For liberties now are liberties that cannot be elaborated in ways that lead to basic inequalities (in the way that the liberties tied to incentivized talent and to privatized property do) since they have been reconfigured in a framework quite different from the Enlightenment's framework for them. In the new framework, the social effects of those specific liberties, understood in the ways that they were elaborated in the earlier framework, would be a major source of the malaise that I identified above as alienation because they would fall afoul of both ideals that I presented in my two encapsulated slogans.

A word of caution. It would be wrong to think that these two aspects of an unalienated life are entirely or even notionally separate, the one having to do with our relations with nature, the other with the more social relations between one another. That would be to quite fail to see the *integrations* that Gandhi sought when he presented four seemingly miscellaneous transformations as, au fond, one transformation.[30] There is a great tendency in us to ghettoize questions of nature as purely ecological questions, independent of the deepest social and economic issues that confront us. (It partly explains why those who for decades showed callous indifference to global injustice and global poverty have now suddenly become greatly preoccupied with global warming.) And there is a converse tendency to think that human beings and their social relations are laden with value considerations but nature itself is something that contains no value properties and is exhaustively studied by the sciences. This is the modern form of superstition that I was earlier inveighing against. Both tendencies, in their *opposite* ways, are symptoms of the shallowness in the orthodox Enlightenment that Gandhi and Marx sought to transcend in their radical critiques of different aspects of modernity. I have said a great deal about Gandhi in presenting this refusal of a separation of our alienation from nature with the more social forms of our alienation, so let me repeat in full a precisely apt quotation from Marx that sums up *his* relevance to the integrated diagnosis of these two alienations that I have been trying to present in this essay: "The abstract enmity between sense and spirit is necessary so long as the human feeling for nature, the human sense of nature, and, therefore, also the natural sense of man, are not yet produced by man's own labor."[31] The aptness of these words as a conclusion of this essay's argument can be put summarily in philosophical terms. If the isolated subject of Kantian epistemology was eventually to be redescribed by Hegel as a creature of modern social alienation, my point has been that Marx developed that notion of alienation in the specific terms of the conditions of labor in a capitalist society, and this had the effect of *integrating* it with a more underlying or more nuclear form of alienation that lay in human subjectivity's conceptual entrapment in a Humean epistemology of value that generates what Marx, in this passage, calls the "abstract enmity between sense and spirit," echoed in the enmity between nature and value that emerged in a specific stage of history, and is only overcome by repudiating that epistemology in forms of (secular) enchantment of nature that restore what he, in this passage, calls "the human sense of nature" and "the natural sense of man."

What this essay has actually provided in its analysis is relatively limited. It has presented in some detail the ways in which an ideal of the unalienated life is made distant by the developments of a central stand of modernity in which there have been very specific political and economic effects and accompaniments of a certain increasing outlook of detachment. And it has given encapsulated and sloganized conceptual formulations of what it is to reduce that distance. Liberty and equality, I have said, are necessary conditions for the reduction of that distance, but to see the point of "equality" and "liberty" as in the service of such a reduction amounts to a substantial change in the meanings of these terms, for it is to have recontextualized them in a different theoretical framework where they do not any longer have a self-standing centrality. What I have not done and could not possibly do in an essay already of inordinate length is to say in any detail what the contours of the new meanings are. That cannot really be done unless one first also presents a less encapsulated sense of what the ideal of an unalienated life is than I have done. The two slogans I stated, which jointly give one a sense of that ideal, are little more than slogans because all I have been able to do is to give them negative formulations. The unalienated life is first the negation of the effects of a certain detachment of outlook that has deracinated value properties from the world and, second, the overcoming of a certain pervasive malaise that affects those who are both badly off and well off. To say in *more positive* terms what the ideal is would, of course, require us to show the ways in which the unalienated life, when it is made possible by reconfigured notions of liberty and equality, is *itself* reconfigured to be something entirely different from the unalienated forms of life that are often said to have been present in times prior to the onset of the alienation (genealogically analyzed in this essay) that is peculiar to modernity. This point is vital since the shifting conceptual dialectic between these three key notions (liberty, equality, and the unalienated life) reflects historical changes and, therefore, is in part an historical dialectic.

Though, as I said, I cannot possibly spell these things out much beyond the slogans and negative formulations I have offered so far, a rough sense of this dialectic within which any *further* spelling out would have to be pursued, can be roughly conveyed. The sense of *belonging* that was made possible by the social frameworks of a period prior to modernity was, as is well known and widely acknowledged, highly limited by the oppressive defects of those social frameworks. (To say "feudal" to describe these societies would be merely to use a *vastly* summarizing category that we have all been brought up on.) It is precisely those defects that the sloganized ideals of the Enlightenment, Liberty and Equality, were intended as *directly* addressing. And I have argued that since the methodological and theoretical framework within which those two concepts were then developed made it impossible to so much as conceive how they could be jointly implemented, we should no longer see them as something to be *directly* approached, but rather as indirectly approached by the direct construction of something quite else, the ideal of an unalienated life, thereby theoretically transforming the concepts of liberty and equality. Now if the achievement of an ideal of an unalienated life were to bring, in its wake, *indirectly,* conditions of liberty and equality (however transformed), it is bound to be very different from the unalienated life which is acknowledged to have existed in prior times because the conditions in which it existed then were also acknowledged to be acutely *lacking* in, precisely, liberty and equality. Thus, given this rudimentary conceptual/historical dialectic, what we need to show is how a new framework that breaks out of the dialectic would solve for *three* things at once—a transformed notion of liberty and equality, as I have said from the outset, but also it would now seem a transformed notion of the unalienated life. So this is to be conceived as a holistically triangular transformation—we overcome a certain historical and conceptual dialectic and in doing so together and at once transform all three concepts that feature in the dialectic.

If this is the highly ambitious theoretical challenge to have emerged from our dialectic, how might we begin to think of this triangulated bootstrapping transformation of the notions of liberty and equality *and* the ideal of an unalienated life in concert, all at once? The complexity of the dialectic within which this ambitious task emerges suggests a very general further question to be asked. We have to ask, first, if the defects of the lack of liberty and equality of an earlier time are deemed unacceptable in our own, what can be retained of the general idea of social "belonging" of that earlier time in any revision of the idea of an unalienated life for our own time? This question, put just that way, seems more simple than it is since we know from the labors of this essay's analysis that the attempts to directly overcome those defects were marred by the fact that liberty and equality flowered in conception within a social framework in which deep forms of, precisely, alienation and non-belonging developed, and these in turn were of a piece with the theoretical and methodological developments that generated a highly *individualized* notion of liberty that attached to property, labor, and talent in the ways that made for liberty's conceptual incoherence with equality.

So, a concerted and triangulated transformation of all three notions would have to find its hook, its initial roots, in *individual* liberty being conceived of in *collective* or non-individualistic terms. If liberty is self-governance, the power to make the decisions that shape the material and spiritual aspects of our lives, then what is needed to transform the notion of liberty is for each individual to approach these decisions not primarily with her own interests in mind but the interests of everyone in society. The last few words of that last sentence express something utterly familiar, a cliché, a piety. The critique of self-interest has long been with us. If there is going to be novelty in the pursuit, then, it is only because it is to be essentially connected to the first part of the sentence—for it is far less well known and hardly at all theoretically developed that what such a critique of self-interest amounts to is the construction of a notion of *liberty*. Why is that little known and developed? I repeat: Because individual self-governance (i.e., liberty) has for so long been viewed in individualist terms. What is it to have a non-individualistic conception of individual self-governance? It is not group or collective self-governance but rather something like this.

The world, both the natural and the social world, I had said earlier makes normative demands on us as individuals. That has been central through the entire long passage of this essay's argument. And to be unalienated, I have also said, is for our agency to be in responsive sync with these demands. To perceive these demands from the 'world' (capaciously conceived in both natural and social terms) *for what they are,* our own orientation to the world, as we perceive them, has to be to something that goes beyond the orientation in which individual interests are primary (consider—a physical analogy that should be extrapolated to the social—how, one driving a car, one orients oneself to the road not from the point of view of *one's own body* but from the point of view of the *car*). That orientation, even though it may involve the mentality of individuals, since it requires individuals to exercise *liberty* from the point of view of a more *collective orientation* to the world, i.e., from the point of view of the interests and concerns of all, is bound to *internally* cohere with equality in its outcomes. Equality would, thus, not be seen as something *extra,* but as an outcome likely to be *built-into* the deliverances of the exercise of liberty, when the exercise of *individual* liberty is the exercise of a mentality in this sort of unalienated *non*-individualistic responsiveness to the "world" free of the effects of a detached outlook on that "world" which this essay has tried to genealogically diagnose.

I need hardly repeat that these last closing remarks are the most elementary gestures in the direction of what it takes to pursue the tasks that emerge from the dialectic that this essay has set up. That will be painfully obvious to any reader. But I hope something of the *significance* of what might be achieved if we pursued those tasks along this direction comes through from the detailed elaboration of this background dialectic derived from Gandhi and Marx, in which I have situated them.

The Political Possibilities of the
Long Romantic Period

1.

The assertion of a long period of any movement or tradition is an act of interpretative resistance. What does it resist? Dichotomies, of course, such as, say, Romantic and Classical, and the tidy periodizations they generate. This much is obvious. But beyond the obvious, when it comes to Romanticism, the assertion of a longer than standardly periodized span is not merely an *act* of resistance of this familiar kind—it is, in one sense, an attempt to *describe* a form of resistance.

If Harold Bloom had his way, the long Romantic period would begin with the Gnostics and it would be found in nothing less than an implicit and loosely defined Gnosticism that is recurrently glimpsed—in both canon and periphery—through the literary ages of the West, down to Melville at least.[1] It is never far from the surface of this sweep of his visionary readings that they are intended to describe the trajectory of a resistance. How could they fail to do that? That is, how could the syncretic practices and the strange and fascinating metaphysical doctrines that were so pervasive till they were stamped out by an increasingly orthodox Christianity recur so often in the visions of writers and thinkers for twenty hundred years and fail to be viewed as an abiding, if ineffectual, form of resistance. I don't want to particularly dwell on the Gnostic tradition, nor on Bloom. I begin with him only to mention how a long period can be conceived and also to express a frustration that nothing in this great length, which he presents with such originality and panoramic ambition, is then integrated by him into the metaphysical and political themes that it suggests. So if, for instance, one were to even so much as just ask for a diagnosis of its sustained and repeated defeat at the hands of orthodoxy and even if one were to make a (too) simple initial stab at answering with the thought that those who are better organized, as orthodoxy always is, are always bound to win and that some outlooks and doctrines—exemplified in this version of the long Romantic tradition—are *by the very nature of their metaphysical and political commitments* bound to fall short on the relevant forms of organization, we are already on the path to the kind of integration of themes I just mentioned. But whether by will or by temperament, Bloom has withheld himself from integrations of this kind and we must look elsewhere for the political possibilities of Romanticism than in its most influential theorist.

By contrast, Isaiah Berlin very self-consciously brought a deliberate mix of Romantic metaphysical and political ideas to the attention of English-speaking philosophers;[2] yet (by a second contrast with Bloom) he has no conception of a periodization that is longer than a starting point roughly in Rousseau and going then to the German Romantic tradition from its Jena origins to the flowering of German Idealism. The reason for this focus is quite simply that the fascination he has for these thinkers is in equal parts accompanied by the *anxieties* they create in him and his liberal political commitments. This explains not only the lack of interest in a longer period; it explains too his studied indifference to the English counterpart in Romanticism which, we must suppose, did not prompt in him the same anxieties. So, for instance, we must suppose that Shelley's political radicalism no doubt seemed to him to be something that could be domesticated within his own cherished liberal ideals, which were capacious enough to accommodate Shelley's atheism, his egalitarianism, his feminism, and his commitment to the early stirrings of what would later come to be called Irish Home rule. In Berlin's mind this was a politics that was innocent of the underlying metaphysical ideas of History and of Consciousness or of the Dionysian instinct erected into a source of ideals of nationalist unity; it was innocent, that is, of the claims of what he called "positive liberty" that led to vanguardist slogans such as "forcing people to be free." But he never stopped to notice the deep and close and extraordinarily detailed links between German metaphysics and English Romanticism that are so superbly revealed and traversed in M. H. Abrams's *Natural Supernaturalism.*[3]

On the other hand, Abrams's tour de force is what it is partly because it almost entirely lacks the political dimension that prompts Berlin's interests in the subject. It has about three pages on Marx on alienation and a section called the "Politics of Vision," a phrase borrowed from Mark Schorer's book on Blake, but the section is mostly on what is meant by vision, hardly at all about politics. Part of what gives the book its fierce and illuminating focus is the *conspicuousness* of this absence, by which I mean this: Abrams's conviction of the detailed importance of German metaphysics to English Romanticism leads him, as I will try to show, to the verge of all the right questions of its broader political significance, but it *rests* on that verge without drawing any explicit inferences at all.

Though missing in Abrams, Berlin's is not the only major philosophical treatment that is explicitly political. His general form of political nervousness about Romanticism is actually more interestingly present and much better motivated than it is in a cold warrior like Berlin himself, or in Horkheimer and Adorno, whose philosophical critiques of modern bourgeois society deployed a whole range of concepts that originated in Romanticism's instinctive as well as considered reactions to the orthodox Enlightenment, concepts such as "disenchantment" and "alienation"—yet without any open, detailed acknowledgement on their part of these origins and affinities.[4] This is understandable for obvious reasons. Romanticism in the tradition they inherited at *their* intellectual location was tainted as having been an inspirational source for a whole history of German nationalism that culminated in the events that overtook Europe in the 30s and 40s of the last century. That culmination was the context in which they were writing and it induced in them and other German thinkers an entirely excusable neurosis about the original setting of their own critical categories and so these Romanticist influences were bound to remain unnamed. Thus whereas the political significance of Romanticism produced in Berlin the jitters that led him to describe it

as a "Counter"-Enlightenment, it provided a rich source for Horkheimer
and Adorno's thoroughly *internal* critique of (the more orthodox lega-
cies of) the Enlightenment, with a jitters only about *naming* their source,
and thereby refusing to acknowledge that their own critique was in fact
evidence for a long period of Romanticism's political significance reaching all the way down to the mid-twentieth century.

We have then an intellectual history of a subject (Romanticism) that
has several elements which, though each is in varying degrees acknowledged by the most interesting theorists in the field, they all remain, in
these theorists' hands, as elements more miscellaneous and less *integrated* than they might be. The elements are a distinctive metaphysics summarized in phrases such as "natural supernaturalism"; a moral
psychology that borders on and derives from such a metaphysics and
which is intended to construct some alternative to the cultural detritus
and the psychological desolation that it describes with such terms as
"disenchantment" and "alienation"; a conviction in its political significance and its critical powers of resistance to orthodoxy of one form or
other; a specific reading given to this significance where the resistance
amounts to what is sometimes described, whether rightly or wrongly, as
a "*Counter*-Enlightenment"; and, finally, the scope for a highly elastic
periodization. With this assembly of selective themes from a well-known
intellectual history in place, I must step away and ask: What might a *philosopher* (I am declaring my disciplinary location) contribute to the task
of integrating these seemingly miscellaneous elements?

2.

It should go without saying that the decisions an intellectual historian
makes about periodization depend not just on knowledge but also on
interests. Bloom's emancipatory method was to free one from the assumption that the resistances Romanticism made possible were necessarily to
Classical form and constraint. If the most underlying interest is to find
in the Romantic world-view ideas and attitudes that drive the resistance
to orthodox Christianity, a sea of clichés about the nineteenth century's
reactions to the Augustan age are made to subside, and we are landed

with Bloom's wide swath going back to the Gnostics, the most capacious periodization I know in the study of Romanticism.

Now I say *"going back"* and that expression is intended to suggest a point of some methodological import. The idea that interests are necessarily shaping choices may give the impression of complete stipulative freedom in periodization, but the fact is that, even within this acknowledgement of abundant choice, we are, to use Edward Said's term, constrained by the idea of "beginnings."[5] Let me develop this idea along lines entirely different from Said's, though inspired by his insight that beginnings are not merely generative; they are also a constraint on choice and freedom.

It is a familiar point that much of the modern period is characterized by teleological narratives: of progress, of cumulative development, of convergence, and so on. These progressive ideals have come under much criticism in recent decades for reasons that are equally familiar to us. But I don't particularly want to focus on their rightness or wrongness, only on something general about the sequences of periodization that they reveal. Narratives of progress often define their ideal in terms of the *end* toward which one dialectically moves or aspires: the Prussian state in Hegel (of course he put it in more abstract terms than my rude reduction), communism in another even more familiar story, and nothing less than Truth itself, in Charles Sanders Peirce. The more orthodox Liberal Enlightenment did not define its ideal of progress upon a nameable end, in a way that Hegel, Marx, and Peirce did, but there is no doubt that its progressive commitments are governed by ideals of rationality, which we may achieve in our lives and thought in varying degrees of approximation and in the achievement of which we may improve ourselves or be made to improve by pedagogical projects, large and small ("Liberal Empire" is a large such project and remains so to this day).

My own methodological instinct about these teleological forms of understanding is that, however the narrative is supposed to end, the *sequence* that leads to that end cannot have its *beginnings* at the very inception of social time. To assume that we have been converging and progressing toward some ideal end from the beginning of thought and culture itself is to empty the very idea of progress of its substance and denude it of its interest. One assumes rather that there were many false starts, endless false leads followed without fruitful direction, but then at some crucial point we were set on a path, which we think of as the *right* path, and from then on, there is an accumulation and convergence of history or value or cognitive content toward some recognizable ideal or end. It is this idea of a *right starting point* that gives the idea of progress substance and bite.

Let me quickly illustrate what I have in mind with an interesting philosophical claim made by Hilary Putnam about what we can infer from genuinely cumulative and convergent progress. Putnam has argued that science, alone among cognitive enterprises, has the following property. It builds on past results and thus progresses cumulatively. Hence, Putnam concludes, if it converges by such accumulation upon a certain set of conclusions, we can infer that whatever entities those conclusions posit (electrons, say, or quarks) really exist. Thus what philosophers call "realism" about the theoretical entities posited by science can be inferred from the cumulative and convergent nature of progress in science. We could not infer the reality—the existence—of the theoretical entities posited by other forms of cognitive inquiry which do not possess this property of progressive, cumulative convergence. Science alone *progresses* because it alone builds on past results and that is a sign that it is in the business of tracking what is really there rather than in the business of merely imaginative and instrumental theoretical construction that satisfies us in other ways than the discovery of reality. I am not now interested in whether Putnam's premise about the uniquely progressive nature of scientific inquiry is true. Let's, for the sake of discussion, grant that it is true. What I want to ask is: When in this narrative of progressive scientific inquiry does the narrative begin? Have we been converging (by cumulatively building on past results) on the conclusions we now hold since the beginning of scientific inquiry? Surely not. Putnam would be the first to say that there were several false leads and starts for centuries, and it is only sometime in the seventeenth century that we were set on a path that is the *right* path and from then on we have been accumulating knowledge in a progressive way down that path. But if that is so, it is not obvious that the realism that Putnam seeks in his conclusion is required to be inferred from the idea of convergence via accumulation. It could be inferred by saying that if we can say what it is that makes the *beginning* of the narrative the *right* path, the notion of *rightness* there will by itself deliver his conclusion about realism. If we can say what makes it the right path at that beginning stage of the inquiry, we would already have the realism established there, and there is no need to infer the realism from the subsequent cumulative convergence.

This is just an example of the point I was making earlier which, in every notion of progress toward an ideal or ideals, puts great weight on the notion of a substantial conception of *beginnings,* one that it is worth one's while to unearth with a genealogy that may well reveal more about the ideals in question than is revealed by fully articulated conceptions of the idealized end. If that is right, then the intellectual historian's genealogical task of unearthing beginnings is just as important as the philosopher's task of formulating the normative end. (It is well known, of course, that in Nietzsche's conception of philosophy these tasks were not separable.) If you want a slogan for the point and constraint I've just presented via the notion of "beginnings" as constraint, it might be: no teleology without genealogy.

3.

The idea of a *natural* supernaturalism is at least *prima facie* intended to seem paradoxical. And presumably like many paradoxes—at any rate, the ones that we can solve or resolve—they are generated by an ambiguity and resolved by disambiguation. How exactly shall we disambiguate the term "natural" in Abrams's eponymous phrase?

What makes the book so philosophically interesting is that though it mostly focuses on a two-fold ambiguity, that is to say, on two different distinctions between the natural and the supernatural, it really all but explicitly articulates a third much more modern distinction on behalf of that metaphysics. I will want to make something of this third possibility.

The first of the two contrasts between natural and supernatural in that book is just the idea of natural as it stands in contrast with religious or sacral conceptions. But just so as to acknowledge the *distinctiveness* of the frequently pantheistic metaphysics in Romantic literature and thought, a second distinction is assumed by Abrams between the immanent or phenomenal or perceptible on the one hand and the transcendent as going beyond the perceptible (in Kant's philosophy, this domain that reached beyond the "perceptible" or what gets called, in translations of Kant, the "phenomenal," was specifically described as the "noumenal" realm). The important point is that these two distinctions do not coincide. By that I mean, the two distinctions are not co-extensive, they are not denotationally equivalent. It is obvious enough that they are not co-intensive or connotationally equivalent. That is, it is obvious by even a glance at a dictionary or even one's more informal intuitions about linguistic meaning that the term "religious" does not mean "transcendent" and that "immanence" or "perceptibility" do not *by meaning* convey anything non-religious. But it may have *turned out,* contingently as it were, rather than by definition, that these terms coincide in their denotations and that something that is religious (say, God himself) cannot be an instance of something immanent and perceptible. But that is precisely what pantheism denies since it is the sacral *as immanent.*

Abrams comes close to formulating a *third* and much more modern distinction between naturalism and supernaturalism, which is the distinction between the idea of the natural *as what the natural sciences study* and the supernatural as what falls *outside of the coverage of the natural sciences.* This third distinction does not coincide with either of the other two and because that is so, it opens up a *further* possibility, just as introducing the second distinction that failed to coincide with the first permitted possibilities of identifying, as something distinctive, a sacralized nature. What distinctive thing does this third distinction permit? Abrams's book is thick with poetic examples of what it permits and it is at the heart of its argument to say that they exemplify the idea, perhaps the most central idea in Romantic metaphysics, that not only the words on our pages and on our lips and not only the images on our canvases, but objects and things in the world, including in nature, are filled with properties of value and meaning. Abrams desists from explicitly formulating the third criterion by which such an idea and its many specific examples are permitted. And I have formulated the criterion in my own terms so as to raise the genealogical questions I want to raise about the revealing beginnings of Romanticism—revealing, that is, of its detectably specific form of political significance.

That nature and the world around us should have properties of value and meaning is by no means a new idea. It is in fact perhaps as old as the very idea of nature and of the world we inhabit. But it is religious discourse of one kind or another, including pagan religious discourse, that provided the idiom in which such an idea was understood. However, because this third distinction does not coincide with the first distinction, these properties of value and meaning that fall outside of the coverage of science can inhere in what is immanent and perceptible without being elaborated in anything but *secular* terms. And if the terms of their description are not sacral or religious terms at all, but are purely secular, a question is raised about what it is that makes them significantly different from the *other* non-sacralized properties of nature to which we have become so accustomed for some centuries now since the onset of modern science. It is to capture *this* differential that the third criterion for a distinction is formulated. What makes these properties distinct, even controversial, is that they, for some centuries, certainly ever since the middle or late seventeenth century, fall afoul of a common notion that there is nothing in nature, nothing natural therefore, that is not countenanced by natural science. Nature contains all sorts of properties that natural science studies. The point is that value and meaning are wholly unlike those properties. Value and meaning as properties are precisely what are *not* countenanced by natural science. Science has nothing to say about them. If so these properties are supernatural, by this third criterion. But being immanent and perceptible they are perfectly natural by the terms of the second distinction. That is why "*natural* supernaturalism" is one prima facie startling but perfectly accurate description of them. And once we disambiguate the terms "natural" and "supernatural" by these three distinct criteria, there is nothing startling either.

I have said that values and meanings as inhering in the world, including nature, are made possible by the second criterion of the natural as that which is immanent and perceptible. And I have also said that though in an earlier time value and meaning as properties of the world would have necessarily been elaborated in some form of religious or sacral terms, in much romantic poetry and thought, though not by any means all, that is simply not so and Abrams's readings and expositions display that at length. So these properties can be natural by the *first* criterion of the

natural as well. If so, why is the third criterion of the natural needed at
all? And in a crucial move in my sorting out of these ambiguities, I said,
it is needed because we have since the rise of modern science, which is
well before the canonical Romantic poetry was produced, thought that
nature contained properties so radically unlike the properties of value
and meaning that it would be a form of insouciance to think that there
was *nothing* controversial whatever about saying that they may sit side
by side with these other properties. It is to the extent that we actually do
find it controversial that we are motivated to formulate the third criterion
of what to count as natural, by the lights of which value and meaning are
not properties of nature. And if many have for some considerable time
now found it unacceptably controversial, it is because of this pervasive
metaphysical outlook of scientific modernity that even preceded Romanticism in its canonical period, even so early a figure as Blake, whose passionate outcry against Newton was an avowedly *Romantic* reaction to
that outlook.

What is this outlook's appeal that it should have become as pervasive
as it has? One way of seeing its appeal is to ask what it would be like to
assume that the outlook is quite simply wrong. If it were quite straightforwardly wrong, we would have to say that there is nothing even prima
facie problematic about where exactly value and meaning are found in
the world, including nature. In other words, it is quite unproblematic to
say, for instance, that at the very place in the Colorado River that there
is H_2O, there is also value and meaning. At the very place that there are
caloric counts with a certain number assigned to them, there is a human
need. At the very place there is a meteorological perturbation, there is
a threat, and something like *threats* are—*unproblematically,* remember,
because we are really trying on this view—properties of *nature*. They
are out there in nature, right where the meteorological phenomenon is.
At the *very* place, we are saying? *Just* there? Not somewhere else. Not
in our own minds and in our feelings of vulnerability which we then
project onto the world? Well, and if it *is* at the very place out there, do we
see the Colorado River as containing H_2O and see it as having meaning
and value *in the very same* act of seeing. Can we possibly see both these
things in the same act? Or is there a defection somehow to another act
when we see it as one or the other?

These are all questions which seem to many to be so philosophically intractable that it seems much easier to say the following instead: "No, values and meanings are not perceptible properties of the natural world. They are really products of our mental capacities and dispositions, what philosophers such as Hume and Adam Smith call 'desires' and 'moral sentiments,' which by an act of our own mental projection we then attribute to the perceptible world." So to call something out there, in the visible distance on the horizon, a *threat* is not to describe something out there that no natural science could possibly study. There is nothing out there that is not countenanced by natural science. Thus to call it a "threat" is only to project something—constructed from our own feelings of vulnerability—onto the world. How can threats exist outside us just like, and on a par with, meteorological phenomena? Meteorological phenomena are there, *anyway,* whether we apprehend them or not, but threats wouldn't be threats if they were not threats *for us*—they are not there anyway, so are not really independent of us; they are projections of our own mentalities and psychologies.

And so we are now off and running with the outlook that Blake decried, where there is nothing in nature that is not studied by natural science, no enchantment, however secular and non-sacral, in the world. At best *we* are enchanted with our mentalities and our imagination; the rest of nature is brute and valueless, only metaphorically spoken of by us as enchanted in a sustained and comprehensive fit of projective vocabulary of threats and other such evaluatively loaded terms. Hence there is more than one kind of supernaturalism, not just the one about God, whether transcendent or immanent, but one about value too. We, apparently, then, don't just suffer from a "God Delusion," we suffer from a Value Delusion as well. The latter needs exorcism just as much as the former. And Hume is the most formidable proponent of this picture of value, though its beginnings are earlier, and it is to that genealogy that I now turn.[6]

Before I do, let me just say that Kant, though he was deeply opposed to Hume, in a curious way is hobbled by some of Hume's assumptions. He did not accept Hume's positive ideas about value, which viewed value as essentially reducible to our mental dispositions—our desires, or when more geared to (and reared in) the social, our sympathy and moral sentiments. He famously repudiated this psychologistic picture but, having done so, he also found no place for values within the realm of perceptible phenomena. They were not part of the phenomenal world that we take in with our senses and our understanding, since the phenomenal world for Kant was exhaustively characterized as containing only the properties that were allowed it by Newtonian science. Values, thus, were distinguishable only as the deliverances of the exercises of a *"pure practical will"* that was noumenally distanced in its metaphysical status from both our empirical subjectivity and the phenomenal world that it inhabits.

This, then, sets up a new desideratum for we now need to answer a question about how the noumenal was *given* to us. The valiant struggles over the sublime in his third, most ambitious, if not the most profound of his volumes of *Critiques* should not be treated as a late deconstruction of his earlier writing as they sometimes are.[7] They are responses to this desideratum set up by the earlier critiques which, having asserted a noumenal realm, had then to face the question about how elements of the noumenal were even so much as glimpsed by us in our experience; how were they given to us? This would have to be a question that arises, not just about infinity and the great dynamical forces that Kant discusses in his elaboration of "the sublime," but our much more everyday freedom or agency and its relations to value.

The sublime may seem a last and excessive resort for something so quotidian and ubiquitous as agency and value, but Kant having relegated them to the noumenal, left us with nothing less than the sublime and his ideas of a "productive imagination" that generates our grasp on the sublime to meet this desideratum. However, Romantic theory, in Abrams's hands as I read him through my disambiguations of the term "natural," is not required to accept the sublime as the only resort we have for the availability of value in our experience. Unlike Kant, Abrams insists on applying to value what I called the second criterion of the natural as *immanent,* an option that Kant precisely denies himself by relegating value to the noumenal rather than the phenomenal world. So though Abrams writes well of the Romantic sublime when it comes to subjects such as infinity, he is also able to find in much of Romanticism a far more pervasive *natural* supernaturalism in the availability of value and meaning in the everyday, perceptible world around us. It is just that now, given that availability of values in nature, we cannot think of natural sciences as having full coverage of nature; and that is why I explicitly articulated the third criterion of the natural on his behalf.

If contemporary interpretations of Aristotle, such as John McDowell's, are right, this excessive reach for the sublime is quite unnecessary to understand the nature of value, which needs no relegation to the noumenal since, as Aristotle (in McDowell's reading), claimed, value is everywhere present in the perceptible world around us, including nature.[8] McDowell may be right about Aristotle, but the interesting question is: If value was conceived as available to our ordinary perceptions of the world around us in so abidingly influential a world-view such as Aristotle's which so dominated centuries of mediaeval Western thought, why in the hands of the Romantics, Blake say, does it come off as an act of *resistance* to take this view of nature and the world. It is here I think that the genealogy of the modern in a Newtonianism, to use Blake's term, becomes pressing.[9] It is this *new beginnings* that Blake is protesting and that many of the later Romantics too, as Abrams presents them, are dissenting from. And it is in this genealogy that I want to unearth one aspect of the political possibilities in Romanticism. If I am right about this, it will turn out that the idea of the long Romantic period will precede even Blake's passionate outcry by some decades and will reach all the way down not only to Horkheimer and Adorno but even more distant figures like Gandhi.[10]

4.

I had promised to make some integrations of seemingly miscellaneous themes that surfaced in the intellectual history of Romanticism. Here are a series of questions toward that task. To understand the nature of Romantic resistance we have to ask: What is the metaphysical doctrine that Romanticism, expounded in such convincing detail by Abrams as committed to a natural *supernaturalism,* supposed to repudiate? And to see not just the metaphysical but also the political nature of this resistance, we have to ask what worldly forces made it important to undertake this metaphysical resistance. And to find the long periodization for this

Romantic resistance, we have to look at the genealogical *beginnings* of both the resistance and the outlook (and the worldly forces that were mobilizing it) that was being resisted.

The metaphysical outlook that Romantic natural supernaturalism was resisting was just the metaphysical outlook I have been expounding in Humean terms. Let us call it "naturalism *simpliciter,*" naturalism with no supernatural element of any sort, not even one formulated with the most scrupulous secularity as Abrams does by allowing for the application of his first criterion of the natural. This is a naturalism that excludes not merely transcendent and sacral properties; it excludes all properties not countenanced by natural science. What is the genealogy of such an outlook, one which not only overturned a once highly influential Aristotelian world-view as McDowell interprets it, but a world-view that was widely prevalent outside the scholastic cloisters, in the neo-Platonism of popular cultures all over Europe, including the radical sects in England that Christopher Hill describes with such excitement in that remarkable work *The World Turned Upside Down*?[11]

Blake was very shrewd to place the name of Newton at the "beginnings" of such a Humean naturalism. This is so despite the fact that Newton came a little later than such figures as Bacon and Hartlib (not to mention Descartes and Galileo, since I am focusing primarily on England), who had already declared nature to be bereft of any properties that were unconquerable by the methods of science. Both had in fact declared something that had integrated political economy with this metaphysics, claiming that, as a result of stripping nature of such properties, it could now be stripped without qualm for extraction and gain as well, since it lacked any sacral constraints on such extraction.[12] But the reason to make Newtonianism more central than these earlier figures is that broad ideological remarks of this kind began to amount to something measurably transformative only when—some decades after Bacon—*worldly alliances* were very self-consciously forged between scientific organizations, commercial interests, and the latitudinarian Anglican establishment. Newton and Boyle along with Samuel Clarke, Richard Bentley, and others constructed, through fora such as the Boyle lectures at the Royal Society,[13] an explicit agenda that articulated a systematic carte blanche for extractive economies involving deforestation, mining, and the setting up of plantation agriculture, what we today call "agribusiness." All societies had taken from nature and both mining and the enclosures system set out to do so in a way that is well known and well studied, prior to the late seventeenth century. But the *systematic* adoption of enclosures and these other forms of extraction entrenched itself in this period, when the declaration that one may now take with impunity from nature's bounty was deliberately fortified in these worldly alliances of commercial interests with *scientific bodies* and the Protestant establishment, first in England and the Netherlands and then spreading elsewhere in Europe where, of course, in some countries it included the Catholic establishment as well.

The alliances forged an elite that was by no means restricted to scientific, economic, and religious interests. A whole conception of political governance and of law emerged out of these alliances. As Blake later pointed out, the world was left bereft of properties of meaning and value because, as the Royal Society's Newtonian ideologues insisted, the universe was set and kept in motion by a push from an *external* and providential God, not a God that was immanent in the world, sacralizing it from within and providing for an *inner* source of dynamism responsible for motion. This enforced migration of God consolidated in doctrine a very specific notion of political governance, where the rule over a brute populace by a monarch and his courts and the propertied elites emerging out of these alliances was the mundane counterpart to an external God ruling over a brute universe, bereft of value and meaning except as a source of extraction precisely because of such a providential God's generous endowment of it with fertility. The elite ideal of governance surfaced in very specific institutional forms, all of which were anxiously foretold by the early radical sects, who had in their time, through their myriad polemical and instructional pamphlets, reached out and created a radical rank-and-file population who protested the rise of such monopoly institutions and began to demand a variety of countermeasures, including an elimination of tithes, a leveling of the legal sphere by a decentralizing of the courts and the elimination of feed lawyers, as well as the democratization of medicine by drastically reducing, if not eliminating, the costs of medicine, and disallowing canonical and monopoly status to the College of Physicians. The later scientific dissenters were very clear too that these were the very monopolies and undemocratic practices and institutions which would get entrenched if science, conceived in terms of the Newtonianism of the Royal Society, had its ideological victory. All this was well known to Blake, who as I said, channeled these dissenting opinions against Newtonianism for his own time.

I have fastened on Blake as a highly perceptive commentator on the effects of the metaphysical outlook of Newtonianism in order to identify an early but still *recognizably* Romantic form of resistance to "naturalism simpliciter." But the fact is that Blake was only channeling for his own time the prescient alarm voiced by a remarkable group of scientific dissenters of several decades earlier, about how the Newtonian laws and concepts such as gravity, which they all accepted without any objection whatever, were being dressed up in a metaphysical outlook of "naturalism simpliciter" that was quite uncompulsory for those laws and concepts. In England, figures such as John Toland[14] and Anthony Collins[15] saw through the commercial and political and religious interests and motives that underlay the adoption of this metaphysics and they openly resisted not just the metaphysics but the new forms of politics and political economy around it, arguing explicitly that if the neo-Platonism of the earlier radical sectaries had its way rather than this Newtonian exile of God, God would be present in all things and all persons, would be available, that is, to the visionary temperaments of the most ordinary of men and women, thus democratizing the values of political governance and bringing to it a form of local and egalitarian participatory collectivity to match the collective participation in cultivation of the commons that the sectaries had demanded, indeed sometimes even locally implemented, and which the systematic spread of enclosures was undermining.

If Romantic natural supernaturalism represents both a metaphysical and a political resistance and if the genealogy of the metaphysics and emerging politics and political economy it resisted is rightly identified by Blake in the Newtonianism of the late seventeenth century as I have tried to expound it, then I am claiming that the long Romantic period precedes Blake himself in the person of these earlier scientific dissenters and the even earlier radical sectaries they invoked. It is only by genealogically excavating these beginnings, to invoke my use of the Saidian point I made earlier, that the full power of Abrams's ideas of Romanticism's natural supernaturalism is revealed. We could, of course, say with

Bloom that the beginnings should be located much earlier still, since such a resistance would not have been possible without the prevalent neo-Platonist metaphysical ideas that themselves emerged from a submerged Gnostic ancestry; but since Bloom never invested his Gnostic sympathies with any explicit political significance, that expansive periodization he offers is idle, from the point of view of my commitment to integrating a set of seemingly diverse themes that emerge in the intellectual history of Romanticism. In that sense, as I admitted, periodization is indeed driven by one's own interests. But I hope I have nevertheless conveyed the genuine constraint on choice in one's periodization within these interests that comes from the notion of "beginnings."

5.

It remains for me now to add to the integrations I have attempted so far between metaphysics, politics, and the idea of a long period of Romanticism the elements of the moral psychology generated by the Romantic aspiration to finding alternatives to a malaise of culture and mind that are so often characterized, by Romantic thinkers themselves, in terms of "alienation" and "disenchantment." These terms have consistently informed both politics and metaphysics in this long tradition. If that were not so Althusser would not have been so concerned to separate and ghettoize the early Marx from the late, in one of the most willfully destructive interpretative moves to target radical Romantic thought.

"Disenchantment" is a misleadingly omnibus term. It has been elaborated in at least two different registers and rhetorics: the rhetoric of the "death of God" and the rhetoric of "the decline of magic." The death of God came later, though not as late as Nietzsche's pronouncement, since Hegel had pronounced exactly that earlier. The decline of magic is more interesting because, as Keith Thomas and others have studied it, it came measurably earlier.[16] But it is more interesting for another reason. The death of God speaks to the first two of the three criteria of natural and supernatural that we have disambiguated in Abrams. The decline of magic speaks as well to the third and it speaks to the third in ambivalent terms. Thomas himself, but since then many others, displayed just how much science itself emerged out of magic.[17] What motivated and propelled Newton to so many of his remarkable hypotheses in his private study, as opposed to the public face of Newton presented by the Royal Society and in which he acquiesced, has been shown by scholars such as Rattansi to be thoroughly caught up in alchemical preoccupations and neo-Platonist notions.[18] Yet despite these inspiring motivations in magic for many scientific discoveries, it was inevitable and right that science develop a logic of confirmation, a method of assessment of its hypotheses that would be independent of this wayward illogic of discoveries. When this set in, some effects associated with the decline of magic were salutary—in particular the decline in the belief that magic had something to contribute by way of answers to *science's* questions.

But in the realm of the *metaphysics* of science, the decline of magic had a quite destructive effect, something much more consequential than the death of God. It completely preempted any possibility of the embrace of secularized versions of enchantment continuous with Aristotle's metaphysics of value, as McDowell reads him, or of value as conceived by the popular forms of neo-Platonism that you find, say, in the writings of Gerrard Winstanley and others.[19] In other words, it had the effect not of the death of God, since God flourished in a providential role outside the universe for some time to come, but what Carolyn Merchant has called the "death of *nature.*" Merchant's fine work,[20] particularly fine on the subject of mining economies, however, focuses much more on Bacon than the later Newtonian period that Blake rightly saw as more threatening, for reasons I have already given. It is this death of nature that was developed with the most sophistication in Hume's picture of an external world without any value properties—and it dominates metaphysics to this day. Such a metaphysics, as I said earlier, removed all value to the domain of mentality, to desire in particular, and to the somewhat loftier states of mind that Adam Smith and Hume called "moral sentiments."

What has this "disenchantment" of the world to do with notions of alienation and how has Romanticism tended to seek in the conceptual resources of natural supernaturalism the grounds for overcoming alienation from the world? The routine answers to this question are disappointing, appealing as they do to the zones of comfort that belief in God and the practices of magic provide in the gratification of basic human spiritual urges. I don't doubt that these clichés carry some truth, but they are open targets for the scorn poured by contemporary atheists like Dawkins on the irrationality of religious belief and on the superstition of unscientific, magical thinking.

The source of alienation is in fact much deeper because this metaphysical version of disenchantment and the Humean moral psychology it generates preempts much more than what I have mentioned so far. *It preempts the very possibility of human practical agency;* and what natural supernaturalism provides are the conceptual resources for secular forms of re-enchantment that are the most basic and necessary conditions for the kind of human engagement and agency upon which the unalienated life is eventually founded. This may seem like a tall claim. Why can't the Humean picture claim to have within its resources the enabling conditions for our practical agency? Why should one need a *world* enchanted, at the minimum with secularized conceptions of value, as a condition for human subjectivity and agency? Why can't one say (with just the resources that Hume's moral psychology offers) that agency consists in our acting so as to satisfy our desires and moral sentiments? On that picture, desires and moral sentiments are not *responses* to demands from desirab*ilities* or values in the world that are perceived by a subject. Rather, desires are *self-standing* states and acting on them is to exercise our agency.

In short the challenge is: Why can't human agency be *self*-standing in us; why does one need to say the further thing, as I am saying on behalf of the Romanticism that Abrams presents in his book, that by nothing short of seeing our desires as responses to the value properties *in the world* can we find agency *in us?*

To answer these questions would bring to the political and metaphysical integrations of the long Romantic philosophical tradition the cement of a plausible moral psychology.

How, then, might we answer the questions we have just posed? Is there an *argument* for rejecting a self-standing view? Here is a stab at providing something like an argument. It comes in three steps which require one to make some fundamental distinctions and then build the argument on them. So this will need patient elaboration.

1. Let's begin with a distinction that is sometimes attributed to Spinoza. Take the two statements "I intend that I will . . ." and "I predict

that I will do . . ." There is a radical difference that they mark. If I predict that I will do something, I am viewing myself as an object of causal forces rather than as a subject or agent. By contrast if I intend that I do something, I am viewing myself as a subject or an agent. Unlike as in the latter, in the former, I take a merely detached and observer's rather than an agentive point of view on myself. We do have both these points of view on ourselves, but we cannot have both points of view on ourselves at the same time. If I predict that I will do something, that crowds out the intention that I will do it; equally, if I intend to do something, then that displaces anything predictive that I might be thinking about its doing. The first occurrence of "I" in both statements is the "I" of agency. In the statement "I intend that I will . . . ," the second occurrence of "I" is also the "I" of agency. It is just that the second occurrence of "I" in "I predict that I will . . ." is not the "I" of agency—rather the first personal pronoun refers to an object, something that is viewed in detached terms by myself. So if I predict that I will do something, though I have the minimal form of agency that goes into predicting, my angle on myself is completely detached and I see myself as an object. I cease to be engaged in any practical sense, i.e., such engagement as I have is restricted to the kind of thing that goes into objective study, not action in any more practical sense than that. In predicting what I will do, then, unlike in intending, I have abdicated the point of view of practical agency. The general lesson here is one that I will exploit later, so I will put it down with italicized emphasis: *If I never had anything but a detached point of view on myself, I would not and could not be an agent in the practical sense at all.*

So to sum up: The difference between the two statements, the difference between intention and prediction, really marks a difference between two *points of view,* the point of view of practical engagement or agency on the one hand and a point of view of detachment on the other. These are two radically different points of view *on oneself.* Why? Because it is oneself that one is viewing as either a practical agent ("I intend that *I* will . . .") or, by contrast, something to be studied in a detached way ("I predict that *I* will . . .").

2. Next, one can notice that such a distinction in Spinoza, which, as I said, is a distinction of two points of view on oneself, should carry over

without strain to a distinction of those same two points of view not on oneself, but *on the world*. We can perceive the world in a detached way (natural science being the most regimented and systematic form of such perception of the world) and we can see the world with a less detached and a more practically engaged point of view. Here again, as above, the point is that we are agents both when we do natural science and when we are practically engaged with the world; it is just that when we do natural science we see the *world* merely as an object of detached study, but not when we are practically engaged with the world.

3. Now if the world (and not just oneself, as in Spinoza's initial distinction) can be perceived both from the point of view of detachment and the point of view of practical engagement, a question arises: What would the world have to be like for us to have the point of view of practical engagement with it? In other words what would the world have to contain such that it not only prompts the detached point of view, paradigmatically exercised when we do natural science, but also prompts our practically engaged point of view? The answer to this question obviously is that, over and above containing such properties as natural science studies (H_2O, etc.), it better contain other sorts of properties as well, properties that trigger responses from the point of view of practical engagement, and this suggests that it contains value properties (more simply, values) that make normative demands on us to engage with it in more practical and not merely detached terms.

In these three steps I have presented a distinction sometimes attributed to Spinoza and extended it further so that it seems to lead naturally and logically, by the time we reach the third step, to the view that Abrams's natural supernaturalism took for granted. That the world, including nature, contains properties that go beyond the purview of natural sciences, supernaturalizes nature, though of course since the idea of supernatural here is simply a presupposition of what it takes to have a practically engaged perspective on the world, it makes no mention of the sacred. It is supernatural by the lights of the third criterion by which we distinguish between the natural and the supernatural.

So it seems, then, that a secular enchantment of nature is an intuitive fall-out of a perfectly intuitive distinction between intention and prediction.

But the skeptic, the Humean naturalist *simpliciter,* who refuses all supernaturalism in nature, however secular, will find the conclusion of these three steps quite unconvincing. Even if we grant step (2), the Humean would insist that step (3) is illicit. Step (2) is the step which says we bring a point of view of practical engagement on the world (and not just a point of view of detached study). That is fine, it will be said, but that engagement or agency requires no prompting from value properties in the world itself, as step (3) asserts. Agency, our practical engagement with the world, simply flows from our acting on our desires (and moral sentiments), our states of mind, and it is not necessary to see these states of mind such as desires as being responses to any special sort of normatively demanding properties in the world itself, such as desirabilities or values. To insist on these latter is to insist on a superfluous metaphysics.

It might seem then that these three steps of argument are pointless since the Humean challenge is still with us. But the challenge is with us only because those who pose it fail to see the important relation that holds not only between steps (3) and (2), but between steps (3) and (1). Let me get to this relation with a little more philosophical argument.

In a brilliant passage in a brilliant book called *The Varieties of Reference,*[21] the philosopher Gareth Evans made the following insightful claim. It is an odd fact about the human self's relation to its own beliefs that when one is asked, do you believe something, say, that it is raining, you don't turn your eyeball inwards, as it were, upon your mind to see if you have the belief that it is raining. You just look outside to see if it is raining and respond. In other words, we do the same thing when we are asked, "Do you believe it is raining?" as we do when we are asked, "Is it raining?," i.e., we look *at the world* whether we are asked about the world or whether asked about our minds.

I want to extend Evans's insight, which he articulates with relation to our beliefs, to our desires as well. When someone asks one, "Do you desire x?," are we prompted to ponder our own minds and scan our interiors for whether or not we have that desire or are we prompted to consider whether x is desirable? (An aside: Of course, x's desirability may not always be perceptible to us, if x is not sensibly present to us, but I am assuming that something like perception is basic and that when we try to *imagine* the desirability of x or just even reflect on its desirability,

these are capacities that depend on some background of past perceptions, if not of x itself, then perhaps ingredients of x or things sufficiently
approximating or analogous to x, and so on. This point is quite generally true of imagination, whether of value properties or any other kind of
properties.)

To return to the question, "What does one do when one is asked
whether one desires x?," I think the answer is that though there may be
special sorts of case where we might ponder our own minds (say, when
an analyst asks a patient to introspect on one of his desires, given that his
behavior suggests a desire that he disavows), for most ordinary cases, I
think, we would simply consider x's desirability. This suggests that our
desires are often presented to us as having *desirabilities* in the world as
their objects. It is these desirabilities or value properties in the world that
step (3) insists on.

The Humean, who is skeptical, will still persist: Why am I so confident that Evans's point, made about beliefs, can be extended in this way
to desires? It is to answer this question that the relation between steps (3)
and (1) is absolutely crucial.

Perhaps the best way to answer this question is to look critically at
what would seem to follow, if one thought my extension of Evans's point
to be wrong? If one thought that a question about whether one desires
something never requires one to consider its desir*ability*, but rather to
step back and consider by scanning our minds whether it is desir*ed* by
us, then that would suggest that our desires were presented to us in a
way that was accessible to us only when our angle on ourselves was a
detached one. And here we need to go back to step (1), which was about
the two different points of view, not on the world, but on *ourselves*. If it is
indeed true, as we said in that discussion of step (1), that practical agency
is abdicated when we take a detached point of view on ourselves, then it
would seem that to exercise our practical agency, the appropriate way to
experience our desires *cannot* always be to experience them as desir*ed* by
us. This was the message of the italicized sentence in (1) above.

What alternative way *is* there, then, for our desires being present for
us and experienced by us? And the answer it would seem would have
to be: by perceiving the desirability of what is desired. In short, if our
desires were always experienced by us only as desir*ed*, our very agency

would be in jeopardy; and it would only be restored if we found a way
of saying that our desires are sometimes given to us *not* as desired and
therefore available only to the agency-threatening detached point of view
but rather in the engaged point of view when we are perceiving the desirability of what we desire, where no stepping back is involved. It is only
when we experience them in this latter form that we are in the perspective that carries our practical agency. In other words, when we step back
and register in a detached way that we desire something, that desire cannot induce the agentive aspect of our mentality. The desire just sits there
as the leaden object of our detached gaze. And so the Humean challenge
before us, with its claim that our agency consists in just our possession
and pursuit of self-standing desires, is exposed as hollow because it is
only when our desires are not self-standing but given to us via the desirabilities that are given to us in our perception that desires will prompt in
us the responses of our practical agency.

Thus, in order to be practical agents, we must be able to experience
our desires not merely *directly* as elements located in our own mentality
but also and primarily *indirectly* via the perception of values or desirabilities in the world. When we directly perceive values or desirabilities,
in doing so, we indirectly experience our desires. By contrast, when we
step back and scan our desires as elements of our mentality, we perceive
our desires directly. This direct perception of our desires, however, voids
their motivational power of agency. They are the mere *objects* of a gaze or
detached observation. Only when we directly perceive desirabilities in
the world do our desires (now given to us indirectly in these perceptions)
have the power of motivating our agency because they are not the object
of our detached observation. And what that suggests is that desires and
moral sentiments are not self-standing at all but they are our ways of or
conduits for perceiving the value properties in the external world.

However, all this has an important theoretical outcome. It shows that
we need to be a little careful when we say that value properties and desirabilities in the world, including nature, make a normative demand on us.
It is not as if the value properties which prompt our desires are a source
of normative promptings that are entirely alien to the kind of sensibility
we have in *having* desires. Though they prompt our desires, *it is through*
the desires they prompt that we even so much as see the normative demands

they make on us. The relationship is mutually interdependent. (This is the interdependence that Marx described as the "humanism of nature" and "the naturalness of man.")[22] Being unalienated in our relations to nature turns on this mutual interdependence. A fisherman on the Bangladeshi coast may see on the horizon something that prompts only his detached point of view on it, and from this perspective he might describe it in terms of natural scientific study, a "meteorological" phenomenon and perturbation. But what he sees in the world is not restricted to such phenomena. In the same place where he might see that phenomenon, he might instead see something that is described in *value* terms and which prompts his *practical agency,* something that would get a description that figures nowhere in the vocabulary or the ontology of natural science—"a threat." If in our ontology, nature contains not just meteorological perturbations but *threats,* then natural science does not have full coverage of nature. The mutuality in the dependency relations of our subjectivity and the elements of this ontology are vivid when we notice that the perception by the fisherman of something like a threat *outside* in the world and nature is not something *separate* from a certain subjective and agentive state of mind inside. Thus for instance, when one perceives a threat without, one feels vulnerable within. It is not as if these are two things, a perception of the *world* and then a *psychological* extra, a feeling of vulnerability. To see the threat *is* to feel vulnerable. That is the mutuality of the dependence that Marx described in the terms that I quoted above. That is what it is to be in unalienated sync with nature, to be responsive to its evaluative aspects and normative demands that the Romantic metaphysics of natural supernaturalism posits.

And once we start giving examples that are more subtle and sophisticated, bringing in *moral and political* aspects of the world and nature, these points I have made, which are relatively simple because geared to simple examples having to do with threats in nature and the agentive vulnerabilities they prompt, get much more interesting and significant. Blake had already seen through to these interesting and significant sophisticated levels when he described the moral psychology of a looming alienation that he found in the "Newtonianism" he raged against, an alienation he explicitly described as owing to an emerging collective outlook of detachment that would put much of our public life at a distance from these, our most ordinary sources of agency, an alienation that could only be overcome by allowing the Romantic metaphysics of the sort Abrams elaborates (not just in Blake but in an entire tradition) to provide the resources to repudiate the effects of this emerging collective outlook. Marx's own sophistications, as is well known, turned to examples having to do with the conditions of labor under capitalism to describe far more elaborate forms of detachment—detachment in our relations with goods, with work, with others, and with our own selves, all of which would have to be overcome so as to achieve unalienated relations, something only possible if we overturned the very large effects of the collective outlook that had emerged first in the period of early modernity that we have identified as the relevant genealogical "beginnings."

There are fascinating questions about how this notion of an unalienated subjectivity relates to other Romanticist ideas such as, for instance, the clichés about the romantic glorification of genius and of the subject's untethered, often Promethean, aspiration and reach. The idea of natural supernaturalism and the subject's responsiveness to the normative demands of nature gives the human subject a far more modest profile than these other notions. Far from claiming a subject, untethered and unconstrained in its reach and capacities, natural supernaturalism demands merely that the subject's capacities be sensitive to the normative demands that are made on it by the properties of value and meaning in the world, including nature. If anything it is *constrained* by the world in these ways. The poet who is most aware of and committed to this form of modesty of subjectivity is Wordsworth. It is possible, I think, to argue—though I won't do it here—that if we place natural supernaturalism of this sort as being central to Romantic metaphysics, as Abrams does, then all the more outsize conceptions of subjectivity should be interpreted as conveying something measurably less grandiose than some of the rhetoric might suggest. They should be interpreted as registering the subject's capacities from within its modesty and within the constraints placed upon it by the external callings of meanings and values, to break the rules by which art and culture might seem to be governed. Someone like Wittgenstein, for instance, who turned his back on the rule-bound Platonism of an entire intellectual tradition was a philosopher quite continuous with this Romantic tradition and presented a profound philosophical framework from within which to elaborate such an idea of the creative capacities of a subject, even though his focus was on concepts and language of ordinary speech more than Promethean aspiration in art or collective nationalist expression. On the last, despite the frequent misunderstanding of his views, Herder's thinking was exemplary, as was Humboldt's. In keeping with this low-profile conception of the Romantic human subject, they presented an utterly attractive modesty about how much there is to be gained by *losing* one's identity in the encounters we might have with other cultures and nations, and with luck acquire new ones. None of this is meant to deny that morally disastrous mobilizations of Romantic ideas were made by nationalism in some parts of Europe. It is merely meant to register that there is something reprehensibly crude in conceiving of these mobilizations as *inherently* present in Romanticism, as crude as the tiresome ideological canard about Stalinism *inhering* in Marxist ideas. If I am right, there is no better antidote to these reductive equations than to do what Abrams does: make natural supernaturalism the pivotal focus of a Romantic metaphysics and proceed to draw some of the humane and radical political possibilities from it, as I have been trying to do in these essays in the section on Enchantment and the first essay in the section reflecting on Saidian themes.

6.

The political significance that I have sought via these arguments and integrations, and via the genealogical efforts of this essay, is of a politics of a long Romanticism that is quite at odds with Berlin's. It is evidently and avowedly a *radical* politics, from its beginnings in the English radical sects through the English scientific freethinkers and dissenters, and I won't rehearse the entire roll call of intervening figures in the canonical Romantic tradition, through Marx (uncontaminated by the spurious distinction between his "early" and late writings) to Horkheimer and Adorno and even, as I've argued elsewhere, to Gandhi. That it should be so different a construction from Berlin's is, of course, just a symptom of the fact that one's periodizations are conceived from the point of view of one's interests. None of this should occasion any surprise or concern. Even so, my own construction, for all its differences from his, is fashioned pretty much from the same repertory of Romantic ideas and thematic clusters that Berlin presents. By filtering those ideas and themes through the lens of Abrams's ideal of a natural supernaturalism and giving that ideal a very specific semantic as well as genealogical analysis, I have presented something that could not possibly—without bending the terms involved—be described as a *Counter*-Enlightenment. True, it finesses, sometimes even implicitly opposes, many of the cherished commitments of the more orthodox Liberal strand of the Enlightenment from Locke through Hume and Adam Smith and Kant to Berlin himself, but if that is so, one would have thought that the more apt label is not "*Counter*-Enlightenment" but the quite different one now in occasional currency, "*Radical* Enlightenment." If intellectual history is right to suggest that there was a Radical Enlightenment, the arguments I have given should be viewed as an attempt to provide *philosophical* support—from within the long Romantic tradition—for that intellectual history.

The term "radical" in the expression "Radical Enlightenment" would mean precious little, or perhaps I should say it would mean something merely precious, if a certain kind of objection that is of some currency and, in my experience, of some insistence, is not addressed.

There is the nagging and widespread qualm that the (long) Romanticist excavation of the sources of the radical in this essay is an exercise in genealogical nostalgia. From the point of view of this qualm, even though the length of the Romantic period that the essay charts comes all the way down to figures of the recent past such as Gandhi and Horkheimer and Adorno, that fact in itself can't be sufficient to claim the radicalism's relevance to modernity. It cannot absolve it of the charge of nostalgia. After all Gandhi, it will be said, was famously critical of the West precisely for generating the modernity he desperately wished India not to embrace. As for Horkheimer and Adorno, did I not myself say that they were silent about the Romanticist sources of their critique of bourgeois society? And doesn't that make them far less relevant in their critiques of bourgeois society than their successors in Frankfurt (Habermas, for instance) who, having recognized the decreasing relevance of their Romanticist categories (disenchantment, alienation, and so on) have fashioned a quite different form of radical politics that is based on a doctrine of "social democracy" that puts constraints on bourgeois societies and capitalist economies in the form of welfare and safety nets for the worse off rather than dig deeper and further back to forms of enchantment articulated in what I have called the Radical Enlightenment. The vision of a Radical Enlightenment (from Winstanley down to the so-called "early" Marx, Ruskin, Morris, Thoreau, Horkheimer, Adorno, Gandhi, etc.) which may have had its possibilities for politics in a past time, now seems merely nostalgic today because those possibilities were never realized, and there is no other vision that a radical politics can articulate any longer but that of seeking "social democratic" constraints on irreversibly entrenched bourgeois political and economic structures.

Before I begin to address this line of objection, I can't resist saying that, in the face of such frequent sneering about nostalgia, I almost always feel an intense irritation because it is most often to be found on the lips and pens of complacent people. Such people need to be reminded that the most creative efforts of the Renaissance were very likely dismissed, by similarly frequent sneering on the part of mediaeval scholastics, as a nostalgia for a bygone classical age. The fact is that the complacence from which this qualm is expressed is actually often not innocent. What people choose to be complacent about and what they therefore choose to be dismissive (as nostalgic) about is rather selective and the selectivity is driven by ideological considerations. Charges of nostalgia are a cousin of a phenomenon we might call the "It's too late . . ." phenomenon. If something is too late to reverse, it is nostalgic to wish to reverse it. "It's too late to return to 1967 borders; there have been far too many settlements over the last decades" is just one among any number of complacencies regarding present conditions that one can cite. But notice that no one here was likely to say through the Cold War: "It's too late; the Soviet Union is here to stay and in a large part of the world, private capital is simply a thing of the past. It would be nostalgic to aspire to return to it." Thus qualms about nostalgia, of what is and isn't too late, are made not only from a point of view of complacence, but also from ideological points of view, with deliberate selectivity. Even so, I want to take the qualms seriously and address them because they have sometimes been spoken to me by people for whom I have a high respect and whose temperament is not complacent and whose motivations are not, I suspect not even unconsciously, ideological. And above all, I want to address them because I think it is quite simply *wrong* to think that the radicalism of the long Romantic period that I have presented is nostalgic.

To address this kind of qualm, I want first of all try to remove a possible misunderstanding of the argument and conclusions I have tried to present so far. The objection makes it seem that what I have done is to present early dissenting voices of the (long) Romantic past and to find relevant for today their anxieties, which, in their time, early modernity, were *anticipatory* of developments that they *predicted* would be harmful. And, in turn, this makes it natural to think: Now that those developments are deeply entrenched in our outlooks and our societies, to recall those anxieties today cannot retain the particular significance that they had in their time because these outlooks and the structures and institutions they have spawned are not reversible by us. So it will be said: *We* are *not* anticipating and predicting these effects anymore; we are *amidst* them, coping with them, and such coping cannot have realistic aspirations of *reversal* of these tendencies, but must seek other more sober forms of containment and constraint as have been formulated by social democratic ideals.

There is something that is right in this. The point of the argument was never simply to appeal to the early dissenters' anxieties with a view to merely restoring either the outlook or the material scenario prior to the transformations that first got started in early modernity. The use of words like *"reversal"* in this context can be careless in the presuppositions it makes. Thus, for instance, faced with *dis*enchantment of the sort that the entire dissenting tradition I have expounded was analyzing, one may think that the point of attending to this tradition of dissent, as I have done, is to suggest the idea of some sort of *"re*-enchantment." I actually have no objection to being interpreted as making this suggestion, so long as it is understood that re-enchantment today cannot possibly be to the revival of an enchantment that was provided only by notions of a sacralized nature, among other things. That is partly at least why I have tried to present the notion of disenchantment itself along lines that don't *in particular* turn on the loss of sacralized notions but rather in more general terms of the evacuation of value properties in one's conception of the world (including nature) we inhabit.

Talk of "reversal" suggests a) that there is a *comprehensive* and *global* entrenchment today of developments that the early dissenters were anxiously predicting and wanting to avoid for their time and b) that, as a result of this entrenchment, there is nothing in our subjectivity that is not pervaded by the outlooks that were generated first in that early modern period and which gave rise to the dissenters' anxieties.

Both these presuppositions are quite unjustified. I will start by responding to (b) since it is the more fundamental misunderstanding of the argument and its intention, and it takes more patient argument to repudiate it.

Having fastened on the period since early modernity in Europe (following to some extent Weber's own focus with the term "disenchantment" on that time and place as significant), I had said that a set of conceptual transformations in that period removed from our collective and public mentality a conception of the world (including nature) we inhabit as containing value properties. This, I argued, gave rise to (at any rate, was accompanied by) a certain detachment of outlook that, in turn, had large effects (at any rate, was accompanied by large effects) on society, political governance, and political economy. That was the more secularized gloss on disenchantment that I was presenting, a secularized counterpart to Weber's rhetoric of disenchantment as desacralization.

Now my intention in saying this was *not* to deny that ordinary people everywhere still see the world, including nature, as making *normative* demands on them, something that would not be possible if they did not also possess a perceptual phenomenology of *value* in their apprehensions of the world and if the world did not contain perceptible value properties in the way that Abrams's Romantic natural supernaturalists insist on. Indeed, I have argued in explicit detail that we would not even possess the kind of human practical agency we do if the world did not contain value properties to which our agency responded. Thus, I could not possibly be denying that we do, in our everyday agency, in fact perceive the world to be shot through with value properties, that is to say, to be enchanted in the low-profile sense that requires no sacralization.

But if this is so, a question arises: What then was the intention in giving the particular genealogy of "*dis*enchantment" that I did, if I am also insisting that our capacity for practical agency to this day requires that there is this form of enchantment?

Much turns on answering this question adequately. Here, then, is a way to think of it.

In order to make sense of these large disenchanting transformations I presented, even as we retain (and necessarily retain) our quotidian responsive relations to a world suffused with value properties, we need to begin by drawing a distinction between two levels.

The conceptual transformation by which nature came to be conceived as natural resources (along with the other accompanying transformations I mentioned) is one that occurs at a level of *collective, public* understanding, a form of understanding generated by alliances made between powerful forces in society that control governance, political economy, and a slowly emerging and increasingly consciously determined public opinion on these large collective and public matters. It is at this level that policy gets shaped and implemented and though that happens on sites distant from quotidian life, many ordinary people often acquiesce, sometimes even enthusiastically, in these transformative outlooks and policies.

By contrast, there is a level of understanding in these very same people that is and remains *quotidian* in its responses to the world (including nature and human others), often instinctive, but often cultivated too, though cultivated in the habits of *local* forms of solidarity and concern rather than via the inculcation of the wider public, collective understanding I mentioned in the last paragraph, and often implicitly and mostly unknowingly, at odds with the latter.

We should enter some obvious qualifications here. Though the general contrast and distinctness of these two levels is, as I will try to convey, striking and highly significant, there is no reason to think they are not also often scrambled. So, for instance, it is often the case that there are areas of concern and sympathy shown at the more collective level, but these are formulated in terms that are part of the conceptual vocabulary of the detached outlook that these transformations have wrought—and when pursued at this public level they will surface in various forms of poverty measures, of safety nets for the worse off (broadly welfare and social democratic policy) as well as constraints on pollution of nature via taxes on polluters or the enforcing of "cap and trade" agreements, etc. Conversely, there is also no doubt sometimes vicious inhumanity that surfaces in the local lives of ordinary people in their instinctive individual everyday responses to one another as well as individual disregard for one's environment. But acknowledging all these qualifiers does not spoil the general point that there have been a set of transformations at the public and collective level, which I have presented via the critique offered by a long Romantic tradition, transformations which are not necessarily echoed in the everyday and local, communal lives of individual responses to nature and to others.

With the distinction between these two levels in place, I want to now invoke a notion familiar to psychologists under the name "the frame problem."[23] The really important point here is that we need not just a distinction between the collective level, on the one hand, and the individual (local) level, on the other, but also, as a result of that distinction we need to register the following: *Individual* mentality finds itself in *two quite different frames.* On the one hand there is the frame of quotidian life, where responses are shaped by one's instincts and locally, communally developed habits, even in metropoles though obviously there the localities and networks within which the responses are reared will be quite distinct. On the other hand, the individual human mind, unless it has very deliberately and self-consciously resisted it, has also surrendered itself to a different, more collective frame which is dominated by the ideas and ideologies that have had such a longstanding run since they took hold in the period that I have identified genealogically. And *because it is in two separate frames, these two ways of thinking are insulated from each other and individual subjectivity cannot see the many inconsistencies that may exist between judgments and responses that it makes in the two different frames.* One may show great concern and regard for others and for one's environment in one's everyday individual responses and not see that as broadly inconsistent with the support one gives to outlooks and policies in the other frame within which one thinks and acts.

The idea of such differential framing no doubt has existed throughout history. So it is not as if the *distinction* between two frames emerged only in early modernity. What occurred in early modernity is a significant transformation of *one* frame, a significant transformation of individual mentality as it is shaped by the *public and collective level* of thought, a transformation away from the public and collective outlooks of an earlier period, which were no doubt bad in their own different ways—something that we should acknowledge explicitly even as we delineate, as I have tried to do in this essay, the *distinct* ways in which the collective framework that emerged in early modern Europe was bad. And I am making this point about two frames so as to make clear that there may be a great deal of *continuity* in human mentality in one frame (the frame in which the individual subject makes quotidian responses to the world) even as there are large transformations in the other frame. So when one is critical today of the outlook and its effects that have developed at the public and collective level, one need *not* be doing so nostalgically from the beliefs and convictions of an *earlier collective* outlook that has been superseded by the transformations at the collective level, but rather by the lights available in one's *current quotidian* frame of ordinary individual responses to each other and to the natural environment around us.

Even if the foregoing analysis has said something very briefly to address the charge that the radicalism of the long Romantic period is an exercise in nostalgia, the question remains about whether this apparatus of differential frames allows us to say anything plausible against the related objection that the only feasible radicalism that is possible today is not what I have presented via my long Romanticist genealogy but, at best, a series of social democratic constraints to be placed on the economic and political structures of capitalist modernity. I believe the apparatus does have something persuasive to say about this question as well.

The focus of a humane and radical politics in our time should seek not merely to put constraints, salutary though these constraints might be, on the harmful outcomes of the collective framework we have embraced in the last two or three centuries, but rather also seek to *remove* for us *the boundary between* what I have called *the two frames* within which our subjectivity engages, making it one single and unified frame. To the extent that this is possible,[24] it may also become possible for one to see the inconsistencies in one's thinking (inconsistencies that were not visible to one while the two frames were in place) and resolve them in a specific direction—by finding, as I have already suggested, in the resources of one's thinking in the more quotidian frame, the possibilities for criticizing in a more fundamental and radical way the outlooks developed at the collective level that have shaped our thinking when one's mind thinks within the other frame. Why do I say that the resources in this more quotidian frame might well make for a more fundamental and radical criticism and politics? Because, as I have pointed out a little earlier, it is in this frame that our minds have not been contaminated by the public, collective transformations that I, following the radicalism of the long Romantic tradition, have been so critical of. It is in this frame, as I said earlier, that we still possess the sensitivity and responsiveness to the enchantment of the world, to the value properties in the world, including nature, that make the deepest normative demands on us.

So the idea really is this: A politics that is more radical than the social democratic ideal of putting constraints on the runaway effects of our collective outlook and frame must *first* seek to remove the boundary between the collective and the quotidian frames of individual human mentality. If the boundary and the dual frames remain then such radical politics as we can configure remain limited to the conceptual resources available in the collective and public framework and those, as I said, will be ameliorations conceived in the relatively limited terms of the constraints that come from social democracy. It is when the conceptual resources (available in the more deep-going ideal of an enchanted conception of nature and the ideals of an unalienated agency that it makes possible) which are to be found in our more quotidian frame are brought to bear critically on the collective frame that the most creative possibilities of a radical politics that is much more *fundamentally* critical of the collective frame can emerge.

The objections about nostalgia that I am responding to are important (and insistent) enough that I will risk tiring the reader's patience and repeating in summary the argument against them which appeals to the "frame" idea. The boundary between the two frames is what keeps the two frames in place and prevents us from seeing the inconsistency of the judgments and responses we make at the collective and the quotidian levels. Being in two frames, they are insulated from each other and we cannot detect the inconsistencies between them. But if a politics first brings to our consciousness that we have been locked in two frames and succeeds in removing that boundary and allowing our subjectivity to function in a single, unified frame, it would have, in doing so, brought to our consciousness the inconsistency in our responses and judgments that we were hitherto unaware of. If this happens, there is, as I said, a serious chance that we will be able to remove these inconsistencies in a certain direction, seeing in the resources of the quotidian frame the possibilities of radical criticism of the thinking that takes place (and has taken place for some three centuries) in the collective frame. And moreover, if this happens, the criticism will *not* be from the *collective* outlook of some *bygone* period available only in nostalgic fantasies but from the resources within the quotidian frame of our mind *in one's own time.* And moreover, once we recognize the inconsistencies between judgments and responses we make as a result of removing the boundary that keeps the frames in place, some elements in the collective outlook we have acquiesced in may seem to be *fundamentally and radically* wrong by the lights of our own quotidian thinking today, showing thereby that we are not only not harking back nostalgically to some *previous* collective outlook but also that we are not restricted to the critical resources of the *collective* outlook in our own time that have been domesticated by the very transformations they aim to criticize, reducing all criticism to merely placing constraints on those transformations.

Now, of course, it is perfectly possible that *some* of these lights or critical resources to be found in the more *quotidian* of our two frames of the present will *coincide* (or cohere) with *some* elements of the *public and collective* frame of the past. That cannot be grounds for indicting us with nostalgia since these would, given their presence in the everyday responses of ordinary people today, be merely the critical resources we find ourselves with in the *present* to fundamentally resist (rather than merely contain with thought of safety nets and other marginal constraints) what collective assumptions and public policy impose on us. If what were available to us in our everyday responses to the world today did not *at all* coincide, *even in part* with any of the ideas in the collective framework of the past, there would be no possibility for what is called "tradition" to inhere in pockets and interstices of our mentality and help with criticizing our present collective understandings, with a view to forging newer and more creative developments of collective thought. This, it seems to me, is to conceive the modern as a tyranny, where one asserts not merely that one is within modernity, which is hardly deniable, but that we must be completely domesticated by it into a complacence that allows no dialectic between tradition and modernity to emerge in a way that gives rise to critical resources for one against the other, in *both* directions. It is this insistence that *all* criticism that is not to be dismissed as nostalgic will only be *of* tradition *by* modernity that I am calling a complacence in the dominant outlook of the present. Such a complacence in past times would have prevented or preempted the very changes that are often described, and described with pride, as "the Renaissance," which presumably emerged precisely via a dialectic in which elements of the collective frame of a past Classical period inhered as aspects of "tradition" in the responsiveness of individual quotidian agency and talent to the normative demands of the world, to resist some of the collective understanding of the mediaeval period.

What I must admit, of course, is that it is perfectly possible that once the boundary between the two frames I have identified is removed and inconsistencies in one's thinking are revealed, the deliberations by which the inconsistencies are then resolved might have the opposite effect from the one I am holding out the possibility for—it may have the effect of bringing our individual responses more in line with the large transformations we have wrought and which Gandhi, Horkheimer, Adorno, and their entire trajectory of Romanticist antecedents were lamenting. There is no reason to think that there is any inevitability in it happening in one direction or other. But that still does not mean that it is not a worthy goal of a radical politics to seek these possibilities of deliberation and to hold out for a possibility that we will find, in the instincts and concerns that get their play in our individual responsiveness to the normative demands of others and of the environment, critical resources that make us see through the harms of having acquiesced in outlooks that have been formulated at the more collective and public level. As I said, these resources may well be the basis for a more radical politics than one that merely seeks ameliorations of the sort that social democracy does, worthwhile as these latter might be in their own limited terms; and the idea that there is no form of radical politics that is not simply what social democracy offers is a dogma conjured up by a too quick tendency to convict everyone who seeks such a more radical resistance of nostalgia.

What such a radical politics would look like and what it would seek is too large a subject to pursue here. (As I have suggested in another essay in this volume, to theorize it in fuller terms one would have to reorient the relations between a range of notions such as alienation, liberty, and equality, and link Gandhi's and other Romanticist ideas to those of Marx and a range of other dissenting voices in the early modern West that I have briefly presented here.) All I wanted to do in these closing remarks about the effects of there being two frames is to begin to provide a rudimentary conceptual framework and analysis by which it doesn't seem compulsory for us to think that in finding a radical politics today to be of a piece with dissenting voices in early modern Europe, one is merely indulging in an exercise in nostalgic genealogy.

Let me close then with a brief response to (a), the first presupposition which encourages the thought that my genealogy of the long Romantic tradition restricts its relevance to an earlier time now superseded by late modernity. This is the presupposition that the outlooks whose emergence in the early modern period was alarming to the dissenters in Europe in that period are by now too *comprehensively* entrenched and so the radical resistance to them offered by the ideas of the long Romantic period I have been expounding is a nostalgic aspiration to reverse a fait accompli.

The question "Is the reach of those outlooks, the reach of this sort of modernity that this genealogy critically analyzed, now really comprehensive?" is, of course, an empirical question. But in assessing the evidence to answer it, one has to use one's judgment about what is so entrenched as to be beyond resistance, what it means for outlooks and the material conditions that they spawn to affect the *entire* globe's mentalities and economies. Some of this judgment that is needed may have to fight the tendency to think that what holds of Europe and North America today holds for the rest of the world tomorrow—a familiar struggle for those who have resisted and are resisting the intellectual assumptions of a past and present imperialism.

Let me only consider the question in the light of the theme of nature and our unalienated relations with it that I have drawn from my extension of Abrams's idea of "natural supernaturalism."

Consider the fact that the broad idea of what I have presented as an unalienated relation to nature (even if in secular rather than sacralized terms) is echoed in detail in the indigenous societies of many parts of the Southern world today, from Latin America to Australia, who assume without strain that nature has "rights" that have to be honored and respected. Though "rights" was not initially their vernacular idiom for it, it is now working its way into the language of the legal systems of societies like Bolivia and Ecuador with powerful indigenous actors in the leadership. These are not remote or idle metaphysical principles that reflect out-of-date outlooks; they have had direct policy implications like leaving oil in the ground in Ecuador and ending the mining of uranium in Australia. These are present enough today as alternatives for us to be able to say without any strain of nostalgia that instead of ridiculing it, other so-called "advanced" and advancing societies who have glibly claimed the comprehensiveness of their own world-view should take this sensibility seriously and should try to embrace some of it themselves, if they are not to be doomed and drag everyone else to their doom as well. Bolivia takes the lead in this campaign in the global South and is known to have dismissed the posturing in the Copenhagen meeting on the environment a few years ago on the grounds that the naked capital-driven policies of the more powerful governments were insincerely tinkering with the problems rather than asking fundamental questions about the relations between capitalism and the destruction of the environment. To generate alternative fora for policy-making, the Bolivian president, Evo Morales, organized a meeting not just of governments and their mandarins but a massive "summit" with voices from well over a hundred countries and with almost 40,000 people in attendance, voices from below demanding a variety of detailed anti-pollution measures and a systematic legal right, not restricted to regions but possessed of universal status, a right given to the planet's natural properties that would prevent their further transformation into natural resources. Bolivia is only the leader in all this. It speaks for what is assumed to be right by similar indigenous communities *all over the globe.*

And there is much *theoretical* consolidation of these practical and political efforts in the work, for example, of the Economics Nobel prize-winner Elinor Olstrom and others, who have shown how water, pastures, forests, fish stocks, were they left in the control of users rather than in the control of capital and states which serve the predatory intent of capital, would have the effect of seriously combating the repeated appeal to the notion of the "tragedy of the commons" to give the impression of the inevitability of the outlook that the long Romantic tradition is inveighing against. These voices of traditional societies may lose in the end but I think it is fair to say that they are more vociferous and more organized now than they have been for a very long time and that is surely a sign that the reach of that outlook is not comprehensive.

No doubt the possibilities of resistance to the outlook that these efforts and policies offer are still local and regional, and they may well remain so for quite some time to come. But nothing in the relevance of the long Romantic tradition that I am offering asserts that resistance and reversal could either come by a global revolution or overnight. Patience and accumulated effort in such a resistance should be in the service of a *bricolage* of reversal, and from these angles in which the partial light of reversal comes into view in some places, there is wisdom to be learned for other places in the rest of the world, whose complacence is precisely what this wisdom refuses to adopt. In the success of these more regional efforts there are exemplary sources for growing the resistance, and they owe conceptually and philosophically to local ideals of enchantment, often secular versions of enchantment, that deserve to this day to be described as the legacy of a long Romanticism viewed as the "Radical Enlightenment."

Identity

SEVEN

What Is a Muslim?

Fundamental Commitment and Cultural Identity

1.

In recent years, the concept of identity has had its corset removed and hangs loosely and precariously in the domain of culture and politics. This is largely a result of a gradual realization in theoretical work in these subjects that local contexts of study determine our individuation of cultural phenomena quite variously, and that it is much too tidy and distorting to demand, or proceed as if there were, stricter criteria for their identification. The point cannot be dismissed as some arcane, post-modern development in the theory of culture. It accurately captures the experience of individuals and communities. I recall that some years ago in India, almost to my surprise, I heard the words "I am a Muslim" on my lips. It is not just to meet a theoretical demand that I had better specify the context. I was looking for paying-guest accommodation in a neighborhood with a predominantly lower-middle-class Hindu population, hostile to Muslims. A landlord who was interviewing me asked me what my religion was. It seemed hardly to matter that I found Islamic theological doctrine wholly non-credible, that I had grown up in a home dominated by the views of an irreligious father, and that I had then for some years adopted the customary aggressive secular stance of those with communist leanings. It still seemed the only self-respecting thing to say in that context. It was clear to me that I was, without strain or artificiality, a Muslim for about *five minutes*.[1] That is how negotiable the concept of identity can be.

Lying behind and consolidating the contextualization of "identity" is a somewhat more abstract point. Quine had argued that the concept of identity occupies the minds of theorists only in the primitive stages of inquiry.[2] In this phase one is prone to anxiety over one's lack of exact criteria of identity of given phenomena, anxieties which are often released in strict stipulations or in taxonomical theorizing, which one then sheds as investigations become more theoretically sophisticated. Quine was concerned primarily with the phenomena and concepts studied by natural science, but the point, it seems to me, is no less valid for questions such as "What is a Muslim?," "What is an Indian?," and so on. As inquiry advances, the absence of strict criteria need no longer be seen as a sign of one's confusion. It is justified by the fact that the concept in question ("Muslimness," "Indianness," as it might be, or "electron," "the unconscious," and so on) is to be understood as having a place in a more or less systematic theory, with its own particular role in the inferences and transformations that the theory sanctions. This point is not the same as the point about the local and contextual nature of these concepts, but it allows one to embrace their locality with some methodological right. If, after all, these concepts depend on their place in a network of theory, then shifts in theory due to cultural difference or historical change will shift the inferential place and role of the concepts without any anxieties about losing our hold over them.

One might think that these methodological observations should have made us realize that our obsession with questions such as "What is a Muslim?" is irrational and, as with all neuroses, that that realization should by itself be the basis of cure. But things have not been that simple and more work needs to be done to properly diagnose the persistence not merely of an intellectual yearning which such questions reveal, but also the social and cultural phenomena which these questions are undoubtedly tracking. One needs to explain our interest in these questions, not merely dismiss them. And in any case, the best among those who have ushered in the localizing revolution would be the first to say, "Context is only the beginning of wisdom." It does not sweep conceptual problems away nor does it herald the end of theory; it merely removes the rigidities and reifications of a longstanding theoretical tradition.[3]

2.

The context of my own interest in the question of Islamic identity is shaped by a prior political interest in the possibilities for change within the social life of Islam, changes which—whether they are articulated *de jure* as "reform" or not, and they certainly need not be—can properly be described in terms of a shift toward a *de facto* secularity.[4]

The distinction I have just registered between de facto and de jure secularity is intended partly to echo an acknowledgement of a distinction in our understanding of religion, between practices, on the one hand, and a doctrinal and legal discourse, on the other. It is a perfectly general distinction (that is, not one specifically about Islam) and it is pervasive in the contrast between how people live and how they speak. If you a put a microphone to someone's lips in Teheran or Cairo or Bradford (indeed do so in Nebraska or Kansas) and ask, "Do you believe in the dictates of the sharia?" (or "Do you believe that the world was created in six days a few thousand years ago?"), you may well get an affirmative answer. But if you look at the extent to which the sharia (or creationist doctrine) plays a role in the person's life, it may amount to nothing much at all, possibly not much more than just the disposition to affirm in this way when asked, thereby showing the affirmations to be not much more than performatives indicating the desire to be *counted* as devout in ways that have little to do with the legal (and doctrinal) commitments that are being affirmed. If this is right, the deliverances of inquiries based on polls and other such methods of investigation may massively exaggerate the absence of secularity among religious groups. So my interest, then, is to inquire into the possibilities of increasing movement toward such secularity where it does not exist and, if in these pages, I deploy the idiom of *"reform"* (of "internal transformation") to describe such a movement, it is not necessarily intended to convey a shift away from *explicit doctrinal articulations* but rather to probe and monitor the possibilities of internal changes *in the practices* of the social and personal lives of devout people, which may, as I said, be at considerable variance from what they explicitly articulate. "*De facto* secularity" is a good term with which to describe it.

The possibilities of a movement toward greater secularity of this kind within Islam would depend on the extent to which Muslims will consider the details of their practical identification with Islam as negotiable, in the face of other values that they also cherish. There may be some for whom Islam is nothing short of a monolithic commitment, overriding all other commitments, whenever history or personal encounter poses a conflict. But I think it is safe to say, despite a familiar tradition of colonial and post-colonial caricature in Western representations of Islam, that such an *absolutist* project is the exception in a highly diverse and internally conflicted religious community. For the most part, there is no reason to doubt that Muslims, even devout Muslims, will and do take their commitment to Islam not only as one among other values, but also as something which is itself differentiated internally into a number of, in principle, negotiable detailed commitments. If so, there is a pressing question that arises for anybody who comes to this subject with the motivating interest that I have declared. What are the difficulties that recent absolutist assertions or reassertions of Islamic identity pose for the prospect of transformation in Islamic social and legal *practices?* Like most questions about the determinants of culture, this question can also be posed from the opposite direction: To what extent is the relative absence of such transformations among ordinary[5] Muslims responsible for the susceptibility of Islamic polities to constant threat from powerful minority movements which would have it that Islamic identity is, for the most part, non-negotiable?[6]

The complexity of this pair of questions does not lie merely in the conflict between a minority of Islamic absolutists[7] (or "fundamentalists" as they are sometimes misleadingly called) and the far larger class of ordinary Muslims who oppose their vision of an anti-secular polity based on Islamic personal and public law. There is widespread today a more interesting conflict *within* the hearts of ordinary Muslims themselves, a conflict made the more excruciating because it is not always explicitly acknowledged by them. This is the tension generated by their opposition to Islamic absolutism on the one hand and, on the other, their faith in a religion that is defined upon detailed practical commitments with regard to the polity, commitments which Islamic absolutists constantly invoke to their own advantage.[8] But this requires a capacity to criticize one or other detail or even central features of one's practices. It therefore requires a careful scrutiny—in part philosophical—of what the specific demands and consequences of one's particular practices are in specific historical or personal circumstances.

There is a tradition of political and moral thought which might be thought to finesse these detailed tasks because it assumes that philosophical truth is on the side of the secular and the liberal ideal, and that a full grasp of the objectivity of this ideal will itself provide the basis for a deep and destructive philosophical critique of absolutism. From this point of view, and to put it more crudely than it deserves, philosophical argument by itself will give one the right to describe the conflict within ordinary Muslims as a conflict between moral truth and falsity.[9]

I have not yet come across the philosophical argument which would support this claim, and so will proceed on the assumption that liberal and secular values have no purely philosophical justification which puts them outside the arena of essentially contested substantive moral and political values. They happen to be my values and my commitments but I will not pretend that philosophical ethics affords them a more objective status than the values of those who reject them or other values that I myself espouse.

This position is, to some extent, a specific application of Bernard Williams's critique of some of the more ambitious claims of traditional "Ethical Theory."[10] The targets of Williams's argument are philosophical theories (e.g., Utilitarianism, Kantian theories) which offer principles that stand outside a man or woman's fundamental projects and commitments (such as Islam, say, or even more immediate commitments to one's family, lovers, close friends, deep and driving intellectual or artistic interests, and so on), principles whose justification depends on considerations that make no specific reference to those commitments, principles which would in fact, when called upon, be the basis for assessing and adjudicating between those commitments. Though I will not argue for it here, I believe that Williams is right in concluding that, on inspection, such principles are simply unavailable.

However, there is a tendency, present in Williams's own writing (and much more so in the writings of the existentialists who, I believe, are his unacknowledged philosophical antecedents in this critique of Ethical Theory) to conclude that what this leaves us with is a moral life filled with fundamental commitments, and no particular space to stand on from which they can be subject to our own moral criticism. Criticism requires a theoretical position outside the arena of these commitments, and that is exactly what the critique of Ethical Theory has removed. Thus when these fundamental commitments conflict, there is little scope for anything but moral "tragedy," something that apparently ancient Greek playwrights understood better than ancient Greek philosophers or philosophers since. For those who have graduated from contempt and fear of the Islamic world to an alienated despair about it, this offers a cheap theoretical confirmation of their mood. Thus, in a curious way, in Williams's picture, identity remains non-negotiable; it's just that now a number of different non-negotiable identities stand in (possibly) tragic conflict with one another.

But the picture is not compulsory, even if one accepts his skepticism about Ethical Theory.

Many have found the very idea of a "fundamental commitment" or fundamental project (an idea and phrase that goes back to Kierkegaard) obscure. They would have us simply think of them as values, adding perhaps that they are "thick" values, if that helps to bring out the particularistic nature of these commitments. (Not justice or goodness which are "thin," but a whole variety of less abstract values ranging from properties of character such as kindness, sympathy, and loyalty to commitments that people might have such as to religion or theatre, say.)[11] To them there seems nothing distinctive about fundamental commitments over and above thinking of them as one among many others in this range of specific values.

But that is not my complaint against Williams in this discussion of Islamic identity. There very likely *is* something distinctive about a devout person's commitment to Islam, over and above its particularity. Though he never spells out explicitly and in detail what he has in mind by fundamental commitments, Williams says enough for us to infer that they lead up to the existentialist idea (and even perhaps ideal) of authenticity.

And it is this connection between a person's fundamental commitments and the idea of the authentic self that explains the persistence of questions about identity (questions such as "What is a Muslim?") despite an acknowledgement of the radical negotiability of the concept of identity.

A way to expound this theoretical connection is to look to the sorts of effects brought upon a person by his or her abandoning—or the prospect of abandoning—such commitments. I once shared a flat with a close friend, who was an appallingly successful drug-dealer. He had made far more money than I thought was decent, and it was money made on the steady destruction of people's lives, some of whom were talented, even brilliant minds in the university. One day, while he was out, the police arrived at the door and asked me if I had any suspicion that he was a dealer. They said that they did not have sufficient evidence to produce a warrant and search the place, but they were morally certain that he was guilty, and all they needed was for his roommate to express the slightest suspicion. That would give them enough to legally search his premises. I had long quarreled intensely with my friend about his cynical profiteering from drugs and had come to find him utterly reprehensible in this respect. But faced with the question from the police, I found myself turning them away.

Conflicts of this kind are not by any means unusual, nor is the sort of decision that I made. The right description to put on my decision, in the context of the present discussion, is that I could not abandon the fundamental commitment to friendship, even in the face of thorough and deep moral pressure from within my own moral values.

Here one finds oneself saying that what this amounts to is that I placed the value friendship over the sorts of values that made me disapprove of his drug-dealing; and there is nothing false about saying it. But I suggest that it is not *all* that it amounts to.

The suggestion is not that one could never give up a fundamental commitment. That is not what is "fundamental" about it. One can imagine oneself allowing the police in, even if one had a fundamental commitment to one's close friends. What makes the difference is the kind of effect that the relinquishing of a commitment would have upon one. I think it would be fair to say that for many people, in such a conflict, their betrayal of friendship would amount, in their own self-conception, to something of a different order of wrong (though not necessarily moral wrong, certainly not wrong from the point of view of utilitarian principles) than a betrayal of the values which take profiteering from destructive drugs to be reprehensible. It is notoriously hard to describe why there is a different order that is at stake in the comparison rather than merely a difference in degree. But one thing to say is that if I had betrayed my friend, I would have felt a deep and *integrated* destruction of my self which is missing from the more ordinary, though undoubtedly genuine and severe, bad feelings induced in me by my having failed to act on those other values. It is not merely that I would have had *more* such bad feelings or *worse* feelings. It is rather that I would have felt (as many people in my place would have felt) that I had lost something much more defining of what held my self-conception together. The existentialists described the source of this integrity of the self as "authenticity," an obscure term no doubt, but examples like this help to convey what they intended.[12] The idea is delicate and difficult but it is not incoherent nor irredeemably obscure.

So it is not the very idea of fundamental commitment that I am balking at in Williams. On the contrary, even Muslims with no absolutist aspirations may well have such a fundamental commitment to their religion, and I think it is important to acknowledge this, or else one might make things much too easy for oneself in the effort to think of a way out of one's state of conflict. It is partly because the commitment to Islam has this deeper and more integrated place in the ordinary Muslim's self-identity that the conflict seems so entrenched, that internal transformation toward greater secularity in practice has in some places been slow to come, and in those places absolutist minorities have gotten away with the sort of exploitative appeal they have. But on the other hand, having acknowledged that there is this more fundamental level of commitment, there is still the danger that one might settle down with the idea of being locked helplessly in a conflict, a sort of "tragic" stasis, and that would make things too easy for oneself in another way—something akin to the familiar intellectual laziness that accompanies existential anguish. In short, in the study of Islamic identity and the conflict that it generates in ordinary Muslims today, it would be premature either to dismiss the idea of a fundamental commitment or to rest with it in the form that Williams's own writings leave us with.

What is missing in Williams is any interest or effort to offer an explanation of what sort of animal any particular fundamental commitment is, what its origins are, and what particular role or function it has in a person's or community's moral-psychological economy. Different kinds of fundamental commitment will naturally have very different roles, but it is only if one pays attention to them that one will come to some understanding of what is particularly disabling about any particular conflict in which any such commitment figures, and what the rehabilitating elements might be. Once Williams abandons the pretensions of Ethical Theory, which would deliver from on high general principles with a power to criticize particular values and commitments on the ground floor, he does not return to focus on the theoretical possibility that one might, in the process of resolving conflicts between fundamental commitments, come to a fuller understanding of the critical power and generality that is *built into* the commitments on the ground floor.

I have made this last point with such abstractness that it might help here to repeat it with the more concrete theme of Islamic identity and conflict. Ordinary Muslims, I have said, are conflicted between their opposition to anti-secular absolutist forces in their countries and their fundamental commitment to a religion some of whose ongoing practices as well as some parts of its Book speak with detailed pretension to issues of the law and of the state. They may often not perceive the conflict but there is plenty of evidence for it in their own behavior.[13] Confronted with this conflict it is tempting, as I said, to think that this is like any ordinary conflict between any two sets of values (in this case modern and traditional) and that sooner or later the conflict will resolve itself, with one side victorious. Even if one discards the Whiggish tendency to think the modernist victory inevitable, there is this temptation to think that there is nothing particularly distinctive or difficult about the conflict and its eventual resolution. There is also the other temptation. Acknowledging that there is something special and difficult about this conflict, which traditional moral philosophers are especially blind to, there is a temptation to say that ordinary Muslims have a "fundamental" commitment to the conflicting values of Islam and of modernity and that it is the arrogance of abstract philosophy to think that it has anything specific and useful to say by way of diagnosis or cure about something so deep-going in a community's moral psychology. I have already said something to resist the former temptation. In doing so I have registered sympathy with Williams's dissatisfactions with Ethical Theory. The latter temptation, I'm saying, issues from a lack in Williams's own approach to moral philosophy. It is a failure to give moral philosophy the task of mixing it up with (in this case) history in order to say something about the specific functional sources of given fundamental commitments (such as to Islam) and then, relatedly, a failure to consider a more bottom-up approach to the study of moral principles.

3.

What, then, are the sources of a devout but non-absolutist Muslim's "fundamental" commitment to Islam today?

In answering this sort of question, there is yet another temptation that philosophers are prone to. And that is to make a general and ahistorical claim about the human need for some sense of identity that is not merely determined by their material and social circumstances, a sort of Hegelian nod of acknowledgement that a long tradition of Marxist and Marxist-influenced social thought has neglected the sense of identity that Spirit and non-materially determined consciousness has to offer. Here is G. A. Cohen, chiding his own earlier work for precisely such a neglect.

> In *Karl Marx's Theory of History* I said that for Marx, by contrast with Hegel, "the ruling interest and difficulty of men was relating to the *world,* not to the *self*" [his emphasis]. I would still affirm that antithesis, and I now want to add that, to put it crudely, Marx went too far in the materialist direction. In his anti-Hegelian, Feuerbachian affirmation of the radical objectivity of matter, Marx focused on the relationship between subject to an object which is in no way subject, and as time went on he came to neglect the subject's relationship to itself. . . . He rightly reacted against Hegel's extravagant representation of all reality as ultimately an expression of self,

but he nevertheless over-reacted, and he failed to do justice to *the self's irreducible interest in the definition of itself* [my emphasis], and to the social manifestations of that interest. . . . I refer to the social manifestations of the interest in self-identification because I think that human groupings whose lines of demarcation are not economic, such as religious communities and nations, are *as strong and as durable* [my emphasis] as they evidently are partly because they offer satisfaction to the need for self-identification. In adhering to traditionally defined collectivities people retain a sense of who they are.[14]

I don't wish to enter into a discussion of the details of Marxist theory, and my interest in criticizing these remarks is not prompted by a desire to defend economic determinism or Historical Materialism. The issue between us is entirely over the question as to whether we should *rest* our analysis of the concept of religious identity with the self's primitive or "irreducible interest in the definition of itself."[15] I think it both unnecessary and wrong to assign one's understanding of a particular community's religious commitments, in a particular historical and cultural context, to this kind of irreducible interest in self-definition. That would only distract us from what I really wish to emphasize, namely the historical and functional determination of a community's fundamental commitments and the sense of identity they impart. I agree with Cohen that it is a crucial function of their commitment to Islam that it does indeed give Muslims a sense of autonomy and dignity, so I am not suggesting that there is a materialist dissolution of religious commitment. But, as I argue below, that function is *itself* to be understood as a function of historical, social, and material circumstances in precisely the sense Cohen wishes to abandon for some concession to the Subject's "*irreducible interest in the definition of itself.*" In explaining what he rightly notices as the "strength and durability" of religious and nationalist sentiment, Cohen swings from materialist prejudice to an equally unsatisfactory and unhelpful explanatory resting-point.[16]

In contemporary Islam, the further historically determined function is not hard to trace. It is hardly questioned by any but the most stubbornly resistant "Orientalist" that a good deal of Islamic revivalism in various countries in the Middle East, South Asia, and North Africa, not to mention some of the northern cities of England, is the product of a long colonial and post-colonial history, which has shaped a community's perception of itself in terms of the Other. It is a defensive reaction caused not only by the scars and memories of Western colonial rule but by the failure of successive governments to break out of the models of development imposed by a dominating neo-colonial, neo-liberal presence of Western corporate interests in their region, and even more so now with American and European interests more entrenched than ever in the Middle East, after successive humiliating wars. The failure of Egypt under Nasser and of pan-Arab secular nationalism to provide leadership, and the general Arab failure to pressure the West to force Israeli compromise on the Palestinian issue, have also contributed to the appeal that Islam holds as a source of dignity and autonomy in the face of what is perceived to be successive defeats in the hands of an omnipresent, controlling West in their midst. These points are familiar by now. I stress them here in order to say that if Islam is a "fundamental" commitment today, in the sense I had characterized earlier, it also has recognizable historical sources and a vital defensive function in a people's struggle to achieve a sense of identity and self-respect in the face of that history and the perceptions formed by it.[17] Hence the "strength and durability" of Islamic identity has a much more situated and local explanation than Cohen offers.

To be fair, it is not that he thinks religion (or nationalism) are irreducible needs; it is rather that he thinks that the need for a sense of identity is an irreducible need, and a fundamental commitment to religion (or nation) often fulfills that need. But my objection is that once one sees that these identity-constituting commitments have specific functional roles in particular historical circumstances, the very idea of an underlying, explanatory, *irreducible* need for identity that they fulfill is undermined as superfluous and misleading in the study of identity. That different fundamental commitments constitute different identities under different historical circumstances does not at all imply that there is an irreducible need for identity that is *anyway* there and that is fulfilled by some sense of identity or other at different times. There is simply no such irreducible need. To posit it is to posit an explanatory dangler.

The issue between us is so large that it would be surprising if there were not problems remaining for my functional account. Though I cannot deal with them all here, it would be evasive not, at least, to mention the most obvious. A central problem with a functional treatment of identity, such as the one I'm proposing, is the tendency of some social and cultural phenomena (in the present case, conviction in a religious doctrine) to *exceed* what is required by their functions, and thereby to attain an independent phenomenological status in the communal psyche. Islamist sentiment, like many nationalisms, in this way impresses an identity on many Muslim communities that outruns the sort of function we have diagnosed it to have. The source of the commitment may lie in its historically local function, but the commitment then acquires a momentum of its own which may survive even after the function has lapsed. I will call this phenomenon the "surplus phenomenology of identity." It is a surplus quite literally in the sense that it is more than the functional analysis can account for. It is an excess, a residue; and it is properly described as phenomenological precisely because it has no functional role in the psychological economy of the community. It is an experience without a point.

Now it is possible for Cohen to step in right here and claim that this is precisely what he intends by the idea of the sources of identity as being in "the self's irreducible interest in the definition of itself." He says as much a little after the passage I have quoted, noting that "people engage themselves with people and institutions *other* than to secure an identity, and then the engagement persists when whatever its original rationale was has gone, so that it becomes an identification ungrounded in further reasons" (p. 157). In saying that the surplus has phenomenological rather than functional status, I may have given the impression of a concession to this claim. But that impression would be wrong. It's not so much that I want to deny that these engagements might persist. I want to say rather that if they persist in a form that genuinely confers identity in the sense that I have defined above, if they persist in terms of authenticity and fundamental commitment as I have sketched them, then it cannot be that they are ungrounded in some further reasons in the way that Cohen allows. Conversely if they are now ungrounded, then they have lost their blue-chip, identity-imparting aspect and they no longer count as fundamental commitments in the sense that this essay is concerned with. If they really were ungrounded in any important function, relinquishing these engagements and commitments (due to pressure from conflicting values and commitments) would no longer have the traumatic, authenticity-destroying or integrity-destroying effects on the psyche which is special to fundamental commitments, as I defined them earlier.

So if these engagements persist as *fundamental* commitments and confer identity in the sense that is relevant to this essay's theme, then, I would argue, that it is only *in appearance* that this surplus commitment is ungrounded; it is only at first sight that it has a self-standing validity. In emphasizing the functional explanations of identity-forming fundamental commitments, in refusing to treat them as flowing from a primitive and unanalyzable need in our consciousness, I am insisting that this slide from the requirements of the function to a residual surplus phenomenology of identity is, from the point of view of *one* level of functional explanation, a form of communal irrationality. And like all irrational phenomena it demands *another* level of functional explanation. Neuroses, for example, are often identified as neuroses only because at the level they are being identified they do not seem to have a function, they do not fit in with the normal assignation of roles to mental states. This does not preempt there being another level of functional explanation of the behavior identified *initially* as neurotic. Indeed all of psychoanalytic theory is founded on this assumption.

Perhaps a better and closer analogy is with the phenomenon that Eliot located in much Romantic poetry and other writing, and which he scathingly described as lacking an "objective correlative."[18] The sentimentality he noticed in such poetry—missing, in his opinion, in the finest examples of what he and others called "metaphysical" poetry—was the product of a surplus emotion, emotion that exceeded the demands of its ground or object. Here too it is possible for someone to reply that such excess sentiment is a primitive and irreducible fact in the poetic consciousness and in reader response, but that again seems to me to misdescribe the facts. Eliot's negative evaluation of the phenomenon depended precisely on its not having this sort of rock-bottom justification *within poetics*, i.e., the phenomenon demanded another level of explanation in the poet or reader's person, which Eliot considered an irrelevant, egotistical intrusion into the poetic and critical tasks at hand. So also what I have called the "surplus phenomenology of identity" is to be seen as an irrational tendency in the life of cultures and communities because it too outpaces the level of functional explanation we have offered, and similarly demands a further, extrinsic level of functional investigation.

It may be helpful to move from these analogies to an example. Take the survival of Hindu nationalism in India today. Its early sources are sometimes analyzed in terms of the function it served in some part of the mobilizing of some sections of the Indian masses against British colonial rule, but it is evident everywhere that the communal sentiment has survived that function since colonial rule ended. This would, from the point of view of that level of functional analysis, be correctly viewed as a form of irrationality. And I'm saying that it would be quite wrong to claim that, whatever its functional sources, once the sentiment comes into existence it meets a self-standing rationale in the subject's irreducible need for self-definition. There are clearly *other* functions it has served, especially in the last two decades or more, which would require another level of functional investigation, thereby explaining the irrationality. (For instance, the wave of Hindu nationalist feeling that started in the very late 1980s may to a large extent be quite correctly analyzed in terms of the function of creating a mythological Hindu unity in the face of efforts that began around then to expose the deeply divided nature of Hindu culture by the implementation of affirmative action policies in favor of backward Hindu castes.)[19]

I conclude, then, that there is no reason to take a theoretical stance that would deny the irrationality of these surviving or surplus phenomenologies of identity and glamorize them with obscure, unanalyzable philosophical notions such as the subject's search for irreducible definition of itself. It is true that it is not a form of irrationality which has been much studied by philosophical anthropology or the theory of culture.[20] But that may well be just *because* it is too often relegated to some rock-bottom need for self-identification, which then absolves these disciplines from further diagnostic historical work.

4.

Let me return to how the identifying of the specific historical and functional sources of the commitment to Islam opens things up in the study of the conflict under discussion.

It is because their commitment to Islam today is to a large extent governed by the highly defensive function that Muslims find it particularly difficult to make a substantial and sustained criticism of the practices that absolutists would seek to endorse or revive. Their defensiveness inhibits them with the fear that such criticism would amount to a surrender to the forces of the West, which have for so long shown a domineering colonial and post-colonial contempt for their culture. Thus it is that the historically determined function of their commitment, the source of their very self-identity, loops back reflexively upon Muslims to paralyze their capacities for self-criticism and internal transformation.

That a fundamental commitment could be further diagnosed along these lines—something that Williams's theoretical framework has no particular place for or interest in—opens up various other lines for thinking about its unsettleability in the face of conflict. For it gives us space to examine whether there might be aspects of the commitment and its function, in one's psychological economy, which are superfluous or even incoherent. It thus gets us beyond the stultifying idea of being locked in a tragic and irresolvable conflict between such commitments. Let me pursue this general point further with the specific issue of Islam.

I think that it is possible to argue that critical reflection on the inhibiting effect of the defensive function of their contemporary commitment to Islam should lead Muslims to the conclusion that there is a simple but deep philosophical malaise at the heart of it; and that, in turn, should open a path to distinguishing between different aspects of their faith and practice in a way that allows for its internal transformation, and so eventually allows for the conflict they find themselves in to be resolved in favor of a more determined opposition to Islamic absolutism than they have been able to produce so far.

What do I mean here by a philosophical malaise? I have already granted that the contemporary reassertion of Islamist sentiment in many countries as well as a good part of the ordinary Muslim's commitment to

Islam is the product of a certain history of subjugation and condescension, which continues today in revised but nevertheless recognizable forms. Why, then, am I not showing the appropriate sympathy toward these defensive stances? It is in answering this question that the specifically abstract character of the malaise is revealed.

The answer is that Muslims themselves have taken the wrong attitude to this historical determination of their Islamist sentiments. Their own observation of the role of colonialism and the West in shaping their commitments and identity ought to—but alas, *does not*—have a strictly limited and circumscribed role in their own self-conception. The acute consciousness of and obsession with the historical cause of their commitment has made them incapable of critical reflection about the commitment itself. For too long now there has been a tendency among Muslims to keep saying, "You have got to *understand* why we are like this," and then allow that frame of mind to dominate their future actions. This has destroyed their capacity for clear-headed, unreactive political thought and action.

There is an air of paradox in my claim: One's coming to an understanding of the historical source and function of one's commitments can put one in an unreflective and uncritical state of mind about those very commitments. But the paradox is only apparent. Understanding a phenomenon is something that occurs in the third person. And, of course, we do often take such a third person stance toward *ourselves*. But to allow such a stance to develop into defensive and reactive commitments is to *rest* with a third person conception of ourselves. It is to deny the first person or agent's point of view. Thus (when considering the spread of absolutist sentiment in their countries) ordinary Muslims are often heard to say that "this is how things are with us because of colonial and neo-colonial domination." Or to take another not unrelated example, Muslims are often heard to say, "This is how things are with us because of Israeli intransigence and America's refusal to come through with serious pressure on Israel." And so on. These remarks are impeccable. But they are bits of knowledge that one has when one takes a third person stance toward oneself. And that stance, I'm saying, cannot be allowed to exhaust one's self-conception. On the lips of sympathetic others ("this is how things are with *them*") these remarks *are* the *only* stance to take. But on *our* lips, on the lips of Muslims, they cannot be the only remarks we make unless we treat ourselves as objects, unless we think of our future as we think of our past, as something that we cannot make a difference to. The philosophical malaise is quite simply that in allowing the third person point of view to dominate our political responses we are failing to live up to the basic conditions of free agency.

This point echoes, in a much more specific and political context, a point made famous in the third section of Kant's *Grundlegung*.[21] In the form that it occurs in Kant, the point's relevance to politics is not obvious; indeed its relevance to anything outside the very general conditions for the possibility of agency is not obvious. The idea of seeing ourselves primarily as objects, the idea of taking an *exclusively* third person point of view upon ourselves, in that very general Kantian setting, should have the effect of making us altogether passive; extreme versions of the eponymous figure, Oblomov, in Goncharov's novel. After all if one did not think that the future was *any* different from the past, why would one act at all? Though that is the extreme and logical end of taking such a perspective on oneself, my claim is that, when the concerns are not as purely general and metaphysical as they are in Kant's discussion, there are less extreme effects of adopting such a perspective—or at any rate of being dominated by this perspective—which consist, not in passivity, but in reactive and defensive actions, rather than fully autonomous actions.

A failure to see through the implications of their opposition to the absolutists, a failure to press for the transformations that will undermine the ground upon which the absolutists stand, is just one among the many examples of such reactiveness and defensiveness on the part of Muslims. Their sulking, censorious response to Salman Rushdie's book in which there was a complete blindness to the book's own anti-absolutist polemic and importance (not to mention the novel's indictment of Thatcherite Britain's attitudes toward the immigrant poor) is another example, as is the disposition of ordinary Muslims to sometimes lend silent support to third-rate, vainglorious leaders such as Saddam Hussein, who offered instant autonomy and dignity in the face of Western domination with ineffectual war-like stances. Their understanding of themselves as the victims of a history of Western domination constitutes the third person perspective which then perpetuates just these sorts of defensive actions.

If this third person point of view did not so overwhelm their vision of themselves, it would leave space for the *first* person point of view, essential to the very idea of agency. The first person point of view would not allow the context of understanding the colonial past to breed the defensiveness that weakens their opposition to the absolutists.[22]

I should add that this philosophical fallacy informs a great deal of defensiveness not only in the more obviously political arena, but in the academy as well. Recent powerful, trenchant, and much-needed critiques of Orientalism have forced scholars to shun the essentializing tendency in studies of Islam and the third world, and pay greater attention to the detail and diversity of their subject.[23] This effect is laudable. But they have also created a bandwagon effect that inhibits self-criticism in the fear that one is playing into Western and "Orientalizing" caricatures of Islam and the third world. Criticism and transformation *do* mean abstracting from diversity and detail in order to identify a core doctrine or tendency to which one is opposed. Indeed, it is arguable that it is not merely criticism and internal change but even the very idea of *explanation* of social phenomena which requires such abstraction. This methodological ploy does not amount to essentialism or caricature and we cannot afford to be tyrannized into thinking so by bandwagon intellectual trends. It is not essentialism because quite simply no social science, no historical understanding, no agenda for social and political change can afford to ignore this simple methodological canon. Moreover every scholar in this bandwagon has (quite justly) abstracted from the diversity of the West to explain the West's colonial and neo-colonial domination of these regions. It then seems methodologically inconsistent to discourage such abstraction from the diversity within the Islamic people and nations for particular contexts of explanation and of internal change within Islamic culture.

So, speaking initially in the third person, Muslims might correctly say: "In the face of colonial history and in the face of recent frustrations and defeat, Islam has an appeal for us, it is grounded in a doctrine we embrace and which has comprehensive pretensions and claims on us, including—crucially—on our polities, and this gives us a sense of autonomy and identity." If I am right that this defensive attitude reflects a predominantly third person perspective on ourselves, it will do no violence to the use of "us" and "we" here to substitute "them" and "they." This is, after all, the voice of a community's understanding of its own condition and its causes. It is the voice of the subject that takes itself to be an object.

But then, if I am right, there should be place and possibility for the switch to the first person, for the voice of the subject as agent to say, "This appeal of Islam is something we have uncritically and indiscriminately embraced out of demoralization and defeat, often allowing it to dominate our political actions, and it has gotten us nowhere; it is up to us to assess the relative merits of its diverse commitments, up to us to work toward its internal transformation, up to us to oppose the elevation of the sharia to centrality in social practice, to fashion a more depoliticized Islam so that its appeal and relevance is spiritualist and universalist rather than to the polity, so that it does not remain perpetually exploitable by the fundamentalist political factions whom we oppose." This is not merely not the passive voice, it is not the reactive voice either. It is, bending language a bit, the active voice.[24]

5.

These are of course very general things to say about the need for internal transformation of practice and they require detailed and specific study and analysis, as well as a systematic and strategic agenda for political action. That is beyond the province of this essay. But certain general lines of direction should flow obviously from points I have made so far. The idea of a shift in practices in the particular context of the conflict we have been discussing means downplaying the central significance only of those passages of the Quran which are exploited by the absolutists for ends which ordinary Muslims oppose, those portions which speak to questions of the polity and to personal and public law. Internal shifts of practice thus can leave intact the great significance of all the verses with the more purely universalist and spiritual claims and commitments. It is a well-known[25] and highly significant fact that the early verses written in Mecca are all of the latter sort. It is only some of the verses which follow upon Muhammad's arrival in Medina which make detailed claims about the state, the economy, inheritance, marriage, divorce, the status of women in the home and society, and so on. Once they have shed their defensiveness, it is possible for Muslims to argue that after the initial, deep, spiritual, defining pronouncements of the new faith in Mecca, the post-Medina verses were intended to address a very specific historical context in which conversion was paramount in the concerns of the prophet. Conversion was bound to be more effective if the faith addressed itself to a variety of social and interpersonal themes so that Islam could present itself as offering the (often nomadic) regional populations a hitherto unavailable sense of belonging to a unified community. It should also be possible for Muslims, therefore, to argue that since that historical context of seeking conversion has lapsed, the verses to be emphasized now are the Mecca verses which have no specific political commitments. This would indeed constitute a very measurable internal transformation. It would not necessarily emerge, as I have already said, in explicit articulations of doctrinal "reform," but in the actual practice of social life it would have the effect of what is often described as reopening the gates of *ijtihad* (reinterpretation) that are said to be closed in the demands for more rigid applications of the sharia.

Notice that this conception of internal change, and this argument for it, will not be overturned if it turns out that I'm wrong about the functional analysis of Islamic identity. That analysis was intended to counter an unnecessarily limited notion of fundamental commitment and an unmalleable notion of conflict that it generated. But the actual conclusions and argument about internal change are independent of the analysis. Even if my functionalist claim (that a good deal of the ordinary Muslim's fundamental commitment to Islam is out of an historically determined defensiveness) is exaggerated, even if one emphasized the view I have downplayed (that their commitment is primarily out of the need for some purely spiritual basis for self-identification), the point of this proposal for a less overtly politicized Islam of the absolutist, which stresses precisely the universal and spiritual commitments in the early verses of the Quran over many of the later verses, would still retain its validity.

My use of terms like "universalist" should not be made to carry more weight than is intended, so let me make the intention a little clearer. It may appear that in asserting the primacy of the Mecca verses and their "universalist" appeal, I think of internal transformation as requiring an abandonment of what is specific and unique to Islam, leaving some deist core which is hardly recognizable as relevant to the subject of this essay, viz., "*Muslim* Identity." That appearance is not only not intended, but I would argue that it is conjured up only within a framework of thinking about communal identity that thoroughly misdescribes a community's psychology of identity. It is only if one saw communal identity as a highly codifiable phenomenon, as a list or code of necessary and sufficient principles, that one would even be tempted to say that a relaxation or abandonment of some set of principles would have the effect of changing the subject. Though I won't argue for it here, I think it is an egregious misconception of religious identity to see it as a codifiable phenomenon. The idea that without an exercise in practice on the specific doctrinal commitments of public and personal law, Islam would be indistinguishable from all other universal and spiritual claims would be, in the spirit of this codificatory misconception, to divorce the message of the Mecca verses from their origins and history, as well as the abiding set of specific Islamic institutions and practices of prayer (*namaz*), pilgrimage (*hajj*), fasting (*rozah* or *sawm*), funerals (*janazah*), various religious feasts (*id*)—to name just a very few—which they have spawned. No such idea underlies my use of terms like "universalist" and "spiritualist" to characterize the message of these verses. Their use is meant merely to mark a contrast with the specific political and legal commitments that are sometimes stressed by the absolutists today. Depoliticization, however, does not imply deracination. Thus, though such a transformation in Muslims' fundamental commitment to Islam would now leave no particular stress on elements that absolutists insist on, it would all the same be a transformation *within* a commitment to Islam. It would, therefore, still constitute an answer to the question "What is a Muslim?"

Fazlur Rahman, who wrote with learning and acuteness on these subjects,[26] seems to have been struggling to make this point as part of a plea for what he describes as "modernization," but botches it somewhat by describing the *Quran* as a *unity*. The suggestion of Quranic unity is precisely what intellectuals of the absolutist movements themselves invoke to resist internal change, arguing that change of this sort would violate such a unity. The practices that are proposed by what is said to be the revealed word of God may tolerably be transformed precisely because the revealed word is not a unity. Different revelations can now be seen as indexed—even qua revelation—to different historical contexts. It is really the *non-codifiability* that Rahman should be stressing rather than unity, and not of the text but of the sense of identity in which the text has a place among other identity-shaping practices and institutions. This point about non-codifiability of identity should allow one's religious identity (of even a highly devout Muslim) first, to take within its stride, the idea that some revealed verses may be stressed over others as historical contexts lapse, and second to do so not necessarily in some explicitly articulated *counter-code* (after all, if it is not taken to be codified in the first place the need for doctrinal counter-codes also lapses) but in the quotidian practice by which one lives.

But to return now to the larger point, for such internal shifts of practice not to seem to themselves a total surrender to longstanding, hostile, alien cultural and political forces, Muslims will have to take the first step in resolving the present conflict by overcoming their acute defensiveness which, as I said, comes from taking an overwhelmingly third person perspective on themselves. How a community acquires the alternative perspective (of autonomy) in specific historical contexts is a subject that I cannot address in this essay,[27] whose aim is merely to uncover the malaise that makes a conflict seem irresolvable. But I will say this. A failure to overcome the defensiveness, a failure to acquire the first person perspective, will prove a point of the bitterest irony. A failure to come out of the neurotic obsession with the Western and colonial determination of their present condition will only prove that that determination was utterly comprehensive in the destruction it wrought. That is to say, it will prove to be the final victory for imperialism that after all the other humiliations it has visited upon Muslims, it lingered in our psyches in the form of *genuine self-understanding* to make self-criticism and free, unreactive agency impossible.[28]

6.

An underlying theoretical point of this essay has been that if fundamental commitments and the questions of cultural identity that they bring with them (What is an X?) are understood in terms of functional analyses of the kind I have tried to give in the case of Islamic identity today, then there is scope to see these commitments as susceptible to various criticisms in the particular context of a conflict in which they might figure. All this seems to me to offer far more scope and interest to moral philosophy than Williams allows it, even after granting to Williams the validity of the central role he gives to the idea of fundamental commitment and the validity of his critique of traditional moral philosophy.

The essay has studied the question "What is a Muslim?" in the dialectic of a conflict arising out of a concern for transformations in Islamic practice toward greater secularity. The conflict is one that arises because of Muslims' fundamental commitment to certain features of their faith that are often effectively invoked by the absolutists whom ordinary Muslims fundamentally oppose. If a full analysis of the commitment reveals its defensive function which has disabled Muslims from a creative and powerful opposition to the absolutists and if, moreover, this function of the commitment is diagnosed as itself based on a deep but common philosophical fallacy, it should be possible then for Muslims to think their way out of this conflict and to transform the nature of their commitment to Islam, so that it is not disabling in that way.

The question of identity, "What is a Muslim?," then, will get very different answers before and after this dialectic about transformation has played itself out. The dialectic, thus, preserves the negotiability of the concept of identity and the methodological points I began with, at the same time as it situates and explains the urgency and fascination that such questions hold for us.

EIGHT

Notes toward the Definition of Identity

This essay's somewhat encyclopedic analytic mode was prompted by constant dismissals on the part of philosophers of the possibility of a rigorous treatment of the notion of identity in the study of politics. Some have even denied that it even needs to be studied because each person possesses multiple identities, which contextualize the notion to such an extent that it lacks the stability needed to carry the weight it is given in the idea of "identity" politics. I had satisfied myself when I wrote the previous essay, "What Is a Muslim?," that there is no reason to be bullied out of being interested in interesting things because of these superior attitudes of philosophical colleagues. It is a banality that we have multiple identities—a banality presented by those who assert it with banal examples, such as that someone may be, in turn, a professor, a spouse, a father, a cricket-lover, an Indian, a Muslim, and so indefinitely on. Nobody should deny any of this on the simple ground that nobody should deny facts. But asserting such a thing of each person hardly cancels the equally undeniable fact that many persons in certain political contexts may allow (and have allowed) some, even one, of these multiple identities to loom larger than the others and allow themselves to be mobilized in large numbers in politics on its basis.

Another much more familiar source of criticism has been not the philosophers' skepticism of the very notion of identity in politics, but the
broadly Marxist and *traditional* Left skepticism of the specific forms of
identity politics, tied to race, caste, gender, ethnicity, that have emerged
in the last few four decades or so. This is not a skepticism about the very
notion of identity but rather the assertion that it is the concept of class
(economic class) that should determine the primary identity from which
a politics should emerge, rather than these other conceptual categories
I have just mentioned. Many have defended identity politics against this
skepticism by pointing out, rightly in my opinion, that this leaves out
the fact that societies have been ridden not just by class inequalities
but also by inequalities that flow from forms of *disrespect* and *exclusion*
that have sources other than the distinctions of class. Even so, there is a
truth in the Marxist claim that class is the more fundamental category
of social analysis than these other factors, and it should be presented
in a way that does not cancel the importance of acknowledging these
other sources of disrespect and exclusion. Class is indeed more fundamental in the following sense. Should it have turned out that such
(no doubt partial) *elimination* of social inequalities based on disrespect
and exclusion, on the basis of one or other of these other grounds (say,
gender) as we have witnessed in some metropolitan areas of Europe or
North America in recent years, had the effect of undermining the domination of the corporate sector in these societies, the elimination *would
never have been allowed to happen.* If I am right in this speculation, it is
only so because class is more fundamental than these other categories.
That is to say, it is a reflection of the primacy of class as a category of
analysis that we can rightly make the following plausible speculation:
It is only because improvements in gender equality or racial equality
or caste equality have not had the effect of fundamentally undermining capital and corporate interests that these improvements have been
allowed and tolerated. (I think it would be an interesting mirror speculation to the one I have just made to ask: Would the elimination of
class inequalities be tolerated if it undermined patriarchy? But I won't
pursue that further here.) Suffice it to say that even if I am right about
class having this more primary determining role in the analysis of our

societies, the way I have presented what is primary about it does not in any way skeptically undermine (as other ways of stressing the Marxist analysis have) the importance of these other identities in the political arena which contest other forms of disrespect and exclusion than the one based on class.

What, then, is meant by identity? In "What Is a Muslim?" I had somewhat unanalytically announced that someone may be described as having an identity, if she conceived of giving up some commitment of hers (say, to friendship) as having the effect on her of a collapsing sense of who she is, a collapse expressed in thoughts such as "I would not be able to recognize myself if I betrayed a friend." Friendship, on this picture of identity, is a "fundamental commitment" and it constitutes one's self-conception, unlike other more routine commitments one has. Such an idea of self-conception, I had said, could conceivably be what people had in mind when they spoke of identity. And when we turn to examples of commitments of a less personal kind than the commitment to friends or friendship, we may begin to see its potential for being mobilized in the political and cultural arena. These are, I think, true but not very analytical things to say. The effort in the present and very brief essay to provide "notes toward a definition" is really an effort to redeem these more lightly made remarks in "What Is a Muslim?" into some sort of underlying analysis.

Though the essay is primarily interested in characterizing the notion of identity as it affects politics, I will begin with some rather more general remarks and then, even when I go on to consider identity in politics, I will throughout view the political issues through the lens of moral psychology and considerations of what is sometimes called "practical reason."

It is doubtful that the concept of identity is susceptible to a substantial philosophical treatment at a high level of generality. This is so not so much because there are too many disparate theories of identity, but more because such things as the question of whose identity is taken up by philosophers are too disparate to get a uniform treatment. Broadly speaking, two conspicuously different sets of interests make such a treatment especially difficult. The concept of "identity," when applied to such very basic categories as objects, properties, events, and persons, forms a cluster of themes in metaphysics and these receive a kind of analysis far removed from such themes as national, ethnic, racial, or sexual identity, which are usually discussed in political theory. No obviously common notion of identity which is either tractable or interesting spans both sets of interests.

One point of intersection between the more metaphysical and the more sociopolitical themes might be this. Philosophers have long treated the concept of a *person* as something distinct from the concept of personal *identity,* viewing the former as an ethical category and the latter as presenting a focus on metaphysical issues. But more recently the most interesting accounts of the metaphysical issue of personal identity have begun to stress these normative and ethical considerations in a rigorous way, thereby infusing metaphysics with value.[1] Though this turn is often resisted, it should not really come as a surprise since the metaphysical question of personal identity has always been one of the criteria of identity of a person *over time,* and if that question was answered wholly in non-normative terms, then the answer would be disappointing in having no relevance to evaluative questions such as why should a person accept responsibility for actions of a *past* self that is identical with her, or why should a person particularly care—as she does—for the well-being of a *future* self that is identical with her. To insist that any answer to the metaphysical question should have such a relevance would be to begin to unify the two sets of disparate interests in the notion of identity mentioned earlier. Having said that, I will not take up the metaphysical issues any further and will focus entirely on the concept of identity that is of more *direct* interest to the politics and the social sciences.

Here too the issues are diverse. There is the familiar question as to the identity of collective social phenomena: of classes, of nations, and of society itself, and whether or not their identity is in some sense dependent ("supervenient," as philosophers like to say) on the identities of individual persons who belong to them. Much has been written on this subject but it is less current than another subject, which is: What is it for an individual person to be a social type, a Muslim, say, or a white male, a Quebecois, a gay or lesbian? The currency of the subject is a result of the importance it has come to have in politics. The rest of this brief essay will further restrict its focus to this question.

As I said at the outset, philosophers are prone to say that though the extremity of "identity" politics in many parts of the globe in the last few decades has given rise to the constant use of the term "identity" as well as to a glamorous theoretical interest in the concept it expresses, there has been little clarity or rigor in its theoretical deployment.

One initial step toward imposing some theoretical order on the notoriously haphazard concept of "identity" in politics is to distinguish at the outset between its "subjective" and "objective" aspects. When a person is said to have a certain identity owing to some characteristics she has and with which she identi*fies,* then identity is being thought of in its subjective aspects. If a person is said to have a certain identity owing to some characteristics she has but with which she does not necessarily identify, then we are speaking of her objective identity. I have very deliberately used the word "identify" here. It would be a mistake (and it is a frequently made mistake) to use the idiom of a subject "choosing" his or her identity to describe the subjective aspects of identity. That would misleadingly give the impression of far greater freedom than we possess in the identities we might subjectively adopt. I prefer the idiom of "identifying" with characteristics one possesses because it captures the fact that even when we are speaking of subjective identity, we can't help *starting* with what is quite considerably *given to us.* This does not mean that we cannot sometimes identify with things that are not given to us, characteristics that we don't actually have. This can be done out of self-deception or fantasy or even sometimes out a willful form of radical dissent in oppressive circumstances (cross-dressing, for example, can sometimes—though of course not always—be a way of identifying with a gender that is not given to one in order to express dissent against various oppressive forms of conventionality in matters of gender and sexuality); but it is not the routine basis on which mobilization takes place in politics, and so, having acknowledged its possibility, I will not make much of it in the rest of what follows and will restrict the discussion to subjective identities formed by identifying with what is given to one, such as the ethnic or national or gender or racial characteristics that one already possesses.

Let me, then, explore the subjective and objective aspects of identity, in turn.

Subjective Identity

This is the notion of identity that is most immediately relevant to politics since people sometimes tend to allow themselves to be mobilized in the public arena on its basis. (It is not—not by any means—that subjective identity is always mobilized in politics; it is more that, where it exists, it is *poised* so as to be mobilized if other conditions, which I will not discuss here, are present.)

What is it to identify with some characteristic one possesses, thereby making it an identity-imparting characteristic in the subjective sense? This is a more complicated question than it might seem.

A first stab at answering it might be to say that someone identifies with a certain characteristic if she values it. Thus one must value the fact that one belongs to a certain nationality or ethnic community or even a certain profession, if one can be said to have the identity (in the subjective sense) of an Indian or Korean-American, say, or a teacher and writer. That seems to be a minimal initial condition for identifying with it. But it is clearly not sufficient since one may have values from which one is oneself alienated. This can be a fairly common phenomenon. To be alienated from one's values is structurally akin to being alienated from one's desires. Just as an alcoholic may be disgusted with his addictive desire for alcohol, so also someone may disapprove of his own patriotism or find his pride in his profession intolerably smug.

So a further condition has to be added to our minimal condition before a characteristic imparts subjective identity. One has to endorse one's valuing of that characteristic. That would presumably ensure that one is not alienated from its valuing. There is another reason why endorsement of this kind is necessary apart from the attempt to solve the problem of values one is alienated from. The topic of *subjective* identity is not merely about what one is but also about what one conceives of oneself to be. This idea, therefore, brings with it, in any case, the reflective endorsement of the relevant valued characteristics.

To endorse a value, it is often said, is to have a second-order value.[2] Someone must value the fact that she values the characteristic of belonging to a certain nationality or profession, before she can be said to have the identity of an Indian or a teacher, in this subjective sense. (We should add that something like a second-order valuing may not be necessary in order to ensure that there is no alienation from one's own first-order values; all that may be needed is something negative: that there is no second-order disapproval of one's first-order value. However, as I've just said, the second-order level comes in a more positive form, in any case, because subjective identity is unavoidably about reflective matters such as what one takes oneself to be.)

With this second-order valuing in place have we said something sufficient about subjective identity? Not yet, since one's second-order values can be highly neurotic, and when they are they can be values that one is also alienated from. For example, someone may feel his second-order value which disapproves of his first-order valuing (of his role in his profession as being too smug) as itself being too prim, too censorious, too much of a super-ego phenomenon.

What yet further condition must now be added to give a sufficient account of subjective identity? One possibility is to conceive of it as requiring a receding hierarchy of orders of value. At each order, one is not alienated from a value if one endorses it at a higher order. So in our example, any neurosis regarding a person's second-order disapproval of his pride in his profession is ruled out if he has a third-order approval of his second-order disapproval. This solution raises worries about an infinite regress.

In order to avoid such a regress, a second possibility is to conceive of subjective identity not as emerging in a receding hierarchy but as requiring a coherence among one's values, no matter what order of value is being considered. So in our example, the second-order disapproval is neurotic, not because there is a lack of third-order approval of the second-order disapproval, but rather because the latter does not cohere with one's other values at all levels, including the first-order values. The second-order disapproval is something that one is not alienated from, something that one identifies with, only if it coheres well with the first-order values and other second-order values one has. Here no infinite regress threatens, but some philosophical account of coherence among values must be worked out to match the coherentist accounts of belief and knowledge that we already have available with some degree of sophistication. It is worth noting that if this coherentist way of thinking of subjective identity is right, it is very closely tied to rationality in values, since the point of a coherentist account of value is presumably that it is an account of when one's values are rational. In a word, one identifies with one's values to the extent that the value is rational, in the sense of being fortified by coherence with our other values. The conclusion is attractive like any conclusion that allows two seemingly separate themes (rationality and subjective identity, in this case) to be united.

The trouble however is that if subjective identity is given by a rationality-imparting coherence among our values, then we will be identified with all the values we have which are rational in this sense. But that is of not much help with the idea of identity since it follows from this that our identity (in the subjective sense) is never going to be anything very distinctive. It will pick out nothing very special or identity imparting among all our coherent values, such as the ones we have been discussing: Despite valuing the fact that one is an Indian, a teacher, a writer, a Muslim, no one of these will be more importantly relevant to one's identity than other characteristics which we value coherently, such as one's weight, one's love of cricket or of dessert. Precisely what seems attractive about this view is what makes it of no particular help on the subject of identity, with which we are concerned.

Perhaps this difficulty teaches a deflationary lesson. Perhaps it is a sign that there is something inflated about the very idea of identity, that our thinking there is something specially distinctive about some characteristics is misguided, that it is not something we should expect, and that we have come to expect it only because of the recent rise of "identity" politics which has elevated some characteristics—nationality, ethnicity, linguistic and religious allegiances—beyond anything warranted by or echoed in the actual moral-psychological economies of ordinary citizens. There is some point to this qualm, a point in fact that needs much nuanced development in longer discussions of the subject. But it can also be a point that is too glibly made. For it does seem, at first sight anyway, to be quite accurately descriptive of at least a small, vocal, and influential body of citizens in many polities that they display a strong identification with these very characteristics and allow themselves to be mobilized on that basis. And of them at least, some notion of identification must be given, which shows why these characteristics are valued more distinctively than the many others that are also coherently and rationally valued by them.

We are therefore still lacking a sufficient account of subjective identity. To repeat, what we need is not merely endorsement (of one's own valuing of some characteristic of ours) by some higher-order values or by coherence with other values, but some further element that makes the value endorsed more central and distinctive in our psychological economies.

An obvious thought here might be to say that the values which are more central are those that are more *intense* than other values, especially since it does seem as if Muslims, Quebecois, Serbians, etc., who seem most visible in identity politics value their Muslimness, etc., very intensely, more intensely than other things they value. It is a question, however, how theoretically useful it is to plonk down "intensity" as a primitive and unanalyzable property that values have, but even apart from this problem, the thought is wrong, for in some cases of weakness of will, we act on values that are very intense but which we do not endorse.

A better thought at getting at the required further element is to say that the endorsement of the value must be such that it makes the value concerned, in some sense, more *unrevisable* (rather than more intense) relative to the other values one holds. For it is surely intuitive that a Muslim or Quebecois whose identity is caught up with his valuing these characteristics of his is less likely to give up valuing them than the other values he holds, or perhaps—a more subtle variation of the intuition, one that will be developed briefly below—is less likely to *conceive of himself* as giving up the value.

For this thought to be genuinely promising, we need (1) to show what sort of endorsement of a value makes the value relatively unrevisable, and we need (2) to ground the idea of unrevisability in something which would not show the reluctance to revise to be irrational by the lights of the agent herself (in the way cases of weakness of will show that acting on or even holding some of our most intense values is irrational by the agent's own lights).

(1) is the most fundamental task: Which among all the values that equally cohere with one another are the more unrevisable? As we said, it is only if we answer this question that we would have captured what is distinctively identity imparting about valuing being a Muslim

or Quebecois, for the sort of agent we are concerned with. Here is a way of bringing out why that should be so. Any answer to the question would have an analogous effect to what W. V. O. Quine intended when he argued that in a scientific theory some beliefs or propositions are in the very center rather than further out toward the periphery.[3] The idea behind this metaphor was intended to replace misguided traditional ideas of "analytic" propositions. His point was that the quality that allows the theory *to be the theory it is* is given by the beliefs or propositions which are at the center of our physical theory since they are more immune to revision than the ones further out on the periphery which are more exposed to what Quine called the "tribunal of experience." If those central beliefs *do* get revised, then it is not clear whether the initial theory has been improved or whether we have changed the subject because the meanings have changed, and we have a different theory. So also, analogously, we might say that a person's identity is given by his or her relatively unrevisable values—however we characterize them—and if those are given up, then it is not clear whether it is a change in the ordinary sense where the overall identity remains constant but a change in value takes place, or whether the overall identity itself is changed. This analogy, though inexact, is all the same roughly intuitive and reflects our ordinary talk, when in a fit of nationalist sentiment, we say things such as "I will lose my sense of self, of who I am, if I betray my country" (or, as in Forster's British schoolboy morality, "I will lose my sense of self, I will not recognize who I am, if I betray my friend"), the sorts of things we are not likely to say of other things we value. Compare these to "I will lose my sense of self, if I give up my love of desserts," which because of its implausibility, shows such first-order values to be more analogous to beliefs or propositions at the periphery for Quine. (These are mere examples intended to convey the structural point of the analogy intuitively. Of course it is possible, though perhaps not routine, that someone may value his sweet tooth in the way a stereotypical nationalist or British public schoolboy values country or friendship, that is, analogously to Quine's center of the web rather than the periphery. The possibility in no way spoils the analogy; it merely shows that identities might be eccentric or bizarre on occasion.)

So much for why unrevisability of values seems like a plausible thing to focus on in giving a clinching criterion for subjective identity. But (1) was the task of saying what exactly unrevisability amounts to. We are seeking to define a way of endorsing one's valuing of some characteristic one possesses which shows that value to be relatively unrevisable compared to other values one holds. Since we have already seen that coherence cannot provide such a special way of endorsement, let us return to the idea of second-order valuing of a first-order value to explore the sort of endorsement needed. What do we need to add to a second-order value to make the first-order value endorsed (relatively) unrevisable in one's psychological economy? An example may help to make the question and an answer to it less abstract.

Let us take some of the more absolutist Muslims in Iran over the last two decades. They have often urged something that approximates unrevisability of their Islamic values. One way they have done so is to argue that Iran needs to protect itself—in fact not just others in Iran, but even they the absolutists themselves—should protect themselves against their own "moral" weakening and corruption in the face of the inevitable spread of the pernicious values of modernity in general and the West in particular. And they have argued (like Ulysses did, anticipating the Sirens) that this protection should be ensured by entrenching Islamic values so deeply now that were Muslims ever to be so weakened, the social, political, and legal institutions would not make it easy for them to shed their Islamic ways of life. Such a form of endorsement of one's Islamic values vividly shows it to be more unrevisable (in a very special sense) than other values one has and endorses having. What is crucial in this case is that the endorsement takes a counterfactual form: We value something in a way that we want ourselves to be living by the value, even should we (counter to present fact) not value it anymore. At the time of valuing it, then, such a value stands out as very distinctive. The sort of unrevisability here is quite special because it is not so much that the value (at the first-order level) itself is permanent or immutable. But even if we may revise it and cease to value it at some later time, the fact is that at the time of valuing it in this way, one (at the second-order level) yearns for the value to be unrevisable and relatively permanent, unlike all the other values which we endorse in the more ordinary way. That surely makes it part of one's deepest self-conception. Another way to put the point is that since one would so utterly disapprove of oneself upon losing the value at some future point, one *now* tries to make sure that one's self, at that future point, *will* live according to the value. "Identity imparting," "self-constituting," etc., seem apt descriptions for values held and endorsed with such deep commitment.

Task (2) remains. Not all values which are unrevisable in this way are rational. What needs to be added is that these unrevisable values must also cohere with our other values. Coherence of a value, conceived as unrevisable in this special sense, with one's other values, allows for the rationality of this form of unrevisability since reluctance to revise could only be irrational if the value one does not revise is one that does not have rational support from one's other values.

Before closing, I should make one important cautionary remark to protect against a misunderstanding of the notion of subjective identity as just defined. One should not be put off by the specific example given above to think that the sort of endorsement that generates identity in this way is a sign of fanaticism or illiberalism, just because we have become used to thinking of Islamic absolutism to be fanatical and illiberal. That would be to allow substantive opinions on the particular example I have used to illustrate the point to blind us to the merits of the theoretical analysis we have come to, that is to say, blind us to the structural feature of the endorsement of a value that generates subjective identity. After all, the special way liberals value their own basic constitutional rights reflects just such an endorsement of their identity-generating values *as liberals,* since it reflects the same structure as the Iranian absolutists in our earlier example. Liberals elevate a very few of the many values we more or less coherently hold to fundamental constitutional "rights"—for example, free speech—precisely because they want to protect our future selves from giving in to any weakening of those values, as when in the face of strong dislike of another's substantive views, we might in the future find ourselves wanting to censor him. What our elevating these values into fundamental rights does is express the fact that we now want to make it impossible to later censor someone we strongly disagree with if we later have indeed weakened enough to wish to censor him. A liberal's deepest self-conception, i.e., a liberal's identity, and a Muslim's identity, therefore, whatever the differences between them on other matters may be, is given by the same counterfactual structures of endorsing and identifying with their cherished values that our theoretical analysis has proposed. Neither is any more fanatical than the other, at least in matters of subjective identity.

Because liberal doctrine and liberal politics have so often been dogged by identity politics, this parity between the liberal and identitarian that I've just drawn often goes unnoticed by liberals, who feel that their own outlook is in some sort of stark contrast with identity as it affects politics. In general, it is a good question to ask: What in liberalism holds identities in suspicion, and why do identitarians find themselves being thwarted by liberals? There may be more than one reason for this broadly theoretical opposition. Our definition, at any rate characterization, of subjective identity has *one* interesting diagnosis to offer. Ever since (indeed perhaps even before) Mill's celebrated argument for free speech (discussed at length in the essay entitled "Liberalism and the Academy" in this volume) appealed to our fallibility as grounds for tolerance of dissenting opinion, liberal doctrine has cast a suspicious eye on the very idea of the unrevisability of one's values. Mill's appeal to fallibilism in arguing for free speech takes the following form: We have been wrong in the past and so we may be wrong in our current opinions; therefore let's tolerate dissent against our current opinions in case they are wrong. Fallibility (the possibility of being wrong) and revisability, though they are certainly different ideas, are close enough cousins. In philosophically justifying free speech, we may appeal to our tendency to revise just as Mill appeals to our tendency to be wrong. After all we revise when we find ourselves to be wrong. Now I have been highly critical of Mill's fallibilism in the essay I just mentioned. But even in my criticisms, I did say (indeed insisted on) the following: In inquiry, it is rational to—and we should be prepared to—revise our views if *specific* evidence is provided against some *specific* belief we hold. However, if we take subjective identity, as I have defined it seriously, it requires of us to resist any change of mind in the values that constitute our subjective identity, viewing the tendency in us to make such changes as a kind of moral weakening. The Islamist identitarian asks us to protect ourselves from future weakening by making our current values unrevisable. Does this mean that subjective identity really is irrational? Does it amount to saying that we should not change our minds even if specific evidence surfaces against a present commitment held in the subjective identitarian form?

The identitarian has a *prima facie* answer to this charge of dogmatism. He may grant that it is irrational to hold onto a specific belief in the face of specific evidence against it, but can point out that *values* are not like beliefs in being beholden and answerable to *evidence* in the same sense. Thus, what is irrational in inquiry into what is true or false (beliefs) is not irrational in the matter of values, which are not the sorts of things that are true and false. So long as our value, held in this identity-imparting form of resistance to future revision, is coherently reinforced by our other values, then the question of evidence overturning it does not arise. The question of evidence is not relevant to values as it is to beliefs. There is no answer to this defense by the identitarian unless we take up the entire question of whether values are distinct in this way. My own view is that they are not and I argue for this view at length in other essays in this volume. See in particular the essay "Gandhi (and Marx)" and "The Political Possibilities of the Long Romantic Period" where I present reasons for taking values to be properties in the perceptible world around us which makes normative demands on us. If values indeed are perceptible properties, they will be susceptible to revision on the basis of perceptible evidence and not just on the basis of coherence relations with other values. But it is not until we bring in considerations of that kind that liberals can even so much as take up the threat (leave alone repudiate) a politics based on subjective identities, with its stress on the unrevisability of values, poses. And were they to take it up and repudiate this form of unrevisability of values and the identity politics based on it, they would do well to question their own liberal identities which, as I pointed out above, are based on the same structures of unrevisability bestowed on certain values such as free speech which are treated as special among values by being protected as a constitutional right against future weakening that might consider relaxing them or abandoning them.

Objective Identity

When we turn to the objective aspects of identity, identification on the part of the subject in question with the identity-imparting characteristic(s) is not a necessary condition. Thus, for instance, identities when they are thought to be given by characteristics of descent, such as "race" is sometimes said to be, are objective in this sense. Chromosome-based ways of defining gender identity are similarly objective. But biological criteria are not the only criteria that are routinely invoked. Inter-subjective and social criteria are also much favored. Thus, for instance, Marxists often claim that one's identity is given by one's place and role in a particular economic formation in a given period of history, that is to say, one's class identity as "class" as defined by Marx.

Many oppose the purely biological ways of thinking of various kinds of identity, such as racial and gender identity, claiming that these identities are "socially constructed" by the perceptions and attitudes of one's fellows, by the zeitgeist of a particular period, by the conceptual categories and social institutions at a given time. Foucault and those influenced by him have made much of this and Foucault himself gave detailed historical and social accounts of particular concepts and institutions in Europe as determining identities. In fact it is interesting that Foucault and his followers claim that it is not only the biological and other scientific criteria that are caught up in social factors of this kind, but the subjective ones we discussed in the last section as well. These too are shaped by conceptual and institutional formations far removed and hidden from the exercise of our reflective self-understanding, thereby showing the ideals of individual autonomy that we assume to reside in the idea of identification or subjective identity to be illusory.[4] I will not pursue any further these issues raised by Foucault's influence.

I will look instead briefly at the motivations for looking at objective factors of identity at all, over and above the subjective ones.

Many subjects may identify with some characteristic they possess which is *not* what is most salient about them to others. And it is thought important by many political philosophers that nevertheless, it is these latter, the ones that *others* think are more salient, that often define identity in these subjects, no matter what the subjects may conceive themselves

to be. A good example of this can be seen in Stalin's well-known definition of a "nation," which stresses the importance of historical and economic criteria for national identity, with a view to providing a corrective
to what were seen as somewhat premature and ungrounded subjective
identifications of "nationality" found in many secessionist demands in
different parts of the world.[5] Here the motivation for objectivist criteria
of identity is (at least implicitly) political.

But underlying these is a more interesting theoretical rationale that
points to important issues of a more philosophical nature. The claim
that agents may have a certain identity, even if they do not take themselves to do so, implies that what one takes oneself to be can be mistaken,
a kind of self-deception, or at least a self-myopia. (The latter does not
involve the motivated element often associated with self-deception, but
involves instead the idea that one may sometimes simply be too deep for
oneself—where "deep" is not intended as a bit of eulogy.)

It would be philosophically clarifying to make a distinction between
two different sorts of appeal to objectivist identities which are said to be
(possibly) hidden from a subject's own self-conception. 1) One claim—
the weaker one—is that subjects often betray signs of a certain identity
in much of their behavior, even if they do not endorse and identify with
what is reflected in their behavior. 2) The other, stronger claim does not
even require something in the subjects' behavior to reflect the identity
given by the unendorsed characteristic; rather, the characteristic and the
identity are given by the delivery of some (social, political, economic, or
biological) theory regarding these subjects.

The weaker claim (1), not surprisingly, is less controversial since it
requires that the characteristics of a subject which are going to define
his identity are something that he at least reveals in his behavior. The
subject may not endorse them, he may not even acknowledge them, but
if the only good explanation of his behavior is that he has those characteristics, and if those characteristics are salient compared to others,
then some claim can be made regarding how they impart his identity.
Within this view, the more extreme cases will be where the subject
does not even acknowledge the characteristics as being revealed in the
behavior. Many of the identities that surface in Freudian and psychoanalytic theories make much of this sort of case (Oedipal or narcissistic

identities, for example). The less extreme cases will be those where there *is* acknowledgement of the characteristics, but no endorsement of them on the part of the subject. These are likely to be more common. What may be called "silent" identities, as in "silent majorities," often belong to subjects who are not self-identified with a certain pattern of behavior but will not be in any particular state of denial (as they are in the more extreme cases) about whether their behavior reveals the characteristics they are seen to have. It is very likely, for example, that many ordinary Muslims who do not identify with absolutist or fundamentalist Islam may all the same admit that much in their behavior mutedly plays along with these Islamist elements in their societies.

The stronger claim (2) very often appeals to biological criteria, but is most interesting when it does not. Since the biological criteria are in any case usually caught up with social factors (see the point made about them above during the brief discussion of "social construction" of identity), they will be ignored here. Perhaps the most well known, well worked out, and widely discussed of the stronger objectivist versions of identity, not biologically based, is due to Marx and those influenced by him. What makes for having a class identity, say a proletarian identity, is not any kind of self-identification with the working class, not even any behavior that suggests certain unacknowledged or unendorsed allegiances to that class, but simply the objective fact of having a certain place and function in the relations of production during the modern capitalist period of economic history. What is remarkable and controversial about this view, more so than anything found in (1) above, is that something regarding the self and its identity is being attributed, without any basis or manifestation required in the conscious or unconscious behavior of the selves or agents concerned. A working-class person who exhibits no proletarian consciousness nor any of the solidarity and forms of behavior appropriate to the class, and none of whose behavior reflects an unconscious betrayal of such solidarity or consciousness, is nevertheless said to have proletarian class identity, albeit with a "false consciousness." It is only because he has this identity that there can be cause to call such a subject's consciousness "false." It is false precisely because he fails to conceive himself aright, fails to see his deepest self, which is determined by objective historical and material relations.

It is such a view of self and identity (where self and self-conception can come so radically apart) which filled Isaiah Berlin with anxiety in his discussion of "positive liberty," since what it encourages is the idea that the achievement of *self*-realization of individual citizens, that is, the achievement of their own autonomy and liberty (in the positive sense), is now left to states or to the "vanguards" of political parties, which lay claim to greater understanding of what some subject's self really and objectively is. On such a view, according to those alarmed by the view, there is no paradox in the expression "forcing someone to be free."[6]

Underlying political anxieties of this kind is a more philosophical issue, which is much discussed in contemporary moral psychology, the issue of external as opposed to internal reasons. An internal reason is a reason for one to do or believe or value something which appeals to some other evaluative element in one's moral-psychological economy. An external reason makes no such appeal to an internal element; it requires only some objective fact that need not even be recognized by the subject for whom it provides a reason. Thus in the orthodox Marxist tradition, a proletarian, given his historically determined identity, has (an external) reason to be a revolutionary even if there is no element in his moral-psychological economy which values it. Berlin's anxieties about statist tyranny carried out in the name of self-realization, autonomy, and positive liberty were thus implicitly and more deeply about the very idea of external reasons, even though he never quite articulated them as having that underlying target; however, it becomes very explicit in a denial of the cogency of the very idea of external reasons in a brilliant essay by Bernard Williams (a philosopher much influenced by Berlin), though the point is marred in that essay by a somewhat confused equation of internal reasons with a Humean notion of value and motivation.[7]

This last set of points provides a good resting point for these brief analytical notes toward the definition of identity, which has distinguished fundamentally between the subjective and objective aspects of the concept. To a considerable extent, which of these two aspects we emphasize in our study of the concept will be a matter of theoretical decision, a decision which, in turn, depends on non-arbitrary philosophical considerations having to do, as we have just seen, with themes at some distance from identity, such as autonomy and moral reasons. In itself, this is to be expected since self, freedom, and reason have been closely connected themes in philosophy ever since Kant, both in the analytical and the European traditions of the discipline. The stakes for these themes in the subject of practical reason are measurably elevated when we connect them further with themes in politics and political philosophy.

NINE

After the Fatwah

Twenty Years of Controversy

1.

Philip Roth once said about the literature of Eastern and Western Europe that in totalitarian regimes, "Everything matters, so nothing goes," while in modern liberal democracies in the West, "Nothing matters, so anything goes."[1] That, if it is true, cannot, of course, be literally or perfectly true; but even as an approximation, it registers a familiar distinction often reflected in discussions of liberal democracy and its various "Others." The distinction is particularly worth exploring in the context of a novel like *The Satanic Verses* written *from* a world which has routinely come to be perceived by its critics as falling within the caption "Nothing matters, so anything goes" and which (at least partly) is *about* a world (the world as conceived by so-called Islamic "fundamentalism") that its author claims, at length and with brilliant irreverence, to fall within the contrasting slogan "Everything matters, so nothing goes."

Roth expresses things slightly misleadingly in his formulation of this latter ideal. He must surely have had in mind to say, "Only one thing matters, so nothing else goes." But the misformulation is understandable on the assumption that if only one thing matters, it is taken to be everything, so that other things are not so much as visible on the horizon. The idea then must be that when other things surface and intrude on the horizon to present conflict, they are, by these monolithic lights, intolerable.

I am pressing on with this abstract caricature in Roth to bring into focus an image not of Islamic fundamentalism but of Islam itself, an image familiarly presented in semi-literate Western imaginings and equally familiarly repudiated by a recent intellectual tradition of ethnography as well as of literary and philosophical criticism.

My subject in this essay is the perception of Rushdie's novel in the context of this image *and* its repudiation because it seems to me that something important gets lost or, at any rate, cramped in such ideological disputation.

In earlier writing[2] on Rushdie and on Islam, I had tried to subvert the distinction Roth appeals to from two different directions.

From one direction, by arguing that the liberal ideal, as it is expressed in the slogan, quite apart from the exaggeration, fails to describe liberal doctrine accurately because the idea of "anything goes" is sanctioned only if one erects the concept of tolerance as the first freedom, the *one thing* that matters above all. On this conception of modern liberal society, the slogan cannot any longer read "Nothing matters so anything goes," but rather "Because one very specific thing matters above all else does anything go." Such an understanding of liberalism is often criticized by those who argue that "You can't just say anything; free speech is not without limit or constraint." John Le Carre's criticism of Rushdie, for instance, took this form.[3] But that is hardly the interesting question raised by Rushdie's book, and it is only if one understands liberal commitments in this simplistic way that such a simplistic form of criticism could surface as the relevant objection. Perhaps some will be inclined to such an understanding of liberalism but I had argued that the more subtle and difficult problem with standard versions of liberalism lies elsewhere. It lies in the fact that so much of classical liberal doctrine, which still dominates modern thought and practice, has taken the form of a priori philosophical argument in favor of liberal principles of tolerance. By "a priori," I mean something very specific; I mean an argument that appeals to no substantive value commitments of citizens. So, for instance, Mill argued that principles regarding freedom of speech are derivable from roughly the following argument. "Our opinions have been wrong in the past. That is evidence that our present opinions may be wrong. Therefore, we should tolerate dissent from our present opinions, just in case they are wrong." Such an argument is a priori in the sense that it is supposed to appeal to *anyone capable of reason,* whatever they might value. Rushdie has sometimes spoken with admiration for this argument in Mill.[4] This strikes me as a mistake. I think the argument, intuitive though it may seem, is a rather gross fallacy because it is based on a wholly non-credible epistemology.[5] Mill gave other arguments for free speech as well, much more modest ones, such as the argument that we should adopt free speech as a principle because it allows for diversity of opinion. This argument is more modest because it does not lay claim to being persuasive to anyone capable of reason, but only to those who value diversity. It rests therefore not with some universal conclusion about the rationality of free speech but rather, because it appeals to a substantive value (the value of diversity), which some people may embrace and others may not, it rests with a conclusion about its reasonableness only for those who do embrace it. I had defended Rushdie against the efforts of Muslims in many parts of the world to censor him, not by the first, ambitious form of argument, but rather the second, more modest form. I did so because I don't believe that there are *any* effective arguments for free speech (or indeed *any other* political or moral principle) that ought to be persuasive to anyone, so long as they are rational, independent of any substantive values they hold.[6]

And from the other direction, I tried to undermine Roth's distinction by arguing that the moral-psychological economy of ordinary Muslims was far more internally contradictory (even if only implicitly and latently so) than the distinction would acknowledge, and that the best case that can be made for Rushdie is to argue that *The Satanic Verses* critically addresses many of those aspects of religious doctrine that the large majority of ordinary, non-"fundamentalist"[7] (though devout) Muslims were themselves implicitly repudiating in many of their de facto secular social formations and habits. He was, in short, their ally against fundamentalist conceptions of Islam, and it was inconsistent therefore to entirely dismiss him and his book in the way that most of these very Muslims had done. If a realization of this implicit internal inconsistency eventually brought, in its wake, an increasing commitment to principles of freedom of speech among Muslims, even in the context of Rushdie's blasphemous novel, that would not be because these principles were plonked down as some philosophically established universal truths of Millian liberal doctrine, but rather because they issued from the resolution of such internal tensions within Muslim values.

This form of internal criticism by Muslims had a much better chance of coming to a viable defense of Rushdie, I claimed, than the one which aspired to ulterior forms of universality and objectivity for liberal principles. But it was constantly blocked by a picture of the dispute that was to be found in the stark distinction that Roth's slogans described. Internal criticism of laws of blasphemy from within Islam by appeal to other values that Muslims hold is only possible if Islamic populations are *conflicted*—conflicted between their commitment to a religion in which there are doctrinal elements regarding prohibition of blasphemy as well as their commitment to values that lend support to greater freedom of speech. In general, internal arguments can only be given when there is internal conflict of this kind. One set of values can then be deployed to give reasons to shed the other opposing value commitments. That is what is meant by "internal" criticism or deliberation deploying "internal" reasons. But if Roth's slogan is true of Islam (as he says it was of Eastern European nations) and only one thing matters, then presumably *there is no* internal conflict and no scope for defending Rushdie against their religious commitments that would censor blasphemy.

2.

What is much more surprising, however, is that The *Satanic Verses* has been particularly difficult to defend along these internalist lines I had proposed, not because of such caricaturing slogans but because of a much more considered challenge coming from scholars and critics who are highly sympathetic and knowledgeable about Islam. I don't mean sympathies and challenges of a superficial sort which simply say, "Tolerance does not mean that you can say anything, however offensive," such as those voiced by John Le Carre. The really difficult and interesting issues are not addressed by such simply stated reactions to Rushdie, and for all my admiration and respect for Le Carre, I think Rushdie's

irritable response to him was to some extent justified, given how crudely
he had presented his objections. What I have in mind when I say there
is an especially difficult challenge that one has to meet if one is going to
defend Rushdie is a criticism of him that goes something like this. (A
good example of its proponents is Talal Asad.)[8]

First, some background. Before looking at the local Muslim response
to Rushdie in Britain, which is Asad's main focus, it is worth recording
the response at the global level, and the material and psychological condition of many of the nations with predominantly Muslim populations
from which that response came. In an interesting way the issues at the
global and the more local level are structurally the same.

In the global picture nobody any longer really denies (except perhaps
a writer such as Naipaul who in his pursuit of surface cultural criticism
of various Islamic peoples has cultivated a deliberate ignorance about
both their histories and their political economies)[9] that the Muslim
reaction is to a large extent a product of a certain attitude of resentment
that has developed over years of colonial rule. Even after decolonization
the West's corporate-driven undermining of the material lives of many
Muslim populations today, its support for Israel against Palestinian aspirations for the most elementary of freedoms, the failure in the past of
Arab Nationalism to shake that support and generally to forge a sense of
post-colonial autonomy and dignity, and the humiliation by the imperial
invasions of Afghanistan and Iraq have all contributed to a continuation
of that attitude even among ordinary, non-fundamentalist Muslims. As
a result the West's support for Rushdie, a novelist who is perceived as
being offensively critical of Islam from the point of view of modernity
and with the literary techniques of post-modernity, is bound to be seen
as just another arrogant symptom of longstanding Western domination
and postures of condescension and contempt.

This psychology at the global level among nations with predominantly
Muslim populations is replayed at the local level among the immigrant
Muslim minorities in European nations like Britain where Rushdie lived
and wrote, and this cannot be surprising because it is the product of very
similar material relations. It should go without reminding but perhaps it
will not, so I will remind you, that the first large wave of Muslim immigration to Britain and other European nations was a result of the relative

privileging of the metropolitan proletariat due to surpluses produced by more than a century of the international spread of Western capital by colonial rule, and also a result of the need to meet the labor shortage in European countries in the decade or more of reconstruction after the Second World War. This wave of immigration was the product of deliberate policy decisions by the governments of many European nations, and it led in subsequent decades to further immigration of families in a pattern that is now well known and well studied. Once again, therefore, as with colonial rule, and once again due to causes that emerge from the movement of the forces and demands of capital, non-white populations were brought together with Western populations, this time *in Western nations.* The inequalities first created by colonial rule at the global level were in fact now being echoed *within* the borders of Western nations themselves.

With this background of colonial history and post-colonial migrant formations in place, the sort of argument I am considering can be summarized as roughly this. Though these immigrants are granted various forms of political equality as the liberal state conceives of them, it is not allowed as a negotiable question, in the context of a "blasphemous" book, whether the first freedom is indeed first. In the global picture, this liberal position is presented as the culmination of hard-won historical progress in the Western world to which the lagging colonies and neo-colonies must now also aspire to evolve. In the local migrant context in Western nations, the argument is more straightforward: The liberal perspective is simply one of "this is how we are. These are our liberal values of free speech, and if you have come to live here, these are the laws you must learn to live under." The point is often extended of course to a far wider range of values than freedom of expression, to include such things as what is worn on one's body and head, what is taught in one's schools, what is paraded on the streets, and so on. Sometimes there is a concession to cultural autonomy in the exercise of such cultural values so long as it is restricted to a sphere in which the basic defining features of the liberal state are left untouched. That is the ideal of multi*culturalism* as we have come to know and love it. But as soon as the Muslim demands something that runs up against the *political* values of free speech upheld by the state, as happened in the aftermath of the publication of Rushdie's book, the limits of multiculturalism are immediately revealed. The British liberal state would not make any concessions.

Such a critique is a much harder and more sophisticated challenge to meet than the simplicities of Roth's distinction and Le Carre's heartfelt sympathies for Muslim sensitivities. How should one respond to it, if one still wishes to defend Rushdie? Is there still some relevance to the general line of defense I had given of Rushdie in responding to this critique?

The first thing to notice is the way in which this critique presents the matter, implicitly at least, as one of a rather straightforward relativism—though in someone like Asad the relativism is not really made explicit. British society simply lays down the law: "This is how we are, these are our laws, so you better adapt to them if you are here." But the Muslims, who were allowed there by international immigration policies to fulfill British economic ends and are now full and rightful citizens of the land, can with equal right claim their own alternative *nomic* structures, which in the context of a "blasphemous" book, will clash with liberal laws. That is the relativist impasse. It is law versus law. And multi*cultural* accommodation is not to the point, or not the primary point. It is wrong of the state to insist on something that is genuinely disputable by its legal citizens. Granting those citizens superficial cultural concessions of headdress, etc., is not the accommodation that is needed. What is needed is an acknowledgement that there is an impasse here on fundamental values, and minority rights require the Muslim demand for censorship not to be dismissible by the liberal state.

Now it was partly my point in those early writings that introducing relativism in this way into the dispute is not to introduce anything very precise or instructive. The positing of a relativist impasse between two nomic systems—one making free speech primary, the other prepared to place free speech second in the context of what everyone acknowledges is a book that writes of a community's most deep and cherished notions with satirical contempt—is to land one with a framework for the dispute that impoverishes the theoretical possibilities.

A first step in revising the framework that Asad's sort of critique imposes is to ask what underlies the British state's attitude. The attitude, I think, is a statist assertion of what I had earlier described as the doctrinal refusal to look for "internal" arguments for free speech, arguments that might appeal to some of the substantive values of ordinary, non-fundamentalist Muslims. On such a view, the assumption is that British society has evolved into values which have a greater or more objective right on their side, and so with that right behind it, the state has no other option but to impose liberal laws. These laws alone have the right on their side. Asad denies them this right and instead asserts a relative (or relativist) right on each nomic side (the values of both the liberal state and the Muslim community).

When the formulation of the framework of the dispute is revised in this way, one can start to find a way out. To begin with, notice a curious thing. *Both* sides in the dispute, when the dispute is formulated in these revised terms, make an assumption that is quite wrong. It is basically an assumption about the nature of reason in politics and morals. The assumption is that if one cannot get reasons that all rational people are going to accept, then one is not in the realm of reason or reasoning with one another at all and there is an impasse, with a relativist right now on each side. This reduces the options, a reduction that *both* sides to the dispute, *despite* their deep opposition to one another, *share,* because of their shared assumption that there is nothing by way of reasoning when reasons of a classical liberal sort are found wanting.

Yet there are theoretical resources by which one may resist this narrowing theoretical assumption that they both take for granted. What that shared assumption does not admit in the space of rationality is any position for what I have called "internal" reasons. But there still is scope, if we allow for a notion of internal reasons, to finesse the dichotomy on offer—either reasons that establish the high-profile objectivity of the liberal principle of free speech or a concession that the principle is just one among others, with only a relativized truth on each side. Allowing internal reasons would still require the liberal position to resist the claim that Muslims have an equal right to their laws when it comes to a matter of such depth of belief and feeling, but it would equally require the liberal *not* to do so by simply declaring that this is because they have come to a more modern and advanced society and must therefore live according to its liberal laws. Asad's complaint is against the latter position taken by the liberal state and the complaint is perfectly justified. But such justification as it has in no way sanctions his further claim that therefore the liberal must admit in the name of minority rights that his own liberal principle of free speech is only one among others (even others which contradict it), each of which has a right, a relativist right, on its side. Rather it behooves the liberal to look for values *within* the Muslim populations (that is what makes the reasoning internal) which might lead them to conclude, despite their depth of feeling about Islam, that free speech may after all be primary. There is nothing in Asad's critique which rules this theoretical and practical possibility out. In fact, it is not clear that there is anything that *can* rule the *possibility* out.

I have written elsewhere about what the scope and the difficulties are for making these possibilities a serious prospect, so I won't rehearse those points here. But I do want to note here that once one sees things in this broader framework, it ought to become clearer why it is increasingly unfair to blame Rushdie's novel (as Rushdie's critics such as Michael Dummett[10] who are sympathetic to Muslim immigrants have done) for being the source and trigger of the hostile reaction in European nations against Muslims for their defensive and censorious response to it. That backlash can now be seen rather as having its real and original source *not* in a deliberately insensitive work of literature, *nor* in the rigidity of a "backward" religious population migrated into alien liberal terrain, but as emerging from a prior refusal on the classical *liberal* state's part to acknowledge that the migration of cultural difference into one's midst should have the effect of laying it open to internal argument, which the state must use its conceptual and other resources to provide. And on the other side, the problem is compounded because this refusal by the liberal state to see values as emerging in negotiable internalist outcomes (a refusal coming from a conviction that they express a universal, philosophically justified truth which allows the state one has adopted therefore to simply impose it with a sense of self-justification) produces just the defensiveness among Muslim immigrants that we recorded in the global picture of colonial rule and which makes it impossible for them to see Rushdie as a partial ally, despite his perceived rhetorical excesses.

This diagnosis should help to deflect Asad's and Dummett's and Le Carre's understanding of *The Satanic Verses,* as the willfully destructive ethnography of a Western-minded liberal author, deaf to the voices of unequal nations of the world and unequal citizens within the Western world.

The diagnosis views the magnitude and vehemence of the Muslim response to Rushdie as deriving from the fact that much more than private faith has been perceived to be under attack, since Islam in many parts of the world is a religion that has a very high political profile. Many of its political aspirations, however, are also the source of considerable anguish for ordinary Muslims since they are sometimes exploited to foist upon Muslim societies policies (and even sometimes regimes) which ordinary Muslims find highly objectionable. Zia's Pakistan, Hekmatyar's Afghanistan, Khomeini's Iran were just some of the examples that were vivid in Rushdie's time of writing *The Satanic Verses*. There is repeated proof that such qualms pervade the thinking of ordinary Muslims. Democratic national elections in any of these countries, when they have occurred, have never yielded more than a fractional vote for the Islamist parties. In general ordinary people have never supported such parties nor are they ever likely to, except where Islam has been suppressed, as in Algeria and perhaps now in Egypt. Even in places where an absolutist Islamic political organization like Hamas does have support among Muslims, that is not because of its absolutism but because it is the only organization that is working hard and with some effectiveness to provide basic services (such as medical, educational, communicative) as well as minimal structures of civil society for one of the most brutalized peoples in the world.

How might this distaste for absolutism among ordinary, usually devout, but non-fundamentalist Muslims be exploited to give an "internalist" defense of the author of a book that has given these very same Muslims such deep offense? By first asking them not to forget that Rushdie has shown great sympathy for their condition in his excoriating critique in the very same novel of Thatcherite England's attitudes and policies toward its immigrant populations. And then, having done that, urging them, despite their feelings of hurt, to also now direct their attention to Rushdie's own anguish, to his own scorn and detestation for the absolutist Islamist vision and to ask them to respond to what seems to be a challenge thrown down by those sections of the novel in which Islam is most obviously the subject: Can we any longer separate the tyrannies of social and political practice in which Islam is so often invoked in Iran, say, or in Afghanistan under the Taliban, without being more critical of *ourselves* and our uncritical susceptibility to such absolutist exploitation of our justified resentment of Western domination of our lands and people? To try to meet this challenge would be to take the novel more seriously than Asad or Dummett or Le Carre would have Muslims do; it would be to awaken to the novel's significance for one's own goals as ordinary non-fundamentalist Muslims, and not simply to dismiss it with the charge of being offensive. Even if the challenge was successfully answered, an honest effort to think it through could not proceed without acknowledging that Rushdie was, for all his differences with the devout commitments of ordinary Muslims, their supporter in a common and worthy agenda. With that acknowledgement crucially in place, a non-absolutist Muslim reader, even if he found the self-consciously post-modern irreverence of the novel alien and offensive, even if she disagreed with Rushdie's wholesale skepticism about the revelation and about Muhammad's unfaltering monotheism, could nevertheless be in a better psychological position to see it as merely Rushdie's own individual mode of pursuit of that shared agenda. Now the excesses (if that is how one views them) of an ally's rhetoric may still offend, but he can hardly any longer be convicted of treachery.

These efforts to put the novel and its author under a more sympathetic light than where his critics, whom I have mentioned, have placed him are of course fraught with the difficulties created by an attitude of defensiveness against the West which I have said is pervasive among most Muslims today, despite their dislike for the fundamentalists in their own society.

However, Muslim defensiveness with regard to the West is a very nuanced thing. In thinking about it historically, one must distinguish between hostility and defensiveness. For centuries the relations between Christian Europe and its growing Islamic neighbor were defined by a hostility in matters of territory and doctrine, and were displayed in the violence of wars and in the most vilifying propaganda against the other. But there was a robustness in this exchange and there was a perverse form of respect for each other that was shown by more or less equal foes. There was a genuine appreciation of and instruction in the achievement of the other in the wide span of culture, science, philosophy, and literature. It was only with the rise of Western colonial domination that this health of hostility eroded into a feeling of defensiveness bred upon the loss of autonomy and upon colonial attitudes of superiority and condescension. These are the attitudes which I said continue today in revised forms for the reasons I mentioned earlier. I stress all this to point out that it is not the so-called "clash" of civilizations that is in itself the issue. As I have just said, there were sustained such clashes for a long period in the past where such attitudes were quite absent. It is only when there is *conquest passing itself off as a clash* that these sentiments surface, as they continue to do today. It is the utter and deliberate sleight of hand and willful deception in the use of the term "clash," knowing perfectly well that for some centuries now and for the foreseeable future "conquest" is the more apt description for the relations between Islam and the West, that is the deepest flaw in Huntington's paper. The fact that today (since decolonization, that is) these conquests do not always take the overt form of invasions (thought clearly they have started doing so once again), but rather the form of corporate-driven foreign engagements as well as cruel and crippling embargoes and sanctions, should not conceal the manifest element of conquest, of materially unequal and exploitative engagement. It is the psychology issuing from these subtle or blatant forms of conquest that has blinded ordinary Muslims to the point and usefulness the novel might have for his or her own value commitments.

Their response to Rushdie has tended to be that he has not helped their case at all in the struggle against Islamic fundamentalism. It is often said that he has provoked rather than condemned the fundamentalist, that he has—at best—shown bad judgment by having failed to see the extremity of the feelings he was going to provoke or—at worst—he saw it all clearly and deliberately sought the publicity it brought him.

But it can surely be replied on his behalf that the fundamentalists have been and will be provoked by much less than Rushdie serves up, so it may be overscrupulous to worry about provoking them. By focusing on the fundamentalist response they are failing to explore the questions that Rushdie's novel and the aftermath of its publication pose for *their own* goals, for the goals of the vast majority of Muslims who are as opposed to the fundamentalist element in their societies as they are hurt by the novel. The deepest issue, then, is whether the answers that such Muslims will, on reflection, provide to these questions are compatible with their own condemnation of the novel. If not, there is a fundamental but implicit contradiction in their position and it is a matter of enormous consequence that they become alive to it. To be hurt and offended by the novel is one thing, a natural thing, for a devout person. But to take up these questions and answer them with reason and intelligence is quite another thing for it does not permit the offense to breed a stultifying defensiveness. I am not suggesting that Muslims will or should agree with Rushdie in his wholesale religious skepticism or his ideas about how the religious impulse is better gratified in our world by art and literature than by orthodox religions. But to disagree and to criticize him amount to taking his novel seriously and therefore to rejecting the sort of condemnation of it one finds so widespread among Muslims. Such disagreement will require that they provide a detailed answer to the question: How can Muslim nations work to build a just and free society in the sort of legitimizing religious framework that even the non-absolutists among them have adopted, without surrender to or constant threat from the fundamentalist elements?

Recent history has repeatedly shown that the progressive possibilities of a politicized Islam amount to a dangerous myth. Rushdie's *Shame* and *The Satanic Verses* have done much to make this evidence vivid. If his novels are remembered for having raised once again the possibilities for Muslims of internal transformations within the practices of Islam, it is hard to see what his bad judgment is supposed to consist in. It is hard to see why the publicity he has sought is selfish. As far as I can see it has—at hideous cost to himself—publicized the need for a more depoliticized Islam. It would be an ungenerous people that focused only on the satirical and parodic "excesses" of an author who has raised questions of such deep and primary significance for them.

3.

When we move the focus from what I have been calling "ordinary" Muslims to those critics of Rushdie who have grown up with the literature and culture of the West, it is much worse than a lack of generosity. It is a failure to grasp the claims that Rushdie has always made for the very idea of writing, and especially of the novel and its inherent potential for cultural and political criticism, a potential with which his Western critics should be perfectly familiar. One crucial element in these claims is to be found in the stance that Rushdie takes on the *mode* of political and cultural criticism, a stance that all of Rushdie's novels brilliantly exemplify, viz., that the novel's power to criticize existing hegemonies cannot be restricted to the mode of argument and counter-argument; it must if necessary take in, in its criticism, the hegemonizing compromises of that mode itself. It must commit itself to providing a clash of modes and languages. No doubt this runs the risk of being perceived as creating excesses, but the stance has always claimed that anything less comprehensive in its polemical and critical intention and effect would only perpetuate the forms and pieties that frame the hegemonies in question.

This stance is not hard to discern in *The Satanic Verses* unless one is distracted by one's own defensiveness as Muslims might be, but presumably his Western critics have no reason to be at all. Anybody who notices that a novelist is disrespectful, not merely to a religious prophet and his family with the play of proper names, but to everything else he touches in every novel he writes, must surely pause to wonder whether there is a considered point underlying this comprehensiveness, and whether the particular things that offend him might have flowed from a more general conviction of what the possibilities of a novel are in the author's own conception of his work.

Nor, obviously, is the stance Rushdie's invention. It is admittedly true that in the last several decades in the West, the target of this stance has always been the bourgeois hegemonies of a culture shaped by a seemingly decaying but, in fact, highly resilient capitalism. Walter Benjamin quotes a Brechtian maxim at the end of his "Conversations" with Brecht: "Don't start with the good old things, start with 'the bad *new* things.'"[11] So it might seem startling and injudicious that an Anglo-Indian novelist brings this stance to a target which his Western critics would have us consider a "bad *old* thing," pre-Enlightenment religiosity, something that the West itself has outgrown, but to be discussed and criticized where it does exist in a more appropriately solemn mode. Rushdie is very well aware of this and has all along resisted the idea of the unsuitability of his adopted mode of writing for his subjects. The question Edward Said once rightly posed—Why did Rushdie fall into this Orientalizing misrepresentation of Islam?—therefore, has an answer. In making a "bad old thing" the target of a post-modern cultural critical stance, *The Satanic Verses* repudiated the historicist restriction of appropriate stances for appropriate targets; it repudiated the restriction as *itself* another Orientalist withholding of the creative possibilities of Islam for its own self-understanding and self-criticism.

Fredric Jameson has written of the appropriateness of pastiche rather than parody in the context of post-modernist culture.[12] Though I happen to find this restriction unconvincing (for reasons that I can't possibly elaborate here), that is not because I am committed to the strong *general* claim that periodicity imposes no constraints on the effectiveness of such modes and stances. If that were so, my concern in the next paragraph for a politicized humanism, fitting for the post-modern literary sensibility, would have no validity. My claim is weaker and more particular. Putting aside Jameson, I am only claiming of Rushdie's stance as I have described it first, that there is a tendency to see it as yielding Orientalizing distortions and excesses in the context of its particular target—Islam—because of a perceived inappropriateness of that stance for that target, and second, this perception of inappropriateness, this restriction of what Islam may employ for its own self-criticism, smacks of the very Orientalism that it charges the stance of having fallen into. Why should well-known antecedents to Rushdie within this stance, such as for example the films of Bunuel and Arrabal (sickening to devout Christians), be any more justified in their intended power to undermine the seemingly perpetual conserving tendencies of bourgeois European culture than Rushdie's intentions, in his own novel, to undermine the constricting and conserving dimensions of the holy for internal changes within the practices of the social life of Muslims?

Literature and criticism, in the world in which Rushdie was educated and lived and wrote *The Satanic Verses,* has witnessed the passing of Leavisite humanism and modernism; and more recently it witnessed the inabilities of an avowedly anti-humanist structuralist and post-structuralist ideology, which succeeded it, to cope with its own urges for cultural criticism. It is struggling to forge a more politicized humanism.

The older humanist paradigms seem manifestly naive and irrelevant, so much so that a vexed question looms for the whole literary culture: How can a humanism, however politicized, fail to seem so? The stance Rushdie has chosen, drawing on and echoing diverse literary and critical strands—from Surrealist Manifestoes to Bakhtin, to name just two, is one effort to answer this question. The irreverent, blaspheming polemical potential provided by the familiarizing speech of popular culture, the "carnival" which "marks the suspension of all hierarchical ranks, privileges, norms and prohibitions," which "opposes all that is ready-made and completed, all pretence at immutability"—these are the explicit adoptions of an answer which attempts, on the one hand to move out of existing apolitical formalisms and relativisms, and on the other to finesse the outdated, pious, legitimizing modes of traditional humanisms. The answer may not, in the end, satisfy and undoubtedly there are other possible answers. On that I take no particular stand, at any rate not here. But it is *an* answer and Rushdie's critics should acknowledge that novels which struggle to provide such answers are struggling with one of the most urgent demands of their culture.

4.

I have spent this essay defending a book against a range of criticisms from a variety of sources. The defense is of a book. If someone were to ask why, if you defend this book, do you not defend the invasions of Afghanistan and Iraq, for which similar claims might be made—that is, that they were carried out to undermine fundamentalist and other forms of tyranny—my answer is not merely that those are invasions (and not books) in which thousands of innocent people have been killed, but that I do not for a moment believe that the *motives* behind those invasions were as these claims suggest. Nor do I believe, as anybody who is not utterly uninformed and devoid of common sense could, that the *consequences* of these invasions will have been to undermine Islamic fundamentalism or the terrorism associated with it. If anything, the opposite is true. Rushdie has sometimes written and spoken with sympathy for some arguments given in favor of a military intervention in Iraq, a sympathy which is in some sense, I suppose, intended to be continuous with his efforts in *The Satanic Verses,* to oppose despotic regimes, including regimes that support Islamic fundamentalism and jihadi groups. Nothing whatever in this essay defending that book should be seen as joining him in this sympathy. For (I wager) nothing in the arguments provided in this essay in defending that book could be continuous with any arguments that he might provide for having that sympathy.

Reflections on Edward Said

Occidentalism, the Very Idea

*An Essay on the Enlightenment, Enchantment,
and the Mentality of Democracy*

1.

It wouldn't be too lofty to describe the extensive debate in many related disciplines over the last few decades about the inherited ideas and ideologies of the "Enlightenment" as our intellectual efforts at self-understanding—in particular, our efforts to come to a more or less precise grip on the sense in which we belong to a period, properly describable as our "modernity."

These ongoing efforts on our part, however, gain a specific interest when they surface in the context of a new form of cold war that has religious rather than communist ideals as its target. Since religion, at least on the surface, in some fairly obvious sense runs afoul of the demands of the Enlightenment, our modernity may seem to be much more at stake now than it was in the contestations of the original Cold War, where the issues seemed to be more about a conflict *internal* to the ideals of the Enlightenment.[1] But in the passage of analysis in this essay, I will have hoped to raise one serious angle of doubt about this seeming difference.

A recurring complaint among critics of the Enlightenment is about a *complacence* in the rough and cumulative consensus that has emerged in modern "Western" thought of the last two centuries and a half. The complaint is misplaced. There has, in fact, always been a detectably edgy and brittle quality in the prideful use of omnibus terms such as "modernity" and "the Enlightenment" to self-describe the "West" and its claim to being something more than a geographical location. One sign of this nervousness is a quickness to find a germ of *irrationality* in any source of radical criticism of the consensus. From quite early on, the strategy has been to tarnish the opposition as being poised in a perpetual ambiguity between radicalism and irrationalism (including sometimes an irrationalism that encourages a fascist, or incipiently fascist, authoritarianism.) Nietzsche was one of the first to sense the theoretical tyranny in this and often responded with an edginess of his own by flamboyantly refusing to be made self-conscious and defensive by the strategy, and by explicitly embracing the ambiguity. More recently Foucault, among others, responded by preempting the strategy and declaring that the irrational was, in any case, the only defense of those who suffered under the comprehensive cognitive grip of the discursive power unleashed by modernity, in the name of "rationality."[2]

I want to pursue some of the underlying issues of this confusing dialectic in such disputation regarding the modern. There is a great urgency to get some clarity on these issues. The stakes are high and they span a wide range of themes on the borderline of politics and culture. In fact, eventually, nothing short of the democratic ideal is at stake, though I will get to that theme more briefly than it deserves in the last third or so of this essay.

A familiar element in a cold war is that the warring sides are joined by academics and other writers, shaping attitudes and rationalizing or domesticating the actions of states and the interests that drive them, in conceptual terms for a broader intellectual public.[3] Some of this conceptual work is brazen and crass and is often reckoned to be so by the more alert among the broad public. But other writing is more sophisticated and has a more superior tone, making passing acknowledgements of the faults on the side to whom it gives intellectual support, and such work is often lionized by the intellectual elites as "fair-minded" and "objective" and despite these marginal criticisms of the state in question, it is tolerated by the broad consensus of those in power. Ever since Samuel Huntington wrote his influential article "The Clash of Civilizations,"[4] there has been a danger that a new cold war would emerge, one between the "West" and "Islam" to use the vast, generalizing terms of Huntington's own portentous claims. Sure enough since that time, and especially with two or three hot wars thrown in to spur the pundits on, an increasing number of books with the more sophisticated aspiration have emerged to consolidate what Huntington had started.

To elaborate this essay's concerns, I will proceed a little obliquely by initially focusing closely and at some length on one such book and briefly invoking another as its foil, and then situate the concerns in a larger historical and conceptual framework. The focus is worth its while since the conclusions of the book I have primarily chosen, as well as the attitudes it expresses, are representative of a great deal of both lay and academic thinking on these themes.

The subtitle of Ian Buruma and Avishai Margalit's *Occidentalism* elaborates its striking title as "The West in the Eyes of Its Enemies."[5] The book's aim is to provide an account of a certain *conception* of the West which is named in their title and which they find today in hostile Islamist reactions to the West, a conception which they claim is just as unfair to and dehumanizing of the West as "Orientalism" was said to be of the Orient, in Edward Said's well-known book bearing that name.[6]

The book is slight and haphazard in argument and my interest in it is not so much intrinsic as it is to use it instrumentally in the dialectic of this essay's analysis. It furnishes—in its way—some of the fundamental theoretical notions needed to present that analysis. Given their various, somewhat unsystematic claims in the book, it is a little obscure, and perhaps even a little arbitrary, what they mean by the "West" and therefore what they have in mind by "Occidentalism." At times they write as if the term "the West" is to be defined by two basic *ideals or principles,* which had their origins in seventeenth century Europe and settled into what we have come to call "the Enlightenment," the tenets of scientific rationality and the formal aspects of democracy, including the commitment to basic liberal individual rights. The "Enemies of the West" are said to be opposed to these principles.

But for the most part, the book, in its successive chapters, identifies the targets of these "Enemies" *as much broader cultural phenomena* than these principles, phenomena such as permissive and "sinful" metropolitan life in the West that has abandoned the organic links that individuals have to nature and community, such as commercial rather than heroic ideals, such as a mechanistic and materialistic outlook which stresses instrumental rationality and utilitarian values rather than the values of the various Romantic and nationalistic and indigenist traditions, and finally, such as a stress on secular and humanistic values which entirely exclude religion from the public realm and therefore invite the "wrath of God" whose domain must be unrestricted.

It is never made clear what exactly the relation is between the defining principles of the West mentioned earlier and these broader cultural phenomena. Both are targets of the "Occidentalists," but what their relation is to one another as targets is never satisfactorily explained. The book's own response to the two targets is somewhat different. They have some sympathy for the opposition to some of the broader phenomena[7] (as anyone might, however much they are committed to the goodness of the West) but the final message of the book comes through as a firm defense of the scientific rationality and the political principles that the "West" is said to have ushered in as exemplary aspects of modernity, and upon which it has defined itself. This differential response on the authors' part makes it particularly important to sort out the question of the relationship between the defining principles and the broader phenomena.

The response leads one to think that the argument of the book is roughly this. The defining essence of "the West" lies in the two basic principles I mentioned earlier but in the eyes of its enemies there is a conflation of these principles with these wider cultural phenomena. Perhaps the conflation occurs via some sort of *illicit derivation* of these cultural phenomena from those principles. Thus, in the attack on these cultural phenomena, the West, as defined by these principles, is also attacked by "Occidentalism." (The authors quite clearly suggest such an interpretation of their argument in frequent remarks describing "Occidentalist" attitudes toward the West (p. 38): "It was an arrogant mistake to think that all men should be free, since our supposed freedoms led only to inhumanity and sterile materialism.") The suspicion that anti-Western thought among Muslims is guilty of such an illicit derivation of some of its conclusions from partially justified critical observations regarding the

West is quite widespread in Western writing and thinking on this subject, and their book has the merit of articulating it very explicitly.

Toward the end of the book, they lightly rehearse the by now well-known intellectual antecedents of the contemporary radical Islamist critique of the broader cultural phenomena in Wahabism as well as in the more recent writings of Maulana Maududi and Syed Qutb; but in earlier chapters there are much more intellectually ambitious efforts at finding prior locations for the critique (especially the aspect of the critique that stresses the loss of Romantic and nationalist and indigenist traditions for the pursuit of utilitarian values and a superficial cosmopolitanism) in certain intellectual traditions in Germany, Russia, and Japan—which then presumably would also count as being anti-"West." The interest of these more ambitious diagnostic efforts are not pursued with any depth or rigor. By the end, one does not quite know what to make of these claims to antecedent "Enemies" since no convincing case is even attempted for a causal and historical influence of these intellectual and cultural movements on radical Islam (though see note 8 below), nor—and this is much worse—is there any effort to sort out what is implied by this recurring critique of "the West" and the principles that define it. One is, at best, left with the impression of an interesting parallel.[8]

The sophistication of the book, therefore, lies not at all in deeply exploring the implications of its own ambitious efforts to connect politics with broader cultural issues. Its sophistication lies entirely in the kind of thing I had mentioned earlier, the fact that its cold war voice comes with a veneer of balance: There are parenthetical and somewhat mildly registered remarks about how Islamist groups also target the long history of colonial subjugation as the enemy, including the West's, especially America's, *continuing* imperial presence in economic (and more recently political) terms in various Muslim nations, as well as its extensive support of either corrupt, brutal, or expansionist regimes over the years as in Saudi Arabia, Israel, Egypt, Indonesia, and so on. But no one should go away with the impression that any of this is more than a veneer. The authors are clear that these do not constitute the main issue. The main issue is that the "Enemies of the West" have first of all confused what is the essence of the West—as I said, scientific rationality and liberal democracy—with the broader cultural phenomena discussed in the four main chapters and second, have again unfairly and *illicitly extended* their perhaps justified anger against Western conquest and colonization and corporate exploitation to a generalized opposition to the "West" *as defined by those principles.* The West is advised not to be made to feel so guilty by these illicit extensions and derivations that it gives up on its essential commitments to its defining principles. Whether one may conclude that it is also advised to stop its unending misadventures in foreign lands over the centuries is not so obvious from the text, since its focus is primarily on characterizing a confused and extrapolated state of mind called "Occidentalism."

To now pursue something that this book leaves superficial and incomplete, it is useful to compare its argument with another recent book, Mahmood Mamdani's *Good Muslim/Bad Muslim,*[9] because its emphasis is entirely elsewhere and it in fact provides something of a foil to Buruma and Margalit's understanding of some of these issues. Those they call the Islamist "Enemies" of the West are the "Bad Muslims" of his title. Those who support American interests in the Middle East, Central Asia, and South Asia (the Chalabis, the Karzais, the Mubaraks, and the Musharaffs, to name only leaders) are the (ironically phrased) "Good Muslims." And he is highly critical of this dichotomy, as being both self-serving and ideological on the part of the West.

He stresses much more than they do the systematically imperialist nature of the US government's actions in these and other parts of the world. He gives an historical account, first of its many covert operations (described by him as "proxy wars") during the Cold War period when it primarily invoked the threat of communism as a justification, and then of its more overt campaigns in the waging of real wars since September 11th when the justification shifted to combating Islamic terror (though, of course, as Mamdani realizes, this justification did not have to wait till September 11; it was put into place immediately after the Cold War ended, and the operations continued in covert form till the atrocities of September 11 gave the United States the excuse for the more overt action in Afghanistan and Iraq).[10]

His analysis is familiar from a lot of writing over the years which has been critical of the United States government, but there is a useful account of the covert operations in the African theatre that are usually ignored in this critique, which has mostly tended to focus on the Middle East, Latin America, and Asia; and he is also courageous to put on center stage the question of Israeli occupation and expansion since 1967 and the successive American governments' support of it as a central diagnosis of the legitimate source of anger against the West.

Apart from the sketches of America's corporate and geo-politically driven wrongdoings in different parts of the world, the book's intellectual burden is to repudiate those who are evasive about these wrongs by changing the subject to, as he puts it, "cultural talk" about civilizational conflicts or conflicts of broad principles. By his lights the main principles at issue are not those of scientific rationality or of democratic liberalism but rather the principles by which one does not occupy another's lands and brutalize the people there, the principles by which one does not support corrupt and authoritarian regimes, the principles by which one does not overthrow perfectly honorable leaders and governments such as those in Iran in the 50s and in Chile in the 70s and replace them with monstrous, tyrannical governments that serve one's economic and generally hegemonic political ends. Everything else is secondary and a distraction from this main issue. By his lights, then, Buruma and Margalit's book will certainly count as typical of such "cultural talk," which he dismisses. To the question I put earlier, do Buruma and Margalit think that the West should be made to feel guilty over the litany of self-interested destructive interventions which Mamdani expounds, his own answer is bound to be that they not only do not think so, they want to distract us from thinking so by putting into the air such trumped up culturalist notions as "Occidentalism."

If I am right in placing *Occidentalism* as a sophisticated cold war intervention, Mamdani would be quite right to have such suspicions of the book. But the issue of culture's relation to politics is a more general one and this tendency on Mamdani's part and on the part of much of the traditional Left to dismiss the cultural surround of political issues is a theme that is essential to the argument of this essay. As I said, it is his view that talk of "Occidentalism" and other such notions should be seen as a sleight of hand, a sly, though not necessarily always conscious, changing of the subject. What he fails to see is that the deepest analysis of what goes wrong in this sort of cold war writing will require not merely seeing these authors as changing the subject from politics to culture, but rather bringing to bear a critique of the *integrated* position that links their politics to their cultural and intellectual stances. This would require linking his own leftist political stances to an absolutely indispensable cultural and intellectual surround. Mamdani's failure to situate his subject in a larger set of intellectual and cultural issues reflects a limitation of his own book, one that prevents a proper analysis of the claims of a full and substantial democracy in the mix of Enlightenment ideas that are associated with our "modernity." The book's failing is the mirror image of the failings of *Occidentalism.* The latter understands that the politics of so-called anti-"Western" thought must be connected with broader cultural phenomena, but its superficial analysis of these connections leaves it as just one more contribution to the new cold war. The former's politics honorably refuses to play into the cold war understanding of Islam, but its understanding of its own worthy politics remains superficial in that it precisely fails to make its analysis connect with the deeper cultural issues.

In order to reach toward the kind of analysis that both books in their contrasting ways fail to make, one needs to first take a critical (rather than dismissive) look at the eponymous "culturalist" idea of "Occidentalism" and to see what relation it bears to its obvious alter-referent, "Orientalism."

2.

The argument of Said's celebrated book is now widely familiar, but it is still worth a brisk walk through its main causeway in order to set up a comparison with Buruma and Margalit's inversion of it. To put it in very rudimentary and schematic terms, it had, among other things, five broad points to make about Western writing on the Orient which, as Said puts it, erected into the "Other" non-Western cultures in various parts of the world. (His attention was, of course, chiefly on writing about countries and cultures of predominantly Arab and Muslim peoples, so in that limited sense, his title is a suitable one for Buruma and Margalit to mimic since that is their focus too.)

First, and most obviously, the material inequalities generated by colonization gave rise to attitudes of civilizational condescension and the societies and peoples of the Orient were as a result presented as being inferior and undeveloped. *Second,* a related but quite different point, it stereotyped them and reduced their variety to monolithic caricatures. *Third,* even when it did not do either of the first two, even when it made the effort to find the Orient's civilizational glories, its attitude was that of wondrous awe, and so it once again reduced the power and living reality of those civilizations, only this time it reduced them to an exotic rather than an inferior or monolithic object. And *fourth,* he argued that all of these three features owed in more and less subtle ways to the proximity of such writing on the Orient to metropolitan sites of political and economic power. This fourth point is absolutely central to the critique and the tremendous interest it has generated. The critique's effectiveness lay in precisely refusing to see literary and scholarly productions about the Orient as self-standing, by linking seemingly learned and aesthetic efforts to (at their worst) mandarin-like self-interest and (at their best) to a blindness regarding their locational privilege. A scholar who can write a whole book on modern Turkey with a just a few tentatively and grudgingly formulated sentences about the treatment of Armenians and pass off as a man of integrity and learning in metropolitan intellectual circles of the West is a good and well-known example of the worst, and Said is devastating about such shabby work. But he is in fact at his literary-critical best when he half-admiringly takes on the more subtle Orientalist writing, such as Kipling's, where nothing so shameless is going on. A *fifth* point that pervaded a great deal of Said's writing on the subject was that all of these four features held true not just of the ideas and works of fringe or extremist intellectuals and writers, but rather of the most canonical and mainstream tradition. The fifth and fourth points are closely connected. It is not surprising that the *canonical* works should have the first three features if those features flowed from the deep links that writing has to *power.* The canon, after all, is often constructed by the powerful, in some broad sense of that term.

It is hard to find anything like the same interest in Buruma and Margalit's claims for "Occidentalist" ideas. The first feature is not to be expected since, as they themselves say, Occidentalist ideas and hostility emerge in Muslim populations out of a sense of material inferiority and humiliation rather than out of a sense of economic superiority. The second feature is plausibly present.[11] The third feature, which is one of the more interesting in Said's critique, is altogether absent and they themselves don't make any claims to it. The subtitle of their book, as I said, is "The West in the Eyes of Its Enemies." Said's subtitle, for good reason, is the more general "Western Conceptions of the Orient." Indeed Said's ideas could be faithfully summed up in a subtitle which reads "The Orient in the Eyes of Its Enemies *and Its Friends*."[12] Then again, by the nature of the case, the fourth and absolutely pivotal feature in Said's critique is not present. That is, the "Enemies" of the West who are presented in this book, far from being close to power, are motivated by their powerlessness and helplessness against Western power and domination. Buruma and Margalit themselves point this out repeatedly. Finally, the fifth feature is also completely absent since it is the extremist, fundamentalist Islamic groups and their ideologues who are "the Enemies of the West" invoking the "wrath of God," and they are far removed from the great and canonical works of Arabic, Persian, Urdu, and other writing, some of which (Iqbal, for instance) Buruma and Margalit mention in order to exclude them from their critique.

So such interest as there is in their argument and conclusions criticizing so-called "Occidentalism" lies not in anything that parallels these five points and the rich integrating relations between them which constitutes the critique of Orientalism, but rather in a line of argument which goes something like this. Among a colonized and powerless Muslim population, where there is a longstanding feeling of humiliation and helplessness, a fringe of religious extremists has emerged, who out of a deep sense of resentment against the colonizers are blinded to the diversity of the West, to its great achievements of the Enlightenment—the temper and ideals of scientific rationality and democratic pluralism—and so by distorted appeals to their religion they have instead focused on the worst aspects of Western life—rampant materialism, shallow commercialism, alienating loss of values and morals—elevating these latter to a picture of a realm of hellish sinfulness ("jahiliya") to be combated by the "wrath of God." Perhaps readers will out of sheer topical interest be drawn to this analysis, but it seems to me to altogether lack the texture and depth and power of the critique of Orientalism.

This absence of the texture and depth in the position taken by the book that it mimics in its title points in the end to a far more principled weakness in its own position, which needs to be exposed in some detail because it raises issues of a kind that go well beyond the interest in this particular book.

As I said, some interest certainly does lie in the book's comparisons and analogies with elements of what they call "Occidentalist" or "anti-Western" thought in other intellectual movements, such as the German Romantic tradition and the Slavophile and Japanese intellectual traditions. To take the first of these, Buruma and Margalit contrast the ideal of a certain kind of cultural *unity* which went deep in some of the German Romantics and led to *nationalist* casts of thought with the ideal of political *pluralism* in Enlightenment thought. There is truth in this contrast but even here the contrast actually integrates more ideas than they notice. Even in an early work of Nietzsche's such as *The Birth of Tragedy,* the Romantic ideal of a mystical unity of experience is traced by him to the undifferentiated quality of the effect of the chorus on the audience in Attic tragedy, and the "Dionysian" possibilities of this in music and dance are invoked with a view to providing a critique of the Apollonian ideal as it is found in the representational and intellectual-izing arts of the late Classical tradition. This is then deployed to assert the special status of a *non*-representational form such as music among the arts, and then German culture is singled out in Europe as the one culture to which music is absolutely central, and from this a broad philosophi-cal argument emerges for a more public and modern revival of such a Dionysian unity in a single German nation, undiluted by the civilities and diversities owing to the shallow cosmopolitanism and pluralism of the French Enlightenment. These heady connections make for fascinat-ing intellectual history, though of course one should "handle with care" when such seemingly diverse regions of human thought and culture and politics are being brought together in an argument.

Buruma and Margalit make the less complex, less philosophical, and more routine point that ideas of *racial* purity in Nazism grew out of quasi-metaphysical arguments for nationalism of this kind and there very likely is scope for such further intellectual integration of racialist attitudes and metaphysics. But it is equally true that Hitler himself invoked with great admiration the system and efficiency of the extermination of the American Indians by the colonists, and historians such as Richard Drinnon have convincingly elaborated the remarkable metaphysics underlying the racial hatred in that particular holocaust as well.[13]

It might be said that it is not quite keeping faith with their argument to invoke the case of these colonists in the West because they are *pre*-Enlightenment examples of "ethnic cleansing" and ideas of racial purity, and the authors are defining the West in *post*-Enlightenment terms. In fact, of course, the "cleansing" went on well into the high Enlightenment period and after, but still they may excuse themselves from a consideration of it on grounds that it was relatively distant from the prime location of the high European Enlightenment, which is their subject.

Even if we do allow them to excuse themselves from considering it, and even if we allow the focus to be exclusively on the period of high European Enlightenment, there are very obvious signs of how uncritical they are of their own basic notions. There is a bounty of extremely familiar evidence of European colonial racism based on similar philosophical rationales, in the heyday of the Enlightenment. It is hard to believe that the authors of *Occidentalism* are not aware of it. Why, then, do they ignore it? Presumably because to invoke it would be to depart from their focus, which is on *anti*-Enlightenment ideas. That is why the example they cite of German Romantic roots of German nationalism and eventually racism depends on an *anti*-rationalist critique of the Enlightenment, whereas colonial racism, they would claim, grew (at least partly) out of a desire to actually *spread* rationality to non-Western lands. This is fair enough: Writers can focus on whichever theme they wish.[14] But there are theoretical consequences of such a claim that are destructive of their own book's main argument. Let me explain.

If one accepts this understanding of colonialism as being (at least partly) motivated by the desire to make the rest of the world more rational, it has to then be granted that that, in turn, presupposes a moral-psychological picture in which there is a notion of rationality that colonial peoples did not possess, a sort of basic moral and mental lack. If so, a distinction of profound analytical significance in the very idea of rationality is generated by this. By the nature of the case, the lack cannot, therefore, be of a "th*in*" notion of rationality, one that is uncontroversially possessed by *all* (undamaged, adult, human minds); rather, it would have to be the lack of a "th*ick*" notion of rationality, a notion that owes to specific historical developments in outlook around the time of the rise of science and its implications for how to think ("rationally") about culture and politics and society. But this has the effect of logically undermining the central argument of the book because there is now a real question as to whether there is not a much tighter and perfectly *licit* derivational connection between such a commitment to rationality, which the authors admire, and the harms that Western colonial rule perpetrated in its name, which the Occidentalist with some justification (even according to the authors) resents. Yet this is exactly the derivational connection which, as I pointed out in the exposition of their argument, they find to be *illicit* and a fallacy. The book's own implicit assumptions are, therefore, devastating to its main line of thought.

3.

It is really hereabouts that we can find the more obvious sources for a critique of the Enlightenment that no cold war sensibility such as theirs could possibly acknowledge. I say it is obvious but the exact structure of the critique and its longstanding historical underpinnings are not always made explicit. Let me begin with a locus of this critique at some distance from the West and then present very early antecedents to it in the dissenting traditions of the West, itself.

The anti-Western figure who comes closest to the form of intellectual critique that Buruma and Margalit elaborate in their various chapters, under the label "Occidentalism," is Gandhi. He wrote and spoke with passion against the sinful city that took us away from organic village communities; he was a bitter opponent of the desacralizing of nature by science and the scientific outlook; he urged the Indian freedom fighters not to inherit from the British the political apparatus of formal democracy and liberal institutions because it was a cognitive enslavement to "Western" ideas unsuited for indigenous political life in India; and he did all this in the name of traditional religious purity which would be corrupted by modern ideals of the Enlightenment. And to add to all this there is one last point of particularly illuminating fit between Gandhi and their "Occidentalist." If they were looking for someone who took the view that there was indeed a more or less strict *derivation* from the ideals of Enlightenment rationality and political liberal institutions to the shallow and harmful cultural aspects of modernity (a derivation which, as I said, they are bound to describe as illicit and a fallacy), it is Gandhi, rather than Muslim intellectuals and writers, where they will most clearly find it. It is he (much more than the German, Slavophile, and Japanese traditions that they invoke) who echoes in detail the Islamic Occidentalist's critique of the broader cultural phenomena that Buruma and Margalit expound; and (much more explicitly than they can be said to), he would absolutely resist the charge that it is a conflation or illicit extrapolation to link the ideals of scientific rationality and modern forms of democratic politics with that broader cultural phenomena—of materialism, uncontrolled technology, the alienating, sinful city, etc. He insisted and argued at length that the notion of rationality, which was first formulated in the name of science in the seventeenth century and developed and modified to practical and public domains with the philosophers of the Enlightenment, had within it the *predisposition* to give rise to the horrors of modern industrial life, to destructive technological frames of mind, to rank commercialism, to the surrender of spiritual casts of mind, and to the destruction of the *genuine pluralism* of traditional life before modernity visited its many tribulations upon India. As he often claimed, it is precisely because this more authentic pluralism was destroyed by modernity that modernity had to impose a quite unsatisfactory form of secularist pluralism in a world that it had itself "disenchanted," to use the Weberian rhetoric. Before this disenchantment, which for Gandhi has its origins in the very scientific rationality that Buruma and Margalit applaud, there was no need for such artificial forms of secularized pluralism in Indian society. The pluralism was native, un-self-conscious, and rooted.

Even those who do not agree with every detail of Gandhi's criticisms (and there are many details that I would certainly resist)[15] could not help but notice that, given this almost perfect fit with the subject their title announces, Gandhi is not so much as mentioned in this book. No doubt this is because Gandhi was the great spokesman of *non*-violence and one of the book's recurring objections is to the dehumanizing violence of the "jihadi" Occidentalists. (So also, their German, Japanese, and Slavophile intellectual antecedents, discussed in the book, are described as having laid seed for eventually well-known violent descendants.) But if their ideas and arguments overlap so closely with Gandhi's[16] and it is only the objectionable commitment to violence and the dehumanization of those whom one opposes violently that makes the Occidentalists they are most interested in different from Gandhi, then those ideas and arguments are only *contingently* related to what is objectionable about Occidentalism. There is therefore no interesting integrity in the doctrine, something one cannot say of the deep integrating links between power, violence, literature, and learning claimed for the doctrine of "Orientalism" which I briefly tried to convey earlier.

The primary aim of *Occidentalism* (to quote my own words when I first introduced the book in this essay) is to "provide an account of a certain *conception* of the West which is named in their title and which they find today in hostile Islamist reactions to the West, a *conception* which they claim is just as unfair to and dehumanizing of the West as 'Orientalism' was said to be of the Orient, in Edward Said's well-known book bearing that name." I am stressing the term "conception" in my own words quite deliberately. It is essential to how the book's aim is formulated. So if I am right and the book's characterization of the "Occidentalist" conception of the West is echoed almost perfectly in Gandhi's critique of the West, and if the crucial mark of difference is that the Islamists have brought to this critique's conception a contingent element of violence, which Gandhi would deplore, then it is not the *conception* that they have established to be dehumanizing. The parallel with Gandhi shows, therefore, that they have not met their aim at all.

The subject is deepened and complicated if we notice that Gandhi's criticisms have antecedents in a tradition of thought that goes all the way back to the seventeenth century in England and elsewhere in Europe, *simultaneous* with the great scientific achievements of that time. It goes back, that is, to just the time and the place when the outlook of scientific "rationality" that Buruma and Margalit place at the defining center of what they call the "West" was being formed, and it is that very outlook with its threatening cultural and political consequences that is the target of the critique.

This critique, in a broad and somewhat crude and undifferentiated version, was made familiar at a somewhat later time by Weberian epithets such as "disenchantment," a rhetoric, which though it conveys something perfectly well, also hides a lot of significant detail that was present in the full and detailed substance of the critique. There is a widespread tendency, which is understandable ever since Nietzsche's celebrated slogan, to elaborate the notion of disenchantment in terms that summon the image of the "dead Father." But there are pitfalls, if one does so without care. This carelessness is rampant in the current revival of tired Victorian debates about the irrationality of belief in a God and in his creation of the universe in six days a few thousand years ago. It is a common thread in recent tree-killing tomes[17] which pour scorn on such irrational beliefs that they view them in terms of a continuing immaturity, one's persistence in an infantile reliance on a father whose demise was registered by philosophers (Nietzsche, but also Hegel before him) much more than a century ago, one's abdication of responsibility and free agency in the humbling of oneself to an authority non-intelligible to human concepts and scientific explanations. What goes entirely missing in this simplistic picture is the intellectual as well as cultural and political *prehistory* of the demise of such an authority figure. And it is this that the earlier critique stressed and which is worth expounding. Well before his demise, brought about I suppose by the scientific outlook that we all now admire and which is rightly recommended in these tedious tomes by our up-to-the-minute atheists, it was science itself and nothing less than science, which far from registering his demise, proposed instead, in the late seventeenth century, a quite different kind of fate for the father, a form of *migration,* an *exile* into inaccessibility from the visions of ordinary people to a place outside the universe, from where, in the now more familiar image of the clockwinder, he first set and then kept an inert universe in motion. And it is the theology and politics and political economy surrounding this deracination of God from the world of matter and nature and human community and perception that the critique focuses on so as to understand its large and abiding effects.

There is no Latin expression such as "Deus Deracinus" to express the thought that the late seventeenth century critique made central. The closest they had was "Deus Absconditus" which, though it is meant to convey the inaccessibility of God, conveys to the English speaker a fugitive fleeing rather than what I want to stress—the idea that it is from the roots of nature and ordinary perceptible life that God was quite assiduously removed. "Racine" or roots is the right description of his immanence in a conception of a sacralized universe, from which he was torn away by the exile to which the metaphysical outlook of early modern science (aligned with thoroughly mundane interests) ushered him. There is no understanding the "infantilism" of our current religious yearnings that does not acknowledge the significance of these intellectual developments of that earlier period.

I have said that my (somewhat grotesque) neologism "Deus Deracinus" would have served the thought I want to express best, but the words we have "Deus *Absconditus*" in another respect suggests something of what I want to capture. The phrase, quite apart from standing for the inaccessibility of God that was insisted upon by the late seventeenth century ideologues of the Royal Society, conveys a certain anxiety that lay behind their insistence. "Conditus" means "put away for *safeguarding,*" with the "abs-" reinforcing the "awayness" and separateness or inaccessibility of where God is safely placed. So we must ask why should the authority figure need safeguarding in an inaccessibility, what dangers lay in his immanence, in his availability to the visionary temperaments and capacities of all those who inhabit his world? And why should the scientific establishment of *early* modernity seek this safekeeping in exile for a father whom its successor in *late,* more mature modernity would properly describe as "dead"?

To put a range of complex, interweaving themes in the crudest summary, the dispute was about the very nature of nature and matter and, relatedly therefore, about the role of the deity, and of the broad cultural and political implications of the different views on these metaphysical and religious concerns. The metaphysical picture that was promoted by Newton (the official Newton of the Royal Society, not the neo-Platonist of his private study) and Boyle, among others, viewed matter and nature as *brute and inert.* On this view, since the material universe was brute, God was *externally* conceived, giving the universe a push from the *outside* to get it in motion. In the dissenting tradition, by contrast, matter was *not* brute and inert, but rather was shot through with an *inner* source of dynamism that was itself divine and which was responsible for motion. God and nature were not separable as in the official metaphysical picture that was growing around the new science, and John Toland, for instance, to take just one example among the active dissenting voices, openly wrote in terms he proclaimed to be "pantheistic."[18]

It should be emphasized right at the outset that the achievements of the "new science" of the seventeenth century were neither denied nor opposed by the critique of these dissenters that I have in mind, and so the critique cannot be dismissed as Luddite reaction to the new science.[19] What it opposed was a development in *outlook* that emerged in the *philosophical surround* of the scientific achievements. In other words, what it opposed was just the notion of "thick" rationality that Buruma and Margalit describe in glowing terms as "scientific rationality."

The link with Gandhi in all this is vivid and explicit in the dissenting voices. One absolutely central claim of the freethinkers of this period in the seventeenth century was about the political and cultural significance of their disagreements with the fast-developing metaphysical orthodoxy of the "Newtonians." Just as Gandhi did, they argued that it is only because one takes matter to be "brute" and "stupid," to use Newton's own terms, that one would find it appropriate to conquer it with the most destructive of technologies with nothing but profit and material wealth as ends, and thereby destroy it both as a natural and a humanitarian environment for one's habitation. In today's terms, one might think that this point was a seventeenth century predecessor to our ecological concerns but though there certainly was an early instinct of that kind, it was embedded in a much more general point (as it was with Gandhi too), a point really about how nature in an ancient and spiritually flourishing sense was being threatened. Today, the most thoroughly and self-consciously secular sensibilities may recoil from the term "spiritually," though I must confess to finding myself feeling no such self-consciousness despite being a secularist, indeed an atheist. The real point has nothing to do with these rhetorical niceties. If one had no use for the word, if one insisted on having the point made with words that we today can summon with confidence and accept without qualm, it would do no great violence to the core of their thinking to say this: The dissenters thought of the *world* not as brute but as *suffused with value.* That they happened to think the source of such value was divine ought not to be the deepest point of interest for us. The point rather is that if it were laden with *value,* it would make *normative* (ethical and social) demands on one, whether one was religious or not, normative demands therefore that did not come merely from our own instrumentalities and subjective utilities. And it is this sense of forming commitments by taking in, in our perceptions, an evaluatively "enchanted" world which—being enchanted in this way—therefore *moved* us to normatively constrained *engagement* with it that the dissenters contrasted with the outlook being offered by the ideologues of the new science.[20] I say "engagement," and mean it. A brute and disenchanted world could not move us to any such engagement since any perception of it, given the sort of thing it was, would necessarily be a *detached* form of observation; and if one ever came out of this detachment, if there was ever any engagement with a world so distantly conceived, so external to our own sensibility, it could only take the form of mastery and control of something alien, with a view to satisfying the only source of value allowed by this outlook—our own utilities and gain.

We are much used to the lament that we have long been living in a world governed by overwhelmingly commercial motives. What I have been trying to do is to trace this to its deepest *conceptual* sources and that is why the seventeenth century is so central to a proper understanding of this world. Familiarly drawn connections, like "Religion and the Rise of Capitalism," are only the beginning of such a tracing. In his probing book *A Grammar of Motives,* Kenneth Burke says that "the experience of an impersonal outlook was empirically intensified in proportion as the rationale of the monetary motive gained greater authority."[21] This gives us a glimpse of the sources. As he says, one had to have an impersonal angle on the world to see it as the source of profit and gain, and vice versa. But I have claimed that the sources go deeper. It is only when we see the world as Boyle and Newton did, as against the freethinkers and dissenters, that we understand further why there was no option but this impersonality in our angle on the world. A desacralized world, to put it

in the dissenting terms of that period, left us no other angle from which
to view it, but an impersonal one. There could be no normative constraint coming upon us from a world that was brute. It could not move
us to engagement with it on *its* terms. All the term-making came from us.
We could bring whatever terms we wished to such a world; and since we
could only regard it impersonally, the terms we brought in our actions
upon it were just the terms that Burke describes as accompanying such
impersonality, the terms of "the monetary" motives for our actions. Thus
it is that the metaphysical issues regarding the world and nature, as they
were debated around the new science, provide the deepest conceptual
sources. It is not without reason, then, that Buruma and Margalit speak
of a "scientific rationality" as defining "the West."

The conceptual sources that we have traced are various but they were
not miscellaneous. Religion, capital, nature, metaphysics, rationality,
science are diverse conceptual elements but they were *tied together* in
a highly deliberate integration, that is to say in deliberately accruing
worldly *alliances*. Newton's and Boyle's metaphysical view of the new
science won out over the freethinkers and became official only because
it was sold not only to the Anglican establishment but, in an alliance
with that establishment, to the powerful mercantile and incipient
industrial interests of the period in precisely these terms, terms which
stressed a future of endlessly profitable consequences that would accrue
if one embraced this particular conception of the new science and build,
in the name of a notion of rationality around it, the institutions of an
increasingly centralized political oligarchy (an early version of a certain
form of centralized state) to help promote these interests. These were
the very terms that the freethinkers found alarming for politics and culture, alarming for the local and egalitarian ways of life, which the radical elements in the English Revolution of some decades earlier, such as
the Levellers, Diggers, Quakers, and other groups had articulated and
fought for.

It is a travesty of the historical complexity built into the thick notion
of scientific rationality we are discussing to think—as is so often done—
that it emerged triumphant in the face of centuries of *clerical* reaction
only. That is the sort of simplification of intellectual history which leads
one to oppose scientific rationality with religion (the "Occident" and

its "Enemies"), without any regard to the highly significant historical fact that it was the *Anglican* establishment that lined up with this thick notion of rationality in an alliance with commercial interests and it was the *dissenting, egalitarian radicals* who opposed such "rationality." It was this scientific rationality, seized upon by just these established religious and economic alliances, that was later central to the colonizing mentality that justified the rapacious conquest of distant lands. It may seem that it is a conceptual leap to go from the seventeenth century conceptions of scientific rationality to the liberal justifications of colonial conquest. But if one accepts the initial *conceptual* connection between views of nature, God, and commerce that were instantiated in these *social and political* alliances between specific groups and interests of the earlier period, there can be no reason to withhold acceptance from the perfectly plausible hypothesis (indeed merely an extension of the connections that have been accepted) that the colonized lands too were to be viewed as brute nature that was available for conquest and control. This hypothesis is wholly plausible *so long as one was able to portray the inhabitants of the colonized lands in infantilized terms,* as a people who were as yet unprepared—by precisely a *mental lack* of such a notion of *scientific rationality*—to have the right attitudes toward nature and commerce and the statecraft that allows nature to be pursued for commercial gain. And such an historically infantilizing portrayal of the inhabitants was explicit in the writings of John Stuart Mill, and even in a few passages in Marx.[22]

There is a fair amount of historical literature by now on this last point about the intellectual rationalizations of colonialism, but I have introduced the salient points of an *earlier pre*-colonial period's critique here in order to point out that Gandhi's and apparently the "Occidentalist's" social and political attack on the "scientific rationality" that is elevated as a defining principle of the "West" has had a very long and recognizable tradition going back to the seventeenth century *in the heart of the West,* and it is this tradition of dissent that seems to keep resurfacing in different forms throughout the intellectual history of the West and elsewhere since the seventeenth century. Buruma and Margalit, as I said, cite later Slavophile, Japanese, and German Romantic and nationalist writing as being critical of this notion of rationality, but my point is that it is the writing and thought at the very site and the very time of the scientific discoveries themselves which anticipate in detail and with thoroughly honorable intent those later developments.

Once that point is brought on to center stage, a standard strategy of the orthodox Enlightenment against fundamental criticisms raised against it is exposed as defensive posturing. It would be quite wrong and anachronistic to dismiss this initial and early intellectual and perfectly *scientific* source of critique, from which later critiques of the Enlightenment derived, as being irrational, unless one is a cold warrior waiting to tarnish all criticism of the "West" along these lines. It is essential to the argument of this essay that far from being anti-West, Gandhi's early antecedents in the West, going back to the seventeenth century and in recurring heterodox traditions in the West since then, constitute what is, and rightly has been, called "the Radical *Enlightenment.*"[23] To dismiss its pantheistic tendencies that I cited as being unscientific and in violation of norms of rationality would be to run together in a blatant slippage the general and "thin" use of terms like "scientific" and "rationalist" with just this "thick" notion of scientific rationality that we had identified above, which had the kind of politically and culturally disastrous consequences that the early dissenters were so prescient and jittery about. Buruma and Margalit's appeal to scientific rationality as a defining feature of the West trades constantly on just such a slippage, subtly appealing to the hurrah element of the general and "thin" terms "rational" and "scientific" to tarnish the critics of the West, while actually having the work in their argument done by the thicker notion of scientific rationality, which the "Occidentalist" tradition and the "Enemies of the West" oppose.

As far as the thin conception of "scientific" and "rationality" is concerned, the plain fact is that *nobody* in that period was, in any case, getting prizes for leaving God out of the world-view of science. That one should think of God as voluntaristically affecting nature from the outside (as the Newtonians did), rather than sacralizing it from within (as the freethinkers insisted), was not in any way to improve on the *science* involved. Both views were therefore just as "unscientific," just as much in violation of scientific rationality, in the "thin" sense of that term that we would now take for granted. What was in dispute had nothing to do with science or rationality in that attenuated sense at all. What the early dissenting tradition (and its many successors, whether in German, Japanese, or Slavophile traditions or in Gandhi) was opposed to is the *metaphysical* orthodoxy that grew around Newtonian science and its implications for broader issues of *culture and politics*. This orthodoxy with all of its implications is what has now come to be called "scientific rationality" in the "thick" sense of that term and in the cold war intellectual's cheerleading about "the West," it has been elevated into a defining ideal, dismissing all opposition as irrationalist, with the hope that accusations of irrationality, because of the *general* stigma that the term imparts in its "thin" usage, will disguise the very specific and "thick" sense of rationality and irrationality that are actually being deployed by them. Such (thick) irrationalism is precisely what the dissenters yearned for; and hindsight shows just how honorable a yearning it was.

The point here is so critical that I will risk taxing the reader's endurance and repeat it. Buruma and Margalit mention only the later Slavophile and German and other "Occidentalist" criticisms of such a notion of the "West." But if I am right that all of these, including Gandhi's criticisms which they conveniently do not mention, are continuous with this much earlier critique in the very heart of the West and its scientific developments, then the terms in which Buruma and Margalit dismiss those criticisms must apply to the antecedent critique as well. It is precisely the point, however, that to say that these early dissenters were unleashing an irrationalist and unscientific critique of the "West" as they define the "West" is to confuse and conflate science and its ideals of rationality with a notion of rationality defined upon a very specific metaphysical outlook that started at a very specific historical moment and place and grew to be a presiding orthodoxy as a result of alliances that were formed by the scientific and clerical and commercial establishment in England and the Netherlands and then spreading to other parts of Europe. It is this outlook and its large consequences for history and culture and political economy which made Gandhi and his many conceptual predecessors in the West anxious in a long tradition of dissenting thought. What this helps to reveal is that while one works with a "thin" notion of rationality and an innocuous notion of the "West," it is absurd to call these freethinkers either "irrational" or "unscientific," or "Enemies of the West."

But if one works openly and without disguise (in a way that Buruma and Margalit do not) with a thick notion of rationality, understood now as shaped by this very specific intellectual, political, and cultural history, it is quite right to call them "irrationalist" and "Enemies of the West"—for those terms, so understood, reveal only the perfectly serious, legitimate, and, as I said, highly prescient anxieties of the dissenters. It is only when we make plain that these thick meanings are being passed off in disguise as the thin ones that one can expose the codes by which an edgy and defensive cold war intellectual rhetoric tries to tarnish an entire tradition of serious and fundamental dissent.

4.

Sometimes this tradition has surfaced in violent activism, at other times in critiques that have stressed more pacifist, religious, and contemplative ways of life. Since colonialism and the West's reach into distant lands which persists after formal decolonization in revised forms today, this very same dissenting tradition has quite naturally surfaced in those distant lands as well, again both in non-violent forms such as Gandhi's and in the violent forms which Buruma and Margalit characterize as coming from the Occidentalist "Enemies of the West" among a fringe of Islamist extremists.

The unpardonable atrocities committed recently by some of the latter in acts of violent terror are in no way absolved by the analysis I am offering. All the analysis does is to show that when the cold warriors of the West try to elevate one's understanding of these atrocities as deriving from a politics that owes to a certain culturalist conception of the West that they call "Occidentalism," they have it only partly right. A full understanding of that conception requires seeing "Occidentalism" as continuous with a longstanding and deep-going dissenting tradition in the West itself. That tradition was clear-eyed about what was implied by the "disenchantment" of the world, to stay with the Weberian term. It is a tradition consisting not just of Gandhi and the early seventeenth century freethinkers, whom I have already mentioned, not just the Slavophile, Japanese, and German critics that are mentioned in their book, but a number of remarkable literary and philosophical voices in between that they don't discuss: Blake, Shelley, William Morris, Whitman, Thoreau, and countless anonymous voices of the non-traditional Left, the Left of the "radical" Enlightenment, from the freemasons of the early period down to the heterodox Left in our own time, voices such as those of Noam Chomsky and E. P. Thompson and the vast army of heroic but anonymous organizers of popular grass roots movements—in a word, the West as conceived by the "radical" Enlightenment which has refused to be complacent about the orthodox Enlightenment's legacy of the "thick" rationality that the early seventeenth century dissenters had warned against.[24] This is the tradition of "Enlightenment" that Buruma and Margalit show little understanding of, though "Enlightenment" is the avowed subject of their book. That should occasion no surprise at all since it is impossible to come to any deep understanding of their own subject while they succumb to the temptations that cold war intellectuals are prone to.

The freethinkers of the seventeenth century, even though they were remarkably prophetic about its consequences, could not, of course, foresee the *details* of the trajectory of the notion of "scientific rationality" whose early signs they had dissented from, that is to say, the entire destructive colonial and corporate legacy of the alliance of concepts and institutions and material interests they were warning against. But their successors over the last 300 or more years, some of whom I have named, have been articulating and responding to these details in their own times.

It goes without saying that not all of these responses are based on a clearly articulated sense of these conceptual, institutional, and material alliances that have developed over the centuries. They are often much more instinctive. And it is undeniable that there are sometimes monstrously violent manifestations in these responses among a terrorist fringe in, among others, Muslim populations (including the Muslim youth in the metropolitan West) who, as Buruma and Margalit acknowledge, feel a sense of powerlessness in the face of an imperial past (and present) in different parts of the world. That some of the political rhetoric of these terrorists appeals confusedly to distortions of their religion, much as talk of "Armageddon" in the heartland of America does, is also undeniable. But if Buruma and Margalit are right that their religious politics and rhetoric are not separable from a cultural understanding of their past and of a certain cultural understanding of the West which has intruded into their past and their present, and if I am right that that cultural understanding has deep affinities with a dissenting *Western* tradition's understanding of "the West" and its own past, then we are required to take very seriously the words of terrorists and of the many, many more ordinary Muslim people who will not always publicly oppose these terrorists despite the fact that they share no "fundamentalist" ideology with them and in fact detest them for the violent disruption of their lives that they have wrought. By "take very seriously the words," I mean take the words to be saying just what they are saying and not self-servingly view them as a fake political front for a runaway religious fanaticism.

We will have to take their words much more seriously than Buruma and Margalit do in their passing, lightly formulated acknowledgements of the wrongs committed by the West. The words have been spoken again and again. They are not just on the recordings of Osama Bin Laden's voice and image, they are constantly on the lips of ordinary Muslims on the street. And they are clear and perfectly precise about what they claim and want: that they are fighting back against centuries of colonial subjugation, that they want the military and the corporate presence of the West (primarily the United States) which continues that subjugation in new and more subtle forms out of their lands, that they want a just solution for the colonized, brutalized Palestinian people, that they want an end to the cynical support by the West (primarily by America) of corrupt regimes in their midst to serve the West's (primarily America's) geopolitical and corporate interests, that they will retaliate (or not speak out against those who retaliate) with an endless cycle of violence unless there is an end to the endless state-terrorist actions both violent (in the bombings and in the bulldozing of their cities and their occupied lands, killing or displacing thousands of civilians) and non-violent (the sanctions and embargoes that cause untold suffering to ordinary, innocent people).[25] To not take these words seriously and see them as genuinely motivating for those who speak them is as morally cretinous as it is to absolve the terrorist actions that a fringe of those who speak these words commit.[26]

The two books I have discussed, as I said, provide an interesting contrast on just this point. Mamdani, who rightly takes these words seriously but (unlike Buruma and Margalit) is suspicious of "culture talk," quite fails to locate the words in the historical and conceptual framework of a cultural and political critique within the West itself of a very specific notion of rationality that we have been discussing; Buruma and Margalit, who rightly see the need to connect issues of politics with cultural critique, therefore correctly situate these words in the broader reaction to such a notion of rationality, yet nevertheless (unlike Mamdani) fail to take the words seriously because they are wholly uncritical of the brutal and inegalitarian political and cultural implications of such a notion of scientific rationality that the "radical" Enlightenment warned against.

But having said this, it would be wrong of me to *rest* with the criticism that the two books are symmetrically unsatisfactory in this way. Since we are undoubtedly in a cold war, Mamdani's is the book that will be unpopular in "the West," not only with those in power but also with the large class of intellectuals and writers and journalists who keep a cold war going and who, as I said at the outset, even when they are often critical of those in power, will not disturb a broad consensus within which those in power can get away with what they have done over the years. Buruma's and Margalit's is the book which may, in some passing detail or other, not entirely please those in power, but it will on the whole be warmly received by this intellectual surround.[27] Even if it conveys something about the moral courage of the respective authors, there is nothing surprising in any of this. If you spend your time writing a book criticizing those in and around power and control, you will get a quite different reaction than if you spend your time writing a book criticizing those who are a fringe among the powerless.

The analysis so far has refused to treat the cultural critique of the West (whether accompanied by violence or not) as being wholly unconnected (or fallaciously and illicitly connected) to the dissent from the thick notion of scientific rationality that developed in the "West" and mobilized itself into one underlying justificatory source of the West's colonizing of other lands. It has, on the contrary, tried to show the connecting threads between them in historical and conceptual terms. It has also acknowledged that sometimes the cultural critique comes with a layer of religious rhetoric and commitment, of a conservative and "fundamentalist" or (a better term) "absolutist" variety. It is often true that those commitments and that rhetoric are the things to which an alienated and powerless people in previously (and presently) colonized lands will turn, and Buruma and Margalit don't particularly wish to deny this. Like most intellectual cold warriors, their focus is on the religious commitment and rhetoric of the immediate cold war target, Muslims who are the "Enemies of the West." However, if there really are conspicuous intellectual and critical affinities between the "Occidentalist Enemies of the West" and Gandhi on the one hand and a longstanding and continuous dissenting tradition *within the West itself* on the other, then we ought to pay some attention to religiosity in the West too, a religiosity which is often (especially in America) a response to the more local rather than imperial consequences of "scientific rationality," in the thick sense of that term.

5.

Earlier, I had—despite registering how undifferentiated the description had come to be in our understanding—followed Weber, in describing the cultural consequences of the thick notion of scientific rationality, as a "disenchantment" of the world. The term captures *some* of what the early dissenters had in mind, as well as what Gandhi much later feared when he saw all around him the eagerness of the elites of the colonized lands to embrace for their formally decolonized nations the models of liberal democracy with its deep links to a corporate and commercial culture of the West. When he famously quipped, "It would be a good idea" to the question "What do you think of Western civilization?" he was not expressing something very distant in basic respects from what Buruma and Margalit describe with the Islamic notion of "jahiliya."[28] But quite apart from this distant and outsider's perspective of a Gandhi or the absolutist Muslim in Arabian and colonized regions of the world, the *local* experience in the West of the disenchanting consequences of "scientific rationality" in the thick sense are bound to be very different from what is experienced by the colonized lands. The conquest and the extracting of surpluses from colonized regions of the world may have created feelings of powerlessness and humiliation there, but what "scientific rationality" (in the thick sense) created in the West's own midst was a quite different form of alienation. Moreover, it is a form of alienation that is not dismissible as "jahiliya" by its own inhabitants. That may be a perspective of the *outsider* (the Occidentalist, including Gandhi) but in the local habitus of the West itself, ordinary people have to *live in and cope with* the disenchantment of their world, seeking whatever muddled forms of re-enchantment that are available to them. Nowhere is this more evident than in the mass of ordinary people living in what has come to be called "red state" America.

It is sometimes said today, as if it is some sort of a peculiarity, that the *majorities* in the red states present themselves as having the mentality of victims. When one compares their condition to those in sub-Saharan Africa or even to the impoverished inner cities of America's metropoles, there is certainly something peculiarly ignorant and impervious about it. But if it is analyzed as an instinctive grasp of the condition of living in a pervasive and longstanding disenchantment of their world, it is not peculiar at all.

So once the full detail and scope of this combination of elements of a disenchanted world brought about by the "exile of the father" in the highly constructed "scientific rationality" that I've expounded are fully understood, it may be worth exploring some of the reactions in our own time to its cumulative effects, which in some parts of the world might rightly be described as having the proportions of a backlash that, as I said earlier, our contemporary atheists describe as an infantile regression to and submission to a dead father. An appreciation of the analysis of the detailed effects of the father's *exile* in an *earlier* period should, I am claiming, make no small difference to how we are to understand this "irrational" failure in our own times to acknowledge his subsequent death. Before closing then, let me speak not to Buruma and Margalit's focus, the Islamist rage against what is perceived by it to be a pernicious modernism of Western society, but to the pervasively conservative religious ethos in the heartland of America about which, given this long historical analysis, it ought, at least as a *first thought*, be utterly natural to say that it is (at least partly) a reaction to this slowly accumulated disenchantment, a way of seeking solidarities and community in a disenchanted world.[29]

Two protests will be made to this natural thought—no doubt by a shrill liberal orthodoxy which seems these days perpetually poised to defend its own self-congratulatory ideals. Before I mention the protests, let me just remind you of the ideals as they were announced by Buruma and Margalit. They are scientific rationality and liberal democracy. So far in this essay I have addressed the former and for the rest of the essay, I want to connect that discussion so far of the first ideal with a consideration of the second, arguing that once we have uncovered, as we just have, the "thick" and cumulative construction of the first of these ideals, they are highly revealing of some acutely contradictory attitudes underlying how the second democratic ideal has turned out.[30]

The first protest will be that the conservative religiosity in the American heartland today is not at all, not even partly, a reaction of the sort I am suggesting to a longstanding process of "disenchantment" because the phenomenon has really been carefully and artificially *engineered* by the Republican Party ever since the Goldwater defeat, as a way of building a constituency for its own success. But the rightness of this protest doesn't refute the claim that there was something for such an engineered phenomenon to tap, something in the yearnings of people, and it is those yearnings, I am claiming, that are natural to see as a reaction to the cumulative effects of disenchantment.

Second, it will be protested, again with some justification, that Western Europe is part of that disenchanted world, as I have described it, and it has nothing like the same kind of pervasive religiosity. To this a plausible rejoinder might be to observe that in Europe, the natural human yearnings for solidarities and community have long found measurable fulfillment in an entrenched social democratic tradition of labor politics and the active presence of unions in the everyday lives of ordinary people,[31] something only fitfully present and present only in some parts of America and at present faded almost to non-existence, even where they once had life.

I don't intend this rejoinder to the second protest to be the sort of explanation offered in President Obama's remark during his first campaign that got him into all that trouble—that working people in America have turned to religion, not out of genuine religious belief and conviction but because of poverty and deprivation. That remark, put as simply as that, seemed to deny genuine agency to working people and their religious commitments. What I am saying instead is this: Human beings have a natural tendency to seek substantial bonds that make for an unalienated life.[32] Family life is not always—perhaps never has been—sufficient to satisfy this tendency. What the church and its pulpit offered in early modern Europe transformed itself there into a social democratic labor politics in late modernity, a politics that often itself grew out of non-conformist religious traditions. For reasons that may have something to do with the fact that predominantly immigrant populations seek not social activism but assimilation in the political economy and the political establishment, such a tradition of politics never developed to the same extent and with the same depth in America. As a result the church continued to provide the chief source of satisfaction for such a substantial human need.

But having made it, I want to worry a little more again about this rejoinder I am making to the second protest. I have said, roughly and crudely in the short space I have in an already rather lengthy essay, that this conservative religiosity in America's heartland is partly at least really a yearning for something that could just as easily have secular outlets too, as in Europe, but given what is far more available in middle America, is provided not at sites such as labor unions, but rather the church. Though I do think the rejoinder, properly elaborated, is plausible, it has to be carefully formulated because, unlike as with Obama's remark, one doesn't want to withhold agency and transparency or self-knowledge from the people one is discussing; and saying that their religiously formulated convictions are really a front for something else, yearnings and values of a much more general kind that could have just as easily been fulfilled in entirely secular forms, as in Europe, comes close to just such a denial of self-knowledge (and therefore full agency) to them.

To put it very summarily, in Obama's case, the denial of agency and self-knowledge to the subjects in question lies in the impression that a remark like his is saying about the religious commitments of the poor, white working class in some parts of America: "You don't really have the beliefs and motivations you seem to think you have. What you really want, without knowing it, is something other than what you say." And somewhat more complicatedly, in my case, the impression of attributing a lack of self-knowledge and agency lies in the following. If, as I am suggesting, the European differential is explainable by the availability to ordinary people of a tradition of different sources and sites than religion to fulfill the yearnings for solidarity and community, then one is in danger of saying that ordinary people in America, *even though they do not know this about themselves,* have the same yearnings as those of ordinary people in Europe, yearnings that are not transparent to themselves, because the only sites available to them to fulfill these yearnings are religious sites, and so all they acknowledge are the more religiously formulated yearnings they explicitly avow. This will seem to many to be analogous to saying what has also often been said, viz., that even the most bourgeois of working-class populations really have revolutionary yearnings because of their objective role in history as "the proletariat," even though they may have no explicit consciousness (that is to say, no *self-knowledge*) of these yearnings of theirs, since what they explicitly avow is only their economistic or, worse, their bourgeois aspirations. I give this example deliberately to bring into focus the crudest and perhaps the most implausible version of the idea of false consciousness. The issues here are complicated and my task for the rest of this essay will be to find a way of making the points I want to go on to make about the democratic mentality so that no such transparency-threatening or self-knowledge-denying and therefore, in the end, agency-threatening[33] version of false consciousness is being assumed by me—but even so something is being acknowledged about these deeper longings of ordinary people.

To explore how this balance might be achieved, let's focus on the hardest case, a particularly egregious manifestation of the reactionary aspects of the religiosity we are discussing. It is well known that in polls until fairly recently, a large majority of Americans were in favor of waging wars against both Afghanistan and Iraq, and a lot of these warmongering attitudes were voiced within an overall conservative religiosity in "red state" America. How shall we think of this? Well, we know how the most sophisticated cold warriors, often voicing elite, Left liberal opinion, who write and applaud books like *Occidentalism,* would think of it. They would, no doubt, be prepared to be consistent and despise the electorate of the red states as an anti-Enlightenment anomaly within the West itself, especially since these conservative regions of the country have explicitly repudiated "scientific rationality." It too is "Occidentalist," they will assert (as they did, for example, regarding the earlier Slavophile tradition). I have heard the large majority of the ordinary people of this part of the country, including the conservative Christian, Republican-voting electorate, frequently described with such terms as "vile" and "stupid" by liberal Left opinion, without a hint of awareness of the deeply anti-democratic nature of such remarks. The curiosity of this, coming as it does from those who *uphold* liberal democracy as one of the ideals that define "the West," therefore, needs some diagnosis.

I say I was struck by remarks such as this because, on the face of it, such an attitude is simply incompatible with a belief in democracy. You cannot believe in democracy and dismiss the electorate of roughly half of the country as a moral abomination. Winston Churchill, whose thinking on civil, rather than military matters was feeble, is said to have pronounced that democracy was a terrible form for a polity to adopt and the only reason to adopt it was that all other forms were more terrible. But I don't get it. Why would one choose democracy over, say, enlightened monarchy, if one thought ordinary people of the electorate to be vile and stupid, and thought a single man or woman to be of great moral judgment and worth? Perhaps Churchill and others who say things like that have in mind that at least democracy allows people the autonomy to choose their government, even if they consistently choose with their "vileness" and "stupidity" governments which wage wars, cut taxes for the rich, create a large handful of billionaires at the expense of millions of ordinary, working people, and so on. But why should we fetishize such a species of autonomy that reduces to a mere formal property if it should turn out that it will always, given the moral weaknesses of the electorate which exercises it, result in what, by our own lights, are morally deplorable verdicts?

We are faced, then, with a central paradox in the very idea of democracy, at least as central as the more familiar paradox of majoritarian tyranny, the paradox of how one can both believe in democracy and the indescribable moral badness of the electorate.

How might we address such a paradox?

When "progressive" opinion finds it natural to blame people before they examine and criticize the institutions that affect them, there has been a measurable departure from the great traditions of democratic dissent that gave rise to some of the more genuinely radical ideals of the Enlightenment. Those traditions allowed no such chasm between "progressive" ideals and the mentality of democracy, that is to say a mentality of *trust in the judgment of ordinary people*—and by "ordinary people" I mean people away from the centers of power and privilege (I have no desire to underestimate the vileness of those who are close to centers of power). Such a mentality, I am arguing, is precisely the mentality that is missing in the ideal of democracy that the sophisticated cold warrior has claimed defines the West, along with the ideal of scientific rationality—and it is missing in large part *because* the ideal has been shaped by the carefully constructed details of the political and economic fallout of the thick features of the ideal of "scientific rationality." The hard theoretical question that needs an answer, then, is: How can that trust, so essential to the mentality of democracy, be *genuinely felt* by us toward an electorate whose decisions we rightly deplore and whose conservative religiosity we often find to be at odds with our most basic political commitments? Much can turn on the answer to this question.

The issues here are in a sense very obvious and I have already hinted at what they are in describing the details of the alliances that first formed the process of disenchantment, but we can approach the obvious a little indirectly by looking at a case far away. Take the extraordinary developments in the very recent past in the Middle East that came to be called the "Arab Spring." Though much has been made of the new social media and its effective role in the remarkable movements that generated change in Cairo and Tunis, that role was primarily mobilizational in a rather more immediate sense of alerting activists to immediate events, including even such things as where a despot's police forces are being deployed in a revolutionary space like a square. The real difference was made not just in Egypt and Tunisia but an entire Middle Eastern region of the world by an agency of much more *conventional* media. Though no doubt many factors were responsible for what led up to the uprisings of the "spring" (including a long-simmering labor unrest in the regions away from the two capitals Tunis and Cairo), one most undeniably salient and dramatic factor was the extraordinary impact of *one television station* for over a decade on ordinary citizens, injecting the healthiest form of conflict into Arab societies and polities by the most basic service of providing information to them of just how much their countries were being run by corrupt and self-serving states and their power elites, in thrall to globalized financial capital and its neo-liberal tendency.

The implications of this for how to diagnose the situation in the United States should be obvious. By contrast with Al-Jazeera, the mainstream media in America (that is, the media read and viewed by ordinary people, who are too busy making a basic living to seek information out at non-standard sites), are cravenly unwilling to provide the most basic information about their government's actions and the consequences of those actions, not to mention the actions and consequences of the governments elsewhere that it supports. And the point is not just about media and information but much more broadly and pervasively about subtle forms of internalization of pervasively orthodox and uncritical thinking on public matters from very early on in the mainstream educational institutions. I am focusing on the institutions of media and education in my diagnosis, but the point goes really much deeper and further into the constructions of attitudes via the "thick" notion of rationality whose long genealogy I have tried to analyze, creating deep epistemic deficits in the population and preventing a democratized *cognitive* public sphere. These were just the sort of developments that the radical sectaries and the scientific dissenters had foreseen when they predicted the disastrous effects of the scientific, religious, and mercantile alliances that were forming all around them to corner all the cognitive and commercial bases of power for the propertied elites.

All this suggests the obvious point that ordinary Americans have all the moral strengths that ordinary people in Europe or any other place have; their weakness, in comparison, is rather *epistemic*, not moral. In fact, I think one can state it as something like the First Law of Political Psychology that "One cannot exercise such moral strengths that one has, if one is pervasively epistemically weak," weak on information, and information, not just in the narrow sense, though that is bad enough, but also in the broader sense of having easily available, in one's education and cognitive life generally, alternative frameworks for thinking about politics, political economy, and public life.[34]

But it is precisely here that a question will be raised about whether I am not, in attributing moral strengths to the very electorate whose moral and political verdicts I find wholly wrong, assuming a discredited notion of false consciousness, somewhat akin to historical materialism's dismissal of the proletariat's bourgeois aspirations as a spurious state of mind on the grounds that such a class, by its objective historical status in a particular economic formation in a particular period of history, had revolutionary consciousness, its true consciousness, which was screened off from it by thick layers of falsifying ideology. The conceptual and methodological issues here are delicate and have to be handled with some care. First of all, I want to insist that I am making a conditional claim: *If* you believe in democracy, you must have confidence in the underlying strengths of ordinary people, over and above respecting their autonomy of choice. But quite apart from the conditional modesty of the claim, what is needed to make the claim grounded in a plausible argument is not merely to say that I am possessed of some *objective theory* of the moral judgment and capacities of ordinary people, *no matter what they say or do*. I don't believe in that form of objectivity, and it is not at all obvious that Marx believed that he possessed an objective theory of history and class (some superlatively strong version of "historical materialism") such that the proletariat must be said to have an underlying true revolutionary consciousness no matter what bourgeois aspirations were reflected in their sayings and doings.

I think that a proper understanding of Marx's ideas about false consciousness can only be had by a proper placing of them in a Hegelian dialectic which, of course, he explicitly endorsed and made his own, and which makes central appeal to the notion of *internal conflict*—a point that I have been stressing for many years now in my writing on secularism.[35] Having mentioned Hegel, I will say immediately that his method will be most clearly and briefly displayed if I invoke ideas of internal conflict not via an exposition of Hegel himself, in whose work the ideas are buried in a gratuitous ontology, but quite another kind of thinker, Freud; and in doing so, the goal will be to make explicit how I think we can, within Marx's general ideas about their false consciousness, *preserve* the transparency and self-knowledge and agency in the attitudes of the ordinary people under discussion.

This may seem perverse. How, it might be asked, can I appeal to Freud to preserve the idea that there is nothing unconscious and opaque or

non-transparent about the attitudes that amount to the moral strengths I
am attributing to ordinary people?

To respond to this and elaborate the argument, I need to set up some
elementary conceptual apparatus first, which though it may initially
seem to be some distance from the subject at hand, is straightforwardly
relevant to it. What I would like to bring to center stage is a distinction
within the Freudian framework between two quite different aspects of its
overall understanding of the mind and its pathologies.[36]

The first is a *structural* hypothesis that is presupposed in the very
idea of the explanation of "irrational" behavior, in one sense of that term.

The second is a series of *empirical* hypotheses about these hypoth-
esized structures.

This broad methodological distinction between the structural and
empirical side of the framework is so elementary and basic that it tends
to get lost in the much more interesting and exciting detail of Freud's
more substantive psychological claims.

If one begins with the basic datum of our psychological lives that is
central to Freud's interests—the fact of irrational behavior—a question
arises as to what form it must be taken to have. The word "irrational"
is widely and loosely used but what is clear is that Freud is not primarily interested in its usage to mark behavior that is anomalous. That is, it
is not behavior that runs afoul of *social* norms. Such anomalousness of
behavior does not amount to irrationality in any sense that is of interest
to psychoanalysis, unless it is *also* a source of anxiety or neurosis in the
agent himself. Hence to the extent that we have a relevant form of irrational behavior for psychoanalysis, it must in some sense seem to be irrational by the lights of, or the point of view of, *the agent himself.* He must
feel the anxiety or the neurosis and therefore there must be *some sense* in
which by his or her own lights (lights, that is, which are to be found in
his or her own attitudes and aspirations and commitments), the behavior
is problematic and needs psychoanalytic attention. This suggests that
irrationality of the relevant kind divides the mind in two frames and the
two frames are in conflict with one another. He argues explicitly that the
mental states that are 1) causing the irrational behavior and the mental
states 2) by the lights of which that behavior is viewed critically, in some
sense, amount to two separate psychological profiles which are "at war"

within a single subject. For the purposes that I want to deploy these very basic ideas in Freud, they seem to provide just the right sort of frame-working—and as will emerge, I mean that word *frame*working to do some serious work—to be able to show that the populations in question are not merely wrong by the lights of something attributed to them on some ultra-*objective* basis (some sort of objective claim about the moral goodness of the judgment of ordinary people in a democracy, or in the case of Marx some objective theory of history according to which a particular class in a particular period has revolutionary consciousness), but rather by lights which we attribute to them on the basis of their own *actions as agents,* that is to say actions which are fully self-known to them because their motivations are fully self-known to them.

What needs stressing, then, is that in Freud's overall conception of the mind in his study of its pathologies, there is *first* a conceptual claim made on what he himself conceives as a priori grounds. This is the claim that, given the fact that irrationality of a kind that he is interested in is not mere anomalousness from social norms, the mind *must*—as if by logic— be seen as divided into two structures or segments or frames (Freud's metaphor is two "chambers"), which are in conflict with one another.

And *then second,* once these structures or frames are well in place as a conceptual and structural prior, Freud *further* goes on to add a quite distinct claim that is *not* structural and conceptual and not made on a priori grounds, but rather made as a subsequent *empirical* hypothesis, viz., that one of these segments of the mind is *unconscious.* (And then even more specific empirical hypotheses about the sorts of mental states that populate this unconscious segment of the mind, empirical hypotheses about the sexual etiologies of our neuroses which we summarize with such omnibus terms as "Oedipus," "Narcissus," and so on.)

Now if the position *conceptually prior* to these specifically empirical claims is that the relevant behavior can only make sense if we think of the mind as often being framed in two segments (with no mention yet of the unconscious, which is a further and subsequent empirical hypothesis), then we are allowed scope sometimes to construct quite *other* empirical hypotheses about one of the frames than that it is unconscious.[37] If so, these two different frames that characterize the mind would explain our seemingly irrational behavior very differently from Freud's explanation because neither would be unconscious and all mental states and attitudes would be transparent and self-known to subjects, thereby preserving their full intentional agency.

So what is important to be clear about is that, theoretically speaking, these two aspects of Freud are entirely separable. You first notice that the *logic* of irrationality requires two frames. This is independent of anything you go on to say about one of the frames on the basis of *evidence*. Freud's empirical claim about one of the frames being unconscious is not a matter of logic and is *not an intrinsic* part of the idea of dual frames. And that is what leaves it open for some sorts of irrationality (by one's own lights) to be able to get a dual frame explanation *without* the empirical hypothesis of the unconscious playing any role in the explanation of one's behavior. It is this possibility allowed by the distinctness of the structural and the empirical hypotheses in the understanding of irrationality that is highly relevant to the particular question about false consciousness we are concerned with in the populations we are discussing.

How, then, does this methodological apparatus get specifically applied to that question? Let me apply it schematically first, and then fill in the schema with some more details.

We can begin by first noting that there is much contradiction in the thinking of these populations and so they are *not* by any means *devoid* of responses (including *religious* responses) that are *inconsistent* with their warmongering, politically conservative religious attitudes. One can then quite plausibly claim that they are inconsistent only because their thinking on many issues occurs in two quite different "frames" that I expounded above via Freud's conceptual and structural point prior to his empirical claims. And then, when turning to empirical hypotheses, *instead* of positing that one of the frames is unconscious (i.e., instead of positing that they lack self-knowledge of what they are doing and why), as Freud did, we can claim plausibly that empirical evidence shows that one of the frames is distorted by institutions that have produced epistemic deficits. That is the general schema by which it becomes perfectly clear that no agency-threatening form of false consciousness is being proposed by me when I submit that we should be more democratic in our mentality and not dismiss the ordinary people whose political verdicts we deeply disagree with.

How is this general schema filled in by our particular case of the mentality of the American heartland?

To fill it, we must ask what gives one the grounds to say that, however egregiously bad we find some of their political opinions, there is relevant inconsistency or contradiction in their thinking? There are widely detectable grounds in the behavior of ordinary people in the electorate of the red states to attribute moral strengths to them and therefore to see them as being in a state of at least *latent* internal conflict with some of their attitudes and responses we find morally deplorable. The most conspicuous such grounds are to be found in the results of polls. Thus, for instance, it is quite commonly the case that when questions in polls are put in terms of values that individuals instinctively hold, the answers go overwhelmingly in a humane and compassionate direction, but if formulated in terms of economic or foreign policy jargon, on the very same issues, it goes in the opposite direction.

Of course, it could be said that the answer to the second sort of question is a sign that the answer to the first sort of question was *insincere* and, therefore, there is no internal conflict in these agents. But that sort of cynical interpretation (to which many on the liberal Left are prone) is quite premature. It takes no account of what I have (invoking Freud) just posited as a conceptual prior of two frames or segments that account for social behavior, which is of obvious relevance here, because how one might think in different ways in different frames can help to explain the seeming inconsistency in these responses. Their answers in these polls suggest that when these people think (and indeed act) as individuals instinctively responding to normative promptings made on their individual moral agency, their views are not, at least not typically, inhumane and destructive, and this is the side that is revealed by them when they respond to the first sort of question in the polls, questions that are framed in terms that don't seek to probe much beyond their individual and instinctive responsive sensibilities. And furthermore, a point of crucial importance for the challenge I had set myself, much of this tendency to give humane answers may well be prompted in many or most of them by a basically *religious* cast of thought and value. So it is not as if one is deracinating them from their religiosity and claiming that their values are at their deepest to be thought of as no different from the humanity of those who are not religious at all and who give the same answers.[38] Call all this the first frame.

But the second sort of question presents itself to them *in a quite different frame,* one that addresses their minds and even their religions (thus making clear that their religiosity surfaces quite differently in each frame), not as individuals instinctively responding to the perceived demands of individual values and ideals, but as their minds have been subordinated to institutional structures of state, corporations, and to the media and educational system that presents these structures to them, and in this frame (shaped by these epistemic deficits) the answers are quite different, indeed quite inconsistent with the other answers given in the other frame. Here, it should be noted I have brought in the other aspect of the distinction in Freud that I mentioned; I have brought in an *empirical* hypothesis rather than the a priori detection of frames and structures in the first place—it's just that the empirical hypothesis being made is not the Freudian one that the responses in the second of these two frames are unconscious because of a desire to suppress thoughts and desires that are uncomfortable to one's psyche, but rather a quite different empirical hypothesis that the responses in this second frame are pervasively shaped by the influence of media, education, and other public forms of cognitive determination that produce epistemic deficits.

Examples of such inconsistency are pervasive in polls. Here is just one very common and uncomplicated sort of example of inconsistency of response in polls, and there are literally scores of others.

"Yes, the conditions of the poor in Harlem are wretched and must be improved" (this might be a response to a question put in the first frame, i.e., a question about what would be their individual response to what are perceptible conditions of great poverty around them making immediate normative demands on their moral agency). And, as I said, one should acknowledge that a lot of these humane responses might issue from genuinely held religious commitments, so one is acknowledging and not denying their *agentive* commitments to religion, not explaining them *away* as owing to one or other sort of material circumstance, as Obama's too quick remark did.

Then, in the same poll, "No, we absolutely must not raise taxes and government spending" (this is a response to a question put in the second frame, i.e., a question put in economic jargon and thus addressing their minds as they have been cognitively shaped into "epistemic deficits" determined in upbringing in homes, then fortified in educational institutions, in the media, etc.).

But being in different frames the inconsistency or conflict in these two responses is not apparent to them, a quite clear and unmistakable attribution, then, of an *unconscious conflict,* even though *each frame* and each thought and attitude in each frame is entirely *within consciousness,* that is within their full agentive awareness.

It is this last point, that *both* frames and the thoughts in them are entirely within consciousness, which staves off the agency-threatening and self-knowledge-threatening version of false consciousness that I am trying to disavow on behalf of Marx. There is nothing—no value, no belief, no attitude, no commitment—in either frame that is not self-known to the agents. There is, of course, inconsistency between the thoughts and commitments of the two frames and that inconsistency is, of course, not self-known to the agent, *precisely because* the inconsistent thoughts and commitments are in *two different frames.* Thus, it is only when the border between the two frames is removed (in Freud's metaphor the "door" between the two chambers is opened) and there is only one frame that the agent will be able to see the inconsistency between his thoughts and commitments, and do something (deliberative and reflective) to get out of the inconsistency.

So, finding such internal conflict or inconsistency in subjects, as I have, is crucial to distinguishing the moral psychology involved in my analysis from notions of false consciousness attributed to the so-called *late* Marx, which in its implausible scientistic versions, appeals to no evidence of conflict *within* the minds of agents as the more Hegelian Marx does and which my appeal to Freud was intended to make vivid. It appeals instead to an objective and ultra-scientific theory of history and mind, independent of what the subject thinks and knows about his own states of mind (self-knowledge) as well as independent of a subject's agency and his or her motivations and conceptions of things.

This issue (of false consciousness) is closely linked with how to understand the entire vexed issue of the anti-democratic mentality in what is labeled "vanguardism." The legacy of Marx (criticized by Bakunin as already being inherent in Marx himself, but most particularly associated with Lenin) has it that a vanguard party leadership brings theoretical analysis to the masses. But if I am right, this is not a straightforward claim but an ambiguous one. There are two ways to understand this idea of this function of a vanguard. One is to simply think that the masses are an empty vessel in the matter of theoretical understanding and receive the theory that is brought to them by the party. The other is to insist that theory itself has its tacit, instinctive version already present in the quotidian individual responses in the speech and practice of ordinary people who comprise the masses, and these responses are available in something like the second of these two frames of their subjective consciousness that I have presented in the Hegelian/Freudian analysis above. And what the vanguard does is elevate it to the level of systematic articulation for the masses. On this reading, the vanguard is not the possessor of "expertise." Expertise, by its very nature, is not the sort of thing that can reside in the mentality of the vast mass of ordinary people without ceasing to be expertise.[39] But on this reading of vanguardism, the masses do already possess in this instinctive and unarticulated sense, evidenced in their responses and behavior from within the second frame, the very knowledge that is theoretically possessed and brought to them under a more systematic description by the vanguard. On such a reading, there is nothing really invidiously anti-democratic in the mentality of a politics in which a vanguard, so conceived, has a leading political function. And now that it has been disambiguated, it is a real question which of these two notions of a vanguard was intended by Marx or indeed even by Lenin, *theoretically* speaking, quite apart from the actual *practice* of communist parties.[40] Indeed, I think it would be fair to say that it is quite possible that someone like Walter Lippmann has a far more anti-democratic understanding of the political mentality of elites and ordinary people than Marx or Lenin.[41]

An essential element in my "frame" analysis was to appeal to a quite different empirical hypothesis from Freud's regarding one of the frames that govern the thinking of the populations I am discussing. Rather than to appeal to the unconscious generated by self-censor mechanisms, my appeal was to evidence of "epistemic weakness" that were responsible for the responses to questions in polls issuing from one of the frames.

These are weaknesses in the *cognitive* realm generated by a political and economic culture and institutions deriving from the metaphysical shifts that I had genealogically traced to the late seventeenth century, which in their entrenchment over the centuries ensure that ordinary people have the epistemic deficits I am stressing.[42] It is the longstanding institutional causes of these deficits that should be the real target of our criticism and contempt, not the ordinary people who are its victims.

The theoretical analysis provided here implies that the boundary or border between these two frames (which ensures that a mind or mentality is in two frames rather than a single, unified frame) that govern the mentality of ordinary people needs erasing, so that there is no segmented division in their mentality and they can explicitly recognize the conflict that is only latently present to them when the border between the segments is in place. If they are able to grasp the conflict within themselves and if the epistemic deficits that afflict them are removed so that the attitudes and outlook of one of the erstwhile segments shaped by those deficits is subject to critical scrutiny by the humane instincts of the other erstwhile segment, then there is scope to expect that such internal deliberation will enable the full flowering of the judgment of the electorate that we count on when we believe in democracy. In such an outcome, there can be hopes for a genuine and substantive democratic culture, quite distinct from the attenuated notion of democracy in the liberal ideal that the cold warrior thinks is a defining ideal of the West.

So one preliminary urgent task for a radical politics today might well be described as that of helping to *erase* that cognitive border in the minds of the electorate that gives rise to the two frames of their political mentality. In other words, a preliminary task of a radical politics is to remove the epistemic deficits in the minds or mentality of the electorate. A real question remains as to how this might be achieved, given (as I have been tracing in the first half of this essay) how deeply entrenched and genealogically fortified this longstanding political and economic culture is that erects the border in their mentality and generates epistemic deficits. All the sites that they are exposed to (their homes and upbringing, the media, the educational institutions, etc.) are too implicated in the conceptual accumulations of the thick "scientific rationality" that pervades their societies, so public education of the sort that would remove the border and thus remove their epistemic deficits cannot any longer be realistically expected to occur on *those* sites. Where then might it occur? I suspect such public education as is needed will happen, at least initially, only on the sites of *popular movements,* as it did in the labor movements in the 1930s and the civil rights movement in the 1960s, where people were educated far more deeply into the economic and racial issues than they could be expected to be by the media and in the educational institutions.[43] Of course, this is not a conclusion that is likely to be welcomed by the liberal Left outlook that I have been criticizing. There has been such a spook induced in the liberal mind by the Jacobin aftermath of the French Revolution that mass movements have come to be associated with everything but public education, a site if not of mob violence, then of the irrational radicalism of the rabble—in other words the site of any radical questioning of the cold warrior's ideal of liberal democracy, which allows at best the constraints of social democracy on the liberalism that promotes capital, but no more fundamental critique of the sort to be found in the early dissenters and the "Radical Enlightenment" that followed in figures such as Marx and others I have named all the way down to Gandhi. The plain fact of the matter is that these anxieties about the Jacobin specter are precisely what the idea of viewing mass movements as a site of public education should be hushing rather than inducing. It is precisely when *public education* to remove epistemic deficits is a goal of mass movements that movements are likely to be peaceful—on the elementary principle that if you have to carry everyone with you, you are bound to have to be moderate, however radical your message is. That, however, remains a large subject for another occasion.

The analytic points of the last many pages that I have struggled to articulate were intended to defend the idea, often dismissed by the high-minded liberal mentality, that the deeply conservative religiosity in the heartland of this country may be, in its way, an honorable expression of something very deep which is *reacting* to something very deep and longstanding, described—too summarily and crudely—with terms such as "disenchantment" and "instrumental rationality."[44] Though my remarks have merely scratched the surface of the issues of alienation and disenchantment in contemporary democratic politics, I hope I have conveyed something of the historical depth that is needed to understand the theoretical issues at stake and the analytical clarity we need to protect ourselves from the growing and undemocratic contempt we have ourselves come to feel toward the ordinary people who react to a phenomenon of such historical depth with the only resources that are available to them.

Returning then to the two defining ideals of the West that Buruma and Margalit had identified, scientific rationality and liberal democracy, what I have tried to present in the overall argument of the essay is how differently integrated these two ideals are from the way they are presented in their book and their analysis. Once their notion of "scientific rationality" is exposed as having a very specific culturally and politically "thick" sense, then it becomes much clearer how the second defining ideal (that of a very specific notion of "liberal democracy" in the cold warrior's understanding of it) is *circumscribed* and made limited by the political, economic, and cultural consequences of that form of "thick" rationality, creating, as a backlash, "Occidentalists" *in their own midst as well* whom the cold warrior would consistently (as I said) dismiss as unworthy of the West's ideals—a whole electorate dismissed as unworthy of the high and hard-won commitments of the "West," which it inhabits only geographically but not in terms of the values by which it votes. My diagnostic account in this long last section of the essay has tried to reveal how undemocratic this mentality is and how, moreover, it reflects the inadequacy and incompleteness of the defining ideal of liberal democracy its possessors congratulate themselves as upholding, how little understanding it has of the yearnings of ordinary people for "enchantment," for belonging, for the solidarities of community, for some control at a local level over the decisions by which their qualitative and material lives are shaped, in short, for the kind of *substantial* democracy that the seemingly irreversible consequences of "scientific rationality" (in the thick sense) have made impossible to achieve. The diagnosis reveals too why in a scenario where these consequences are perceived as simply given and irreversible, these yearnings manifest themselves in muddled articulations of and affiliations to a conservative Christianity that is paradoxically in a masked alliance with the very agencies of the thicker "scientific rationality" to which these yearnings are a reaction.[45]

It would be a mistake to ignore the fact that I am putting so much weight on—that it is a reaction to the larger social and cultural consequences of the thick notion of "scientific rationality"—and instead *rest* in one's diagnosis with the idea that the scenario to which these articulations are a response is merely the desolation brought about by a "market society." To rest with that diagnosis and to fail to go on to subsume the point about market society in these broader and more longstanding social, political, and even philosophical alliances is part of the shallowness of the liberal Left diagnosis I am protesting. It is beginning to be widely understood that the Republican Party's changing of the political agenda in the minds of ordinary people in the red states from issues in political economy to cultural issues surrounding religion is what has made it possible for them to be so resoundingly victorious in those states. If my account is right, then no matter how repugnant one finds their political stances, one has to acknowledge that the Republicans have, in their perverse way, been less shallow than their opposition (at any rate, one kind of Left opposition) which *merely* registers, and then rests with, the idea that it is the consequences of the market that are responsible for the cultural and political desolation of the society in which these citizens find themselves. If my account is right, it shows why these conservative religious articulations of the electorate, which the Republicans have so cynically encouraged—even engineered—and tapped for some forty years, are "the roots that clutch, the branches that grow/out of this stony rubbish," out of this cumulative effect of something with a much wider and longer reach than market society, something which subsumes market society, viz., the phenomenon we have identified as the thick ideal of "scientific rationality"; and the account demands that we ask a large and pressing question: How might we think about alternative and more secular articulations?

T. S. Eliot, who is recognizable in the quoted words of my last sentence,[46] of course, articulated thoroughly *non*-secular alternatives. Indeed it is a measure of how little he understood of the early and absolutely central role of the Anglican establishment in the trajectory that led to the disenchantment he was lamenting in those cited words that it was Anglicanism he turned to for re-enchantment.

Since Eliot, there have been proposals of other quite inadequate alternatives. Thoreau says in his section on "Economy" in *Walden* that "the mass of men lead lives of quiet desperation. What is called resignation is confirmed desperation. . . . A stereotyped but unconscious despair is concealed even under what are called the games and amusements of mankind." Writing as if these words were never written, American social scientists have offered many an *a*political vision of "bowling alleys" and the like, enchanting the lives of ordinary Americans.[47] Apart from failing to perceive what Thoreau did (suggesting as a cure for the malaise what he rightly saw to be one of its symptoms), it is a measure of how little American social science understands of what is needed to *politically* withstand the cultural and political fallout today of the alliances formed in the late seventeenth century under the brave, new, thick, "scientific rationality."

By this I don't mean at all that the ideal of secular forms of re-enchantment to cope with the "stony rubbish" of which Eliot writes has to be understood in terms of the replacement of religion by politics. Such talk of "replacement" is glib and silly, as unsatisfactory as the oft-heard aestheticist slogan: "Art and literature must have the function that religion once had." All I mean is that merely proposing recreational forms of association as providing such alternative and secular forms of enchantment misses out on the fact that it is *values* to live by that are being sought by the vast mass of ordinary people, even if sometimes confusedly in rigidly religious terms (a confusion, which I have been saying, is to some extent quite understandable in the context of the impoverished options they have been allowed); and, therefore, a great deal of *moral-psychological* resources will have to be summoned in the *public* realm so that they can get some sense that they are participating in the decisions which affect their material and spiritual lives. The aesthete who stresses art and literature does at least get something about these normative and evaluative necessities right, but proposes something that shares too much with the "bowling alley" paradigm, where the sites of participation could not possibly be host to the kind of public deliberation and organization that is needed to withstand the *political* culture of isolation and destruction of solidarities that the long era of "scientific rationality" (in the thick sense) has wrought, and which the dissenters had foreseen. It is not that politics must replace religiosity, but rather that an appreciation of the underlying political ground which prompts the religiosity requires that other more secular sources of enchantment than religion will have to emerge out of an alternative configuration of the underlying political ground. Dewey, who was temperamentally shy of the Weberian rhetoric of "enchantment," which I have been wielding with such unblushing relish, and who preferred the more purely psychological vocabulary of "consciousness," was hinting at the point that I have made more explicitly, in his marvelously cryptic remark: "Psychology is the democratic movement come to consciousness."[48]

Once we have acknowledged the great and primary claims of *global* justice, there remains no more urgent intellectual and political task in the West for our times than to frame the possibilities of such alternative, less confused, and more secular forms of re-enchantment which—if my genealogical analysis is right—are quite *intrinsically* related to questions of justice and the resistance to capital that that entails. Nothing less can make for a genuinely substantial notion of democracy, freed from the cold warrior's self-congratulatory ideals or, if not freed from them, connecting them to the lives and yearnings of ordinary people in the way that the "Occidentalist" dissenters *in the West* demanded no less than three centuries ago.

ELEVEN

The Freedom of Beginnings

In a distinction derived from Vico—but developed along very distinctive lines of his own—between the concept of "Origins" and the concept of "Beginnings,"[1] Edward Said raises a whole range of fundamental issues: about the nature of writing, and indeed more generally about the nature of human freedom.

Vico had spoken of how the very notion of a chosen people, by the privilege it endowed them with, protected them from the acts of imagination and intellect by which they might probe their own origins. These acts, which since his time came to be described in terms of "genealogy" but which Vico himself described as "divination," were acts that acknowledged a fundamental fact about those who are allowed their indulgence—that they were always in history, stuck in it, outside of the privilege of the sacred domain, and therefore these probings were essentially the Gentile acts of an enforced secularity. The discipline of history (and indeed of philosophical anthropology and the very idea of what later came to be called "Geisteswissenschaften") therefore was by its nature a secular one.

Said's use of this distinction is suggestive and varied. In this brief essay, I will only be able to explore one strand of suggestion, ignoring many other more familiar and well-mined Saidian themes, such as the contrasts he draws between filiation and affiliation, repetition and departure, social constraint and individual talent, and ignoring too his vast range of references from Marx and before to Auerbach and after.

The contrast I want to focus on is the one he himself strikingly expresses: "As consistently as possible, I use *beginning* as having the more active meaning and *origin* the more passive one: 'X is the origin of Y' while 'The beginning A leads to B'" (p. 6).

The essential passivity which he finds in the notion of origin is his way of developing Vico's understanding of the "chosen" people. Said says that this latter status necessarily amounts to a passive condition, the condition of "*being* chosen." And now Vico's point about divination (acts of inquiry into origins) being forbidden to one by the certitude of that status of being placed outside of history and contingency can also be redescribed in terms of passivity. It is a deprivation of agency because it is the *acts* of beginning that are excluded by the passivity inherent in the very notion of origin. The idea of divination in Vico is therefore broadened by this to include all acts of beginning; as a result his claim about how we must understand the secular probings that will constitute the discipline of history and of philosophical anthropology becomes, in Said, a point more broadly about writing and the exercise of imagination or inquiry itself.

But notice a curious thing. The contrast he has himself made between passive versus active offers Said a parallel contrasting term to "*being* chosen," which is "*choosing.*" But he refuses the offer. He is very careful in the quoted passage not to make his contrast quite so schematically. The idiom he adopts instead is one of "*leads to*"—something at once more unobvious and less voluntaristic. That is a point of some significance. Let me explore it.

The choice of "leads to" instead of something more unambiguously voluntaristic in describing the active voice of beginning (as opposed to the passive voice of origins) is significant in Said's own mind presumably because—as he seems to announce in the subtitle of the book—beginnings are constrained by the *intention* of the agent who writes and imagines; and intentions bring with them a *method*, a method of inquiry. Now it is true that Said himself explicitly introduces the notion of "intention" in tandem with "beginnings" in order to escape the passivity of "origins," i.e., it is his way of introducing the full and final possibilities of *agency* which are denied when one speaks of "origins" and of the chosen people living only in a privileged, sacred history. The idea here, one assumes, is that intentions are on the active rather than the passive side of things because they are states of mind that don't befall one; rather, one *forms* intentions. But what I am stressing just as much as the agency is that "intention" for him brings with it a notion of "leads to" and in particular "leads to" in line with a "method," and that *constrains* the way in which one might understand the notion of agency itself—as something less than pure choice and invention. It is this philosophical pulling in of the reins on agency even as he insists on it (already displayed in how the subtitle of the book immediately qualifies its title) that underlies and allows his appeal to agency to be unembarrassed by the fact of other sorts of constraining phenomena, phenomena such as that of filiation, repetition, etc., which he then exploits with shrewd and rich critical resourcefulness throughout his career. But it is worth focusing just on the underlying philosophy for a moment that allows all this.

At various points, Said conceptually joins "origins" with *"originality"* and *still* pursues its distinctness from "beginnings." Why? Is not originality a more natural property of one's acts rather than what is given to one? Why, then, does originality fall on the side of "origin" which is passive, rather than on the side of "beginnings"? It cannot just be because of the *surface* grammar of the cognates (origins, so therefore originality). That would be—well—shallow. There must be a point of greater depth at stake. Said does not take up this question but, if we make the appropriate interpretative and dialectical links within his own framework, we can construct on his behalf a point of some real conceptual penetration.

When he refuses to pay the compliment of originality to writing and imagination conceived as acts of beginning, he does so saying that they deserve the more modest description "points of departure." The assigning of agency to beginnings *via intention* (rather than invention) now impresses with its relevance. It is this assignment which makes it quite incoherent to place originality on the side of "beginnings." For it is built into the very idea of originality that one cannot *intend* to be original. That literally makes no sense. Just to make the point with an illustration, it is precisely this non-sense, for instance, that accounts for the discomfort we feel in reading the famously flamboyant "beginning" of Rousseau's *Confessions*.[2] It might seems at first sight that we are just a little embarrassed by its egotism, but in fact we are unsettled not by the boast of his announcing his originality so much as by the conceptual oddity of his announcing his originality as a *goal,* as what he is setting out to do or be.

What Aristotle said of pleasure—that it is an experience or property provided *in* or *by* other things we pursue, but it cannot itself be an object of pursuit—is more acutely true of originality. All an act of beginning, in Said's sense, can set out to do, all it can do by way of announced *intention,* is to say what by one's own lights is worth saying—because it is, by one's own lights, roughly and approximately true, true of one's experience, true of how one perceives the world and others, and so on. So if, contra Rousseau, one can have no other goal or intention in beginning an inquiry but to say what is (by one's lights, of course; what other lights are there?) true, then it is these lights which also then implicitly provide the *method* of one's inquiry. Originality may of course *be* a property of what one says. That is not being denied. All that is being denied is that what one says can be *intended* as original. What one says *is* original, if no one has said it before or said it in just that way or said it with the same right and conviction and persuasion. But these are all circumstances independent of what is intended by one. They are circumstances relating to how what one says relates to what others have said.[3] Not being something one can intend, originality can only be a fallout of these other things that may (or may not) hold of what one can and does intend to say. In that sense, appearances to the contrary, it falls on the passive rather than the active side. It is Said's stress on intention as a constitutive feature of beginnings therefore that accounts for why that is so.

But there is danger here. In giving such emphasis to intention and method, one might lose what there is to the *freedom* of writing and thought. Said himself says repeatedly that intention and method bring with them a path of inquiry, they "lead to" places that are generated by the intention and the method. Wherein lies the agency, then? Is it not all given over to a causality, even if it is not one of a sacred origin? Have we not lost our freedom, only this time to our own human natures and secular social and discursive contexts within which intentions and methods are generated and determined? This problem which surfaces in this early book recurs for Said in all of his work, and indeed James Clifford in a now well-known review of *Orientalism*[4] chastises him for the pervasive inconsistency of having all sorts of humanistic aspirations which demand agency, while at the same time surrendering precisely agency in his thrall to a Foucauldian historicist framework in that work. In his way, Said responded to this dilemma through all his work, and before he died he returned to address it (among other things) in his book on humanism. But already in *Beginnings*, there is an explicit awareness of the difficulty and the need to respond to it, even if the actual response is somewhat obscure and less than fully developed. Properly elaborated, however, it says enough if not to preempt Clifford's anxiety, to set him on the path to doing so.

Two kinds of beginnings or aspects of beginning are distinguished by Said, and they are named "transitive" and "intransitive."

He says of the first, "The one leads to the project being realized: this is the transitive aspect of beginning—that is beginning with (or for) an anticipated end" (p. 72). A little later he adds, "One, which I call temporal and transitive, foresees a continuity that *flows from it.* . . . This kind of beginning . . . allows us to initiate, to direct, to measure time, to construct work, to discover, to produce knowledge" (p. 76, my emphasis). All this is just recapitulating the "leads to" idiom of following through on an intention in inquiry according to a method. If this is all there is to beginning, the danger of loss of freedom would be realized.

The other kind or aspect of beginning is motivated explicitly as a resistance to just this outcome.

He says: "The other aspect [of beginning] retains for the beginning its identity as radical starting point: the intransitive and conceptual aspect, that which has no object but its own constant clarification" (p. 73). And then adds a little later: "In attempting to push oneself further and further back to what is only a beginning, a point that is stripped of every use but its categorization in the mind as beginning, one is caught in a tautological circuit of beginnings about to begin. This is the other kind of beginning, the one I called intransitive and conceptual. It is very much a creature of the mind, very much a bristling paradox, yet also very much a figure of thought that draws special attention to itself.

Its existence cannot be doubted, yet its pertinence is wholly to itself"
(p. 77). This passage and others like it are not as transparent as one
would have liked. What is clear is that Said feels the need to introduce
the second aspect of beginning in order to resist the dangers of his own
way of elaborating the first aspect. But it is not obvious how the infinite
regress of beginning that is being proposed can by itself resist the threat
of the loss of freedom. Why, it might be asked, does it not in fact deepen
the difficulty? The trouble with an infinite regress is that it can cut both
ways. It may seem to resist the inevitable "leading to" ends as determined by the method generated by intention because it leaves us always
at the beginning in an endless regress, but what freedom it would register in doing so is one that goes nowhere. It is freedom as stultification.
That does not seem to be what one wants from the notion of agency, in
the first place. And in any case, Said's own insistence that the rhetoric
surrounding beginnings be deflated to "points of departure" implies
that a regress should not be given the weight that his second, intransitive aspect of beginning places on it.

Other remarks, however, suggest a more fruitful line of resistance
(and they in fact even suggest a more sympathetic reading of the passages
already cited, though I will not be able to say how in this brief discussion). One in particular comes close to saying what is crucially needed:
"*From the point of view of the writer,* however, his writing—as he does
it—is perpetually at the beginning" (p. 74, my emphasis).

If we focus on the second half of this remark, we make no advance
on the issue. That some writing or inquiry should perpetually be at the
beginning, I have said, is either an obscure idea or (to the extent that
it is clear) an idea implying a regressive aspect that does no particular
favors to Said's own attempt at resisting the difficulties raised by the first
"intentional" and "methodical" (what he calls the "transitive") aspect
of beginnings. But the first half of the remark makes a vital difference
to how we might understand and reorient this otherwise disappointing
second half. "From the point of view of the writer" is the real source of
the resistance that is needed.

What is really important about Said's insight about there having to
be two aspects of beginnings is not that the first leads forward and the
second is regressive, but rather that there are two perspectives or *points*

of view upon one's acts of beginning. They are viewable from the outside, from the perspective of reflection, from the third person point of view, but they are also viewable from the point of view of the agent (in his quoted remark, the particular agent is of course "the writer"), that is to say the reflexive (not reflective) or the first person point of view. When viewed from the third person point of view the "leads to" idiom provides a natural description of it. That is what threatens with the loss of freedom. But from the first person point of view, "leads to" is a quite inapt description.

What needs amending or reorienting is the claim that when one brings onto center stage the first person point of view (in Said's words, "From the point of view of the writer"), one is generating a regress or an inescapable vortex of beginnings. A proper appreciation of the centrality of the first person point of view in fact allows us to escape the vortex and arrest the regress. Such a proper appreciation is sometimes hard to come to because we can lose sight of the fact that one can take a *third* person point of view *on oneself,* and when one does so one is not oneself in the agential or first personal mode, one is not a subject but rather the object of one's own gaze. The regress is something that one only falls into if one keeps looking at one's beginnings from the *third* person point of view (reflecting on oneself from the outside) and realizing that each last reflection requires another. Such a regress is precisely finessed if one *switches points of view,* switches from self-perception or reflection on oneself and one's beginnings, to the perspective of *being an agent,* the point of view from which one *makes* (or "acts") the beginning rather than reflects on it.

I have said that Said spoils his own insight captured in "From the point of view of the writer" by how he completes the remark in which that phrase occurs. This happens again and again in all the passages where he elaborates on the "intransitive" aspect of beginning. How should we diagnose this tendency on his part? I think it has to do with the fact that in this work he has an imperfect grip on the role of intention and method that he so insightfully introduces into the very idea of a beginning. The fault-line of reasoning in the tendency runs roughly as follows. "The notions of intention and method are to be described in the '*leads to*' idiom of the transitive mode of beginning. But in doing so, we are in danger of losing the freedom of writing and thought. If one is led to something, it would seem one's agency is less than in play. For Said, to resist this danger, we must find some notion or aspect of beginning which excludes intention and method for which that offending idiom is apt, and he proposes that we can do that only if we acknowledge an inescapable regress of beginnings, the "*in*transitive" mode of beginning.

The conclusion of this (fault)-line of reasoning is quite uncompulsory, if it should turn out that from the *first* person point of view, intention and method are *not* aptly described in the "leads to" idiom. So it is not—as he argues—that we need to supplement the "intentional" notion or aspect of beginning by another notion or aspect of beginning that abandons intention because intention always implies an agency-threatening "leads to" idiom. Rather what we need is to find a way of denying that intention always or (better) only implies a "leads to" idiom. And the first half of his remark about the writer's or first person point of view offers him just such a way. From the first person point of view, from the point of view of the person who forms the intention, an intention does not *lead to* any action that "flows from" (to use Said's own words above) the intention with the guidance of the method (the "transitive" aspect). That causal idiom of "leads to," "flows from," etc., is quite apt while the point of view on the intention is one of the self-*observer* rather than the actor, i.e., while it is the point of view of the subject *as object* rather than as agent. But the idiom is mismatched with the first person point of view, since in the first person one asks not what action *will my intention lead to* but what action *should* or *ought* I to do to be in *accord* with my intention and its implied method. Thus the switch from the third to the first person point of view that Said rightly demands in that remark will only generate a regress if one (not having seen the full point of the switch) is still tethered to the idiom of causality, of "leading to." But it will generate no such thing if in full appreciation of the switch, one switches also to notions of "ought" or "should" and "accord" which are the *normative* rather than the *causal* idiom that agency demands.

When I began the consideration of this issue, I applauded Said for having refused the empty and unexplained voluntaristic term "choosing" to express the contrast that "beginnings" provide with the "being chosen" of "origins." The talk of "intention" and "method" instead of "choosing" was his way of making that refusal. But in elaborating the notions of intention and method only from a third person point of view, he allows those notions to be exhaustively understood in the "leads to" idiom of causality. And even when he insightfully brings the first person point of view into focus, as in the remark I cited, he does not see through to how this insight necessarily brings with it the deep relevance of value (ought) or norm to agency.

This relevance, as I said, consists in the fact that when we view intentions from the first person point of view of the agent, we cannot see our intentions in the "leads to" causal mode. That is to say, we cannot step outside of the first person point of view *while we are in it* and view ourselves from the outside, from a third person point of view. In a word, we cannot both be *agents* and at the same time be *observers* or predictors of ourselves and what our minds will cause us or "lead" us to do. While we are agents we ask what *ought* we to do and we say what we are *committed* to doing by our intentions. Talk of "oughts" and "commitments," however, is paradigmatically a normative and evaluative way of talking.

By "normative" and "evaluative" talk, I don't necessarily by any means have in mind moralistic talk. It is not moral or social norms that are at stake. It is a confusion (at any rate, reductive) to think that the realm of value is exhausted by the realm of the moral. The norms and commitments in question here are generated by one's own intentions, not by something external to us as morality is often taken to be. But it is normative all the same. Consider the most trivial of examples of an intention. I intend to take my umbrella when I go out. But, let's say, when the time comes I don't take my umbrella. In that case, *by the lights of my intention*, I did something *wrong*. I failed to live up to the commitment generated by the intention. This is not a moral wrong. But that we can all the same use the term "wrong" quite appropriately makes it uncontroversially an evaluative phenomenon. The triviality of the example may show that evaluative and normative vocabulary does not always have to have a high profile. Weightier examples may increase the stature of the profile, but even the trivial examples reveal that there is an *intrinsic* link between intention and norm or value.

And the point of contrast with all this is that while we are observers of ourselves and not agents, while we have a third rather than a first person angle on ourselves, we ask or say what we will be *"led to"* do by our intentions rather than what we should or ought to do, given our intentions. That is a non-normative, causal way of talking. And the two ways of talking (normative and causal) are strictly incommensurate. We *cannot straddle* both ways of talking. We can only switch from one to the other. The impossibility that the "cannot" here is conveying is analogous to the impossibility in our perception of that notorious figure in Wittgenstein: We can see it as a duck and we can see it as a rabbit but we cannot see it as a duck *while* we see it as a rabbit. To see the one rather than the other one has to make a switch in perspective or point of view. Wittgenstein in that example of course was not meaning to point to perspectives of the first person and the third person, agent and observer. So I invoke him only by way of analogy. But the analogy is a good one because it conveys that a perspectival shift is required in each case.

It is because Said does not see through to this last step implied by his own insight in invoking "the point of view of the writer" in that cited remark that he lands us in the end with the impoverished options of the empty rhetoric of "choosing" versus the agency-threatening causal idiom of "leads to." But if the interpretations and diagnoses offered in this brief discussion are right, we are in a position now to say that what is needed to explain and fill out the otherwise idle voluntaristic idiom of choosing is to conceptually link it along these lines with norm and value. Now it is no longer a dogmatically asserted voluntarism, it is one with our normative, deliberative exercises involved in inquiry or writing or action.

I say "*one* with" and mean it. We have, anciently, thought there are two mysteries: the very possibility of free agency in a causal universe and the very place of value in a naturalistic world. If I am right, these are the *same* mystery. And reducing two mysteries to one is surely some sort of progress.

This normative and evaluative dimension *built into* the very idea of agency and intention is what is struggling to get out in Said's insight that something about the first person point of view will provide the resistance to his transitive and causal aspects of beginnings which threaten freedom and agency. Because it doesn't quite get out, there is all that unhelpful talk of an infinite and perpetual regress of beginnings. That talk distracts from the fact that questions asked and assertions made about one's intentions from the first person point of view (unlike from the third person point of view) are not predictive; they are evaluative and speak to one's commitments rather than one's causal tendencies. It is really only where agency and value ("intention" and "ought") join that Clifford's anxiety about the tensions in Said's twin commitments to historicism (causality, "leads to" . . .) and humanism will be calmed. There is much more to be said here of course, and I regret that I must end, having hardly begun.

TWELVE

Edward Said

An Intellectual and Personal Tribute

There are a very few intellectuals—Bertrand Russell, E. P. Thompson, and Noam Chomsky come to mind in the English-speaking world—whose writings and whose lives provide a kind of pole that thousands of people look toward so as to feel that they are not wholly lost or marginal for possessing instincts for justice and humanity, and for thinking that some small steps might be taken toward their achievement. Edward Said was, without a doubt, such a man. The daze and despair so many of us here at Columbia feel, now that we have taken in that he has gone, is only a very local sign of what is a global loss without measure. And to think of what it must be like for his own brutalized people to lose him is unbearable.

1.

Edward was, as they say, "many things to many people," and though he was too vast to be contained by a mere university, even one as uncloistered as Columbia, he was a teacher and took great pride in being one. So let me say something about that first.

To put it seemingly frivolously, he was deeply "cool." I say "deeply" and mean it. One day, the best undergraduate I have ever taught and my very favorite student said to me, "Prof. Said is really cool." Now I, who have been trying to be cool for decades, was mildly annoyed by this, and said, "Look, I can understand that you think he is a great scholar and intellectual and a peerless public figure, but why 'cool'? He doesn't wear black, he despises popular music, he hangs out with well-heeled professors and other rich and famous people, and he is preposterously handsome—how uncool can you get!" She looked at me dismissively and said, "All that's really not a big deal. It's—like—really on the surface."

Edward's influence on the young came from his refusal to allow literature to offer merely self-standing pleasures. The connections he made in even our most canonical works, between the narrations of novels and the tellings of national histories, between the assertions of an author and the assertion of power by states, between the unconscious attitudes of a seemingly high-minded writer and some subtle illiberal tendency of social or national prejudice, drew to the study of literature numberless students who, out of a quest for worldly engagement, or more simply out of a cosmopolitan curiosity, demanded just such an integrity of words with morals. Not long ago while giving a lecture in Hong Kong, I found that students were passing around a faint and barely readable photographed parchment of one of his unpublished manuscripts—a contribution to a symposium held 10,000 miles away—as though it were a handwritten poem by a Renaissance courtier. No other literary critic has had such a, literally, planetary influence. And he achieved this without any of the heart-sinking, charmless prose of the literary avant-garde, nor the natural, unaffected dullness of the old guard. His writing, like his speech, had the voltage of dramatization and (it has to be said) self-dramatization, which no young person could find anything but cool.

2.

Because of his great political courage, because he repeatedly broke his lion's heart in the cause of Palestinian freedom, because so much of his most familiar and famous writing was intellectually continuous with those political themes and struggles, and because it was expressed with a ceaseless flow of political ardor, Edward's intellectual legacy will be primarily political, not just among the young, nor just in the popular image, but also in the eyes of academic research. There is no gainsaying this. And it must be so. It will be right to be so. This side of him was of course manifest to his own people, but it was also central to so many others for whom the Palestinian struggle is a reminder that the fight for the most elementary of freedoms is not yet over. Since so much has rightly been written about it, I want to briefly situate that most vital part of his life and thought in the larger setting of his humanism, of which we often spoke in our conversations inside and outside the classes we taught together, and on which he had just completed a book, when he died. It was perhaps the only "ism" he avowed (he was, despite being in the midst of an anti-colonial struggle, consistently critical of national-ism), and he avowed it with a stubborn idealism, in the face of its having been made to seem pious and sentimental by the recent developments in literary theory.

Underlying the civic passions and the charged impressionism of his political and literary writing was a deep and structured argument of greater generality than anything that is usually attributed to him. (He was always impatient with arguments, and would tell me that it was a philosopher's obsession, keen to find philosophers as bad as lawyers on this score. But he was wrong about this, and came around to saying that something like this argument was indeed a thread in his work.)

Two elements of frameworking breadth have abided through the diverse doctrinal formulations of humanism, from its earliest classical hints to the most subtle surviving versions of our own time. They can, in retrospect, be seen as its defining poles.

One is its aspiration to find some feature or features which sets what is human apart—apart from *both* nature, as the natural sciences study it, *and* from what is super-nature and transcendental, as these are pursued by the outreach of theology and metaphysics.

The other is the yearning to show regard for *all* that is human, for what is human *wherever* it may be found, and however remote it may be from the more vivid presence of the parochial. The dictum "Nothing human is alien to me," still moving despite its great familiarity (and despite the legend about its trivial origin), conveys something of that yearning.

These two familiar poles framed the argument that Edward presented throughout his life as a writer.

At one pole, to explore what sets the human apart, he invoked early on in his work a principle of Vico's, that we know best what *we ourselves* make—history. Self-knowledge thus becomes special, standing apart from other forms of knowledge. And only human beings, so far as we know, are capable of that self-knowledge.

At the other pole, to make urgent Terence's dictum, he plunged into the topical, warning us of the disasters that will follow, and which indeed are already upon us, if we conduct our public lives as intellectuals with an indifference to the concerns and the suffering of people in places distant from our Western, metropolitan sites of self-interest.

Relatively fixed poles though they may be in a highly changeable set of ideas we call "humanistic," these two features are not "poles apart." They are not merely two unrelated and contingent elements of humanism. They must be brought together in a coherent view. And Edward tried to do just that.

To bridge the distance between them, he started first at one pole by completing Vico's insight with a striking philosophical addition. What Vico brought to light was the especially human ability for self-knowledge, and the special character possessed by self-knowledge among all the other knowledges we have. This special character which has affected our paths of study in ways that we have, since Vico's time, taken to describing with such terms as "Verstehen," "Geisteswissenschaften," or as they like to say in America, "the Social Sciences," still gives no particular hint of the role and centrality of the humanities. It is Said's claim, I think, that until we supplement self-knowledge with, in fact until we understand self-knowledge as being constituted by, self-*criticism,* humanism and its disciplinary manifestations ("the Humanities") are still not visible on the horizon. What makes that supplement and that new understanding possible is the study of literature. To put it schematically, the study of literature, that is to say "Criticism," his own life-long pursuit, when it supplements *self*-knowledge gives us the truly unique human capacity, the capacity to be *self-critical.*

Turning then to the other pole, how can a concern for *all* that is human be linked, not just contingently but *necessarily,* to this capacity for self-criticism? Why are these not simply two disparate elements in our understanding of humanism? Said's answer is that when criticism at our universities is not parochial, when it studies the traditions and concepts of other cultures, it opens itself up to resources by which it may become *self*-criticism, resources not present while the focus is cozy and insular. The "Other," therefore, is the source and resource for a better, more critical understanding of the "self." It is important to see, then, that the appeal of Terence's ideal for Said cannot degenerate into a fetishization of "diversity" for its own sake or into a glib and "correct" embrace of current multiculturalist tendency. It is strictly a step in an argument that starts with Vico and ends with the relevance of humanism in American intellectual life and politics. Multiculturalism has not had a more learned and lofty defense. It may in the end be the only defense it deserves.

James Clifford in a now famous review of *Orientalism* had chastised Edward, saying that he cannot possibly reconcile the denial of the human subject, in his appeal to Foucault in that work, with his own humanist intellectual urges, reconcile, that is, his historicist theoretical vision with the agency essential to the humanist ideal. But if the argument I have just presented is effective, if the *methodical* link between the two poles I mentioned really exists, it goes a long way in easing these tensions. It allows one not simply to assert but to claim with some right, as Edward did, that criticism is *both* of two *seemingly* inconsistent things: It is philology, the "history" of words, the "reception" of a tradition, at the same time as it allows for a "resistance" to that tradition and to the repository of custom that words accumulate.

The argument, thus, gives literary humanism a rigor and intellectual muscle, as well as a topicality and political relevance, that makes it unrecognizable from the musty doctrine it had become earlier in the last century—and it gives those disillusioned with or just simply bored with that doctrine something more lively and important to turn to than the arid formalisms and relativisms of recent years. For this, we must all be grateful.

3.

I first met Edward twenty years ago when I noticed an incongruously well-dressed man at a luncheon talk I gave as a fresh recruit at the Society of Fellows, on some theme in the philosophy of history. With a single

question, asked without a trace of condescension, he made me see why
the issues of substance and urgency lay elsewhere than where I was
laboring them. I knew immediately that he was a good thing, though I
did not know then that I would never change my mind. One had heard
so much about him. No person I knew had more political enemies. They
did not find it enough to hate him; they wanted the whole world to hate
him, and they weaved fantastications and myths in trying to make it happen. For those who admired his indomitable political will, these scurri-
lous attacks against him made him seem even more iconic, and for those
who knew him well, his seductive, self-pitying responses to them made
him even more dear.

An essential part of his great and natural charm was that friendship
with him was not without difficulty, nor without steep demand. He
would do his best sometimes to appear a credible swine, if for no other
reason than to raise a spark in the conversation. I recall when we were on
the stage together at some public meeting, after the idiotic fuss that was
made about his having thrown a stone in the air at a site in Lebanon which
had just been evacuated by the Israeli army. The person who introduced
us began with me, and gave me the modest introduction I deserved, and
then went on to poetic heights about him, and concluded by saying that
he was the author of over twenty books. As she finished, I leaned into
my microphone and said, "Over twenty books! Somebody has to stop
this terrorist! First he throws stones! Now he is cutting down trees!" He
immediately leaned into his own microphone and said, "My dear fellow,
you should worry just a bit that for a man who has not written as much,
that remark will come off as bitter rather than funny." On another occasion, we were sitting in his flat last New Year's Eve for dinner, with a
gathering of his friends from the Modern Languages Association, which
had just had its annual meeting in New York City. The talk that evening
had had much to do with feminism in the academy, the usual drill about
the feminine pronoun, and all of us had self-consciously displayed our
impeccable commitments. The conversation came around to whether
my wife and I would be moving our daughter from Brearley to the newly
started school for the children of faculty at Columbia University, a subject of vexed indecision for us. Edward asked us impatiently, "So are
you bringing her to the Columbia School? What the hell is holding you

up?" And I said, "Well, I am not sure, she is very happy at Brearley."
And he said, throwing a glance around at the women in the room, "Who
cares, she's a GIRL!!!" This teasing sometimes became willfully, even if
delightfully, dangerous. An interviewer once asked him on television if
he had read a recent book on Wagner, which had come to the extraordinary conclusion that his music was so infused with anti-Semitism that
if someone who was not anti-Semitic heard his operas, he or she would
become anti-Semitic by the end of it. What, the interviewer asked, do
you think of that conclusion? Edward, who despised anti-Semitism as
much as anyone I know but perfectly aware of the obvious dangers of the
subject for a person with his political commitments, leaned forward and
said, as if in earnest: "You know, I tried it. I got all my Wagner out and
heard it all day and half into the night." He then paused, allowing the
menace to build up, and then, shaking his head, "It didn't work."

Yes, he was "mad, bad, and dangerous to know," and he was a great
and good and inspiring and beloved man. It is very hard to bear the loss
of someone so large of heart and mind.

As I wrote those last words, I was reminded that that heart and mind
were lodged in a body, which, for all its robustness, was cursed with
a wretched illness that he fought with such heroism for a dozen years.
Reminded too of that more muted and less recognized form of heroism—
forbearing and endlessly giving—with which his remarkable wife Mar-
iam stood by his side each day for all those years, and of that obscure and
nameless thing she will need now that he is gone, to be without the presence of the most present person she, and his children, and his friends,
have known. I wish her vast reserves of it, whatever it is, and of every
other good thing.

Notes

Preface

1. At a lecture given at Columbia University.
2. Salman, a friend, when alerted to my passing reference to his remark, wrote me a note to say that he does not recall having said it, and that if he did say it, he must have meant it ironically. Even if intended with irony, I hope he will not mind my retaining the reference to it since, as I say, despite my finding it unconvincing, it points to what I take to be theoretically and historically fruitful continuities that rigidly made dichotomies between religion and the secular have masked.

1. Secularism

Charles Taylor read a draft of this essay with much care and acute comprehension and responded with a generous and detailed account of the points on which we are agreed and disagreed. Disagreements remain, but I am grateful to him for the considerable improvements that I was able to make as a result of having to address his response. I am also much indebted to Carol Rovane, Jeffrey Stout, Ira Katznelson, Michael Warner, and David Bromwich for detailed comments on the earlier draft in which they made a number of helpful suggestions and criticisms, as well as to Prabhat Patnaik, Aijaz Ahmad, Vivek Dhareshwar, and Al Stepan, who also took the trouble to read the essay and made useful responses. Finally, this essay started life as a Social Science Research Council (SSRC) working paper, put up on its website "Immanent Frame," where it fetched extensive commentary from a number of very distinguished scholars of secularism from a variety of disciplines, which brought much instruction to me. Since I have responded to them in detail on that website, I have not revised the present essay much in accord with those responses, but I would like to record my thanks to them once again for bothering to read my work and for their valuable comments.

1. Akeel Bilgrami, "What Is a Muslim?," *Critical Inquiry* 18 (1992). See also Akeel Bilgrami, "Rushdie and the Reform of Islam," *Grand Street* 8(4) (1989): 170–184.
2. On analysis, this general distinction in Williams does a lot of different work and marks more than one specific distinction. In this essay, I am exploiting just one of the specific

distinctions that are marked. See Bernard Williams, "Internal and External Reasons," in *Moral Luck* (Cambridge: Cambridge University Press, 1981). For an analysis of the different things going on in the distinction, see the appendix to my *Self-Knowledge and Resentment* (Cambridge, Mass.: Harvard University Press, 2006).

3. I am passing from talk of "truth" of a doctrine to whether there are reasons for believing it that carry conviction. This is not a slip. See note 13 for more on this.

4. See Charles Taylor, "Modes of Secularism," in Rajeev Bhargava (ed.), *Secularism and Its Critics* (Oxford: Oxford University Press, 1998). The idea of an overlapping consensus is most fully articulated in John Rawls, *Political Liberalism* (New York: Columbia University Press, 1993).

5. John Rawls, *The Law of Peoples* (Cambridge, Mass.: Harvard University Press, 1999).

6. Charles Taylor, "Why We Need a Radical Redefinition of Secularism," in Jonathan Van Antwerpen and Eduardo Mendieta (eds.), *The Power of Religion in the Public Sphere* (New York: Columbia University Press, 2011).

7. India is sometimes described as a secular state that fits Taylor's neutral, symmetrically equidistant ideal toward India's different *religions*. (I think this is a mistaken reading of Indian secularism as it came to be an explicit commitment after the constituent assembly debates on these issues. This is not an essay on Indian secularism, so I can't discuss why that is so here, though some of what I say at the end of this essay on the well-known issue of Muslim personal laws in India, which has obvious relevance to Indian secularism, conveys one reason for why it is mistaken. More generally, the point I make above about how a state neutralist ideal of secularism that allows the *symmetrical* banning of books blaspheming against different religions in the society applies to this view of Indian secularism that I find mistaken. It should also be noted that, unlike some articulations of this idea of Indian secularism, Taylor explicitly wishes to add *non-religion* as well to the mix of standpoints that the secular state must be neutral toward.

8. For more on this, see my essays "What Is a Muslim?" in this volume; "The Clash within Civilizations," *Daedalus* 132(3) (2003); and "Islam, Conflict and Democracy," in Abdou Filali Ansary and Sikeena Karmali (eds.), *Pluralism in Muslim Contexts*. (Edinburgh: University of Edinburgh Press 2009), pp. 78–93.

9. The best reading of Savarkar and the mentality of Gandhi's assassin is Ashis Nandy's recent work. See, for instance, his "Allure of the Demonic," *Outlook*, August 22, 2005. On his reading, Savarkar desacralized Hinduism and made it into a modern ideology, the very thing Gandhi's Hinduism fought most deeply against. It is ironic, as I am trying to argue in this essay, that if Gandhi had had his way, secularism would not be necessary for India. It is only because the Savarkar ideology with its modern, religious majoritarianism mimicking of European nation-building exercises began to have some serious purchase in the Indian polity, including even in the Congress Party by the late 1980s, that secularism became an absolute inevitability in India as the only way to repair the damages of this increasing tendency. See more in note 11 on this question.

10. Despite greatly encouraging the role of women in the freedom movement, his thought and his activist efforts were not much focused on gender inequality. That was not so with caste inequality, in particular untouchability, which was an issue that was constantly in Gandhi's thoughts, and it has to be said—as it often is—that the politics he

generated on the issue of caste at various points in his political life were often highly problematic, even though he had a genuine and deep compassion for the suffering owing to "untouchability" of the people to whom he gave the name "harijans."

11. There may be some evidence that Gandhi himself changed the substance and the idiom of his understanding of the issues by the time it came to the 1940s when the majoritarian threat loomed much larger even within the Congress Party that he led. That, I think, is the sort of contextual shift we should be tracking in the study of secularism and its relevance. In Section V of his article "Gandhiji, Secularism and Communalism," *The Social Scientist* 32(1–2) (January–February 2004): 3–29, Bipan Chandra cites evidence for such a shift in Gandhi's thinking in the 1940s. He describes this as a shift within Gandhi's secularism, or in other words, in the *meaning* that secularism had for Gandhi, but for reasons I've been sketching at length, I wouldn't follow him on this. In his earlier period, Gandhi is not properly described as a secularist. Bipan Chandra's essay, even so, is valuable for raising the question of such a shift in that later period. And in my remarks on the increasing influence of a majoritarian nationalism (or what Bipan Chandra would call "Hindu Communalism") even within the Congress Party—in its Mahasabhite element—we are given the causes of the shift in context that may have prompted the change in Gandhi's thought on the subject. Gandhi's entire evolution on the subject can, therefore, be seen as *starting* with a fear of this aspect of the post-Westphalian nationalist tendency infecting the Indian polity and a great effort on his part to protect India from that path, but then perhaps *ending* with a resigned acknowledgement of its increasing contagion and therefore shifting to the idiom and substance of secularism to control the damage. That, I believe, should be the right description of the shift that Bipan Chandra is marking in that essay. I say all this, assuming that he is right in his reading of the Gandhi of the 1940s. But we should also ask a more basic interpretative question of how correct that reading of Gandhi is. Might it not be that though Gandhi was prepared to say in the 1940s that there is no great harm in acknowledging some need for secularism to combat the majoritarian tendency that was incipiently rearing its head in Indian politics, he nevertheless held out a hope in his heart that India would find its way to finessing the tendency as a result of its very longstanding and deep-going *popular* syncretic traditions wherein Hindus and Muslims had a relatively unified life of custom and practice, whether in the realm of mutual worship in shared shrines or more broadly in the harmony of their common cultural traditions. In other words, might it not be that it is well after Gandhi died, really only in the period after Indira Gandhi, that the kind of majoritarianism he most feared became entrenched in Indian political life and when—were he alive—the relevance of a doctrine like (S) would come to him to seem inescapable.

12. I give this example of the term "democracy" just so as to show that a word can get a "hurrah" status with all sides wanting it for themselves since there will be seeming merit on the side of those who can claim it, thereby taking away from any precise meaning that it might have. I don't mean to suggest that Taylor has the polemical and propaganda motives that surrounded the Cold War disputes around "free" versus "people's" democracy debates. In fact, in the case of that term, I think, the way to define or characterize it is to see it as a form of government in which ordinary people have a serious

input in the important decisions in their material and other central aspects of their lives. Neither Cold War exemplifications of "free" or "people's" democracy met this criterion. On the one hand, elections in "free" democracies were not occasions or sites on which important issues that made a difference to the material lives of people were even so much as raised (all crucial decisions being made by the corporate sectors of society at some distance from the electoral field). And, on the other hand, the very idea of "people's" democracy was not intended (at any rate, not after the soviets and democratic councils in the Soviet Union were dismantled), to give people *input* into decisions on these matters; it was rather a claim to achieve the fulfillment of people's material and other essential needs—thus, even, when this was genuinely achieved, its achievement, however it is described, can't be described as an achievement of *democracy,* by the lights of the criterion I just mentioned.

13. Apart from the papers mentioned in note 1, see "Two Concepts of Secularism," *Economic and Political Weekly* (July 9, 1994): 1749-1761 vol 29, no. 28 republished in Rajeev Bhargava (ed.), *Secularism and Its Critics* (Oxford: Oxford University Press, 1998); and "Secularism and the Moral Psychology of Identity," *Economic and Political Weekly* 32(40): 2527-2540; republished in Amiya Bagchi, Rajeev Bhargava, and R. Sudarshan (eds.), *Multiculturalism, Liberalism, and Democracy* (Oxford: Oxford University Press, 2001).

14. Of course, it may not always be able to be completely neutral regarding it since such a secularism may sometimes threaten the neutrality.

15. I am going directly from talk of "reasons" to talk of "truth." This is a deliberate collapsing of epistemological and metaphysical notions, on my part. Some may want to keep epistemological and metaphysical issues apart and say that a principled failure to find *reasons* against a position one is in moral or political disagreement with does not yet show that position to be *true.* It still might not be true, even though one can't establish that to be so. If someone insists on making this sharp distinction between "reasons" and "truth," the relativism I am discussing is a relativism regarding *the former only.* There would have to be *another* kind of relativism regarding truth, in that case, that someone may wish to argue for. Having expressed this caveat, I will continue to talk of the relativist as saying that regarding various positions in disagreement with one another, each have the "truth" on their side—and will ask the reader who wishes to make that sharp distinction to simply read my use of "truth" in the text differently from the way it is read when keeping epistemology and metaphysics sharply distinct. Two related caveats. First, I myself have distinguished sharply between questions of the meaning of "secularism" and questions of justifying secularism. But that is a quite different distinction from the one which I am collapsing in this note. All I am doing in this note is to say that I want to formulate a relativism that is generated by a *principled* failure on one's part to provide internal reasons to another position with which one is disagreed in order to get them to change their minds and come around to one's own position. And I am asking the reader's indulgence in allowing me to calibrate the use of "true" and "false" along these lines, allowing me, that is, to say of a position against which one in principle cannot provide internal reasons that it is *true.* The second caveat has to do with the fact that some may think that questions of "truth" and

"falsity" don't arise when it comes to morals and politics—they should be restricted only to questions of science and matters approximating science, where value elements are (more or less) missing. I find this view to be quite wrong, but I don't need to argue for that here. I need simply only ask once again for terminological latitude on the part of the reader, i.e., ask the reader who has a qualm about using "true" and "false" for political and moral positions to substitute some other words for my use of "true" or "false" (right or wrong, or just x and y, would be fine).

16. It is important to understand two things about this evaluative, quasi-humanist stance. First, one must be clear about its role in the dialectic of this essay. It is *not* something that is being wheeled in against relativism *directly*. It is not a matter of saying "I take an evaluative stance that my position is right and not merely one right position among others." That would be glib and utterly unconvincing, a way of avoiding wrestling seriously with the specter of relativism created (prima facie) by the stress on internal reasons and the denial of external reasons. Rather the evaluative stance has been wheeled in on the coattails of the Hegelian argument against relativism that invokes the subject-in-history. It props up *that* argument, which is the primary argument against relativism. The evaluative stance is merely a stance taken on the question of how to interpret history and the prospects it holds out for the possibility of the introduction of conflicts into the psychological economies of those with whom one is in political or moral conflict. It is a stance that gives one the right to take a certain default position on that question. It offers no other more direct certification of anti-relativism. The second thing to understand about the evaluative, quasi-humanist stance is this. It is a stance taken toward each other by disputants who are in *conflict* or disagreement. It, therefore, has bearing only when there is a genuine conflict or disagreement between two positions, say between (S) and some position that opposes (S). And a genuine conflict or disagreement occurs only when (S) can, in the first place, claim to have relevance and application, given certain social conditions, and given the ideals that the polity has set out to achieve. When it can rightly claim this, then, if there is some position that opposes (S), that position and (S) are in conflict. But (S) may sometimes be quite irrelevant, given certain social conditions and certain goals adopted by a polity. Thus for instance, if I am right in what I say in the discussion of Gandhi in Section 4, (S) had no conspicuous relevance to India at the time when Gandhi was initially writing. For this reason, Gandhi did not hold a position that was *in conflict* with (S); he was rather saying that (S) had no relevance, no application in the context of Indian society at that time. It, in turn, follows that the evaluative, quasi-humanist stance that gives support to the entire Hegelian argument is not something that (S) can adopt in that context. There is no genuine disputant to adopt it toward.

17. I repeat that as it happens, of course, the exception was granted only to Muslims, so this is not a good example of the neutralist ideal that Taylor favors, but that is just what I am putting aside from consideration for the purposes of giving this relativistic reading to the Muslims being granted an exception. This differential owes partly to minority rights issues attaching to Muslims, who are a minority in India.

18. Two important points must be made here. First, I am not actually taking any firm stand on whether it was or was not right for the Muslims to be allowed to live by their own

personal laws in post-independence India. To take such a stand would require a very detailed discussion of the historical context, which would be quite out of place in an essay of this kind. I am only saying that a non-coercive or "non-dominating" conception of the politics of secularism (defined as (S)) might well find nothing wrong, from a theoretical point of view, in that particular outcome in India, so long as the outcome was interpreted along the lines of the second reading I gave it, and the second reading was justified by the historical context. Second, and far more important, though I think, in fact, that the concession to Muslim personal laws was exactly such a Hegelian moment in the Indian constitution, I do want to say something to clarify this position since it is poised to be misunderstood in a rather elementary way. In the two papers mentioned in note 13, I argue at length—invoking specific examples, for instance one from provincial history in Bengal in the 1920s—how the *state itself* may play a role in helping religious groups and communities to come to see and to formulate these internal reasons and then to play the role of implementing those changes via reform of laws and customs. Therefore, the idea of *internal reasons for reform* is not to be confused with *internal reform* of a religion from within the religion. The point of the latter is that the state has no role to play in changes within a religious standpoint. That is not the point at all of this essay's argument and its stress on internal reasons. Let me be clear, then, about what is and is not the point. The point *is* a) to view the state as having its own voice in the field of providing reasons, but since these will be *internal* reasons, they will have to be, as I said earlier, articulated in the *conceptual* vernacular of the groups to which the state seeks to provide internal reasons to change, as well as b) for the state to give religious groups a voice in the field of reasons, in the fraternal spirit that Taylor urges, by allowing them to see and articulate their own internal reasons for any change in their position. (A constituent assembly is just one such large and prominent forum where groups can come together for precisely such a fraternal deliberation.) What, then, is *not* the point of the argument about internal reasons? It is not the point to insist that the groups must carry out their own internal changes without any role for the state to play. Of course, if the groups did make their own internal changes (e.g., reform of their personal laws), that may be something a subscriber of (S) can applaud. But there is nothing in the idea of seeking internal reasons for (S) that requires that reform of religious laws must take this purely internal form with no role for the state to play. Sumit Sarkar conflates and confuses this distinction between internal reasons for reform and internal reform in equating my view of these matters with Partha Chatterjee's in his paper "The Anti-Secularist Critique of Hindutva: Problems of a Shared Discursive Space," *Germinal* 1 (1994).

19. I must confess to having written an essay about twenty years ago called "Two Concepts of Secularism" (see reference in note 13), in which I had written of how a secularism based on internal reasons is one concept of secularism and another based on external reasons is a second concept. This is what I am saying in the present essay is a mistake. There is only one concept of secularism and there are two different paths of justification for it. And even in that early essay where I did make a contrast between two concepts of secularism in the title, I was very clear in the details of what I had said that I was not really *defining* secularism differently in each, but merely saying that it

makes a big difference to politics, in particular a politics that avoids some of the subtle coercions that secularism can be party to, if we take internal and external reasons as different *justifications* seriously, and stress the former over the latter. If, in that essay, I was not always as careful to be *explicit* about this distinction between issues of definition on the one hand, and justification and basis of implementation on the other, the present essay can be seen as a detailed corrective to such a lapse.

2. Secularism, Multiculturalism, and the Very Concept of Law

This essay was originally published in Anaradha Dingwaney Needham and Rajeswari Sunder Rajan (eds.), *The Crisis of Secularism in India* (Durham, N.C.: Duke University Press, 2007). I am grateful to Carol Rovane, Steve White, Amartya Sen, Brian Barry, Jeremy Waldron, and Jon Elster for comments and discussion.

1. I am using the term "secularism" in this context pretty much as I defined it in my previous essay. My reason for invoking the term "secularism" and the term "multiculturalism" at all in the context of this essay is simply this. I am interested in the demands made by groups (religious minorities in particular) in a multicultural society that they be exempted from certain laws of a liberal democratic polity because they conflict with their religious practices and customs and convictions. These demands for exemption, though they are likely to clash with secularism as understood by (S) in my previous essay need not clash with secularism as defined as by Taylor's neutralist state ideal or with various other definitions of secularism that may be of interest to others.

2. In Britain, free speech is put aside in the case of blasphemy and in fact there have been cases fought and won in favor of censorship against blasphemy. But they are restricted to blasphemy against the Christian faith.

3. Cambridge: Polity Press, 2001, p. 39.

4. See earlier in the text on the reason for putting aside considerations such as self-defense as not issuing from people's sentiments but from the subject matter itself.

5. Jon Elster, in commenting on this paper, put this objection to me.

6. It is of course also familiarly disputed as being a worthy aspiration in the realm of science, especially by those who think that psychology and even biology are not to be thought as being so highly integrated or subsumable into such a hierarchical conception of science. Indeed there is even a view that ceteribus paribus clauses infect laws not just in the special sciences but all the way up even in the fundamental sciences, such as physics. All these philosophical positions would find the assumption of subsumption that governs the vision of some notions of scientific inquiry and the underlying secularist understanding of legislation that I am presenting in this essay (without approval or disapproval) to be suspect.

3. Liberalism and the Academy

This is the transcript of a lecture given at the New School in New York, originally published as "Freedom, Truth, and Inquiry" in Jean Bricmont and Julie Franck (eds.), *Chomsky Notebook*

(New York: Columbia University Press, 2010). I owe a great debt of gratitude to Isaac Levi for detailed discussions over the years of the pragmatist epistemological themes in Section 2 and to Noam Chomsky for the general tendency of the view taken in Section 3.

1. Actually, it was the *idea* and not the *expression* that Oliver Wendell Holmes put into the air in his dissenting opinion in *Abrams vs. The United States.* His own expression was "free trade in ideas." The expression "marketplace of ideas" was first used in the language of the Supreme Court in *Keyishan vs. Board of Regents of the State University of New York* (1967).
2. R. Hofstadter and W. P. Metzger, *The Development of Academic Freedom in the United States* (New York: Columbia University Press, 1955), p. 527.
3. John Stuart Mill, *On Liberty,* ch. 2 (London: Longman, Roberts and Green, 1869).
4. Qualms about arguments of this kind of ambition in politics are central to the political direction presented in this book and are discussed at much greater length in Essay 1, "Secularism: Its Content and Context," under the topic of "external versus internal reasons," and they surface again in some of the essays revolving around issues of identity, especially "What Is a Muslim?" and "After the Fatwah."
5. There is more on this distinction between cognitive and moral values in the essay "Gandhi, the Philosopher" in this volume, where the differences between Gandhi and the sort of mentality that underlies Mill's argument are discussed at some length.
6. The most powerful pragmatist to whom the anti-Millian views expressed in this essay owe is Peirce, especially in his remarkable essay "The Fixation of Belief," in *Collected Papers,* vol. 5, bk. II, ch. 4 (Cambridge, Mass.: Harvard University Press, 1978). Isaac Levi's many writings—but particularly his *Enterprise of Knowledge* (Cambridge, Mass.: MIT Press, 1983)—are no less deep and powerful and this essay's epistemological tendency owes much to what I have learned from him. The relevant Austin text on these themes is primarily "Other Minds," *Philosophical Papers* (Oxford: Oxford University Press, 1960), p. 98. I have not cited Wittgenstein for reasons of space, but similar attitudes may be found in *On Certainty* (Oxford: Blackwell, 1969). And, of course, Kant's transcendental idealism is presented most fully in his *Critique of Pure Reason,* trans. Norman Kemp Smith (London: Macmillan, 1929).
7. And this could only mean that when we state the conditions which make any particular proposition true or false, the conditions are always something that are specified by the lights of our own background beliefs.
8. Richard Rorty, *Philosophy and the Mirror of Nature* (Princeton, N.J.: Princeton University Press, 1981).
9. Noam Chomsky and Edward Hermann in their rightly celebrated *Manufacturing Consent* (New York: Pantheon Books, 1988), have addressed this subject with the focus primarily on the media in this country.
10. I realize that it *is* a matter of will whether one *presents* in a classroom (or indeed in one's research) what one has evidence for. That is why failing to do so is to be described as "dishonesty." I am only saying here that when the evidence compels us to draw a conclusion, the will is not in play; it is not a matter of choice, even though coming to believe something on the basis of evidence is in the realm of the intentional.

4. Gandhi, the Philosopher

This essay was originally published in *Raritan: A Quarterly Review* 21(2) (2001): 48–67.

1. Sumit Sarkar, *Modern India* (Basingstoke: Macmillan, 1989), p. 179; emphasis is mine.
2. John Stuart Mill, *"On Liberty" and Other Writings,* ed. Stefan Collini (Cambridge: Cambridge University Press, 1989).
3. I have written at considerable length on Mill on the notion of truth and its relation to liberal politics in my essay in this volume entitled "Liberalism and the Academy." What is briefly discussed above gets a fuller and more patient discussion and elaboration there. It has necessarily had to be brief here because the focus is on Gandhi and not liberalism or Mill. But even the brief remarks I had made in this essay (as it was first published) should have conveyed a few things plainly to those whose grasp of English (and philosophical) vocabulary is not imperfect. In criticizing a certain widespread reading of Gandhi, *I made no claims whatever about truth being absolute.* I had only said that in the way Gandhi approached the concept of truth, the pursuit of truth was not the intellectual pursuit of something that is based (in some sort of cognitive forensics) on evidence but rather it was to be seen as an essentially experiential notion in which moral experience and conscience in particular were central. This meant that for him, truth was seen as something that one came to from *one's* point of view, the point of view of one's moral inquiry. And, as such, we should hold the truth with all the confidence that the convictions of our conscience delivered. Does this make truth *absolute?* How on earth could it, since it was *one's* truth, flowing from one's own conscience—*not*, as I said, expounding Gandhi, *to be universalized.* Presumably "absolute" truth is precisely not made modest in these ways that I had elaborated in this essay on Gandhi's behalf. This point is so elementary and obvious as an interpretation of the English words with which I presented my argument that it should have gone without saying. But it has not. (See the opening paragraph and the first footnote in Tanika Sarkar's essay "Gandhi and Social Relations," in Judith M. Brown and Anthony Parel (eds.), *The Cambridge Companion to Gandhi* (Cambridge: Cambridge University Press, 2011). So I am saying it. First of all, the idea that I am confident of some of my beliefs and convictions does not mean that I can never entertain beliefs as hypotheses and 'experiment with truth', to use one of Gandhi's frequent and eponymous expressions. Moreover, the idea of being *confident* in one's convictions of the truth (as one inquires into it from the point of view of one's experience and conscience) is perfectly compatible with the idea of *revision* of one's convictions and, therefore, perfectly compatible with the idea of "experiments" with truth, to use one of Gandhi's frequent and eponymous expressions. This is because it is foolish to think that the common-sense idea that we often revise our beliefs requires us to nonsensically think, "I know that p but for all I know p may be false". It is nonsense to think that because you cannot know something which is false. It is this nonsensical thing that I was protesting as a specious form of diffidence about truth built into Mill's argument, and one can only avoid saying it if one either abandons Mill's idea that we must always be diffident about anything we claim to know or give up on the idea that we ever know anything and become total skeptics, a tiresomely inaccurate philosophy to attribute to Gandhi's moral and intellectual outlook. Sarkar

congratulates herself on presenting a Gandhi who was given to experiments with truth and contrives to suggest that I could not possibly see Gandhi as being so.But that is, just as I say, a contrivance which quite fails to keep faith with what I say because it quite fails to comprehend it.

4. Gandhi, however, was not against criticism of institutions and policies and even of whole civilizational tendencies and himself made such criticism frequently as, say, in *Hind Swaraj* where he is harshly critical of the modern West. But he tried throughout his life to avoid criticism of individuals. And the fact is that even if he was often critical of individuals, that does not overturn his intellectual opposition to such criticism. Failing to live up to what one thinks one should and shouldn't do is not to be inconsistent in one's *thinking*.

5. Robert Louis Stevenson, "Henry David Thoreau: His Character and Opinions," *Cornhill Magazine*, June 1880.

6. Working with this very contrast on responses to notions of brotherhood, I spell out this form of humanism in more detail in the second half of my essay "Secularism: Its Content and Context" in this volume.

7. *Young India*, November 20, 1927.

8. February 11, 1932; see *Collected Works of Mahatma Gandhi*, Electronic Book, vol. 55, New Delhi: Government of India Publications 1999.

9. See his "Is Truth a Goal of Enquiry?," *Philosophical Quarterly* 45(180) (July 1995): 281–300. For more detail on this subject see my essay and his reply to it in Robert Brandom (ed.), *Rorty and His Critics* (Oxford: Blackwell, 2000).

10. See Harry Frankfurt, *On Bullshit* (Princeton, N.J.: Princeton University Press, 2005).

11. This was a hoax perpetrated by Alan Sokal, who wrote a paper making the most deliberately incoherent and ridiculous arguments for the cultural relativity of certain mathematical notions, and submitted it to a well-known journal of literary and cultural studies. The paper was published, and then Sokal publicly announced that the paper was a hoax intended to expose the charlatanism of post-modern tendencies in literary and cultural studies.

12. I somewhat regret putting the point this way because when I first put it this way and published this essay some fifteen years ago, I found others who had cited it with appreciation were also developing what I have said here by suggesting in a most misleading way that Gandhi was an anti-political thinker. He was nothing of the sort. Gandhi had criticized a very specific form of politics, one that emerged in a European context and with aspirations of a specific sort that I have just mentioned. In my essay "Gandhi (and Marx)" in this volume I try to present his critique of this form of politics with this aspiration when I discuss his views on the transformation of the concept of human beings into the concept of citizens. Gandhi was an intensely political thinker with a deep conviction in a form of politics that he theorized with much sophistication and implemented with much, though varying, success. I try to convey some of what its aspirations are and should be in the closing sections of two essays in this volume, "The Political Possibilities of the Long Romantic Period" and "Occidentalism, The Very Idea: An Essay on the Enlightenment, Enchantment, and the Mentality of Democracy."

5. Gandhi (and Marx)

I have benefited greatly from conversations with Carol Rovane, Steve White, and Calvin Normore on one or other of the themes of this essay. James Tully wrote a wonderfully instructive set of comments on the essay when I gave it at a Nomis Conference at the London School of Economics. Noam Chomsky sent detailed comments on a first draft of the essay which helped me to improve it, as did Sheldon Pollock. I am very grateful to all of them.

1. On a detailed response to the general contemporary dismissal of certain sorts of radical dissenting points of view as outdated and nostalgic, see the closing pages of the essay "The Political Possibilities of the Long Romantic Period" in this volume.

2. See Perry Anderson, "Gandhi Centre Stage," *London Review of Books* 34(13) (July 5, 2012): 3–11.

3. Even within the weight and preponderance of his critique of "modern Western civilization," as he sometimes called it, Gandhi, in many of his writings, often felt and exercised the obligation of no small counterweight, first in expressing admiration for much in the West, especially its dissenting traditions, from which he had learned much, and second in expressing concern about what he thought was defective in Indian society

4. It is interesting that these two sources of the tension that is generated between the ideals of liberty and equality—the attaching of the notion of liberty to property and also, via the notion of dessert, to incentivized talent—come together in the notion of *intellectual* property.

5. When I first introduced the term "detachment" above, I deliberately said "detachment of the wrong kind." This is because there is an ambiguity in the idea of detachment that should be made plain. Gandhi himself used the word "detachment" in a quite different way as well, one he commended. This was detachment from the wrong sorts of goods and activities in the world. But that use of the term was quite different from the use of it to describe a pervasive and dominant attitude by which one related to nature, and the world in general, a highly intellectualized, scientific gaze that led eventually to treating it, including people, as a means. This latter detachment was contrasted with the best kind of practical—in the sense of moral rather than opportunistic—*engagement* with the world; indeed it canceled out such an engagement, an engagement which he thought should be our primary way of relating to the world. So a way to expound the ambiguity is to say that he thought of the *former* kind of detachment, which he commended, as something to adopt *within* an *engagement rather than a detachment* of the latter kind.

6. It is this saturation with cognitive mediation of the idea of living in the world that the term "logocentrism" in post-structuralist philosophy is perhaps partly meant to convey. But what is interesting is that in this tradition of European philosophy, the fault-line is placed well before Descartes. Thus for instance Nietzsche who was perhaps the first to have raised the issue in his early work *The Birth of Tragedy* laid blame for it on the door of "Apollonian" ideals of representation that first surfaced in Plato's Socrates and in Greek drama after the passing of Attic tragedy. Heidegger, who was much influenced on this score by Nietzsche, also placed it in ideas going back to Plato, as did Derrida somewhat later. To some extent, Wittgenstein's attack on Platonism in how we

understand the nature of concepts and meaning in general and mathematical concepts in particular is a cousin of these early genealogical identifications. But I think, given Gandhi's diagnostic purposes, having to do with the theme of alienation as owing to a specific emergence of an outlook of detachment, a later identification of the fault-line in the seventeenth century is far more appropriate. It is in this period that the outlook emerging around modern developments in science gave this detachment a far more pointed focus, especially as it was consolidated by scientific organizations such as the Royal Society in alliances it formed with commercial and orthodox religious interests.

7. When in making this point about the sacralized conception of nature I appeal to the dissent of the Early Modern period, I have in mind two quite different groups of dissenters, one earlier the other somewhat later. The earlier dissenters were primarily political dissenters, the radical sects, the most prominent of which were the Levellers and Diggers but joined by a range of other groups all of which are brilliantly surveyed and studied by Christopher Hill in his rightly applauded *The World Turned Upside Down* (London: Penguin 1975) and under his influence by a range of other British historians. Thus, to give just one example among scores in the writing of this earlier period, Jacob Bauthumley: God was "in all Creatures, Man and Beast, Fish and Fowle, and every green thing, from the highest Cedar to the Ivey on the Wall"; quoted in Norman Cohn, *The Pursuit of the Millennium* (Oxford: Oxford University Press, 1970). But these ideas of nature were also urgent commitments of a later, quite different group of *scientific* dissenters that I mention briefly later in this essay and discuss further in my essay "Occidentalism, The Very Idea" in this volume. Theirs was a dissent against a certain ideology of a desacralized nature invoking Newton's views that was perpetrated by some of the more mandarin figures in the newly founded Royal Society such as Samuel Clarke and Richard Bentley, who relied also on the authority and prominence of Boyle, apart from Newton. Major proponents of such dissent were John Toland and Anthony Collins, and their philosophical and political motives are well traversed by Margaret Jacob in the work mentioned further below in this note. It might be thought (Michael Warner in commentary on some of my essays put this objection to me) that it is wrong to think of their dissent as 'scientific' dissent since figures like Toland and Collins, unlike Newton and Boyle (some of whose ideas they were dissenting from) were not 'scientists'. This objection's distinction is anachronistic. Science and metaphysics were not sharply distinguished in the Early Modern period and both fell under the label of 'natural philosophy'. It was quite proper to think of Newton, Boyle, Toland and Collins as all being the *same* sort of inquirers, natural philosophers. What is true and something I have myself repeatedly insisted on is that the dissenters did *not* object at all to Newton's *laws* but only to the metaphysics that he chose to ground the laws in, a grounding the dissenters thought uncompulsory, given the content of the laws. If one makes our current distinction between the laws of science and the metaphysics that conceptually grounds them, restricting the term 'science' only to the former and discarding the equation of science with natural philosophy (a broader form of inquiry that includes metaphysics), then it would indeed be wrong to call the dissent 'scientific'. But that would be to impose a current distinction on an earlier period when it did not exist. For that reason I feel no impropriety about calling the dissenters 'scientific' dissenters. There should be nothing

misleading about that rhetoric if we are clear, as I have always been, that the dissent was not against Newton's laws but against the desacralized metaphysics of nature that the laws were said (by the orthodoxy of the Royal Society ideologues) to promote. Moreover, the very fact that the dissenters knew and understood the laws perfectly well and insisted that they were compatible with a metaphysics of a sacralized nature in which motion was the result of an inner source of dynamism in nature that was divine (rather than an external administering by a providential and distant God as in the offical Newtonian metaphysics promoted by the Royal Society) is proof of the fact that they were fully on top of the 'science' involved. That is perhaps further reason to think of them, even by our current notions, as men of science, though by our current notions we would not count their dissent as dissent against the science but against the metaphysics. One further point worth noting is that their pantheistic and hermeticist ideas were central to the doctrine of a range of other groups, not just in England but also from an even earlier time (ever since the doctrines of Bruno and Ficino), all over Europe. It is also worth observing that in Europe, the later figure of Spinoza was more influential in politics than some of these earlier neo-Platonists, and he was sometimes an inspiration for the *scientific* dissenters in England that I have mentioned. Spinoza too is well known for having equated God with nature, but I don't think that this is properly described as a "pantheism" and it is almost certainly wrong to describe it as "sacralizing" nature. His was too abstract an equation for that. Still, it is interesting to see Jonathan Israel making much of Spinoza's influence on radical groups in Europe in his work *Radical Enlightenment: Philosophy and the Making of Modernity in Europe 1650–1750* (Oxford: Oxford University Press, 2002). This impressively large volume sets out to shift the emphasis from the orthodox liberal influence of someone like Locke to what he calls "spinozism" and its intellectual sway on a more radical side of the Enlightenment. What is "radical" for Israel, however, is measurably less critical of the orthodox Enlightenment than the radical groups that I am focused on in England. These differences are worth a close study. The channel of radicalism I am appealing to in order to understand Gandhi's radical ideas goes from sects such as the Diggers through the scientific dissenters I have mentioned—dissenters who are well presented in another very rich discussion of the radical Enlightenment by Margaret Jacob, *Radical Enlightenment: Pantheists, Freemasons, Republicans* (London: George Allen and Unwin, 1981)—to figures like Blake and even later to Morris and the non-conformist religious Left ideals of Tawney. Israel's discussion, by contrast, seems to be seeking channels that lead to quite different figures such as, say, Condorcet, who have almost no affinities with Gandhian thought. Gandhi apart, even if one were focused just on Europe, there is interesting comparative work to be done here in the intellectual history of the Enlightenment and its legacy for the possibility of a genuinely radical politics. I suspect Israel's historical conception would fall far short of the tradition of radicalism I am seeking.

8. The term "spontaneous" needs explaining here since one might be puzzled by how such a term can be used to describe *deterministic* tendencies, whenever since Kant the term has been used to describe our *freedom*. But a moment's careful reflection makes clear that it is not really inconsistent with Kant's usage. Lange and Patnaik deploy the term to convey that you cannot by any human planning put constraints (say, Keynesian

constraints) that *determine* capital to *stay* on a path that deviates from its "logic." For that reason capital is free ("spontaneous"); it is free from any such permanent constraint on it, a usage that squares perfectly well with Kant's. What needs to be made explicit is that though capital is indeed spontaneous in Kant's sense, human beings, if they stay within the framework of capitalist society, are *not*; they are not free to put abidingly efficacious constraints on capital. So if this is right, capital *determines* human aspirations and limits them, and it is *free* from human constraint. That is why one can, depending on which of these one stresses, use both the terms "spontaneous" and "deterministic" to characterize it. No puzzle, therefore, remains. I should add a qualification to this that makes Patnaik's thought here particularly complex and interesting. He does not say that capital is so completely deterministic of human effort that it can never be *transcended* by human effort. *It just can't be immanently or internally constrained by human effort.* This is because it has its own *irresistible* immanent tendencies. These tendencies are in accord with the logic of *capital*, of a particular formation in a particular period of history, and not a general logic of history. So human effort, though it cannot for this reason resist capital immanently, can nevertheless transcend capital (as Marx hoped that a revolutionary proletariat class would mobilize to do in European nations) and wise human decision and effort can *preempt* or bypass capital (as Gandhi hoped India would). Nothing in the spontaneous (deterministic) tendencies immanent in capital rules either out. For Lange, see Oskar Lange, *Political Economy*, vol. 1 (Warsaw: Pergamon Press, 1963). For Patnaik, see Prabhat Patnaik, "Socialism or Reformism," *Monthly Review*, July 16, 2010.

9. When I use the term "exile" of God ("Deus Absconditus" was the expression used to convey this), I am not innocuously registering the belief in a transcendental rather than an immanent God. Belief in God's transcendence has, of course, a very long history, as long, indeed, as the history of belief in God. But the movement to counter enthusiasm by *exiling* God to a transcendence of this specific providential distance was a very specific movement that came at a very specific later historical moment. It emerged in the alliances that were being formed in this period that I am discussing, alliances between commercial interests, Anglican (or in Europe, other orthodox religious) interests, and the institutional scientific interests that took Newton's views of motion and matter to be central. No belief in transcendence of any earlier period in history had the same significance that these alliances bestowed on the God "exiled" to transcendence in the second half of the seventeenth century.

10. This example is utterly familiar, as I said, as no doubt are criticisms of it, but one should not, just because of this familiarity, underestimate how much and how pervasively it is still to be found in highly hidden assumptions, assumptions which do not get stated explicitly in a wide variety of economic analyses right down to the present day. Thus, precisely because it (and criticisms of it) are so familiar, its proponents tend to submerge it in implicit places that are below the surface of explicit theorizing, giving the impression that it is more outdated than it in fact is.

11. See Prabhat Patnaik, "Globalization and Social Progress," *Social Scientist* 39(1–2) (January–February 2011): 47–59, for an extended criticism of the sort that I am presenting very briefly here. For Sen's elaboration of the analogy, see his "Prohibiting

the Use of Agricultural Land for Industry Is Ultimately Self-Defeating," *The Telegraph* (Kolkata), July 23, 2010.

12. In the pages that immediately follow on nationalism, secularism, and the function of notions of both civility and of rights, I am going to redeem my pledge (made cryptically in the last paragraph or two of the essay "Gandhi, the Philosopher" in this volume) to say something about the specific kind of politics that Gandhi was opposed to as having relevance for the India about which he was writing in 1909. Part of this (the material on nationalism and secularism) recapitulates some of the things I said on Gandhi in the essay "Secularism: Its Content and Context" in this volume. I apologize for this overlap, but I allow myself to do it because it helps to give the full picture of the four sets of transformations that I am trying to genealogically present on Gandhi's behalf.

13. See Ashis Nandy's analysis of Savarkar's Hindutva ideology in "Allure of the Demonic," *Outlook,* August 22, 2005.

14. I try to see through the implications of this Gandhian diagnosis for the entire doctrine of secularism as it was formulated in India and quite generally in more theoretical terms in "Secularism: Its Content and Context" in this volume.

15. It is well known that Newton had another side to his intellectual profile. I have stressed the official Newton presented to the world by the Royal Society, who propagated a "Newtonianism" that was partly mobilized to counter the dissenters dismissed for their "enthusiasm" by the scientific mandarins of the time, which included figures no less than Boyle, and others like Bentley and Clarke. This Newton had a great influence and left an abiding legacy of this form of counter to such dissenting tendencies that was well expressed by Adam Smith in a later time, when he declared that "science is a great antidote to the power of enthusiasm and superstition." What he failed to see, as I will argue later in this essay, is that the outlook emerging around modern science—though not the science, itself—generated its own superstition when it disallowed any value properties in nature and, ironically, it is *this* superstition that the *"enthusiasm"* of the early modern period presciently noted and honorably tried to preempt. But though this is the influential Newton, it is also by now very well understood, however, that Newton in his private study with his alchemical preoccupations nursed ideas bordering on neo-Platonism, strands of which—and this is its own kind of irony—lay behind the ideas of the dissenters and their "enthusiasm."

16. In *A Brief View and Survey of the Dangerous and Pernicious Errors to Church and State in Mr Hobbes's Book, entitled Leviathan* (2nd impression, Oxford, 1676), p. 111. The link between civility and the propertied classes is apparent in the fact that by "propriety," Clarendon meant "property." And the semantics by which the behavior of the propertied classes was distinguished from the rest initially owed to a distinction they bore to *nomads* (which is what the "this" in "this barbarity" refers to), who lacked any ties to property except for cattle. I am grateful to Keith Thomas for bringing this passage and its significance to my attention.

17. For more on just this last point, see the lengthy note 11 in my essay "Secularism: Its Content and Context" in this volume.

18. People always, of course, took from nature. But to see it as natural resources is a quite different thing. It is to form wholly new attitudes regarding one's relations to it backed

by the law and by a variety of institutions of political economy and of the state. It is to see extraction as a *systematic project* one carries out with impunity, exercising one's *right* to nature's bounty.

19. *Grundrisse* (New York: Vintage, 1973), pp. 409–410.

20. John McDowell, "Virtue and Reason," *The Monist* 62(3) (July 1979): 331–350.

21. It is also to say something quite distinct from the sort of angle on natural science made familiar recently by Bruno Latour and, before him, by Kuhn, viz., that we speak implicitly in all sorts of political and sociological ways in our science of nature, while pretending that nature lays itself bare to us directly in that science. What is being said here rather is that there is something *distinct* about the perspective of practical agency on nature, distinct, that is, from the perspective of detachment in natural science, even if the latter is politically shaped as scientific investigation even within this detached perspective might well be. The form of practical agency I am concerned with is dependent on a deeper philosophical *contrast* with detachment, even if the latter, the detached perspective, is, as it must be, exercised within some form of agency in which values and politics play their inevitable part. Moreover, yet another well-known position such as, for instance, Isaac Levi's among others, which insists that science is value-laden, though hardly deniable, is making a quite different claim than is being made here. However much scientists evaluate, in doing so, they don't make any such claim as that there are value properties *in nature itself* which prompt our practical agency rather than our detached theoretical gaze, however much this latter is shaped by value decisions and politics.

22. There is a very natural but elementary fallacy one can fall into here. It is obvious, as I have been expounding the idea of value properties being in nature, that they are properties that one can only perceive if one has our (human) form of agency. Dogs, or frogs, cannot perceive them. It is this that Marx meant when he said that nature was "for man," what he called the "humanism" of nature. This leads people to think that therefore values must really not be in nature but in our minds and merely projected onto the world by us. But that is a non sequitur. It simply does not follow from the fact that a certain kind of sensibility is needed to perceive something that that perceived thing is not a property in the world but a mere projection by the perceiver onto the world. It needs our sort of sensibility to perceive color in the world, as has been pointed out by a long tradition of philosophical writing on secondary qualities from Galileo, Locke, and Newton to McDowell, Blackburn, Crispin Wright, and others in our own time. A variety of creatures don't perceive colors either. Should we, then, be tempted to say that therefore the carpet below my feet is not really blue and I am projecting blue onto it? No doubt some of the philosophers I have just mentioned have been willing to say it, though of course not McDowell himself. But it is a completely mistaken thing to say. In fact, as Wittgenstein might have put it, it is such an absurd thing to say that only a subject as rarefied and perverse as philosophy would be tempted to say it. It doesn't even help here to say something that I believe to be true, viz., that color is something that can be *reduced* to or is in some other *systematic way dependent on* (supervenient on, as philosophers like to say) scientifically specifiable natural *micro*-properties. However, I believe it does not make sense to say (or

for that matter to deny) that value is similarly dependent on the properties that the fundamental sciences study, say, fundamental physics (and this is a point with which I deeply disagree with John McDowell, who thinks there is no difference between color and values on this point). Suppose I am right on this point and McDowell wrong. My point for now is that that would certainly not show that colors are really in the world and value properties are not, unless one believed that there is nothing in the natural world that natural sciences cannot study. But to believe that is to beg the question against my claim since that is precisely the view that I am claiming is dogmatic and a modern superstition. (I should emphasize what I said above passingly: that I don't actually *deny* such a dependency—"supervenience" as philosophers call it—of value on non-normative properties. I would not deny it if I could make sense of the idea, since if you grant sense to the idea, it would be a very extreme thing to deny it. My reason for not granting sense to the idea—or to put it differently, my reason for saying that I neither assert nor deny such a dependency—has to do with the fact that value properties are only perceptible from within a first person point of view of practical agency rather than the point of view of detachment from within which the properties of natural science are studied. For more on all these issues, see Chapter 5 of my book *Self-Knowledge and Resentment* (Cambridge, Mass.: Harvard University Press, 2006) and the exchange with Thomas Baldwin and Calvin Normore in a symposium on that book in *Philosophy and Phenomenological Research* 81(3).

Another elementary fallacy is to think that because different people may perceive in the same place in the world different value properties making different normative demands on them, these properties must not really be in the world. That is a quite invalid inference from a perfectly correct and innocuous premise. After all, such differential perception occurs not just with value properties but also with the properties that natural science studies. This is because of the theory-ladenness of observation in science. Thus to take just one example from an abundant literature going from Norwood Russell Hanson to Kuhn and Feyerabend and Dudley Shapere, someone having internalized one scientific theory may perceive some phenomena (particles, as it might be) at the same place that another, having internalized another theory, perceives something quite different (waves, as it might be). Does this mean that science too does not study any properties that are really present in nature? I have written at length about some of these issues regarding values and nature in Chapter 5 of my book *Self-Knowledge and Resentment* (Cambridge, Mass.: Harvard University Press, 2006) and various papers, perhaps most comprehensively in "The Wider Significance of Naturalism." (in *Naturalism and Normativity* edited by David Macarthur and Mario De Caro (New York: Columbia University Press, 2009).

23. For a similar though not identical distinction that needs sorting out, see my disambiguation of the term "detachment" in Gandhi in note 5 above.

24. For a more patient presentation of this argument (via a distinction in Spinoza) and its implications see "The Political Possibilities of the Long Romantic Period" in this volume. What is important to stress here is that this argument shows that in our practical agency, in our everyday agentive responses to the world, we *do* take it for granted that there are value properties in the world. What I've been stressing is that in our *public*

and collective frames of thinking we *deny* this fundamental fact of a world suffused with value, and thereby pursue policies and outlooks that induce the sort of alienation I am analyzing in this essay. The implications of this divergence between the quotidian and the public/collective frames of thinking are presented in much greater detail in the essay mentioned earlier in this note.

25. If, as I've argued, we cannot even account for our practical agency (as opposed to the sort of agency that goes into detached understanding of the world and ourselves) without seeing the world, including nature, as containing value properties, it is hardly surprising that we would be alienated if we conceived of the world along lines that evacuated it of value properties. If my argument is persuasive, it would leave us with a manifestly alienated conception of subjectivity, a mere passive *receptacle* of desires to be satisfied, without those desires being agentive responses to the world's normative callings. In the concluding pages of "The Political Possibilities of the Long Romantic Period" in this volume, I set up a framework to show how this alienation cannot depend on the *actual* loss of all individual practical agency entirely since we cannot have and obviously have not lost our practical agency entirely as a result of these detached outlooks that emerged in the period in which Gandhi placed them genealogically. Rather what is needed is to show how a *public* frame of thinking gets generated in which such detachment dominates and, in turn, generates a kind of alienation, and that this sits in (not always conscious) tension with a quite different frame, a frame within which we have *quotidian* individual responses to the normative demands of the world in the practical agency we possess and exercise. It is partly in the overcoming of this tension where the political possibilities of Romanticism lie.

26. For deep and probing remarks on Marx's understanding of the objectification of subjects in capitalist society and of the aspiration of socialism to restore subjectivity, see Prabhat Patnaik, *Re-Envisioning Socialism* (New Delhi: Tulika Press, 2010).

27. Steve White from whom I have learned much on these themes over many conversations had suggested that 'positive liberty', 'fraternity', and 'group agency', may be the right notions. I think instead, for a number of reasons, that Gandhi's and Marx's stress on the unalienated life is the right thing to stress.

28. Katherine Boo, *Behind the Beautiful Forevers* (New York: Random House, 2012), p. 20.

29. Macalaster Bell, *Hard Feelings: The Moral Psychology of Contempt* (Oxford: Oxford University Press, 2013).

30. Gandhi often, like Heidegger and Wittgenstein, deploys the term "world" instead of the term "nature" as the more comprehensive term with which to describe that with which we have these *integrated* relations, and I have sometimes used the phrase "the world, including nature" to indicate this integrity. By "world" is meant something quite as capacious and inclusive as "nature and its inhabitants and the history and tradition of the relation between nature and its inhabitants as well as the social relations between its inhabitants." As I said at the outset, though I have broken down Gandhi's initial genealogical question that mentions only the world into four questions that mention more particularly (and tractably) nature and various social relations, Gandhi himself

thought that those four questions fed into a single question that had its more omnibus and integrated formulation as I presented it.

31. *Collected Works,* vol. 3: *Economic and Philosophical Manuscripts* (Moscow: Progress Publications), p. 375.First Published 1932. Reprinted 1959.

6. The Political Possibilities of the Long Romantic Period

This essay was originally published in *Studies in Romanticism* 49(4) (Winter 2010).

1. This is such a constantly recurring theme in Bloom's work that there is no point in singling out the reference of any particular book as a reference. *Omens of the Millennium* (New York: Riverhead Books, 1997) is only the most explicit.

2. See, among other works, *The Roots of Romanticism* (Princeton, N.J.: Princeton University Press, 2001), and *Political Ideas in the Romantic Age* (Princeton, N.J.: Princeton University Press, 2006).

3. New York: W. W. Norton, 1973.

4. See Max Adorno and Theodor W. Horkheimer, *Dialectic of Enlightenment* (New York: Continuum, 1976).

5. See Edward Said, *Beginnings* (New York: Columbia University Press, New Edition, 2006).

6. See Hume's discussion of value and practical reason in *A Treatise of Human Nature,* bk. III, pt. 2 (Oxford: Oxford University Press, 2000).

7. See "The Analytic of the Sublime," *Critique of Judgment* (Indianapolis, Ind.: Hackett, 1987).

8. See in particular McDowell's pioneering essay "Virtue and Reason," *The Monist* 62(3) (July 1979): 331–350.

9. See especially "The Book of Urizen," but also "Jerusalem: The Emanation of the Giant Albion," *The Complete Poetry and Prose of William Blake,* ed. D. Erdman (New York: Anchor, 1997).

10. For such an understanding of Gandhi, see my "Occidentalism, the Very Idea: An Essay on the Enlightenment, Enchantment, and the Mentality of Democracy" and "Gandhi (and Marx)" in this volume.

11. New York: Penguin, 1984.

12. For a fine essay on the conceptual links between changing conceptions of nature and political economy in this period in England, see Simon Schaffer's "The Earth's Fertility as a Social Fact in Early Modern England," in M. Teich, R. Porter, and B. Gustafsson (eds.), *Nature and Society in Historical Context* (Princeton, N.J.: Princeton University Press, 1997).

13. I am focusing on England particularly because the alliances that I mention between scientific bodies and commercial interests and established Protestantism were first most explicitly formulated in England as a result of the Royal Society's openly commercial and religious links, both in the body of its membership, as well as in its self-understanding, as exemplified, for instance, in Boyle's own instructions with which he set up the lectures bearing his name. The Royal Society, as I said earlier, made Newton's

broad claims about the inertness and brute materiality of nature and the providential distance of God the central basis for forging the political and economic aspects of
these alliances. Perhaps the first to have pointed out the role of this "Newtonianism"
in the rise of capitalism is the Soviet scientist and historian of science Boris Hessen in
his address "The Social and Economic Roots of Newton's Principia" to the Second
International Congress of the History of Science in 1931 in London. The claims in that
address are remarkable for their simplicity and their attribution of intentions to Newton himself. It is far more plausible to see it as what Margaret Jacob calls the "culture
of Newtonianism," a mandarin phenomenon in which the Royal Society was the most
active agent. See M. Jacob, *Newton and the Culture of Newtonianism* (Atlantic High-
lands, N.J.: Humanity Books, 1994). Still, there is no doubt that the Hessen thesis was
a great mobilizer in this direction in the cultural History of Science.

14. See, among other writings, *Pantheisticon* (first English translation, 1751) (Whitefish,
Mont.: Kessinger Publishing, 2009).

15. See especially the Collins-Clarke correspondence of 1706–1708 which is published in
full in Samuel Clarke's *Works* (New York: Garland Press, , first published 1738, republished 1928 and 1994).

16. Keith Thomas, *Religion and the Decline of Magic* (London: Weidenfeld and Nichol-
son, 1971).

17. See, for instance, P. M. Rattansi, "Newton and the Pipes of Pan," *Notes and Records of
the Royal Society of London* 21(2) (December 1966): 108–143; Christopher Hill, "Science and Magic," a lecture given in 1976 at the J. D. Bernal Peace Library and published
in the third volume of his *Collected Essays;Writing and Revolution in 17th Century
Englad* (Amherst: University of Massachussets Press, 1985); and Charles Webster's
From Paracelsus to Newton: Magic and the Making of Modern Science (Cambridge:
Cambridge University Press, 1982).

18. P. M. Rattansi, "Newton's Alchemical Studies," in Allen G. Debus (ed.), *Science, Medicine, and Society in the Renaissance* (London: Heinemann, 1972), as well as his paper
mentioned in the previous note.

19. See Gerrard Winstanley, *The Works of Gerrard Winstanley*, ed. George H. Sabine
(New York: Russell and Russell, 1965). See especially his "Fire in the Bush" and "Mys-
terie of God."

20. *The Death of Nature* (San Francisco: Harper, 1991).

21. Oxford: Oxford University Press, 1982.

22. For the reference in Marx of these words and a detailed discussion of what is meant by
them, see my essay "Gandhi (and Marx)" in this volume.

23. In "Occidentalism, the Very Idea" in this volume I put the notion of frames to use in
a quite different context, one of studying certain forms of seeming irrationality, and
in that context, I trace the origin of the notion to Freud's methodology for studying
irrationality.

24. What sort of politics in our time makes it possible to remove the boundary between
these frames to allow us a single frame for our subjectivity is a question I address in the
closing pages of the essay "Occidentalism, the Very Idea: An Essay on the Enlightenment, Enchantment, and the Mentality of Democracy" in this volume.

7. What Is a Muslim?

I should stress at the very outset that this essay, though in an important sense self-standing, is one of three essays on the subject of Islamic identity. The others, entitled "Intrinsic and Extrinsic Explanations of Islam" (*Transition,* forthcoming, eds. Anthony Appiah and Henry Louis Gates, Jr.) and "Islamic Identity and Quotidian Institutions," address aspects of the subject that the present essay ignores. (The substance of these two unpublished essays have now been incorporated in my book *What Is a Muslim?,* forthcoming from Princeton University Press.) The first of these essays addresses issues in political economy and the political sociology of the state, as they impinge on the question of religious identity. The second explores the role of mosques, prayer, pilgrimage, fasting, and other such customs and institutions in the sustaining of identity. The present essay's concern is more with underlying philosophical issues. The reader is urged, therefore, not to assume that the points made here aim at anything approximating a comprehensive treatment of the subject. All the same, the sense in which the essay *is* self-standing is that there is nothing in the other two papers which seriously revise or qualify the claims made in this one. My thanks to G. A. Cohen, Ronald Dworkin, Charles Larmore, Isaac Levi, Thomas Nagel, Carol Rovane, Stephen White, Bernard Williams, the members of the New York University Legal Theory Seminar, and the Fellows of the Whitney Humanities Center, Yale University, for comments and criticisms which have helped to improve this essay. This piece was originally published by the University of Chicago Press in *Critical Inquiry* 18(4) (*Identities*) (Summer 1992): 821–842.

1. No suggestion here that my commitment to being a Muslim has not been more than five minutes long. There are several other contexts, and many more sustained contexts, in which someone with that background and those anti-theological views could identify himself or herself as a Muslim. There is no particular list of *types* of such contexts for identification. If there were, that would undermine the very idea of locality since it would allow us to formulate the very sort of generalizations that stricter criteria of identity demand. Someone with no theological commitments might feel a sense of identity with Islam in contexts as diverse as when he feels shame at the actions of Muslims—as, say, the Muslim response to the publication of Rushdie's *The Satanic Verses;* when he feels concern about the future of Muslims in some hostile area—as, say, in parts of India or England; or quite simply by an intellectual inheritance of public-mindedness from the fact that his family has been involved in Muslim politics for a very long time. There is no interesting common thread running through these different contexts; and I take it to be obvious that birth into a Muslim family is not sufficient nor (given conversion) even necessary to Muslim identity, though, of course, one would expect the relevance of the contexts I have just mentioned to usually presuppose the fact of birth.

2. W. V. Quine, *Word and Object* (Cambridge, Mass.: MIT Press, 1960). See also "Natural Kinds," in *Ontological Relativity and Other Essays* (New York: Columbia University Press, 1969).

3. In saying this I am taking a stand against the more apocalyptic, theory-destroying view of the emphasis on context that is to be found in Richard Rorty's numerous recent writings on the effects of pragmatism. This disagreement may turn on the fact that

pragmatism for him, but not for me, is mixed in with Kuhnian incommensurability and deconstruction.

4. In the first appearance of this essay well over twenty years ago, I had used the rhetoric of "reform" without careful distinctions between practice and doctrine, de facto and de jure, that I am now making clear. In making this change, Talal Asad's writings have had much influence on me, though in the essay "After the Fatwah" in this volume, I have written critically (yet not without some sympathy and partial agreement) of another strand in his writing—on Rushdie.

5. A word of explanation of this somewhat self-conscious use of the word "ordinary" is necessary here since I will use it with some frequency in the rest of the essay. In the original version of the essay, which was written in great haste and some agitation in the days immediately after February 14, 1989 (in fact it was begun on the night of February 14th after an interview I gave on "the fatwah" to Robert Macneil on National Public Television's *Newshour*), I had used the word "moderate" throughout where I now have the word "ordinary." I greatly regret having used that term in the published essay where it was deployed so extensively because of the impression of condescension it conveys, condescension that is well captured in the ironic title of Mahmoud Mamdani's excellent book *Good Muslim, Bad Muslim,* which I discuss (though somewhat critically for other reasons) in my essay "Occidentalism, the Very Idea" in this volume. I don't believe my use of the term was *intended* condescendingly at all but intention is one thing (and it is even possible, of course, that I was self-deceived about what was intended) and effect is another, and certainly the effect of the rhetoric is undeniably one of condescension, a condescension which is especially regrettable because it feeds into the cold war attitudes against Islam that deeply set in after September 11, 2001. When I wrote the present essay in early 1989, I was not so sensitive to these cold war attitudes because they themselves were not so widespread and evident as they became a dozen years later. I doubt that I would write this essay with some of the same rhetoric as I did then, and though I have not done much to change the rhetoric now, I am alerting the reader in the notes (see the previous note too) to one or two of these changes I *have* made and expressing regret for the insensitivity of my previous choice of words. The word "ordinary," though better, is not ideal, but it will have to do to mark some sort of contrast with Muslims who have been described as "fundamentalist" and are perhaps better described as "absolutist" in their conviction of a relatively strict adherence to Quranic doctrine and to sharia law or to a zealous commitment to waging a struggle against the "infidel" and the pernicious influence of the "jahiliya" that is supposed to characterize the "modern West." These notions, as is well known, are not precise and are found on the lips and the pens of a very small fraction of Muslims anywhere in the world, so it is just as well that the contrasting term "ordinary" does not aspire to precision either and is capacious enough to denote the far larger class of Muslims in all parts of the world.

6. The threat is very real and can be seen not just in the spectacular developments in Iran during the 1980s but also elsewhere as well, such as, to cite just a few, "Islamisation" policies in Pakistan under Zia ul Haq, in the complexion of powerful guerilla forces and political parties in Afghanistan in the last few decades, in the accelerating Islamist

reaction in the Middle-East to the Iraqi defeat, as well as, more generally, in the policy commitments in personal law, especially regarding the status of women, in many Muslim populations, even despite the fact of being under *de facto* secular governments. Recoil from "Orientalist" misrepresentations of Islamic countries should not blind us to the reality and threatening promise of these developments.

7. Though it will not be relevant to my concerns in this essay, it should be mentioned that the absolutist minority does not form a unified movement. There has, for some time, been division between the anti-imperialist Islamist groups and some of the Islamist groups who draw resources from and give allegiance to Saudi Arabia. There is partial coincidence of this division with the Shia-Sunni division because the anti-imperialist groups have sometimes been inspired by the Iranian example, but it is only partial. Thus, for instance on the Sunni side, some sections of Islamist politics in contemporary Egypt, with their large business interests, are quite happy to make concessions to neo-liberal policies pushed on their country primarily by the United States and can hardly be counted as "anti-imperialist" in any genuine sense. On the other hand many "Wahabi"-influenced groups, though the ideology emerges from Saudi Arabia, are deeply opposed to the Saudi Arabian government and elite's complicity with the foreign policy interests of the United States and the economic interests of US corporations. Osama bin Laden was, of course, only the most notable and notorious figure in this opposition.

8. This internal conflict in the ordinary Muslim is an essential stage in the dialectic of this essay. The essay's interest is to study the extent to which negotiation and transformation of identity is possible, once one records that there is this conflict.

9. There has also been a partially overlapping intellectual tradition, much less current, which adds to this an a priori historical conviction which makes it an inevitable outcome of the progressive development of social, political, and economic formations that this liberal vision will take hold. This strand of argument has lost its thread in the last few decades but the more purely philosophical claims are still the subject of interesting and lively dispute among philosophers.

10. I will continue to use the expression "Ethical Theory" with capital letters to mark that it is traditional moral philosophy that is the target of this critique. The critique may be found in a number of Williams's writings, including his contribution to J. J. C. Smart and Bernard Williams, *Utilitarianism: For and Against* (Cambridge: Cambridge University Press, 1973). See also "Utilitarianism and Moral Self-Indulgence," in *Moral Luck* (Cambridge: Cambridge University Press, 1981). In more recent work, Williams addresses Aristotelian ethical theory in some detail as well, and his relation to it is much more complex than to Kant and to Utilitarianism. Since this essay is not intended primarily as a commentary on Williams, I will restrict my discussion to the points he makes in his earlier work, which I wish to exploit in the discussion of Muslims' fundamental commitment to their faith. I should also add that in a letter to me Williams quite rightly points out that in more recent work he is far less obviously the target of the criticisms I make of him in this essay. See particularly the Postscript to his *Ethics and the Limits of Philosophy* (London: Collins, 1985).

11. This distinction may be found in Williams himself and is by now common in philosophical discussions of moral value.

12. It is conceivable, though not perhaps routine, that people have fundamental commitments not to things like friendship and religion but to utilitarian and other sorts of principles of traditional moral philosophy that Williams is inveighing against.

13. See my "The Clash within Civilizations," *Daedalus* 132(3) (Summer 2003): 88–93, for more on this conflict.

14. G. A. Cohen, "Reconsidering Historical Materialism," in A. Callinicos (ed.), *Marxist Theory* (Oxford: Oxford University Press, 1989), pp. 154–155.

15. I should stress that the question here is not primarily at the level of individual sensibility and psyche. When in this passage Cohen talks of the "strength and durability" of religious and nationalist sentiment, he is referring to a communal phenomenon. I think that despite his claim that the spiritual search for identity in the individual subject explains the communal phenomenon, Cohen would nevertheless say that these are different phenomena, irreducible to one another. What I say below, by way of disagreement with Cohen, obviously does not amount to a denial of the fact that individuals often have spiritual yearnings. Rather it amounts to a denial that this fact satisfactorily explains the phenomenon of communal religious identity, as we find it in many Muslim countries today. That is, I deny that the phenomenon is, to use Cohen's words, merely a "social manifestation" of the "self's irreducible interest in the definition of itself." It has a quite distinct functional and historical explanation, about which more below.

16. Here I should add that, despite my opposition to Cohen's point, which is advertised by him as a point inspired by Hegel, the view I am promoting is perfectly in consonance with that aspect of Hegelian doctrine which precisely emphasizes historical conditioning of self-definitions. My complaint, then, is that Cohen's essay fails to think through the implications of the fully Hegelian doctrine. The idea of the "self's *irreducible* interest in the definition of itself" which Cohen is stressing in this essay is at odds (in the way I argue below) with a historically conditioned conception. What I below describe as the "rock-bottom" attitude to what I call the "surplus phenomenology of identity," an attitude which Cohen, for all he says in that paper, can claim as his own, is just the attitude which is made unnecessary by the historical conditioning. It is just the attitude that makes the phenomenology un-Hegelian.

17. Two qualifications. First, I am not suggesting that this defensive function exhausts the functional explanation of Muslims' fundamental commitment to Islam. But it is the *central* function to fasten on when the task is to diagnose the failure to think one's way out of the present conflict. More on this below. Second, though identities are often formed in this way under conditions of defeat and demoralization and though often prompted by feelings of helplessness, they are also sometimes formed under quite different conditions—of victory, not defeat, and prompted by triumphalist feeling and pride, rather than powerlessness. Thus, for instance, historians have described how Scots to some extent assumed British identity when Britain became an increasingly dominant imperial power, and sociologists have noticed a measurable increase in Jewish identification in America with Israel after Israeli's highly decisive victory in 1967, described by a manifestly impressed media in triumphalist terms. I think it is even perhaps arguable

that the mujahedeen victory in Afghanistan did much to inspire identitarian Islamist commitments among jihadi youth, an interesting combination of both motivations shaping identity—of powerlessness in their *general* conditions and empowered confidence from a *particular* success.

18. See *The Use of Poetry and the Use of Criticism* (London: Faber and Faber, 1933). Obviously, I am only invoking Eliot's general idea here, not his particular literary-critical judgments.

19. See my "Cry, the Beloved Sub-Continent," *New Republic,* June 10, 1991.

20. Writings in these disciplines, to their detriment, do not mix it up enough with historical and political studies, to develop theoretical (philosophical) treatments of this phenomenon of "surplus phenomenology."

21. *Foundations of the Metaphysics of Morals,* trans. Lewis White Beck (Indianapolis, IN: Bobbs-Merrill, 1983).

22. Incidentally, it should go without saying, but perhaps it will not, so I will say it: It is not a matter of the moral high ground for its own sake. The point is straightforwardly one of *self-interest.* If Machiavelli was given to advising displaced people rather than princes, he too would have said, "Don't give up the moral high ground unless you are absolutely certain that this man in this real world of US military domination will deliver you from displacement."

23. The *locus classicus* is, of course, Edward Said's *Orientalism* (New York: Columbia University Press, 1978).

24. For a brief discussion of why ordinary Muslims find it hard to summon the confidence to get over this defensiveness and make the defection from the third person to the first person point of view, see the points made around the distinction between clash and conquest in the relations between Islam and the West in "After the Fatwah: Twenty Years of Controversy" in this volume.

25. See, for instance, Mahmoud Muhammad Taha's *The Second Message of Islam* (Ithaca, N.Y.: Syracuse University Press, 1996) for an emphasis on this distinction. I had not read Taha's work when I first wrote and published the present essay and I was steered to it fairly soon after when I read the writings of Abdullahi Ahmed An Na'im, who is also the translator of the volume just cited.

26. *Islam and Modernity* (Chicago: University of Chicago Press, 1982), pp. 159–161; also the introductory remarks on pp. 2–3.

27. A first step would be to acknowledge the conflict itself, which for the most part lies hidden; such an acknowledgement might lead to the processes of reflection that are necessary. The specific forms of reflection that underlie the first person point of view constitute a large and important philosophical subject. See Chapters 7 and 9 of Thomas Nagel's *The View From Nowhere* (Oxford: Oxford University Press, 1986).

28. My emphasis on the requirements of the perspective of free agency and the philosophical malaise underlying the ordinary Muslim's failure to acquire it fully may seem as if I have, after all, introduced a purely philosophical argument in favor of reform and of the secular ideal. But that is not quite right. I am happy to grant that the adoption of this first person perspective is itself to be justified on grounds that are internal to other values and commitments of ordinary Muslims, thereby keeping faith with the

point of Williams's initial critique of the philosophical ambitions of traditional "Ethical Theory."

8. Notes toward the Definition of Identity

This essay was originally published by the MIT Press in *Daedalus* 135(4) (*On Identity*) (Fall 2006): 5–14.

1. See Carol Rovane, *The Bounds of Agency* (Princeton, N.J.: Princeton University Press, 1998).

2. For extensive discussion of second-order valuing see the essays by Harry Frankfurt in his *The Importance of What We Care About* (Cambridge: Cambridge University Press, 1988).

3. See W. V. O Quine, "Two Dogmas of Empiricism," in *From a Logical Point of View* (Cambridge, Mass.: Harvard University Press, 2003).

4. See, among several other writings, Michel Foucault, *Archaeology of Knowledge* (New York: Pantheon Books, 1972). See also Ian Hacking, *The Social Construction of What?* (Cambridge, Mass.: Harvard University Press, 1999).

5. Joseph Stalin, *Marxism and The National Question* (Moscow: Progress Publishers, 1953).

6. For Isaiah Berlin's by now much-discussed, somewhat cold warrior's anxiety on these issues, see his classic "Two Concepts of Liberty," in *Four Essays on Liberty* (Oxford: Oxford University Press, 1969). It is worth a detailed consideration as to whether and how the issues that Berlin raises affect the notion of identity, in the objective sense. I discuss it at the end of my essay "Occidentalism, the Very Idea" in this volume and as a general theme it is explored at much greater length in a book I am currently writing, tentatively entitled *Practical Reason in Morals and Politics*.

7. See Bernard Williams, "Internal and External Reasons," in *Moral Luck* (Cambridge: Cambridge University Press. 1981).

9. After the Fatwah

This essay was originally published in Daniel Herwitz and Ashutosh Varshney (eds.), *Midnight's Diaspora: Critical Encounters with Salman Rushdie* (Ann Arbor: University of Michigan Press, 2008).

1. Interview (summer 1983–winter 1984) in Hermione Lee, *Writers at Work: The Paris Review Interviews* (7th series) (New York: Viking/Penguin, 1986).

2. The essay "What Is a Muslim?" republished in this volume captures the dialectic of this subversion, though with minimal reference to Rushdie's novel.

3. The titillating but hardly deep-going exchange between John Le Carre and Rushdie on *The Satanic Verses* began in 1989 and was renewed in 1997 in correspondence in the pages of *The Guardian*.

4. In a lecture/discussion presided over by Lee Bollinger at Columbia University, Rushdie explicitly cited this argument in Mill as convincing him.

5. See "Liberalism and the Academy" in this volume for a much more detailed discussion of Mill's argument.

6. See the first section of "Secularism: Its Content and Context" in this volume for elaboration of this more modest form of argument in terms of the notion of "*internal reasons.*"

7. In keeping with its frequent occurrence in the present context of discussion, I am being sheep-like and lazy in using the word "fundamentalist." I have preferred to use the term "absolutist" partly in other writings because the term "fundamentalist" has a very specific history when used to describe religious stances, one that does not fit the present context perfectly. But the writing on the Islamist reaction to Rushdie is so constant in its use of the term that I will not fuss to keep it out of my own idiom, now that I have warned here that it is not perfectly apt.

8. See the "Polemics" section in his *Genealogies of Religion* (Baltimore: Johns Hopkins University Press, 1993).

9. See V. S. Naipaul, *Among the Believers: An Islamic Journey* (New York: Vintage, 1992).

10. Michael Dummett, "Open Letter to Rushdie," *The Independent on Sunday,* February 25, 1990.

11. See Walter Benjamin, "Conversations," in *Understanding Brecht* (New York: Verso, 2003). I should add that though in the discussion that follows I present the religiosity under attack by Rushdie to be an inversion of Brecht's instruction in the maxim—thus a "bad *old* thing" rather than a "bad new thing"—it is not actually obvious at all that contemporary religious fundamentalism, whether Islamic or Hindu or Christian, isn't a quite distinctly *new* thing, a product of modernity's distortions of the old thing. That is one strand of theme of my discussion of Gandhi in the essays in this volume.

12. See Fredric Jameson, *Postmodernism, or, the Cultural Logic of Late Capitalism* (Durham, N.C.: Duke University Press, 1992).

10. Occidentalism, the Very Idea

I am very grateful to Carol Rovane, Stephen White, Noam Chomsky, Jonathan Arac, Adrienne Rich, Eric Foner, David Bromwich, Ira Katznelson, and Jerry Cooper for their detailed and valuable comments on this essay. Bruce Robbins published detailed comments twice on this essay and though I (regrettably) replied to them with increasing impatience and ill temper because I felt he massively—and polemically—misunderstood my ideas, I am grateful to him for pressing me to present in various places in greater detail what I have meant by secular forms of enchantment and how it is relevant to the understanding of a wide range of issues of our democratic culture. I am grateful too to authors of a number of comments on this essay on the excellent website "3 Quarks Daily." This essay was originally published in *Critical Inquiry* 32(3) (Spring 2006): 381–411.

1. It would, I suppose, be an atrocious crudeness and also thoroughly misleading to put the internal tension of the previous cold war as being between the Enlightenment values of liberty and equality. Certainly anti-communist cold warriors would not describe the tension along these lines and would insist on describing it as a tension between the values of liberty and authoritarianism. Even so, their own support of manifestly

authoritarian regimes and of their governments' role in the overthrow of *democratically elected* regimes with egalitarian aspirations, such as in Iran in the 40s and Chile in the 70s (to name just two) shows that insistence to be mendacious. One can be wholly critical of the authoritarianism of communist regimes and still point this out. On the other hand, there is a parallel mendacity, given how things turned out, in the communist self-description of being committed to egalitarian values. But if the idea here is one of getting right some balance of rhetoric and motives in that cold war, then from the point of view of the rhetoric, liberty and equality were certainly the values that were respectively stressed by each side; and, moreover, there can be little doubt that no matter what their rhetoric explicitly said about being opposed to authoritarianism, the anti-communism was really primarily motivated by an opposition to the egalitarian ideals that might, if pursued and if they gained a wider allegiance than they did behind the Iron Curtain (where they were getting no serious allegiance at all), undermine the corporate interests of Western nations.

2. Foucault's specific response is a much more politically focused and historically diagnostic and, it has to be said, stylistically charmless variation on a response first formulated in the Surrealist aesthetic, whose targets were presented in slightly different, though by no means unrelated, rhetoric—instead of "the Enlightenment," the target was termed as "bourgeois" modernity with its "legitimizing" representational and narrative modes and verisimilitudes.

3. If one is to be scrupulous, one should register a caveat. The concept of a "cold war," though it has had its early versions ever since 1917, really only came to be conventionally deployed in the way we are now used to after World War II. And in this period, most of the academic and "independent" writers and journalists that I refer to were on the side of the West, for obvious reasons. In the Soviet Union, defenders of their government's actions could not be accurately described as "independent writers" or "academics." And in the West, though there were some who took the Soviet side, they were, except in France, rather peripheral in their weight and influence. In the current cold war too, a similar caveat holds and that is why I will speak only about the writing on one side of the cold war.

4. First published in *Foreign Affairs* 72(3) (Summer 1993): 22–49.

5. Ian Buruma and Avishai Margalit, *Occidentalism: The West in the Eyes of Its Enemies* (New York: Penguin, 2004).

6. Edward Said, *Orientalism: Western Conceptions of the Orient*, rev. ed. (London: Penguin, 1995).

7. "And they were not entirely wrong," say the authors (see p. 112), after a summary description of the condition of the world wrought by a corporate-driven Western society.

8. I am merely recording that they do not attempt to provide any evidence of causal influences, but, to be fair to them, causal influences are not required for the parallels they draw to be interesting. That there is only an interesting parallel and not a causal influence would not matter, if the implications of the parallel were pursued in some depth, which they are not by Buruma and Margalit. This essay will try to draw a further parallel from an earlier period with a view to pursuing those deeper implications, but with no particular claim to causal influence. Traditions of thought in politics and culture

can emerge without causal links so long as the affinities in intellectual and political responses, even among responses in far-flung regions and times, reflect a deep, common understanding of what they are responding to. Thus, my claims in this essay will be something that Buruma and Margalit could also make for the parallels they cite: that the parallels are interesting, without causal influence, so long as one can see in them a pattern that speaks to a deeper historically recurring phenomenon which has common underlying sources. This essay is motivated by the need for an analysis of the underlying sources of the critique of the "West" that Buruma and Margalit find in contemporary Islamism and in some European and Japanese traditions of thought; and its claim will be that the sources, in order to be properly identified, must go back to a certain metaphysical disputation in the early modern "West" itself.

9. New York: Pantheon Books, 2004.

10. To say that such justifications were put into place soon after the initial Cold War ended is also too late, actually. One heard these justifications as early as 1981, when the Reagan administration talked first of a "war on terror"—Libya and Palestinians were particularly targeted, and disgraceful stereotyping generalizations and racial attitudes toward Arabs began to be expressed, even among academics and the metropolitan intelligentsia, who had for some years not dared to say similar things about African-Americans and Jews.

11. However, in my own view, this second feature lacks the interest or the conviction of the rest because it is not obvious that its presence *is* always a sign of reducing one's subject of study to the "Other." There is a real question whether one can make any interesting claims or generalizations about a subject without abstracting, and sometimes abstracting considerably, from the diversity and detail of the subject. A great deal of explanation depends on such abstraction. We do after all ignore the diversity of the West when we talk of its colonizing mentality or its corporate-driven policies, and it would be absurd to stop talking in this way in fear that one is abstracting away from other aspects of the West which stand in opposition to this mentality and these policies. And if it would be absurd to stop talking in these broadly truthful ways about the West, consistency demands that we should not always react critically or defensively to generalizations made about Islam, despite the fact of diverse elements in nations with Islamic populations. See "What Is a Muslim? and "After the Fatwah" in this volume for more on these themes.

12. This third feature, though commonly found in much writing, should be deployed more restrictively than Said did. Not to do so would be to miss the remarkable modesty of outlook in some of the most interesting aspects of Romanticism, especially German Romantic interest in the Orient, which was not by any means guilty of always merely exoticizing its subjects. Some of the interest was motivated by the view that the West did not know it all and that one might, in one's absorption in the Orient, even *lose* one's identity and, with luck, acquire new knowledges and identities. In the sequel to this essay, "Democracy and Disenchantment," I will look at the Romantics' (both German and British) understanding of nature and show how it was very much and very deliberately of a piece with the seventeenth century dissenters' anti-Newtonian conception of matter that is discussed further below in the present essay. (Blake, for instance, was as

explicit and clear-headed and passionate about these philosophical and historical connections as anyone could be.) Through such an understanding, they explicitly raised the whole metaphysical and political aspect of the notion of "enchantment" (as Weber would later describe it) which I refer to briefly at the end of this essay, and of which Said himself did not have much awareness because of his keenness to convict them of "othering" their subject. M. H. Abrams's book *Natural Supernaturalism: Tradition and Revolution in Romantic Literature* (New York: W. W. Norton, 1973) is more knowing and insightful on this aspect of Romanticism, though there too the focus is more purely on the metaphysical themes, and the political issues at stake are not explored in the detail they deserve. It is the large theme of "Democracy and Disenchantment."

13. Richard Drinnon, *Facing West: The Metaphysics of Indian Hating and Empire Building* (New York: Schocken, 1980).

14. I assume that the authors will admit that, just as with European colonialism, which they don't write of, the Nazis, imperial Japan, and Stalin, who were the statist inheritors of the early Occidentalist conceptions they do write of, also gave lofty rationales for their racial attitudes. Even so, I am accepting some of these grounds they might give for focusing on the latter and not the former. After all the author of *Orientalism* had his own focus, so why shouldn't they? But still it would have been good to hear just a little bit more from the authors of *Occidentalism* about their view of the racial attitudes shown *since* European colonialism. For example, even Israeli historians acknowledge their government's acts of "ethnic purification," "redeeming the land," and so on. Are the attitudes expressed toward the Palestinians in these actions continuous with the German, Japanese, Slavophile antecedents of the contemporary Occidentalists, of which they write, or are they more akin to the colonial forms of racialism? Has anyone ever rationalized this Israeli action in terms of spreading "rationality"? Or does it owe much more to the Romantic German or Slavophile argument they discuss, invoking notions of land and ancient religious roots as the basis of its nationalism? If it does, should the Israelis be counted among the Occidentalists?

15. See "Gandhi, the Philosopher" in this volume, and "Gandhi's Religion and Its Relation to His Politics," in Judith Brown and Anthony Parel (eds.), *The Cambridge Companion to Gandhi* (Cambridge: Cambridge University Press, 2011).

16. If anyone is skeptical of this link I am drawing between the Islamic "Occidentalist" conception of "the West" and what Gandhi has to say about the Enlightenment, all they have to do is compare the four central chapters of *Occidentalism* where that conception is described and the pages of Gandhi's text *Hind Swaraj* (Cambridge: Cambridge University Press, 1997) to notice the remarkable overlap of responses and opinions to Western culture and imperial attitudes. I have only summarized Buruma and Margalit's description of Occidentalism and Gandhi's views at two different points in this essay. The details of the overlap far outrun my brief summaries.

17. To name just two, Richard Dawkins, *The God Delusion* (Boston: Houghton Mifflin, 2006) and Christopher Hitchens, *God is Not Great* (New York: Warner Books, 2007).

18. In a series of works, starting with *Christianity Not Mysterious* in 1696, more explicitly pantheistic in statement in the discussion of Spinoza in *Letters to Serena* (1704) and then in the late work *Pantheisticon* (1724). These writings are extensively discussed in

Margaret Jacob's extremely useful treatment of the subject mentioned in note 23. She also discusses a vast range of other figures among the dissenting voices of that period, not just in England but in the Netherlands, France, and elsewhere in Europe. Two important points should be added here. *First,* though the dissenting response I am invoking which explicitly addressed the new science appeared late in the seventeenth century, the basic metaphysical picture of matter and nature that it was presenting (in more explicitly scientific terms) and the social, egalitarian attitudes it was claiming to be linked with this metaphysical picture was already firmly being asserted by the politically radical groups of the English Revolution five decades earlier. These are the radical sectaries whose views and writings were memorably traversed by Christopher Hill in his *The World Turned Upside Down* (London: Penguin, 1975). Winstanley, to pick only the most well known of the revolutionary figures of the time, put it in terms that quite explicitly anticipated Toland and others: "God is still in motion" and the "truth is hid in every body"; cited by Hill in G. H. Sabine (ed.), *The Works of Gerard Winstanley* (Ithaca, N.Y.: Cornell University Press, 1941), p. 293. What makes the dissenting scientific position of some decades later so poignant and so richly interesting by being much more than merely scientific and metaphysical is precisely the fact that it was a despairing response to what it perceived to be a betrayal in the name of "scientific rationality" of the egalitarian ideals that held promise during the earlier revolutionary period. The second point that should be stressed is that this metaphysical and scientific debate about the nature of matter and nature should not be confused with another debate of that time, perhaps a more widely discussed one, regarding the "general concourse," which had to do with whether or not the deity was needed after the first formation of the universe, to keep it from falling apart. In that debate, Boyle, in fact, wrote against the Deists, arguing in favor of the "general concourse," of a continually active God. But *both* sides of that dispute take God to be external to a brute nature, which was mechanically conceived, unlike Toland and his "socratic Brotherhood" and the dissenting tradition I am focusing on, who denied it was brute and denied that God stood apart from nature, making only external interventions. The dispute about "general concourse" was only about whether the interventions from the outside of an *externally* conceived God were or were not needed after the original creative intervention.

19. As Gandhi's critique is bound to seem, coming centuries later, when the science is no longer "new" and its effects on our lives, which the earlier critique was warning against, seem like a fait accompli.

20. I have written at greater length about this conception of the world as providing normative demands upon us and the essential links that such a conception of the world has with our capacities for free agency and self-knowledge, thereby making both freedom and self-knowledge thoroughly normative notions, in *Self-Knowledge and Resentment,* ch. 4 and 5 (Cambridge, Mass.: Harvard University Press, 2006). For the idea that values are perceptible external qualities, see John McDowell's pioneering essay "Values and Secondary Qualities," in Ted Honderich (ed.), *Morality and Objectivity* (London: Routledge and Kegan Paul, 1985).

21. Berkeley: University of California Press, 1969.

22. Marx was a very complex figure on issues of nature and human relations to it. As I suggest in my "Gandhi (and Marx)" in this volume, there is certainly a reading of *The Economic and Philosophical Manuscripts* that would place him very close to the dissenters' and to Gandhi's position on this question. But there are some passages in Marx which suggest another somewhat opposed understanding.

23. See especially Margaret Jacob, *The Radical Enlightenment: Pantheists, Freemasons, and Republicans* (London: George Allen and Unwin, 1981), which traces some of the trajectory that gave rise to the Radical Enlightenment from the dissenters in late seventeenth century England that I have been discussing. She is good too on the alliances I have been discussing between the Newtonian ideologues and the Anglicans speaking toward the commercial interests of the time, especially the *conceptual basis* for these alliances as they were spelt out by the Newtonian ideologues who were carefully chosen to give the highly influential Boyle lectures when they were first set up. (See especially Chapter 3.)

24. There is, in the sense of the term that I have been presenting, a strikingly "radical" side to Burke too. There are eloquent criticisms of something like the outlook that I have described as forming around the official ideology of the "new science," which can be found in Burke's diagnosis of what he saw as the massive impertinence of British colonial actions in India. I have no scholarly sense of Burke's grasp of his intellectual antecedents, but there is much in his writing to suggest that he would be sympathetic to the political and cultural outlook of the earlier dissenting tradition I have been discussing, even perhaps to their metaphysics, though that is not obviously discernible in the texts.

25. I don't want to give the impression that these political responses on the lips of Muslims are all that is on their lips. This is not the place to look at all the diverse and complex things that a fundamental commitment to Islam amounts to among Muslim populations in the Middle East and South Asia. I have written about that subject in a number of essays. See, for example, "What Is a Muslim?" in this volume and "Secularism, Nationalism, and Modernity," in Rajeev Bhargava (ed.), *Secularism and Its Critics* (Oxford: Oxford University Press, 1997). What I do want to stress in the context of a cold war climate today is that writers and intellectuals are prone to think that all the rest that is on their lips somehow discounts the importance of what I am calling attention to as being on their lips in this essay. (See the next note, 26, for a little more on this.)

26. "I don't accept they really care about these causes, the perpetrators of this ideology." So says Tony Blair in one of his many incoherent speeches about Islamism, and this quote is a gorgeously explicit example of the "not taking seriously" I am referring to. For a devastating analysis of this speech, see Geoffrey Wheatcroft's piece "Blair's Dubious Logic on Islamism and Ireland," *Financial Times*, August 28, 2005, in which he exposes the inconsistency in Blair's positions on the terror associated with the two issues mentioned in his title. The real difference between the two, of course, is that only one of them is a cold war target at the moment. That quite nicely accounts for the inconsistency. It is only to be expected, I suppose, that the leader of a government which has played so central a role in a war against terror based on a sustained deceit of its people should proclaim such a thing as I have quoted. What shall we say of the

intellectuals and journalists who proclaim it? Wheatcroft's excellent article would have been even more effective if he had exposed some of them too.

27. I mean this to be a general but obviously not an exceptionless claim. No doubt some books that one would expect to be unpopular with the mainstream of opinion in a cold war climate might get some good notices from friends and carefully cultivated writers for the press, and other books that one would expect to be warmly received by the generality of conventional opinion will occasionally be seen through as being the cold war interventions they are.

28. See note 16 for my firm conviction in this similarity.

29. The remarks that follow in the rest of this essay are a very brief, perhaps misleadingly brief, summary of material (on the subject of the relation between my ideas of a "secular enchantment" and democratic politics in America and elsewhere), material which nests within a much longer and thematically larger project on the relation between practical reason, moral psychology, and democratic politics. As should be obvious, my interest in these remarks that follow here is not in a detailed sociological and historical account of the phenomenon of the place of religion in America, of which there are increasingly many fine and instructive examples in the literature of the last many years. Any such account would look at a very wide variety of causal factors and recognize the phenomenon itself to be very diverse and locally differentiated. My interest in the present essay is only in the broad moral psychology at stake but I feel quite confident that nothing in the very general diagnostic "first thought" I have just expressed is at odds with the details and the diversity that needs to be, and increasingly has been, carefully studied.

30. I comment in some more detail on some of the contradictions of the liberal democratic ideal in the classical trajectory of Enlightenment thought and the political practice it has spawned in the essay "Gandhi (and Marx)" in this volume.

31. It is not surprising at all that these fulfillments of yearnings for community and solidarity that religion and the church offers should have their echo in the solidarities and communities offered by the emerging institutions of labor movements. After all these labor movements were often themselves outgrowths of (non-conformist) religious movements, as for instance Methodism in England. So there is in fact much observable continuity between some forms of radical secular politics and some kinds of religious movements, a synergy that goes back to the Puritan dissenters I have been invoking.

32. This point, which should be a banality, is not to be confused with the point I was contesting in my essay "What Is a Muslim?" in this volume, the point made by Gerry Cohen that there is a universal need to seek some kind of *identity* in the fundamental sense that I was characterizing in that essay.

33. To deny self-knowledge to someone is, in the end, to deny to him or her a full conception of agency because full agency does require one to know what one is doing and why one did or does it. That is why, for instance, a standard understanding of Freudian ideas is that the self-knowledge one comes to gain in psychoanalytic treatment empowers one with agency and liberates one. This idea of how coming to have knowledge of one's underlying motives increases one's freedom and agency was explicitly anticipated by Spinoza without, of course, any proposal about psychoanalysis as a method or doctrine.

34. There is a detailed discussion of this issue in a very specific context, the context of the academy, in my "Liberalism and the Academy" in this volume. But speaking without restriction to any such context, it would hardly be an exaggeration to say that the very subject of Ethics should now undergo a reorientation so that the question "What ought we to know?" becomes just as primary as the traditional ethical question "What ought we to do?" or "How ought we to live?" The braiding of the cognitive with the political (and therefore the ethical) is so detailed in our times that the latter two questions are idle without prior attention to the former question. So just to give an example of the relevance of the cognitive to our ethical assessments of people that is pertinent to what I have been saying in the text above: If someone in Kansas, working long hours all days of the week to earn 50,000 dollars a year with a wife and three children to support, fails to spend his time on non-standard media sites to find out what forms of wrong his government has been up to on the international stage for the last forty years and more, his failure to know is far less culpable than such a failure to know on the part of someone with a great deal of time and privileges available to him or her to find these things out—a colleague of mine at Columbia University, say, or a comfortably off, willfully unemployed househusband or housewife on the Upper West or Upper East Side. The latter failure of knowledge, it would be right to say, unlike the former, is a far greater form of dishonesty of the moral intellect.

35. I discuss this Hegelian element at length in my essay "Secularism: Its Content and Context" in this volume.

36. I rely here primarily on his *Introductory Lectures on Psychoanalysis*(London: Hogarth Press, 1924) but the assumption of this distinction is peppered all over many other writings.

37. As I said, Freud described the structural idea of there being two frames or segments with the metaphor of "chambers" and he presented the further empirical hypotheses of one of them being unconscious with the further metaphor that the door between the chambers functioned as a "censor."

38. It is not just what is said by whom in polls that provides evidence of this. In an interesting bit of documentation, *The Chronicle of Anthropology* reports that religious people are the largest donors to charity. See the report on this by David. E. Campbell and Robert D. Putnam, "Charity's Religious Edge," *The Wall Street Journal*, December 10, 2010.

39. For more on the notion of expertise, see my discussion of Gandhi's genealogical analysis of it in my essay "Gandhi (and Marx)" in this volume.

40. What I have said here about vanguardism has obvious relevance too to questions of "positive liberty" raised by Berlin, in his celebrated essay "Two Concepts of Liberty." (See note 6 of "Notes toward the Definition of Identity" in this volume and my discussion of Berlin on this subject in the essay.) Berlin, a cold warrior, was filled with anxiety about the notion of positive liberty as understood in terms of a notion of self-realization because he insisted that the notion of self that is involved in positive liberty is entirely outside of the conscious mental orbit of the possessor of the self that was to be realized—it was constituted rather by an objective theory of history possessed by a vanguard who could then tell you what your self *really* was, even though you did not

know it or reveal it in your behavior, and thus *force* you to be free in the sense of *positive* freedom or liberty . But once we have the Hegelian or Freudian "frame" analysis the notion of self-realization is itself ambiguous in the way I have proposed that the notion of a vanguard is. How Berlin conceives positive liberty, summarized briefly above, is just one of its meanings. The second, alternative meaning of positive liberty offered by the frame analysis would go something like this. If the self or selves of ordinary people already manifest in their behavior and responses in instinctive and unarticulated forms the tacit knowledge that a vanguard brings to them in more systematic articulations, then it is genuine *self*-realization that they would achieve if they achieved it, and not the tyrannical idea that Berlin feared.

41. For critiques of Walter Lippmann's vanguardism, see Herbert Aptheker, "Polemics on the "New Conservatism," in *History and Reality* (New York, Cameron Associates, 1955). See also Noam Chomsky, "Force and Opinion," *Z Magazine* (July–August 1991). In a bizarre appreciation of Walter Lippmann, Bruno Latour endorses this very vanguardism in his political thought. See Bruno Latour, *Le Public Fantome* (Paris: Demopolis, 2008).

42. I say much more in my essay "Gandhi (and Marx)" in this volume on how democratized knowledges to live by were changed in this long process of disenchantment to elite expertise to rule by. In another essay in this volume, "The Political Possibilities of the Long Romantic Period," I make a somewhat different though not entirely unrelated use of the "frame" problem (as psychologists call it, and which I am claiming was already present in the conceptual apparatus in Freud's systematic thought, if we distinguish between its structural and its empirical side).

43. As I say in the early pages and the closing page of the essay "Gandhi, the Philosopher" in this volume, Gandhi fairly early on repudiated the traditional politics by which his lawyerly colleagues in the freedom movement hoped to achieve self-governance. His reason for doing so was perfectly straightforward. He explicitly said that though it was fine to criticize states (unlike the criticism of individuals, which he discouraged for reasons I discuss in that essay), it was futile to do so with a view to thinking that one could persuade them into a different point of view. No argument, no exemplary action really had efficacy in persuading the state and it was a confusion (what philosophers would call a category confusion) to think that it could because states were not moral subjects capable of moral deliberation. States were forces (tendencies and dispositions), not of nature, but forces of political artifice and apparatus. And the only way to get them to do things could be by a counter-force. And since he was against violence, he thought it should be by the force of non-violent movements. Thus, in his scheme of things, one persuades people by the force of exemplary action (as I point out in that essay) but we get states to do things by movements. This just was a corollary of the difference between the kind of subjectivity that individuals possess and the kind of thing (a cluster of tendencies and dispositions) a state is. The words of editorialists in newspapers and teachers in universities that try to persuade people have nothing like the power of movements when it came to dealing with the state on matters of fundamental moral and political import. Arguments, exemplary actions, and so on would be fine in mobilizing people to oppose states in movements but have no real efficacy in direct efforts at

persuading the state. To think they do is to reify them with a kind of subjectivity they do not possess.

44. Mention of the expression "instrumental rationality" brings to mind the work of Frankfurt school criticisms of modern bourgeois society and a question may be raised as to why I don't discuss those criticisms much more than I do. I, in fact, do discuss them in another essay, "The Political Possibilities of the Long Romantic Period," in this volume. It is interesting that Buruma and Margalit don't make anything of Horkheimer and Adorno (focusing entirely on German Romanticism instead), just as they don't make anything of Gandhi (focusing entirely on Islamic jihadis instead). In response, just as I refuse to allow any great *conceptual* distance between Gandhi and their "Occidentalists" in this essay, in my brief discussion of Horkheimer and Adorno in the other essay I just mentioned, I refuse to put any great conceptual distance between their criticisms of instrumental rationality and German Romanticism. However, it is undeniable that Horkheimer and Adorno did *allow* such a distance to become possible because of their *silence* about their affinities with Romanticist ideas and their silence about the sources of their stress on alienation and disenchantment and instrumental rationality in Romantic notions. In that essay I offer one obvious and honorable motivation for their doing so, and it has to do with their anxiety about being contaminated by the association that German Romanticism had come to have with the horrific events of Europe in the 1930s and 40s. The work has yet to be written which definitively demonstrates that there is no *intrinsic* relation between the aspects of Romantic philosophy that I invoke in my essay (which also influences their criticisms of modern capitalist society) and the fascist element that surfaced in nationalistic developments in German politics in the last century. Until that work is written, crude equations between Romanticism and fascism of the sort that Buruma and Margalit present in their book will be swallowed whole by the credulous reader whom they hope to convince. Some of Charles Taylor's writing on Herder is a good place to start in seeking an explicit and detailed corrective account of the kind that is needed to silence once and for all interpretative crudeness of this kind.

45. I hope what I have just said makes it emphatically clear (and I *always have been* very clear ever since I first wrote these words in this essay when it was initially published) that my view here is *not* that contemporary religious political upsurges are themselves a form of re-enchantment for our times. They absolutely are not, and nowhere in my writing have I said that they are. As the present essay, in its first appearance quite some years ago and all other essays following it, make quite unambiguously plain, I see this rather as a symptom of the *yearning* for re-enchantment. In fact, as I point out in the words in the text to which this note is attached, this form of religiosity which is a yearning for re-enchantment is in fact ironically in a masked *alliance* with the very scientific rationality that generates the disenchantment and against which the yearning is reacting. I am keen to point all this out because even such a discerning critic as Michael Warner, with whom I have had some illuminating discussions on the subject, has not quite seen my view in this way. He says in a comment on my view: "But it is open to a strong objection that Bilgrami does not acknowledge. In the best recent work on secular culture, these very same forms of modern irrationalism are interpreted not as

protests against secular rationality, but rather as secularizing performances of rationality's other." And then, after citing some views of Simon During, Leigh Schmidt, and Charles Taylor, he adds: "It seems to me that the work of these different thinkers in different disciplines (During is a literary critic, Schmidt a historian, and Taylor of course a philosopher) converges on the same recognition that modern forms of irrationalist culture, especially in entertainment, cannot be read as 're-enchantment.'" In these two remarks, Warner says two quite different things, but seems to give the impression that he thinks the second point is a recapitulation of the first. It is not. First he says that modern expressions of religiosity are *not protests* against scientific rationality (in the "thick" sense that I mean that term) and the disenchantment it induces because they are, in some inverted sense, of a piece with it. And second, he says (after citing During, Schmidt, and Taylor) that these modern expressions of religiosity *cannot be read as* "re-enchantment." About the second, as I just pointed out earlier in this note, I have myself made clear that they are not re-enchantment (but rather yearnings for it) and nothing in any words I have ever written suggested that they should be read as re-enchantment. As for the first point he makes, it is not quite right. Though it may well be that some expressions of religiosity today are actual performative assertions of thick scientific rationality, but surfacing as its "other," I think it is too obvious to deny that there are also many, many cases in which they are indeed reactions and protests (often unconscious) against the effects of scientific rationality in its "thick" sense. As such, they are (often unconscious) yearnings for re-enchantment. Now I don't deny that even when they are reactions and protests of this kind, they *are* often of a piece with some of the features of thick scientific rationality. But I don't see why the fact that these expressions of religiosity are *of a piece* with a lot of scientific rationality makes it impossible for them also to be protests against it. All it shows is what I said it shows: that there is an *irony* in the "masked alliance" that religiously articulated reactions and protests against scientific rationality have with what they are reacting and protesting against. Human mentality is full of examples of how one may inherit the features of something one is reacting against in articulating and performing the reaction. In a world that is *pervaded* with the features and effects of the thick scientific rationality that has produced a chronic disenchantment, reactions and protests against it are bound to appeal to some of those features in the articulation of those reactions and protests. There is irony in this, of course, as I say. And confusion too. But to say that is not to say, as Warner does, that it is impossible for it to happen. Far from being impossible it is fairly widespread— though often in this ironic and confused relation in which is even partly constituted and constricted by the very features of the aspects of modernity it is reacting to.

46. T. S. Eliot, "The Wasteland," *Collected Poems* (London: Harcourt Brace, 1963).

47. The well-known example of bowling alleys is given in Robert D. Putnam, *Bowling Alone: The Collapse and Revival of American Community* (New York: Simon & Schuster, 2000). For Thoreau, see *Walden* (Cambridge: The Riverside Press, 1960).

48. See John Dewey, *The Early Works, 1882–1898*, vol. 5, ed. Jo Ann Boydston (Carbondale: Southern Illinois University Press, 1969), p. 23. Dewey was stressing "movement" as much as he was stressing the other word "democracy" in this remark, and I believe it is movements alone that can be the sites of the sort of public deliberation that

I mentioned as what was needed earlier in the paragraph to which this note is attached. "Democratic," the other word in Dewey's phrase, is, of course, a description, not a proper name. Heaven knows it is not the proper name of the party, whose learning curve has consistently proved to be flat and which has long lost the nerve and the will to be such a site, or even to pay heed to the opinions that emerge as the deliverances of the public deliberation carried out at the sites of popular movements.

11. The Freedom of Beginnings

This essay first appeared under the title "Interpreting a Distinction" in *Critical Inquiry* 31(2) (Winter 2005), a special issue of that journal devoted to invited essays on Edward Said after his death, edited by Homi Bhabha and W. J. T. Mitchell. The ideas in it were first presented at various points in three graduate seminars that Edward Said and I gave at Columbia University over a period of five years on the subjects of "historicism," "interpretation," and "the power of knowledge." I am grateful to him for his extended responses to them over those years, and to Carol Rovane and James Miller for comments on an initial draft of the essay.

1. In his *Beginnings: Intention and Method* (New York: Basic Books, 1975). The distinction is made throughout the book but is most explicit in the Preface and Chapter 1. Page references are to this text. For Vico, see *The New Science,* trans. T. G. Bergin and M. H. Fisch (Ithaca, N.Y.: Cornell University Press, 1988). The distinction is made in many parts of the book. See page 103 for just one good instance of it.

2. Rousseau, *The Confessions,* trans. J. M. Cohen (London: Longmans, 1944).

3. I suppose if one knew what everyone else had said, one could without incoherence intend to say something different and, thereby, original but even such an intention (based on the scarcely human condition of omniscience) could not be a *self-standing* one. One would also have to intend to say what was worth saying for other reasons—that it got things right, by one's lights, for instance—else the intention to be original would be, if not coherent, some sort of idle vanity, a caricature of Romanticist aspiration.

4. See James Clifford, "On *Orientalism,*" in *The Predicament of Culture: Twentieth Century Ethnography, Literature, and Art* (Cambridge, Mass.: Harvard University Press, 1988). And see Edward Said, *Orientalism* (London: Routledge and Kegan Paul, 1978).

Sources

Essay 2 was originally published in Anaradha Dingwaney Needham and Rajeswari Sunder Ragan (eds.), *The Crisis of Secularism in India* (Durham, N.C.: Duke University Press, 2007), copyright © 2007 Duke University Press; reprinted by permission of the publisher. It appears here moderately expanded from that earlier publication.

Essay 3 was originally published as "Freedom, Truth, and Inquiry," from *Chomsky Notebook*, edited by Jean Bricmont and Julie Franck; originally published in French as *Chomsky*, copyright © Éditions de l'Herne, 2007; translation and new material copyright © 2010 Columbia University Press; reprinted with permission of the publisher. It appears here moderately expanded from that earlier publication.

Essay 4 was originally published in *Raritan: A Quarterly Review* 21:2 (2001): 48–67.

Essay 6 was originally published in *Studies in Romanticism* 49:4 (Winter 2010); reprinted courtesy of the Trustees of Boston University. It appears here moderately expanded from that earlier publication.

Essay 7 was originally published by University of Chicago Press in *Critical Inquiry* 18:4, *Identities* (Summer 1992): 821–842. It appears here moderately expanded from that earlier publication.

Essay 8 was originally published in *Daedalus* 135:4, *On Identity* (Fall 2006): 5–14, © 2006 Akeel Bilgrami; reprinted courtesy of MIT Press Journals. It appears here moderately expanded from that earlier publication.

Essay 9 was originally published in Daniel Herwitz and Ashutosh Varshney (eds.), *Midnight's Diaspora: Critical Encounters with Salman Rushdie* (Ann Arbor: University of Michigan Press, 2008). It appears here moderately expanded from that earlier publication.

Essay 10 was originally published by University of Chicago Press in *Critical Inquiry* 32:3 (Spring 2006): 381–411. It appears here moderately expanded from that earlier publication.

Essay 11 was originally published as "Interpreting a Distinction" by University of Chicago Press in *Critical Inquiry* 31:2 (Winter 2005): 389–397.

Author Index

Abrams, M. H., 177, 181–183, 186–188, 190, 191, 193, 195, 200, 201, 202, 205, 212 354n1, 376n12

Adorno, T. W., 177–178, 187, 201, 202, 203, 211, 365n4, 382n44

Ahmad, Aijaz, 347

Althusser, Louis, 191

Anderson, Perry, 122, 357n2

Arac, Jonathan, 373

Aristotle: McDowell's reading of 153, 187, 192; on pleasure 331; virtue theory, 73

Asad, Talal, 264–268, 270, 368n4, 373n8

Auerbach, Erich, 329

Austin, J. L., 84, 85, 111, 354n6

Bacon, Francis, 188, 192

Bakhtin, Mikhail, 275

Bakunin, Mikhail, 320

Baldwin, Thomas, 363n21

Barry, Brian, 62–68

Bauthumley, Jacob, 358n7

Bell, Macalaster, 168, 364n28

Benjamin, Walter, 273, 373n11

Bennett, Jane, 161–162

Bentley, Richard, 188, 358n7, 361n15

Berlin, Isaiah: on liberty, 258, 372n6, 380–381; on the Romantics 176–178, 201–202

Bhabha, Homi, 384

Blackburn, Simon, 362n21

Blair, Tony, 378n26

Blake, William, 79, 177, 184–185, 187–190, 192, 199–200, 303–359n7, 365n9, 375n12

Bloom, Harold, 175–176, 178–179, 191, 365n1,

Bollinger, Lee, 372n4

Boo, Katherine, 167, 364n27

Boyle, Robert, 154, 188, 295, 297, 298, 358n7, 361n15, 365n13, 377n18, 378n23

Brecht, Bertold, 273, 373n11

Bromwich, David, xiii, 347, 373

Burke, Edmund, 378n24

Burke, Kenneth, 297–298

Burke, Peter, 148

Buruma, Ian, Chapter 12, 374n5, 374–375n8, 376, 382n44

Campbell, David E., 380n12

Chandra, Bipan, 349n11

Chatterjee, Partha, 352n18

Subject Index

Modernity, xi, 10, 22, 25–28, 33, 53, 56–57, 125, 130–131, 139–141, 155–156, 170, 184, 200, 202–208, 210–211, 226, 251, 264, 279–296, 309, 373n11, 372n2, 382n45
Moral: exemplarity, 112–115; judgment, 73, 107–116, 314; perception, 73, 198–199, 205; principles, 73, 111–113, 115, 117, 168, 178, 191, 193, 226; psychology, ix, 54–55, 113, 193, 199, 226, 243, 258, 320, 379n27
Movements: mass or popular movements, 104, 303, 322–323, 366n24, 381–382n43, 383–384n48
Multiculturalism, Chapter 2, 53–57, 147, 265–266, 343, 353n1

Nationalism/Nation-state/Nation-building, 25–33, 55–56, 58–60,102–104, 113, 120, 147–148, 177, 201, 227–228, 231, 244, 264, 282–283, 289–290, 299–300, 340–341, 349n11, 361n12, 370n15, 376n14, 382n44; as anti-imperialism, 102–103, 146–147; European origins of, 25–33, 146–148; German, 289–291, 302; Japanese, 289, 302; Slavophile, 289, 291, 302. *See also* Identity; Romanticism
Naturalism, 151; natural supernaturalism, Chapter 6; scientistic naturalism, 182, 188–191. *See also* Enchantment
Nature: as containing opportunities, 154–155; as containing value properties, 153–165, 193–199; contrasted with natural resources, 133–141, 144–145, 152–164, 362–363n18; defined as 'what the natural sciences study, 152–164, 169, 182–200, 376–377n18; desacralization of, 134, 142, 150–152, 155–156, 205; relation to the concept of the 'world', 173, 364–365n29; three definitions of, Chapter 6: section 3
Neo-Platonism, 134, 188, 190, 192, 361n15
Non-violence, Ahimsa, 102–110, 114–118, 293
Normative, 29–34; relation to first- and third-person points of view, 336–338; versus descriptive, 336–338, 377n20
Nostalgia, xi, 144, 203–214, 357n1

Occidentalism, x, xiii, Chapter 10
Orientalism, 235, 274, 281, 293–294, 332, 343; defining features of, 286–289, 375n11, 375n12
Other, the, 343

Pakistan, 49, 96, 269, 368n6
Palestine/Palestinians, 87, 96, 228, 264, 304, 340, 341, 375n10, 376n14
Pantheism, 181–182, 359n7
Paradox of the preface, 82, 88–89,
Paternalism, xiii,
Periodization, 175, 176, 178–181, 187–188, 191, 201
Phronesis, 73
Pleasure, 331
Pluralism, 16, 26, 27, 28, 31, 45–46, 48, 288–289, 292; about reasons, 47
Politics and Romanticism, Chapter 6
Populations, 133, 143–144; contrasted with 'people', 133
Possessive individualism, 135, 138, 142
Pragmatism, 84–86, 354n6, 367n3
Progress, 80–81, 117, 179–181, 265, 369n9
Property, 126–128, 134–135, 142, 163, 169, 172, 357n4, 361n16
Protestantism, 134, 142, 147, 189, 365n13
Public education, 322–324

Quotidian, the, 117, 186, 206–214, 239, 321, 364n24; individual versus public and collective, 206–214, 364n13
Quran, the, 236–238, 368n5

Race/racial equality, 242
Racism, 289–291
Radicalism (radical politics), x, 148, 202–203, 208–214, 358–359n7, 378n24; relation to religion, 379n31
Rationality, 374n2; instrumental, instrumentality, 107, 108; practical reason, x, 243, 259, 365n6, 379n29; scientific rationality, 281–283, 291–302; thick versus thin notions of rationality, 298–302
Realism, 84–86, 180–181

Reasons: external, Chapter 1: section 2, 259; internal, Chapter 1: sections 2, 5, and 6, 258, 266–268; internal reasons versus internal reform, 352n18, 354n4; relevance of state to internal reasons, 352n18. *See also* Rationality

Re-enchantment, 155–164, 382–383n45

Relativism, Chapter 1: section 5, 120, 266–268, 275; about reasons versus relativism about truth, 350–351n15

Religion, ix–x, xiii, 380n38; and capital, 188, 298–299, 325, 360n9, 378n23, 383n45; doctrine versus practice, 219–220; and radical politics, 309 (*see also* Dissenters; English Revolution); as source of dignity, autonomy, comfort, 59, Chapter 3: section 3, 378n31. *See also* Christianity; Enchantment; Identity; Islam; Protestantism; Secularism

Rights, 149–150

Romanticism, xi, Chapter 6, 375n12; English, 175–177; German, 175–178, 290–291; ideas of genius, 200; linked to fascism, 290–291, 382n44; promethean, 200; versus classical, 175, 178. *See also* Long Romantic Period; Politics and Romanticism; View of Nature

Royal Society, 142, 189–190, 192, 295–296, 358–359n7, 359n7, 361n15, 365–366n13; alliances with commercial and Anglican interests, 188, 358n6, 378n23

Satyagraha/Satyagrahis, 104, 105, 107, 108, 109, 112, 116

Saudi Arabia, 96, 283, 369n7

Science: outlook of science/scientism 131, 142, 294–302, 357–358n6, 361n15; relation to capital, 134–140, 144–145, 297–298, 364n25, 365–366n13; science as itself value laden and socio-politically constituted, 362n20; scientific rationality, 281–283, 291–302, 361n15; scientific realism, 180–181

Secularism, x, xii–xiii, Chapter 1, Chapter 2, 147–148, 353n1; as lexicographical ordering, Chapter 1: section 4; as neutrality between religions, 350n14;

contextual relevance of, Chapter 1: section 3 (e), 351n16; contrasted with 'secular', 5–6; contrasted with 'secularization', 4–5; definition of, Chapter 1: section 1, 352–353n19; in India, 48–50, 348n7, 351n17, 351–352n18; justification of, 352–353n19, Chapter 2: section 2; implementation of, Chapter 1: sections 5 and 6; origins in addressing post Westphalian nation-building, 26–27, 58, 147–148, 349n11; self-interest, 371n22, 377n20; versus multiculturalism, Chapter 2; why Gandhi rejected it, 26–27,147–148

Self-knowledge, 309–310, 342, 374n27, 379n33

Shia-Sunni, 369n7

Social contract, 9, 134–138

Social democracy, 202, 208–209, 211, 323

Socialism/Socialist, 22, 94, 140, 163, 164, 364n25

Social sciences, 88, 147, 155–156, 244, 342

Soviet Union, 23, 96, 97, 349–350n12

State, 5, 10, 12, 352n18, 381–382n43; coercive, Chapter 1: sections 5 and 6; justification of state, 25–26, 146–147; liberal state, 265–268; secular state, Chapter 1; state neutral between religions, Chapter 1; sublime, 186–187

Surrealism, 275, 374n2

Syncretism/syncretic, 28, 175

Teleology, 179–181

Terrorism, 60, 96, 104, 276, 284, 302–304, 375n10, 378–379n26

Third-person (detached) point of view, 193–199, 233–236, 239, 297–298, 334–338

Total evidence requirement, 65–67

Toleration, 26–27, 28–29, 53–57, 77, 78, 111, 113, 261, 263. *See also* Freedom: of speech

Tradition, 55–57, 110, 168, 210–211

Truth, 105–121; as absolute, 355n3; as cognitive value or goal, 106, 116–121; as experiential notion, 116; as a moral value (of truth-telling), 116–121; as relevant to morals and politics, 350–351n15;

Other books in the *Convergences* series

Timothy Brennan, *At Home in the World: Cosmopolitanism Now*

Pascale Casanova, *The World Republic of Letters*

Jean Franco, *The Decline and Fall of the Lettered City: Latin America in the Cold War*

Ranajit Guha, *Dominance without Hegemony: History and Power in Colonial India*

Linda Hutcheon and Michael Hutcheon, *Opera: The Art of Dying*

Jeffrey Kallberg, *Chopin at the Boundaries: Sex, History, and Musical Genre*

Amy Kaplan, *The Anarchy of Empire in the Making of U.S. Culture*

Tarif Khalidi, *The Muslim Jesus: Sayings and Stories in Islamic Literature*

Declan Kiberd, *Inventing Ireland*

Jane Miller, *Seductions: Studies in Reading and Culture*

Masao Miyoshi, *Off Center: Power and Culture Relations between Japan and the United States*

Tom Paulin, *Minotaur: Poetry and the Nation State*

Richard Poirier, *Poetry and Pragmatism*

Jacqueline Rose, *The Haunting of Sylvia Plath*

Edward W. Said, *Reflections on Exile and Other Essays*

Tony Tanner, *Venice Desired*

Tzvetan Todorov, *On Human Diversity: Nationalism, Racism, and Exoticism in French Thought*

Printed in the USA
CPSIA information can be obtained
at www.ICGtesting.com
LVHW090211120224
771317LV00027B/58/J